PILGRIMS

W9-AHY-865

Susan Hardman Moore is director of postgraduate studies at the School of Divinity, University of Edinburgh. Previously, she held positions at the University of Durham and King's College London. She has published on puritan theology and piety, on the New England experiment, and on religious life in revolutionary England; she has wide experience supervising doctoral research in Reformation history and theology.

Pilgrims

NEW WORLD SETTLERS & THE CALL OF HOME

SUSAN HARDMAN MOORE

YALE UNIVERSITY PRESS
NEW HAVEN AND LONDON

Copyright © 2007 Susan Hardman Moore

First printed in paperback 2010

All rights reserved. This book may not be reproduced in whole or in part, in any form (beyond that copying permitted by Sections 107 and 108 of the U.S. Copyright Law and except by reviewers for the public press) without written permission from the publishers.

For information about this and other Yale University Press publications, please contact:

U.S. Office: sales.press@yale.edu   yalebooks.com
Europe Office: sales@yaleup.co.uk   www.yaleup.co.uk

Set in Minion by J&L Composition, Filey, North Yorkshire
Printed in Great Britain by Hobbs the Printers Ltd, Totton, Hampshire

Library of Congress Cataloguing-in-Publication Data

Hardman Moore, Susan.
    Pilgrims: New World settlers and the call of home/Susan Hardman Moore.
        p. cm.
    Includes bibliographical references and index.
    ISBN 978-0-300-11718-9 (alk. paper)
    1. New England—History—Colonial period, ca. 1600–1775. 2. Connecticut—Church history. 3. Massachusetts—Church history. 4. New England—Church history. 5. England—Church history. 6. Congregationalism—History—17th century. 7. Immigrants—New England—History—17th century. 8. Immigrants—England—History—17th century. 9. New England—Emigration and immigration—History—17th century. 10. England—Emigration and immigration—History—17th century. I. Title.
    F7.H36 2007
    973.2 2—dc22

2007012115

A catalogue record for this book is available from the British Library.

ISBN 978-0-300-16405-3 (pbk)

Mixed Sources
Product group from well-managed
forests and other controlled sources
Cert no. SA-COC-001530
www.fsc.org
© 1996 Forest Stewardship Council

The paper used for the text pages of this book is FSC certified. FSC (The Forest Stewardship Council) is an international network to promote responsible management of the world's forests.

10 9 8 7 6 5 4 3 2 1

For Rannoch and Helena

pilgrim, *n.*

1. A person on a journey, a person who travels from place to place; a traveller, a wanderer, an itinerant. Also in early use: a foreigner, an alien, a stranger . . .

2. a. A person who makes a journey (usually of a long distance) to a sacred place as an act of religious devotion . . .

3. *fig.* Originally and chiefly in religious contexts: a person travelling through life, *esp.* one who undertakes a course of spiritual development leading towards heaven, a state of blessedness, etc.; a person who experiences life as a sojourn, exile, or period of estrangement from such a state . . .

4. a. *U.S. Hist.* Usu. in plural and with capital initial. Any of the English Puritans who founded the colony of Plymouth, Massachusetts, in 1620; (*gen.*) any of the other early English colonists.

From the *Oxford English Dictionary*

CONTENTS

ILLUSTRATIONS

1 The title page of William Prynne, *Newes from Ipswich* (London, 1641). © The British Library Board. All Rights Reserved. Thomason E. 177 (12).

2 'The South Part of New-England, as is it Planted this yeare, 1634', William Wood, *New England's Prospect* (London, 1634). This item is reproduced by permission of The Huntingdon Library, San Marino, California.

3 'The Saltonstall Family', *c.*1637, by David Des Granges (1611/13–?1675). © Tate, London 2007.

4 George Wyllys' 'Promise and Oath', Wyllys Papers VII, 24a. Reproduced by permission of The Connecticut Historical Society, Hartford, Connecticut.

5 The Henry Whitfield House, Guilford, Connecticut. Courtesy of Henry Whitfield State Museum, Guilford, CT, Connecticut Commission on Culture and Tourism.

6 John Leverett, Governor of the Massachusetts Bay Colony, 1673–9. Attributed to Sir Peter Lely. Reproduced by permission of the Peabody Essex Museum, Salem, Massachusetts.

7 Governor Leverett's buff leather coat. Massachusetts Historical Society, Artefact 0219. Reproduced by permission of the Massachusetts Historical Society.

8 J. Aikin, *A Description of the Country from Thirty to Forty Miles around Manchester* (London: John Stockdale, 1795), Plate 52: Dukinfield Hall, Dukinfield, Cheshire. Reproduced by permission of the University of Edinburgh.

9 Edward Winslow, by an anonymous artist, school of Robert Walker, London, 1651. Courtesy of Pilgrim Hall Museum, Plymouth, Massachusetts.

10 Penelope Pelham Winslow, by an anonymous artist, London, 1651. Courtesy of Pilgrim Hall Museum, Plymouth, Massachusetts.

11 Embroidered shoe, thought to have been worn by Penelope Pelham Winslow at her wedding in London, 1651. Courtesy of Pilgrim Hall Museum, Plymouth, Massachusetts.

ACKNOWLEDGMENTS

First and foremost, I thank Patrick Collinson for his inspiration and encouragement. Sydney Ahlstrom and Harry Stout at Yale, and Conrad Wright at Harvard, helped me greatly during my time there. Geoffrey Nuttall and Peter Lake were formative in the development of this project. I have enjoyed the company of scholars in the Religious History of Britain 1500–1800 Seminar at the Institute of Historical Research, London – especially Kenneth Fincham and Nicholas Tyacke, my fellow convenors since the seminar's inception in 1991. Many colleagues have supported me in my work over the years: in particular, Kingsley Barrett, Gerald Bonner, Ann Loades, Alan Suggate and Stephen Sykes at the University of Durham; Colin Gunton and Mark Smith at King's College London; Stewart Brown, Jane Dawson, David Fergusson, Bruce McCormack and David Wright at the University of Edinburgh. My doctoral students, past and present, have sparked me to think in new directions: Kim Murray, Gavin McGrath, Jonathan Trigg and Judith Rossall in Durham; Ronald Frost, Joanna Spreadbury and Kelly Kapic in London; Graeme Milne, Scott Spurlock, Jung Woo Shin, Mark Garcia, William Schweitzer, Christopher Ross, Joseph Chi, John Tweeddale, Edwin Tay, Hansang Lee, and Timothy Bridges in Edinburgh. I have appreciated the friendly advice of staff in libraries and archives on the eastern seaboard of the United States and in Britain, notably at Dr Williams's Library in London, and at New College Library and the National Library of Scotland in Edinburgh.

Sears McGee and the readers for Yale University Press made invaluable comments on the initial proposal for the book, and on the manuscript. I owe a particular debt to Heather McCallum at Yale, who not only took me on but also steered the writing with acuity and kindness. I thank Candida Brazil, together with her colleagues Sarah Faulkner, Hannah Godfrey and Rachael Lonsdale, for all their care and professionalism.

My friends Sara Trist, Julie McKinna, Mike Penny and Ilona Anderson have been exceptionally generous in giving practical support as the book neared completion, as have my mother, Celia, and the wider circle of my family – Rachel and Geoffrey, Roger and Clare, David and Christina. Very sadly, David died this last year, as did William Trist. Both are much missed. From my days in America, I recall with affection and gratitude Leonard and Harriet Spear, Fielding and Mary Jukes, Rick and Mary Howard, Ruth Drews and Dean Peckham, and friends at Yale and Harvard Divinity Schools, who welcomed me into their homes.

It has been a running joke in our family that without John this book would never have seen the light of day but another might have been written much sooner. To Rannoch and Helena: thank you for letting me spend so much time with my books. I hope that one day you will read this book and see what it was all about.

Susan Hardman Moore
New College, Edinburgh
February 2007

NOTE ON THE TEXT

Quotations from seventeenth-century sources have been changed to use modern spelling and punctuation.

The word 'Church' has a capital when it refers to the universal, worldwide community of Christians and to the national Church of England. The word 'church' is used in relation to local Christian communities, institutions and officials, and for buildings. 'Presbyterian' and 'Congregationalist' (or 'Independent') have capitals when they refer to parties in the religious and political turmoil of revolutionary England, or to nonconformist denominations after 1660. Often, 'presbyterian' and 'congregationalist' appear less formally, without capitals, as adjectives to describe positions in the fluid debate about church order from 1630–1660.

Some dates are cited in the form 1 January 1640/1. This, in modern terms, is 1641. The Gregorian calendar, introduced in England in 1752, started the new year on 1 January. Before 1752, following the old conventions of the Julian calendar, the year began on 25 March. Documents from the period between 1 January and 24 March are cited in the form 1640/1, to reflect the old and the new style, for clarity.

I thank the owners and keepers of the manuscripts listed in the Bibliography for permission to cite items from their collections. I am grateful for permission to draw on materials I have previously published: 'Popery, purity and Providence: deciphering the New England experiment', in Anthony Fletcher and Peter Roberts, eds, *Religion, Culture and Society in Early Modern Britain* (Cambridge: Cambridge University Press, 1994), pp. 257–89; 'Arguing for Peace: Giles Firmin on New England and Godly Unity', in R.N. Swanson, ed., *Unity and Diversity in the Church*, Studies in Church History, 32 (Oxford: Blackwell, 1996), pp. 251–61; '"Pure folkes" and the Parish: Thomas Larkham in Cockermouth and Tavistock', in Diana Wood, ed., *Life and Thought in the Northern Church c.1100–c.1700* (Woodbridge, Suffolk: Boydell Press, 1999), pp. 489–509.

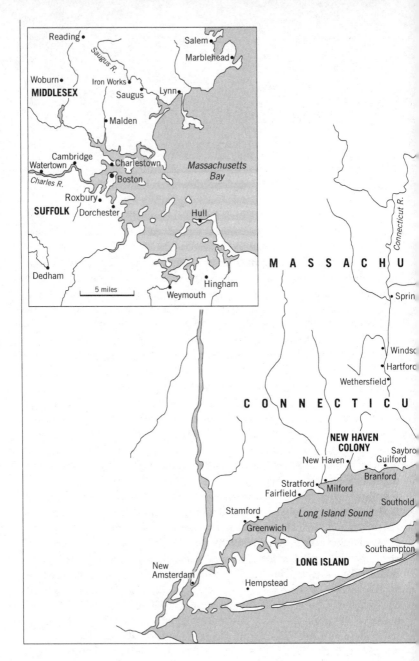

New England, *c.*1660.

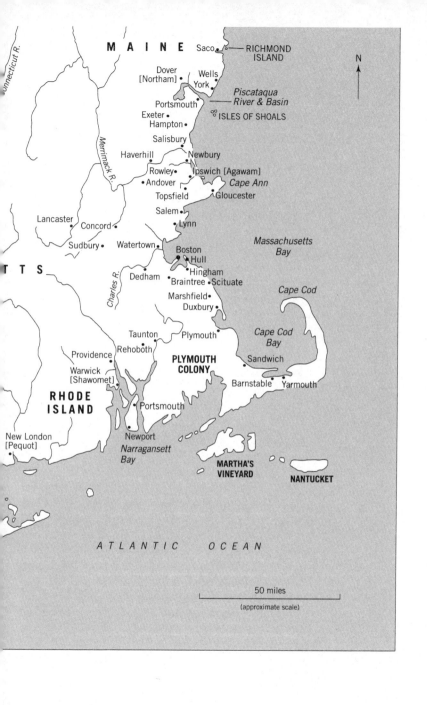

PROLOGUE: THE STORY OF SUSANNA BELL

In 1673 a London printer published first-hand testimony of a life that crossed the Atlantic not once, but twice – to New England and back. *The Legacy of a Dying Mother to her Mourning Children, Being the Experiences of Mrs. Susanna Bell,* was a deathbed speech written down by one of her children, probably at Susanna's home on Seething Lane in the City of London. Almost all that is known about Susanna Bell comes from this deathbed testimony. She had a story to tell: of a traumatic decision to leave England for New England; of the bewilderment of life in the tough conditions of early Massachusetts; of returning home after more than a decade away in America. In the past, no-one really noticed Susanna. Her narrative – nineteen pages long when it appeared in print – was overshadowed from the start by a pious preface twice the length, written by a well known preacher in the City of London, Thomas Brooks. Brooks' nineteenth-century editor reprinted Susanna's account chiefly because it gave glimpses of famous colonial ministers. Yet Susanna's history, lived out between two Englands, is one of many fragments that undermine the traditional understanding of the 'Great Migration' of the 1630s as a one-way ticket to America.[1]

What persuaded thousands of migrants like Susanna Bell to uproot from their native soil in the first place? By the best estimates, somewhere between 13,000 and 21,000 people sailed over to the wilderness of New England in the 1630s, to pioneer English settlement in Massachusetts, Connecticut, and the New Haven Colony.[2] But then in the 1640s and 1650s came an intriguing and largely unexplored migration back to England. Susanna Bell's decision to leave was not exceptional at all. In the decades after 1640, far more people left New England each year than went there.[3] Perhaps as many as one in four settlers returned home: a dramatic possibility, at odds with the conventional story of pilgrims laying the cornerstone for a new nation. Why did Susanna and so many others abandon America?

Susanna set out for New England in 1634, either from London or from Bury St Edmund's in Suffolk, where she was baptised in 1604 and still had 'kindred' in 1672. At first, she refused to leave home. Her husband Thomas wanted to go to New England, but 'I and my friends were very averse unto it. I having one child, and being big with another, thought it to be very difficult to cross the seas with two small children.' Some of the neighbours sided with her. Why go, 'living so well as I did'? Then the baby Susanna carried was born – and died unexpectedly. She pleaded with God to know why: 'so far as it pleased the Lord to help a poor wretch, I begged earnestly of him, to know why he took away my child, and it was given to me, that it was because I would not go to New England'. Susanna believed the loss of her child was heaven-sent to make her change her mind. This way of interpreting events was not strange or unusual in early modern England. Everyone, from Jesuits to Protestant radicals, from intellectuals to simple folk, expected acts of Providence. But it was one thing to share a general belief in Providence, and quite another to agree on how to interpret God's acts. Naturally, one hotly debated matter was the question of whether Providence smiled on the migrants who left to settle New England – a debate conducted more among friends than with enemies, as Susanna Bell's conversations with her neigh-bours suggest. In her private grief, Susanna took her child's death as a decisive intervention from Providence to send her to New England. Once she realised this, 'the Lord took away all fears from my spirit, and . . . I told my husband I was willing to go with him'.[4]

Thomas Bell first broached the idea of emigration, according to Susanna, when 'some troubles' arose in England. These troubles arose from political and religious conflict during Charles I's Personal Rule, a period when the King called no Parliament, from 1629 to 1640. In particular, the 'godly' – as puri-tans preferred to call themselves – accused Archbishop William Laud (Archbishop of Canterbury from 1633, and before that Bishop of London) of making innovations that steered the Church in a Catholic direction, under-cutting England's Protestant Reformation. From the perspective of Laud and his allies on the bench of bishops, it was the puritans who were the innova-tors, jeopardising the 'doctrine and discipline of our Church established'. A Laudian official reckoned England was well rid of them: 'seeing they have found a New England', he wished them all 'safely transported and pitched there that they may triumph and practise their new discipline and fooleries . . . that our Church and state might be quiet'.[5] The volatile tensions of the 1630s exploded in civil wars in the 1640s, in England, Scotland and Ireland. To interpret these tumultuous times, historians have tried to under-stand what the word 'puritan' signified, in the context of the issues that so deeply divided Church, state and society.[6] Although migration to New

England has often been called a 'puritan migration', in what sense migrants like Thomas and Susanna should be thought of as puritan – and, indeed, to what extent it was religion that catalysed the exodus from England to America – has been a source of much debate.[7]

Emigrants like the Bells are sometimes portrayed as religious extremists, attracted to New England to put distance between themselves and the 'ungodly'. From this point of view, these were Protestants of a sectarian temper, at odds with the broad church of parish religion. Religious policy in the 1630s played at most a marginal role: the Thomas Bells of puritanism might well have gone to New England anyway.[8] Cast as militant radicals, New England's settlers can easily be seen as migrants with a mission to work out the Reformation not yet finished in England, to provide a model for their native country – an 'errand into the wilderness' to build a 'city on a hill'.[9] But from another perspective, migrants like Thomas and Susanna came not from a radical fringe. Rather, they came from a movement central to the newly Protestant Church of England, part of a lively campaign to win hearts and minds – a movement far from monolithic, carrying many shades of opinion and practice within a broad commitment to Reformed Protestantism. In the 1630s these zealous Protestants felt threatened by Laudian policies that seemed anti-Calvinist: for example, a prohibition on sermons about predestination, and changes to the communion service that seemed to bring back elements of the Catholic mass.[10] For some, Thomas Bell probably among them, these innovations proved too much. After a great deal of soul-searching about whether it was legitimate to desert England at a time of crisis, people like Thomas plucked up stakes for America. They fled what they saw as 'popery' to find a refuge in which to practise true and pure religion – this was not a militant errand to set up a city on a hill, but a reaction to pressure, a voluntary exile, a search for a safe haven.[11]

Thomas Bell was not only a man unsettled by the troubles of the 1630s. He was also a merchant with an eye for new opportunities in Atlantic trade. Emigrants had mixed motives, and could list a variety of reasons for leaving England. Religious aspirations kept company with hopes of profit and efforts to revive flagging careers. Weavers left the beleaguered textile industry of East Anglia. The promise of furs and timber tempted entrepreneurs. West Country fishermen looked for new ways to exploit North Atlantic fishing grounds: the way to the Great Migration was paved by earlier ventures in the 1610s and 1620s to establish fishing settlements – not so much God as cod. Some migrants went because their families or friends did. Unusually, in comparison to the young, single and rootless adventurers drawn to other Atlantic colonies, New England attracted people of all ages, including well-settled families. The social bonds in godly circles helped to build up the momentum of migration.

Susanna Bell thought first of her children, next of loyalty to her husband, and finally that 'many people of God went for New England and among them my husband desired to go'. (Thomas Bell's sister, Katherine Meakins, emigrated in 1633, the year before Thomas and Susanna – perhaps hers was the voyage Susanna refused to join?) Undeniably, then, an assortment of motives, economic and social as well as spiritual, drew settlers across the Atlantic.[12] Does this reduce religion to merely one of many factors in a decision to sail for America?

No: the life-story of Susanna Bell illustrates something fundamental to the mindset of godly emigrants – their determination to weave a providential story for their lives out of an untidy mass of events and aspirations. Potential settlers who wanted to find the hand of Providence in the New England project looked for a confluence of reasons to emigrate: the more varied, the better.[13] To find inner certainty about a call to leave England, godly migrants weighed up the signs, for and against. Providence would show itself first one way, then another. Everything was grist for the mill: disappointments and losses in old England, incentives in New; in Susanna's case, the death of a child.

Perhaps the strongest evidence for the overarching significance of religious factors is that the flow of migrants reflected the development and demise of Laudian initiatives, diocese by diocese.[14] The pressure – or threat of pressure – that the godly believed would uproot preachers and limit the practice of piety pushed them into evasive tactics which, for some, ended in a decision to leave their native country. Although information about most emigrants is fragmentary, and the harder evidence comes from an identifiable cohort of emigrant ministers, without putting religious motives centre stage it would be difficult to explain why thousands set sail for New England between 1630 and 1639, and only a trickle before or after.

Susanna's memories of her first voyage across the Atlantic were still vivid on her deathbed in the 1670s. She recalled how she sailed to New England, pregnant again and with a small child in tow:

> We were eight weeks in our passage, and saw nothing but the heavens and waters. I knew that the Lord was a great God upon the shore: but when I was upon the sea, I did then see more of his glorious power than ever I had done before . . . I thought I could never be thankful enough to the Lord for his goodness in preserving us upon the sea, I being big with child, and my husband sick almost all the voyage.

She remembered the disorientation of arriving in Massachusetts, and how settlers 'gave us the best entertainment they could'. The Bells settled at

Roxbury, near Boston. Thomas 'would have gone by water higher into the country', but Susanna put her foot down: 'I told him . . . I was not willing to go again to sea'.[15]

She felt unsure of her faith as soon as she stepped off the ship – from 'the first sermon that I heard after I came ashore'. She thought 'if I could but get into the fellowship of the people of God, that would quiet my spirit'. But a shock awaited her. The Roxbury church turned down her request to join, because she could not convince the members that she had personal experience of God's grace:

> They were very faithful to the Lord, and my soul, and asked me what promise the Lord had made home in power upon me. And I answered them, 'Jeremiah 31.3, "Yea, I have loved thee with an everlasting love, therefore with loving kindness I have drawn thee"'. But they told me this was a general promise; that I must look to get some particular promise made home in power upon me, and persuaded me to wait a little longer to see what God would further do for my poor soul . . .

This rebuff, and the quest for spiritual assurance that followed, dominated Susanna's deathbed testimony. (It took up eight out of nineteen pages in print.) In her own words, 'I did not experimentally know what it was to have . . . grace in my heart, nor what it was to have union with Christ, that being a mystery to me'. To find what the church thought she lacked, she travelled from sermon to sermon – to hear John Cotton preach in Boston, and Thomas Shepard in Newtown (later Cambridge), as well as John Eliot, minister of Roxbury. In the end, a word of hope came from another woman, who told Susanna she had heard a preacher say that 'the Lord had more glory in the salvation than in the damnation of sinners'. This lifted Susanna's heart. But when John Eliot and others encouraged her to approach the church again, her sense of unworthiness made her reply 'that all church fellowship would do me no good'; nothing but personal assurance of salvation in Christ would help. Eliot told her she 'was already in the pangs of the new birth; and he did believe it would not be long before the Lord spoke peace to my poor soul'. Shortly afterwards, Susanna recalled, 'the Lord . . . did so quiet my heart, that all the world seemed as nothing unto me'. The Roxbury church invited her to 'come into fellowship with them', and admitted her to the covenant, 'a babe in Christ among them'. She went to see John Cotton in Boston, 'to ask him what he thought of the work of God upon my poor soul. And he told me, that he was satisfied that it was a real work of God'.[16]

Susanna's experiences capture a startling innovation in New England: the test of spiritual experience. Roxbury's church records lend support to her story. Thomas joined the church well before her. It is likely that Thomas and Susanna first applied at the same time, not long after their arrival in 1634, but he was accepted and she was not. Susanna's intense and anxious quest for assurance possibly lasted for more than a year. A church like Roxbury, gathered by a covenant – a common vow that created and bound the community (in itself a dramatic innovation, though not as novel as the test) – restricted membership to those who could show 'a real work of God' in their soul.[17] In English parish churches, godly clergy tried to ensure that only sincere Christians took part in communion, but measured this by knowledge of basic Christian teaching, not by personal testimony. As for baptism, everyone within the geographical bounds of an English parish was expected to bring infants to be baptised (or face questions about their orthodoxy). In New England, as Susanna soon found out, every settler was required to attend sermons in the meetinghouse, but only those who passed the test of spiritual experience could become church members. Only church members could receive communion; only members could bring children to be baptised.[18]

Massachusetts was soon torn apart by the kind of questions that distressed Susanna. She wanted to know God 'experimentally' – to experience grace in her heart and the mystery of 'union with Christ'. She hoped to discover a particular promise in Scripture that went home in power to her soul. Yet how could she be sure God had done 'a real work' in her? The preachers Susanna went to hear in neighbouring towns, John Cotton and Thomas Shepard, came out on opposite sides in a debate about free grace that erupted in 1637, the 'Antinomian Controversy'. All agreed that God's grace in Christ – won at the cost of the Cross – was freely given to the elect. But how was God's eternal decree of predestination played out in time? Cotton preached that assurance of salvation could come in an instant, by a direct revelation from the Holy Spirit, through the personal way Scripture-promises spoke to the believer. Cotton's ideas were taken up by admirers in Boston, led by Anne Hutchinson, her brother-in-law the minister John Wheelwright, and the young aristocrat Sir Henry Vane (perhaps the most eminent migrant to come to New England, who served as Governor of Massachusetts in 1636).[19] Thomas Shepard, in contrast to John Cotton, stressed the need for intense personal discipline and self-scrutiny, to prepare the heart for God's work and then to find the signs of holiness in daily life that brought assurance of salvation. Shepard talked a great deal about the pitfalls of hypocrisy, the difficulty of being a sincere convert.[20] For Cotton and his admirers, costly grace should be free; for Shepard and his allies, free grace was costly. Small wonder Susanna's journey from preacher to preacher left her anxious and confused.

Cotton's spiritual vibrancy and Shepard's strict discipline managed to co-exist in the Bay Colony – a reflection of the wide spectrum of puritan opinion

galvanised into emigration by the crisis of the 1630s – until extravagant inter-
preters of Cotton's message raised the spectre of heresy and moral anarchy,
with too much talk of Spirit-filled mystical bliss, and too little of holy living
rooted in the precepts of Scripture. In January 1637 the authorities put
Wheelwright on trial; in November that year, Hutchinson. Sir Henry Vane –
disruptive, but with highly placed friends in England – was not arrested. The
controversy split Roxbury church. John Eliot and Thomas Weld, who served
together as its ministers, volunteered to testify against Hutchinson. For several
months after her trial, Anne Hutchinson was kept in custody in Roxbury, at
the house of Weld's brother, Joseph. During this time, Eliot and Weld held
many meetings, some lasting half a day, to win round Roxbury church
members who supported Anne Hutchinson's 'corrupt opinions' – with little
success. Five people were excommunicated. Other Roxbury members wanted
to join the Boston church, where they found Cotton's preaching more satisfying, but were refused permission. Susanna seems to have been caught in the
middle: her sympathies with Cotton show in her decision to ask his opinion
about whether God had done 'a real work' in her, but John Eliot remained her
spiritual mentor.[21] In a step typical of their strategy for securing orthodoxy
in Massachusetts, the magistrates banished the convicted dissidents
Wheelwright and Hutchinson outside the Bay Colony's borders. Wheelwright
went north to what is now Exeter, New Hampshire, and continued to live
outside Massachusetts until his death in 1679, although the authorities lifted
his sentence of banishment in 1644. Hutchinson moved south to make a new
settlement in Narragansett Bay; then west into Dutch territory (in what is now
New York State), where she and fifteen members of her family died in an
Indian attack in 1643. Sir Henry Vane left for England, voluntarily. Even John
Cotton thought of leaving Massachusetts – for another part of New England
– but in the end chose to distance himself from the 'unorthodoxy' and to build
bridges with fellow ministers. The Massachusetts authorities rewarded
Thomas Shepard with a decision to locate Harvard College at Newtown (soon
renamed Cambridge, in honour of the alma mater of almost all the settlers
who were graduates): they praised 'the vigilancy of Mr Shepard . . . for the
deliverance of all the flocks which our Lord had in the wilderness'.[22]

Reports of strange innovations in New England, and contention among the
settlers, trickled back to England. Colonists appeared to have deviated from
what had been promised in advance – continued loyalty to the English Church
– and become 'separatist', setting up churches which turned their backs on the
Church of England. The emergence of what was soon called the 'New England
Way' perplexed the godly who had been left behind, particularly those originally most in sympathy with the venture. Rumours circulated that settlers had
to renounce the godly in England if they wanted to join colonial churches. The

Massachusetts authorities tried to end these reports by stifling voices that spoke out for a radical separation from the Church of England: early in 1636 Roger Williams, pastor of the church at Salem, was banished from the Bay Colony for this reason. A year later, reports of an outbreak of heresy – the Antinomian Controversy – threw fuel on the fire of suspicion back in England. In an effort to dampen things down, the ministers John Cotton and John Wilson went aboard a ship in Boston harbour which was bound for England, to ask the passengers to take the message home that New England's divisions over antinomianism were not fundamental. (Wilson, to Cotton's annoyance, said only a few people could fathom what all the debate was about.) But attempts to salvage New England's reputation had limited effect. Three thousand miles away in England, it looked as if settlers had diverted, dangerously, from the path they set out on when they left home. From the mid-1630s onwards, letters from godly supporters in different parts of England insisted New England's leaders should justify themselves: 'If you can show that you walk in the ways of God we shall heartily rejoice to walk with you, but if you have turned aside we shall earnestly desire you . . . seriously to consider the matter and speedily reform what is out of order.'[23]

By their own lights, settlers were not as radical as their critics made them out to be. In reply to hostile questions, colonial ministers insisted, time and time again, that their churches were not separatist: they recognised English congregations as true churches. These were people who had argued vigorously against separatism when they were in England. To justify what they saw as an exceptional step – withdrawing from their native country – they believed Providence provided a route to primitive purity in New England, as a refuge from the threat of popery. Innovations in colonial churches arose from the opportunity to provide a pure Scriptural witness against popery. At the same time, the need to stabilise fragile new communities shaped the evolution of church life. In Susanna's narrative, for example, the church actually seems quite tender towards her; solicitous to set her straight spiritually, and to draw her into fellowship. Arguably, the tight bonds of New England's covenanted churches, and the emphasis on sharing spiritual experience, were intended to be inclusive not exclusive – not so much a sieve to separate the worthy from the unworthy, as a safety-net for disorientated settlers.[24]

As England lurched into the chaos of civil war between Charles I and Parliament, and censorship collapsed, private arguments became public. What former allies in the puritan movement debated in letters and papers sent to and fro across the Atlantic in the 1630s got into print in the 1640s, as the initial salvos of a fierce pamphlet war. (All the texts were printed in London. Colonists sent manuscripts back across the ocean – one or two hit the seabed rather than the English market. New England's first printing press, shipped over in 1638, stood in Harvard Yard more or less inactive for thirty years. Paper had to be imported; ink and trained printers were scarce.) Debate about the New England experiment fused with disputes within England, and between the English and the Scots, about the right way to reform the Church of England. The battle of books stirred up mistrust between the 'puritanisms' of old England and New. English critics blamed New England for the rise of radical sectarian churches on English soil.[25]

Curiously, Susanna's deathbed narrative said no more about her time in New England (no mention, for example, of the birth of a daughter at Roxbury in 1640). What loomed large in her mind were her thoughts and feelings when Thomas went to England.[26] By 1639 he was one of the sixteen wealthiest inhabitants of Roxbury. His trading interests took him back across the Atlantic three times in the 1640s. On the first occasion, in 1642, Thomas joined a swarm of settlers travelling on business, or going home for good.[27] A significant sea change had happened in 1640: English investors and potential emigrants lost interest in New England when Parliament met after the eleven years of Charles I's personal rule, and hopes of reform in England rose. The tide of migrants started to flow the other way. A tract published to revive English interest in the colonies, *New Englands First Fruits*, came out around the time Thomas Bell reached London. One of eight 'frequently asked questions' it answered, to defend New England, was 'Why do many come away from thence?'[28]

In February 1643, 'news came out of England, by two fishing ships, of the civil wars there between the King and the Parliament'. This information took four months to cross the Atlantic (the first battle, at Edgehill, happened in October 1642). Susanna recalled that after Thomas set off across the Atlantic 'we did hear of a war broke forth in England, and friends told me my husband would be in danger of his life if taken'. The hazards of war discouraged colonists from leaving for England – although some members of the Massachusetts Artillery Company, with skills honed in hand-to-hand fighting with Native Americans, went back to join the Parliamentary army. The conflict disrupted shipping. This thinned out the possibilities for sending letters: contact between the two Englands became sparser, leaving imaginations to run riot about the toll of civil war. For settlers caught in England when conflict broke out, it was probably hard to find a passage back. Perhaps Thomas Bell had to stay away longer than he originally intended. John Eliot paid Susanna a pastoral visit in her husband's absence, to talk over 'how the Lord did build up my heart'. She consoled herself with thoughts of a better husband: Christ, her heavenly bridegroom. While Thomas was away in England she had a son, baptised in April 1643 but dead by June.[29]

Thomas came back from war-torn England by the end of 1644 – to judge from the birth of a daughter in September 1645. However, Susanna's hopes that in future he would conduct business from Roxbury were disappointed: 'my husband told me, that he must go again to England, and I was very unwilling to it'. News of Charles I's surrender to the Scots at Newark, which ended the First Civil War in the summer of 1646, reached New England that autumn. A great surge of settlers, earlier deterred by the hostilities back home, now set off for England, Thomas among them. This second visit was brief: he left in December 1646 and reached England in the depth of winter; he sailed from London in the spring of 1647 and arrived back in Roxbury by the summer.[30] Thomas built his business around supplies for New England, particularly cloth and metalwork, which settlers could not yet manufacture. A certificate of goods imported for him on the *Indeavour* of London in 1645 included canvas, cottons, and 'linsey woolsey'; shovels and bellows; 'birding shot of lead'; woollen stockings, shoes, and plain felt hats; sixty rugs for beds; twenty barrels of soap. Other transactions show Thomas as part of a web of merchant activity between old England and New, connected to exporters of New World produce – fish; moose skins; timber masts; two hundred thousand 'treenailes' (cylindrical pins of hardwood, which unlike metal would not rust in contact with water, used in shipbuilding to fasten timbers together).[31]

Towards the end of 1647, Thomas travelled to England again and this time took Susanna with him. On the way back, as on the way over, the Bells had a young child to cope with, aged two, as well as older children.[32] London merchants held the upper hand in trade, with colonial merchants as junior collaborators. It must have been tempting to transfer back to the metropolis. In trading and property records over the next few years, Thomas Bell 'of Roxbury' turned into Thomas Bell 'of London, Citizen and merchant'.[33]

In her *Experiences*, Susanna testified that it 'pleased God to bring me back to my native country'.[34] This was a remarkable turnaround for someone who, at the start of her testimony, declared that God allowed her child to die to convince her to emigrate. How could Susanna – who saw the hand of Providence so dramatically in her decision to go to New England – put her convictions into reverse, to come home?

To unravel the logic that carried them to New England, settlers like Susanna had to find a 'just call' to abandon America. In a mirror image of their deliberations about whether to leave England, colonists now weighed up whether they were called by Providence to make their way back. Settlers brought an extraordinary range of reasons into play to justify leaving America: better opportunities for employment; property to attend to in England; an inheritance back home; an invitation from friends; a sick relative; a desire to see England once more; poverty; New England's harsh climate. The minister John Davenport, who wanted to leave New Haven to avoid another New England winter – for his health's sake – used the commandment 'Thou shalt not kill' to argue he had a duty to preserve his life. Thomas Bell, to judge from Susanna's narrative, persuaded her by arguing that his trading activities in England would ease the pressure to think of worldly things, and free her mind for spiritual thoughts: Susanna 'was glad to hear it from him, and desired him to go'. He pointed out that if she did not let him go, 'the name of God would suffer' (in other words, without supplies the settlements would fail) – 'to prevent which', she said, 'I consented'. Susanna was convinced that 'the Lord by his Providence was pleased to call my husband to come for England'.[35]

Settlers had to persuade not only themselves but also their neighbours. Ties of covenant meant that decisions to leave were scrutinised by the church and perhaps (where there was a plantation covenant) by the town.[36] Communities had to find ways to endorse an individual's call to England without undermining the purpose of Providence for those who stayed on in America. Fellow settlers could be ambivalent, or downright hostile, if someone's wish to leave threatened a town's viability. Even a desire to visit England might be greeted with suspicion. As the history of Thomas and Susanna illustrates, a visit might lead to permanent resettlement. Parents, wise to what their children might do, sometimes made residence in New England the condition for receiving a legacy. Some settlers, to ward off the temptation to leave, tied themselves down with a vow or solemn oath.[37]

Colonists who disregarded the opinion of their neighbours risked the judgment of God. John Winthrop – the first Governor of Massachusetts, and a harsh critic of settlers who deserted New England 'for outward advantage' – wrote that 'all ways were sought for an open door to get out at; but it is to be feared many crept out at a broken wall'. Letters and papers from early New England recorded many instances of the Almighty delivering punishment on the Atlantic – at the hands of pirates or Turks, or by storms and shipwrecks.[38]

Susanna saw her safe passage across the seas as the blessing of Providence on her decision to return to England. By 1651 the Bells lived in Seething Lane in the parish of All Hallows Barking, between the Tower of London and the heart of the City's commercial activity at Cornhill. Truth to tell, Susanna was a little disappointed by what she found. 'I was much troubled that there was no better observation of the Lord's day': Londoners failed to follow New England's practice of starting the Sabbath on Saturday afternoon.[39] She joined the congregationalist circles that flourished in London parishes during the English Republic. Up and down the country, colonists arrived back with experience of New England's churches – but did not necessarily insist on putting this into practice. Some returned with a jaundiced view of New England, and added their voices to the chorus of English critics. Others, although they supported New England's style of primitive purity, were judicious about how far and how fast they brought colonial ways to English soil. The kind of church that could exist in a New World might not be possible – or essential – for old England's parish churches. In terms of how the New England Way reached England, there is an intriguing counterpoint between the flow of settlers back across the Atlantic and the flood of colonial tracts from London presses. In the crucial debates of the 1640s, printed books, not New Englanders, articulated the New England Way. Ironically, the most vociferous advocates of replicating the New England Way in England usually turn out not to be people who had been there, but those who had read about it.[40]

In 1654, seven years after leaving New England, Thomas and Susanna sent back to ask the Roxbury church to release them from covenant. This was a significant step in their detachment from life in Massachusetts, because it freed them to join in covenant with a church in London. But transatlantic loyalties stayed with them the rest of their days. Ties of friendship and business stretched across the Atlantic, and Thomas still owned property and land in Roxbury. In 1655 he signed a certificate to recommend a minister for a Lincolnshire parish: John Wheelwright, notorious for his part in the Antinomian Controversy almost twenty years earlier, who had also returned to England. (Others who gave Wheelwright certificates included David Yale, a Boston merchant who came back to England in 1652, bringing his son, Elihu, then aged three. Elihu became an East India trader who made a fortune in diamonds: he never went to New England again, but left his mark by endowing a College at New Haven.)[41] Thomas Bell, like Susanna, had connections with people from both sides of the free grace controversy. He supported Wheelwright, but also assisted Wheelwright's old opponent, John Eliot, with business for the New England Company (founded in 1649 to promote the conversion of Native Americans). One of Bell's trading partners came to London in 1658 to collect printing blocks and paper for producing Eliot's translation of the Bible into Algonquian on the press in Harvard Yard.[42] In his will, made in 1672 not long before his death, Thomas left all his tenements and land in New England to John Eliot and a church officer, to hold in trust 'for the maintenance of a schoolmaster and free school for the teaching and instruction of poor men's children at Roxbury'.[43]

Other settlers who, like Susanna, stepped ashore again in their native country, scattered to all corners of the British Isles.[44] A good number seem to have gone back to the communities they left in the 1630s – occasionally to the same house, rented out in their absence. Some fought for Parliament in the 1640s. Some joined Cromwellian campaigns in Ireland and Scotland (which continued the British civil wars into the 1650s), or put their seafaring expertise at the service of Cromwell's navy. By the 1650s, Cromwell regarded New England as a project that had outlived its usefulness, except as a good recruiting ground for other ventures at the frontier of his regime.

The diarist Samuel Pepys was a neighbour of the Bells on Seething Lane from 1660. Thomas and Susanna might well have known Pepys' Navy Office house, because a former settler from Charlestown, Massachusetts, Major Francis Willoughby, lived there until Pepys pushed him out at the Restoration. Both Pepys and the Bells stayed in London during the Great Plague of 1665, and survived. Pepys wrote of 'having stayed in the city till above 7400 died in one week . . . and little noise heard day nor night but tolling of bells . . . till whole families (ten or twelve together) have been swept away'. Susanna's recollection echoes his. She remembered:

> the pestilence . . . that swept away many thousands; and under that sad Providence . . . the Lord did help me to rely alone upon himself, from that Scripture, Psalm 91.7, 'A thousand shall fall at thy side, and ten thousand at thy right hand, but it shall not come nigh thee' . . . it pleased the Lord to preserve both my self and all my relations . . . though some of them were often in the midst of danger.[45]

The Fire of London in 1666 narrowly passed them by. Pepys wrote an hour-by-hour record of the disaster – in which he and Sir William Penn (father of the founder of Pennsylvania) devised the strategy of blowing up houses to create a firebreak. On 5 September 1666 Pepys went to bed, only to be roused at two in the morning by his wife Elizabeth after 'new cries of fire' from the foot of Seething Lane. They fled the City. Pepys came back the following day, and, to his amazement, although the fire had scorched the tower and porch of All Hallows parish church at the foot of the Lane, it had gone no further. Without the firebreak, Seething Lane would have gone up in flames. Again, Susanna's recollection echoes that of Pepys: 'a dreadful fire, which reduced to ashes many thousand houses'; God's love was 'manifested to me in the preservation of my habitation, when many better than myself were burnt out'.[46]

It would be good to know as much about the other settlers who went back to England as about Susanna. Most of those who left New England have to be tracked down with a degree of ingenuity. While the English authorities attempted to monitor traffic to New England in the 1630s, and some of these passenger lists survive, no-one in New England kept rosters of those who sailed away. Settlers preparing to embark often left a scrap or two of evidence in the records: a will, a letter of attorney, a request for permission to leave the fellowship of the church. Had Susanna's children not recorded her *Experiences*, virtually all that would be known of her story would be one line in the Roxbury church book: 'Mr. Tho. Bell and his wife had letters of dismission granted and sent to England.' Nevertheless, from small pieces of information a migrant's story can be traced backwards and forwards in time, to construct a life history: from origins in England, across the Atlantic, and back again. All this detective work leads to the conjecture that as many as one in four settlers abandoned New England.[47]

Most migrants' histories are jigsaws with many missing pieces. The fullest information exists for ministers, because eighteenth-century historians collected manuscripts and recollections from families and friends, to document the history of Dissent. This makes the twists and turns of clerical careers easier to follow on both sides of the Atlantic.[48] In the context of migration from New England to England, their histories are particularly valuable. A high proportion – one in three – of the clergy who went to America in the 1630s eventually went back to their native country. In the godly circles from which emigrants came, ministers' words and deeds carried authority. This influence is evident in Susanna's narrative of her life, and in the spiritual testimonies of many early settlers: they made the journey to New England (and back) a journey from sermon to sermon. Because godly preachers articulated and shaped the migrants' world-view, their experience can be used to map more contours onto the landscape.[49]

People like Susanna, who dropped out of the onward march of American history, are easily written out of the story. They can be overlooked, or ignored as atypical, or deemed unpatriotic. Or, going to the other extreme, they can be elevated as ambassadors for the New England Way, taking light to old England from their 'city on a hill'. A search in colonial records soon throws up prominent colonists and noisy dissenters who left New England, but the characters who loom largest are not necessarily representative. A wider trawl catches not only ministers and magistrates, merchants and dissidents, but also wives and widows, children, servants, apprentices, military men, surgeons, shoemakers and shopkeepers. What emerges from the small print of their individual lives is different from what comes out of a single biography, or the study of a particular New England town, or a treatment of religious tensions, or the story of those who stayed on in America. Few of the characters are well known, but collectively their stories add up to an intriguing tale, full of human aspirations and foibles. The relationship between their rhetoric and behaviour is complex, sometimes counterintuitive. The untidiness and ambiguity of individual lives contrasts with the clarity and certainty of their beliefs about the intentions of Providence.

Susanna died in 1673, the year after Thomas. She asked to be buried in the parish of All Hallows Barking, 'as near as may be to the body of my deceased husband'. In her will – written in 1672, twenty-five years after she left Massachusetts – she bequeathed 'to Mrs Anne Eliot, the wife of John Eliot of Roxbury in New England, my black cloth gown and petticoat belonging to it'.[50] At the end of her deathbed speech, her thoughts turned back to early days in New England, when an earthquake shook Massachusetts. A witness at the time described the noise as like 'the rattling of coaches in London'. While her Roxbury neighbours ran up and down thinking the world was at an end, Susanna sat still and drew comfort from Bible texts like Hebrews 11:13, which pictured God's people as 'strangers and pilgrims on the earth'.[51] Susanna's tale was transatlantic; shaped by the complex times she lived in; lavishly embroidered with threads of Providence.

EXODUS FROM ENGLAND

> When I was made a minister, I was exhorted . . . by the bishop . . . to have in remembrance into how high an office I was called; that is to say, a messenger, a watchman, a pastor and steward of the Lord . . . to feed and provide for the Lord's family . . . and to see that I never ceased . . . my care.
>
> Thomas Allen[1]

In 1636 Thomas Allen, Rector of St Edmund's, Norwich, delivered an impassioned defence of his vocation in the Church of England, to protest against a sentence of excommunication imposed on him by a church court. To Allen's dismay, the sentence had been publicly announced in Norwich Cathedral, 'in the time of divine service and presence of many citizens'. Excommunication meant he could not preach – he could not even enter a church.

Allen's clash with the authorities began when he refused to comply with directives from the recently appointed Bishop of Norwich, Matthew Wren. Wren's inspection of his new diocese – the Visitation of 1636 – became notorious, both for its rigour and for the way it expressed controversial policies promoted by the Archbishop of Canterbury, William Laud. Wren's agenda was extraordinarily detailed: the Visitation Articles required the clergy and churchwardens in each parish to answer almost nine hundred questions. The accompanying Orders insisted the Book of Common Prayer – the authorised service book of the English Church – must be followed to the letter. Wren cut out popular puritan pastimes like extra preaching on Sunday afternoons and weekdays, and banned freely composed prayers (often a sermon in themselves) before and after a preacher spoke. Allen objected, in particular, to the bishop's order that the communion table should be set against the east wall of the church, with no seats nearby, and a rail in front for parishioners to kneel at, 'so thick with pillars, that dogs may not get in'. For Protestants used to standing or sitting around a table to celebrate the 'Lord's Supper', these changes reeked of a return to the Catholic Mass.[2]

Allen petitioned Clement Corbet, the bishop's chancellor (a lawyer who presided at the Consistory Court, which handled matters of church discipline), to lift the sentence of excommunication. He deployed arguments put together by a scathing critic of Wren, the London lawyer William Prynne, to claim the action against him was illegal. Corbet dismissed Allen's appeal, and gave him a stark choice: to resign, or to affirm that 'the bishop could not err and command anything that might possibly be against the word of God'. Allen argued that such an exalted view of episcopal authority was repugnant to the doctrine of the Church of England. His petition of protest alleged that Corbet spoke to him 'in a very unbefitting manner, calling me and other ministers coxcombs, and knaves, and fools', saying 'preaching is but mere foolery and no better'.[3]

Loyalty to the Church of England was at stake. But who had become disloyal? In the religious culture of the time, novelty was bad – truth always had a long history. From Allen's point of view, Wren's orders for Norwich contained innovations that went well beyond what Parliament had ever authorised for the Church of England. For Wren and Corbet, Allen was the innovator who jeopardised 'the good foundation of doctrine and discipline' in the Church. Corbet was tempted to wish that, like the Gadarene swine who rushed over a cliff to destruction (Mark 5:11–13), Allen and his kind would be 'all precipitated with their precipitate and silly inventions'.[4]

Within three years Thomas Allen was in Massachusetts – like Susanna Bell, he found a New England. But before this he proved himself stubborn in his efforts to keep a foothold in Norwich. His petition against excommunication failed, but he still would not comply with Bishop Wren's orders; nor would he resign. For a few months he retreated to the Netherlands, a Calvinist refuge closely connected with Norwich through trade, to evade pressure.[5] His flock sent money – so 'addicted' to him, the church authorities reported, they would pay no-one but Allen or his deputies. While he was away his brother took legal action in the civil courts: Robert Allen brought a charge of trespass against the churchwardens and a workman, for digging up the chancel at St Edmunds to put in a communion rail and make steps to raise the altar (in obedience to Wren's directives).[6] When Allen came back to Norwich, Clement Corbet reported he was like a woodcock, an elusive and well camouflaged bird; or an owl, active only under cover of darkness.[7] Allen's discretion was a precaution against arrest. Any excommunicated person who did not make peace with the Church within forty days risked being taken into custody by the civil authorities. In June 1637 Corbet took a sheriff of Norwich and a keeper from the Norwich jail on a night raid, armed with a warrant from the Court of High Commission – the highest church court in the Province of Canterbury, presided over by Archbishop Laud. They set a watch at the house of Allen's brother. At eleven at night they heard 'one very earnest at his devotions', and broke in to search the premises. Thomas managed to slip away (leaving his sister-in-law to argue with the bishop's chancellor about whether she was within her rights to invite someone round to say prayers). Corbet never caught Allen. The Court of High Commission tried him in his absence and stripped him of his post as a preacher.[8] His tactics to play for time, and hold onto his parish by being evasive, came to nothing. After the night raid, Allen next appears across the Atlantic. Early in 1639 he joined the church at Boston, Massachusetts. Within a few months he became one of the ministers to the church at Charlestown, across the Charles River from Boston.[9]

By the late 1630s a whole network of people Allen knew had shipped themselves to the New World: a colleague in the ministry, his lawyer, and other members of his parish.[10] Michael Metcalfe, a weaver from St Edmund's who stood up for Allen in the church courts, emigrated with his wife, nine children and a servant, to evade a summons from the ecclesiastical authorities.[11] To justify his flight, Metcalfe wrote a long letter to fellow Christians in Norwich to denounce Wren's unlawful innovations – drenched in the language of John Foxe's *Book of Martyrs*, the book most favoured by godly English Protestants after the Bible. 'God is about to try his people in the furnace of his affliction', Metcalfe prophesied. (In 1654, in Massachusetts, Metcalfe bequeathed a copy of the *Book of Martyrs*. Since virtually all books in early New England arrived in settlers' baggage, this was probably something he had carried over from Norwich.) Foxe's account of Mary Tudor's fierce persecution of Protestants in the 1550s, when official policy briefly revived Catholicism, struck a chord. Marian martyrs went to the stake only two or three generations earlier, most in East Anglia.[12]

For emigrants like Allen and Metcalfe, the 1630s played out a providential drama in which history might repeat itself – preachers and people thrown together into God's furnace of affliction. Should they stay and see out the crisis, or find a refuge abroad? To leave England could be construed as desertion, but perhaps exceptional circumstances justified an extraordinary journey.

I

Preachers like Thomas Allen stood at the core of the campaign waged by committed Protestants to win England for the Reformation. Although the country turned Protestant by law in the mid-sixteenth century, it took much longer for reformed religion to travel from the statute book to the pew. The puritan movement that started in the 1560s, in the reign of Elizabeth I, was not so much a radical counter-culture as the first flush of grassroots enthusiasm for the new style of faith, stirred up by a generation of ministers educated in the Protestant hothouse of Cambridge colleges like Emmanuel. Preachers captured the imagination and energy of their congregations. What came from the pulpit was reinforced in smaller gatherings where the godly repeated to each other the notes they had taken at the sermon; in private counselling about cases of conscience; and in the intense attention given to 'godly life' in the rapidly growing print culture of puritanism.[13] Committed Protestants travelled from preacher to preacher – the London artisan Nehemiah Wallington once heard nineteen sermons in a week.[14] Admittedly, the puritan movement did not sit neatly with the geographically based structure of the English Church. The godly frequently crossed parish boundaries to hear preachers. Their style of piety meant relations between the zealous few and the rest of the parish were often edgy. Puritanism could take both moderate and divisive forms, in different social and cultural settings.[15] But despite the tendency of the godly to form an inner circle within the Church, most ardent Protestants still looked to parish pulpits as the way to secure and build up England's Reformation.

Loyalty to the Church of England ran deep. By the 1620s the broad boundaries of the puritan movement had been defined for fifty years by opposition to 'popery' and 'separation'. The fragile and incomplete nature of the Reformation in England made it vital to witness against what keen Protestants called 'popery' – traces of the Catholic past not yet purged from the English Church, or any hint of a Catholic revival. This was an age when Christ and Antichrist seemed ready to join battle. Fear and polemic occupied the ground between Protestant and Catholic; religion and politics went hand in hand.[16] To English Protestants, the threat of Catholicism seemed all the more real after Spanish forces overwhelmed Protestants in the German Palatinate in 1620 (a territory linked to England by the marriage of England's Princess Elizabeth, daughter of James I, to the staunchly Calvinist Elector of the Palatinate, Frederick V). A further blow was Charles I's marriage to a French Catholic, Princess Henrietta Maria, in 1625.[17]

At the other extreme from popery, and equally to be avoided, was 'separation'. Some radical Protestants renounced the Church of England as antichristian, and illegally separated from it to form their own exclusive and pure congregations, but only a tiny minority took this path. For the majority, although the English Church was still blemished by traces of Catholicism, it remained a true church. The godly mindset equated truth with unity, and error with division. So most wore their refusal to separate from the national Church as a badge of honour: splinter groups inevitably committed the sin of schism.[18]

Godly preachers relied on access to the pulpits of the Church of England to steer the ship of the Church between Scylla and Charybdis, the rocks of

popery and separation. Pragmatic compromises at a local level, from ministers prepared to moderate their demands for reform and from the bishops
who valued their preaching skills, kept the ball in play until the end of the
1620s. To keep public preaching free and plentiful, puritan clergy were often
prepared to conform (within reason) to what their superiors required – and if
they bent the rules a little to accommodate their convictions, they could
expect the creaky bureaucracy of the Church to be slow to chase them up. [19]

In the 1630s, the goal posts moved. Archbishop William Laud and others on
the bench of bishops conducted business in a brisker style, concerned to bring
order and decency to the Church – in the fabric of its buildings, in worship,
and in the discipline of the clergy. They introduced new ceremonies that
the godly saw as 'popish', like bowing at the name of Jesus. Old rules were
strictly enforced: for example, the requirement that ministers should wear a
surplice – a white flowing overgarment, which some puritans called the
'whore's smock' (a name derived from identifying the Catholic Church with
the antichristian Whore of Babylon in the Book of Revelation). Zealous
Protestants preferred a plain black gown with no frills, as worn in Geneva.
When the church authorities set conditions godly clergy found it hard to agree
to – a rule that preachers should not talk about predestination; a requirement
to read from the pulpit the Book of Sports, which legalised games on the
Sabbath – the godly took it as a sign that the Laudians wanted to cripple the
preaching ministry.[20] They believed that an end to sermons would have
calamitous effects: a rise in popery, an outpouring of divine wrath, the snuffing
out of the light of the gospel. When Thomas Allen and other Norwich ministers were prevented from preaching, godly citizens objected that the number
of 'papists' in the city had increased. It was claimed no danger from France or
Spain could compare with the threat to England from a God angry at the
silencing of his preachers. The image of silent preachers as 'extinguished
lights' became common currency. A minister was summoned to appear before
a church court for preaching that 'the lights of the Church of England were
gone into New England and . . . only the sockets were left'.[21]

The godly had felt under threat many times before: arguably, they often
defined their identity by indulging in a 'charitable Christian hatred' of their
enemies. But in the 1630s it seemed the old room for manoeuvre had gone.
Places of temporary refuge, like English congregations in the Netherlands,
came increasingly within reach of the long arm of Laud. In these changed
circumstances, America looked like a haven.[22]

II

The thousands who left for New England in the Great Migration were hardly typical Atlantic migrants. Settlers of more southerly colonies like Virginia, for example, were usually aged between fifteen and twenty-four, male, single, unskilled, from the lower strata of English society – mostly indentured servants, under contract to work for between four and seven years in return for their passage to the New World. New England's settlers, in contrast, travelled in families. This was the most family-centred migration in America's history. Instead of showing a bias towards the young, New England recruited a spectrum of ages that reflected England's population profile. The social standing of settlers was higher. They came from the middle ranks of English society. John Winthrop, the first Governor of Massachusetts, for example, came from a deeply religious minor gentry family in the Stour Valley, on the Essex–Suffolk border. He had some experience as a lawyer in London; he farmed his estate at Groton, Suffolk, and acted as a county Justice of the Peace. New England released him from falling rents and rising debts, and turned him into a big fish in a small pool. Beside upwardly aspiring gentry like Winthrop, the first settlers were yeomen (small landowners) and farmers; craftsmen like coopers, blacksmiths, tanners, millers, shoemakers and weavers; merchants and traders. New England had a more skilled population than anywhere else in the New World. The level of literacy was much higher than in England, reflecting the connection between print and Protestantism – Bible-reading habits. As a rule, emigrants came from large urban centres or small market towns (which made New England's wilderness more of a shock). Most came from communities in which they had a long family history. All in all, they were unusual migrants.[23]

When the godly were uprooted, they left their native soil not singly but in clumps. Along with the striking proportion of families in the Great Migration, a remarkable feature is the way emigrants banded together to travel in companies. Early in the 1630s, recruits gathered by local gentry – neighbours and friends, tenants and local craftsmen – were quite common. John Winthrop led a company from Suffolk in 1630. Many of the thousand souls who sailed on the seventeen ships in the Winthrop Fleet had set off from home in company with other local families, bound together by kinship and acquaintance over many years. Throughout the decade, puritan clerics travelled over with companies from their parish and neighbourhood. Nearly seven hundred East Anglian migrants made their way over in such pilgrim bands; similar parties left from the West Country, Yorkshire and Lancashire. Even when migrants travelled independently, ties to relatives and friends had often persuaded them to leave home: most came from a dense network of interrelated families.

Susanna Bell and her family, for example, followed her sister-in-law Katherine Meakins; Katherine had sailed on the *Griffin* in 1633, along with the company gathered by the minister John Cotton; Cotton and his clan had followed the Lincolnshire troupe led over in 1630 by Isaac Johnson, brother-in-law to the Earl of Lincoln. The puritan movement drew much of its vitality from strong social bonds. A mentality shaped by many years of 'gadding to sermons' together (as the godly liked to call their travels around the local area to hear good preachers) proved fertile ground from which to recruit settlers for New England.[24]

The Great Migration gathered pace slowly at the start. Only a trickle of migrants had settled in New England by 1633. The flood arrived between 1634 and 1639, and the influx reached its height in 1638. (A colossal endeavour to map out the lives of all the immigrants in the 1630s, the Great Migration Study Project currently underway in Boston, is patiently working its way through the decade. The project made relatively swift progress to 1633, but has now slowed under the sheer volume of new arrivals from 1634 onwards.) The pace of migration increased as the decade went on, with a step-change not long after Laud became Archbishop of Canterbury. Emigration and Laudian policy gathered momentum in tandem.[25]

It is difficult to determine what happened in the years and months before people set sail, to prompt them to leave England. Emigrants like Susanna Bell or Michael Metcalfe are highly unusual because they put on paper the events and motives that provoked their decision. For most migrants, the bare fact that they settled in New England survives, with no information about their reasons for setting out from home.

Ministers like Thomas Allen left more on the record about their movements and intentions on the eve of emigration. Allen was one of seventy-six ministers who went to New England between 1629 and 1640.[26] Although only a handful left personal statements about why they left England, tracing the experience of these migrant preachers in the years and months before they sailed for America can provide clues to wider patterns in the Great Migration – to the motives that gave a wide range of English citizens the pluck to cross the Atlantic to make a New England. The pervasive culture of preaching in godly circles meant these clerics had good opportunities to shape the outlook of their hearers. So the communities they left from, and when, and the chain of events that preceded and perhaps precipitated their departure, are significant. For this reason, it is worth making a journey up and down the dioceses of England, to investigate the circumstances of New England-bound ministers as they made the decision to leave home.

Particularly surprising is the fact that the overwhelming majority of migrant preachers came from a ministry deeply rooted in parish pulpits, not from a restless underworld of radicals well on their way to separation from the Church of England.[27] Many came from parishes they had served for years: John Cotton told his bishop he wanted to leave Boston in Lincolnshire after twenty years as minister there 'by the goodness of God ... and your Lordship's lawful favour'.[28] Only a few had been in posts where it was easier to shelter from the authorities' demands for religious conformity, as lecturers (preachers with no parish, sometimes appointed by a town council) or as household chaplains.[29] Only two had crossed the divide into separatism, renouncing their ordination in the Church of England as antichristian.[30] The rest had not. Richard Mather of Toxteth, Lancashire, took across the Atlantic in 1635 the certificate of ordination he had received from the Bishop of Chester in 1619. He kept it in his study at Dorchester, Massachusetts, where years later one of his sons found it – a torn piece of parchment – and asked what it was. Mather admitted he received the certificate from his bishop, 'and (said he) I tore it, because I took no pleasure in keeping a monument of my sin and folly in submitting to that superstition'. But intriguingly, Mather had not thrown it on the fire, as he might have done if he had totally rejected his English ministry. Like the true Church in England, the piece of parchment was damaged but not destroyed.[31]

The impression that these preachers were people reluctantly detached from the English Church – rather than closet separatists ready and willing to cut loose – is confirmed by the fact that at least half left England only after coming into conflict with the ecclesiastical authorities over requirements that they could not in conscience agree to.[32] Twenty-two of the seventy-six had been suspended or removed from their posts.[33] Sixteen more resigned or left when they were cited to appear in the Court of High Commission, or because they anticipated they could not comply with conditions the authorities set.[34] Many of the rest left when pressure in their locality visibly tightened, or the sense of threat became too much: threats could be as unsettling as direct action.[35]

A close connection exists between emigration and the dioceses where the Laudian agenda was most vigorously pursued. The diocese of London saw the greatest concentration – over a fifth of all clerical emigrants – and their displacement began early, concentrated in William Laud's time as Bishop of London between 1628 and 1633.[36] Laud's hand was strengthened by a document he had a large part in drafting, the 'Royal Instructions to the Episcopate' of 1629. These Instructions aimed to take a tighter grip on the culture of preaching: instead of offering extra sermons on Sunday afternoons, ministers should teach their flocks the catechism by question and answer; lecturers employed to preach by town corporations should not float free of pastoral responsibilities, but hold down a local parish appointment (so the bishop had more control over them).[37] One of those Laud targeted in his campaign was

Thomas Weld, Vicar of Terling in Essex. Initially, Weld was given three months to conform to what the authorities required. Given the slow speed of ecclesiastical machinery, he might have expected to be left alone to go on as before. Not so: Weld was interviewed again and again, until he declared that no amount of extra time would convince him to change his mind and comply. Then he was suspended, deprived of his living, and excommunicated.[38] The stringency of Laud's enquiries, and the efficiency of his administrative machine, sparked off the departures of others. Significantly, the haemorrhage of preachers from the diocese of London all but stopped after Laud became Archbishop of Canterbury in 1633 and was replaced as Bishop of London by the far less efficient William Juxon.

To the north, eleven ministers emigrated from the dioceses of Chester and York after pressure for conformity from Richard Neile, the Archbishop of York. Neile later boasted, 'I never deprived any man, but have endeavoured their reformation with meekness and with patience.'[39] True, his administrative style was less abrasive than Laud's – he preferred to keep ministers on suspension instead of moving quickly to dismiss them. But his velvet glove disguised a steely hand. In the diocese of Chester, Neile pressed Bishop John Bridgeman to enforce conformity. Neile organised his own Visitation in 1633, and saw to it that key officials followed Laudian policy.[40] One of the emigrant ministers, Samuel Eaton of West Kirby on the Wirral peninsula, had attracted attention for 'irregularities' between 1628 and 1630. Eaton was suspended and ejected from his parish in 1632, in the first phase of more rigorous demands for conformity. In 1634 he disappeared to the Netherlands for a while, probably to evade a summons to the Court of High Commission. (By 1640, he had built up a massive fine of £1,550 for failing to appear before the court: more than a minister might expect to earn in twenty or thirty years.) Eaton emigrated to New England in 1637, with his brothers Theophilus, a London merchant – later distinguished as Governor of New Haven Colony; and Nathaniel, an Essex curate and schoolmaster – later disgraced as the first head of Harvard College for feeding the students too little and beating them too much.[41] Across the Pennines in the diocese of York, a Bradford puritan recorded that many thought 'popery was likely to be set up and the light of the gospel put out'; many ministers had been silenced, and great numbers left for New England. Even Archbishop Neile admitted migration might have run out of control. He told Charles I in 1639 'too many of your Majesty's subjects inhabiting in these east parts of Yorkshire are gone into New England'.[42]

In the diocese of Norwich, Bishop Matthew Wren's campaign for conformity led to forty ministers being disciplined, among them Thomas Allen. Fourteen emigrated to New England. After his initial Visitation in 1636, Wren set up a network of commissioners to keep in motion what he had started. His Chancellor, Clement Corbet, was a tough enforcer in Norfolk.[43] Corbet's rigour was more than equalled in Suffolk by the zeal of the Archdeacon of Suffolk's agent, Henry Dade, who allegedly made an off-the-cuff remark at dinner (between bouts of presiding over a church court) that 'he knew the King and Council would be glad that the thousands who went to New England were drowned in the sea'.[44] One migrant from Dade's territory was John Phillip, Rector of Wrentham since 1609. Like Thomas Allen, Phillip tried to keep a foothold in his parish, despite a sentence of excommunication. He left eventually, in 1637, after letters came from the church at Dedham, Massachusetts (which was led by Phillip's former curate), to invite him over.[45] Henry Dade met his match in Ferdinando Adams, a shoemaker and church-warden of St Mary-le-Tower, Ipswich. Samuel Ward, town preacher at the church since 1605, had been suspended from the ministry by the Court of High Commission in November 1635. When Wren's agents arrived in April 1636, Adams would not unlock the Tower church to let them in. They stood outside for two hours, in the middle of a crowd angry at Ward's suspension. Adams refused to paint out a Biblical text daubed inside the building – 'My house shall be a house of prayer, but you have made it a den of thieves.' He would not take out seats in the chancel and move the communion table against the east wall. Henry Dade's fierce pursuit of Ipswich puritans eventually cost him his job, but not before Ferdinando Adams had fled to New England, excommunicated and in contempt of court.[46]

Later, to defend his record, Bishop Wren tried to head off the accusation that emigration resulted from episcopal pressure (by 1641, he and Laud were under investigation by Parliament and imprisoned in the Tower of London). Wren pointed to the large number of emigrants from the diocese of Lincoln, which under Bishop John Williams – long at odds with Laud, and by 1637 suspended by the Archbishop and locked up in the Tower – had been a haven for nonconformists.[47] In fact, the thirteen ministers who left the diocese of Lincoln went only after Laud started to overrule Williams and intervene directly.[48] John Cotton left his parish at Boston in Lincolnshire for Boston, Massachusetts, in 1633. Even though he had been heavily involved in discussions about emigration since 1629, he left only when his activities came under direct investigation by Laud's officials.[49]

Emigration to New England was not an obvious course of action. Far more people thought about America than ever made it to the boat – including an obscure and impoverished gentleman farmer, Oliver Cromwell (whose background was remarkably similar to that of Massachusetts' first governor, John Winthrop).[50] The relatively small number of clergy who eventually left England, and the delay between pressure from the church authorities and emigration, shows a reluctance to go.[51] Ministers played for time, and stayed close to their parishes if they could, perhaps installing a curate to preach in their place.[52] Some retreated to the Low Countries.[53] More moved within England, hoping that by going to a different diocese they would find freedom to preach. Thomas Shepard of Earls Colne in Essex, for example, went first to Yorkshire, then to Northumberland. Only after the authorities caught up with him again did Shepard think of going to the New World: 'seeing I had been tossed from the south to the north of England and now could go no farther, I . . . began to listen to a call to New England'.[54]

Some capitulated to what was asked of them, in order to keep a licence to preach – until, perhaps, the bar for conformity was raised again. Charles Chauncy gave in not once, but twice. As Vicar of Ware, Hertfordshire, he appeared before the Court of High Commission in 1630 for playing fast and loose with the Book of Common Prayer, and for his failure to wear the surplice or use the sign of the cross at baptism. After a meeting with Laud – then Bishop of London – Chauncy agreed to conform. But in 1633 he moved across a boundary, into the diocese of Peterborough, because some of his parishioners decided to rail in the communion table at Ware. Laud (this time as Archbishop of Canterbury) pursued Chauncy to his new parish; in 1635 the Court of High Commission suspended him from preaching. To get the suspension lifted, Chauncy had to read out in court, on bended knee before Laud, a statement accepting communion rails. He reached New England by 1638, on the verge of more trouble – a report to Laud's agent said Chauncy 'mends like sour ale in summer' (in other words, not at all).[55] Chauncy was deeply ashamed of his double submission to Laud. It haunted him for the rest of his life, despite a distinguished career in New England, where he spent almost twenty years as President of Harvard. Around the time of his trial in 1635, he christened his son Ichabod, 'the glory has departed' (identifying the troubles of the Church of England under Laud with the capture of the Ark of God by the Philistines, 1 Samuel 4:21). When Chauncy sailed for New England, he left behind a handwritten recantation of what he had agreed to in court. As soon as censorship of the press eased up, in 1641, he sent instructions for his manuscript to be printed. At his induction as pastor of Scituate, Massachusetts, he told the congregation: 'Alas, Christians! I am no maiden; for my soul has been defiled with false worship.'[56] Chauncy held on to his ministry in England tenaciously, by twists and turns, for most of the 1630s. The decision to go to New England was rarely hasty. Often, as in Chauncy's case, it came at the end of a long war of attrition.

III

Hesitation about emigration, and reluctance to pluck up roots in England, stemmed from doubts about the depth of the crisis and how soon it would pass. Perhaps divine judgment on England could still be averted. Even if things went from bad to worse, God could be relied on to protect his own, just as he had preserved the elect during the centuries when Rome governed England's churches. Was it wise to drain England of godly citizens, at a time when they were needed to witness against popery? A mass migration across the Atlantic had implications altogether different from private, temporary flight to another part of the country, or to the Netherlands. Samuel Ward, minister at St Mary-le-Tower in Ipswich, declared he was 'not of so melancholy a spirit, nor looked through so black spectacles as to write that religion stands on tiptoe in this land, looking westwards'. Ward's remarks have to be taken with a pinch of salt, since he wrote in answer to questions from the Court of High Commission. Yet in the end Ward stayed in Ipswich, suspended by the church authorities, but with his stipend as town preacher still paid by the corporation. Of Ward's extended family – a veritable dynasty of ministers – three scattered to New England or the Netherlands.[57] However, his step-brother Daniel Rogers of Wethersfield in Essex, who was suspended by Laud in 1629, also stayed put. Rogers preached against emigration in the late 1630s: 'Alas! . . . All cannot go. What will become of such as must stay?'[58] The Essex minister Thomas Shepard recalled talking with Rogers and other ministers from the county about whether to 'let such a swine [Laud] . . . root up God's plants'. Of the six people Shepard identified as party to that conversation, Rogers and two others remained in England, while Shepard and two others left for America. The decision about whether to go or stay divided the godly community.[59]

Godly emigrants – people like Susanna Bell as well as clerics – worried a great deal about staying on the right side of Providence. Without the protection of Providence, settlement in New England courted disaster: financial ruin or (even more dire in the eyes of the godly) spiritual disorder. To find out which way Providence wanted them to go, the godly looked to each other to test out the truth, in a corporate, social process.[60] Emigrants thought a common mind would represent a stamp of approval from Providence. The godly who left wanted the godly who stayed behind to share their view of emigration. This required communal scrutiny of the reasons for leaving England. A consensus in favour would avoid charges that they were deserting their homeland, or (worse still) falling into the sin of schism. If the policies of the Laudian regime threatened to unleash God's wrath on England, breaking up the unity of the godly would bring down an even greater heap of Providential coals upon their heads.

A streak of providentialism ran through the debate about emigration, and allowed emigrants to gather many kinds of motive into a religious framework. Providence had a knack of presenting the same truth in different guises, so a habit of puritan piety (evident in diaries and letters) was to look for multiple reasons that pointed the same way. Economic and religious motives did not compete, but complemented each other. A weaver like Michael Metcalfe must have been conscious of a slump in the textile industry in the 1630s – particularly with nine children to feed – but his letter to the people of Norwich shows he was equally galvanised by unpalatable innovations in his church.[61] 'Religion and profit jump together', as one colonist put it. The families that settled New England were not fortune hunters. To recognise the tug of Providence in the call to emigrate, however, they wanted to be sure they could make a living. They looked to Providence to provide a basic 'competency' – enough to get by on, so they could worship God unhindered by worldly concerns: 'nothing sorts better with piety than competency'.[62] A dozen different reasons to follow the compass west to America – religious or otherwise – confirmed the hand of Providence on the tiller.[63]

A remarkable amount of heart-searching went on before potential migrants turned into settlers on board a ship for New England. As colonists later pointed out, to defend their course of action, 'Yea, how many serious consultations with one another, and with the faithful ministers, and other eminent servants of Christ, have been taken about this work . . . which clears us from any rash heady rushing into this place, out of discontent.'[64] In the summer of 1629, meetings in Lincolnshire, Bury St Edmunds and Cambridge thrashed out the prospects for settlement. John Winthrop made a long list of pros and cons. Handwritten copies of his document circulated among the godly (several slightly different manuscripts survive). These discussions led to a decision by Winthrop and others to emigrate. Winthrop was chosen Governor of the Massachusetts Bay Company and – in a neat manoeuvre to evade interference from the English government – the Company resolved to move lock, stock and barrel to the New World.[65] Later on, in Lancashire, Richard Mather drew up arguments for emigration to be debated at local gatherings of clerics and lay people. Mather's case, supported with a battery of references to Scripture, began with the proposition that 'to remove from a corrupt church to a purer is necessary for them that are not otherwise tied, but free'. Christians ought to move, if they could, from persecution to safety, from restriction to freedom, from a place with 'fearful signs of desolation' to a place with 'well grounded hope . . . of God's protection'.[66] On a more intimate scale, the diary of Samuel Rogers – son of Daniel Rogers, minister at Wethersfield in

Essex – contains echoes of many conversations he was party to, or overheard, about New England. Samuel aspired to be a preacher but saw no way to get a job in East Anglia, given the strict requirements for conformity: 'poor Suffolk and Norfolk lying desolate by that cursed wretch Wren . . . oh Lord some way for preaching; oh my soul is in New England'. His father Daniel spoke out against emigration. Samuel swayed towards it, under the influence of people who were about to set sail and settlers who had come back to gather recruits. From 1635 to 1637 he went through an agony of indecision about whether to join the tide of emigrants but, in the end, stayed at home.[67]

Long-standing debates among the godly about how to behave under pressure lay behind these discussions.[68] When John Cotton came under scrutiny from the Court of High Commission in 1632, he travelled with some friends from Lincolnshire to Northamptonshire, to get advice from the veteran nonconformist John Dod. Dod's national standing within the puritan movement made his opinion significant. A generation earlier, similar debates about conformity followed the Hampton Court Conference of 1604 – where James I initiated some religious reform but insisted that all clergy should accept the scriptural character of the Book of Common Prayer, the hierarchically ordered ministry of bishops, priests and deacons, and the Thirty-Nine Articles as a standard for doctrine. Dod could not accept all the conditions. He managed to continue his ministry from within a private household (an arrangement connived at by a series of bishops), and so proved that being a suspended preacher need not mean outright separatism or an end to pastoral work. The purpose of Cotton's visit was to find out if Dod would advise him to take the same path. In the circumstances of the 1630s, Dod thought not: 'I am old . . . and therefore must stand still, and bear the brunt; but you, being young . . . may go whither you will, and ought, being persecuted in one city, to flee unto another.' In a striking reversal, Dod changed his mind about emigration within a few years, and started to discourage it. But in 1632 he told not only Cotton but also his Lincolnshire friends to go, saying 'the removing of a minister was like the draining of a fish pond: the good fish will follow the water, but eels, and other baggage fish, will stick in the mud'.[69] After his conversation with Dod, just before he set sail for Massachusetts in 1633, Cotton took part in a secret meeting at Ockley in Surrey about how far to conform to ceremonies. All but one of the ministers present eventually left for the Netherlands or New England. The departure of ministers like Cotton tempted more than the 'good fish' of Boston in Lincolnshire to cross the pond.[70]

Good precedents existed for a tactical retreat from England. Emigrants found examples going back to the days of Israel, but the Marian exiles – the Protestants who fled abroad during the reign of Mary Tudor – came most quickly to mind. John Cotton contrasted these wise exiles of the 1550s, whose actions protected Reformed religion and helped to preserve the Church of England, with the unwise German Protestants of the Upper Palatinate, who in the 1620s stayed on after their ministers were banished, and found their church snuffed out. Richard Mather pointed out that the Protestant martyrs Nicholas Ridley and John Bradford, who died at the stake in 1555, advised fellow Christians to flee England.[71] Looking further back, John Davenport cited examples from the Bible and early Christian history, to show how voluntary banishment – self-imposed exile – could be a real confession of faith, not cowardice: it witnessed 'that our faith is dearer unto us, than all the enjoyments from which we fly'.[72] Richard Mather cited one of the Ten Commandments, 'Thou shalt not kill', to justify an escape from danger, since a Christian who buckled under persecution committed spiritual suicide – 'soul murder'.[73]

With eyes trained by Foxe's *Book of Martyrs* to follow in the footsteps of Marian Protestants, the godly had a razor-sharp perception of change stirring: a revitalisation of Catholic influence. This, like Providence, became a thread that tied many things together. John Winthrop and his circle implicated popery in the decay of justice, the malaise in trade, the stagnation of 'fountains of learning and religion'. To justify their journey out of England, emigrants pitted popery against purity, threat against opportunity. Anxiety about the return of Catholicism to England loosened inhibitions about leaving home, and whetted the appetite for purity. If Laudian policy posed an extraordinary threat, the empty landscape of New England presented an unusual opportunity to build a godly society from scratch, in a Reformation by evasion.[74] This is not to say that emigrants sailed for New England with a sense of divine mission – an 'errand into the wilderness' to light a torch for purity that would show the way to a complete Reformation, to the millennial rule of Christ at the end of time. That vision of New England's unique purpose came later, from the settlers' children and grandchildren, who wanted to portray the heroism of the first generation in order to stir up in their own time a strong and united sense of purpose.[75] What motivated migrants in the 1630s was a search for primitive purity – for biblical patterns of life, rather a millennial dream. These radical conservatives looked backwards, not forwards.[76]

If emigration could be construed as a protest against popery, this was checked and balanced by the other theme familiar in godly circles: resisting schismatic separation from the Church in England. To show they had left lawfully, the pioneers of New England set a high premium on making right use of the freedom America offered. Purity must be matched with peaceful, orderly settlement. John Winthrop believed emigrants could not afford to forfeit the good opinion of the godly at home. To do so would undermine perceptions that the venture had the blessing of Providence. Concern for New England's reputation lay at the heart of Winthrop's famous words to fellow emigrants on the way to America:

> we shall be as a city upon a hill, the eyes of all people are upon us; so that if we shall deal falsely with our God in this work we have undertaken . . . we shall be made a story and a by-word through the world, we shall open the mouths of enemies to speak evil of the ways of God . . . we shall shame the faces of many of God's worthy servants, and cause their prayers to be turned into curses upon us.[77]

Winthrop's city upon a hill was not a 'world-redeeming beacon', the 'hub of the universe', the 'New Jerusalem'.[78] His attitude was altogether more defensive and anxious. Winthrop feared New England could become a by-word for error, a cause for shame, the object of curses. A city on a hill is exposed. Winthrop wanted to be sure he and others would not be found in the wrong – either by the godly, or by God. A letter to his wife Margaret, written a few months before he set sail for America, expressed a mixture of confidence in Providence and fear of what might happen if settlers did not live up to divine expectations:

> Is he not a God abroad as well as at home? Is not his power and Providence the same in New England that it hath been in old England? If our ways please him he can command deliverance and safety in all places, and can make the stones of the field, and the beasts, yea, the raging seas and our very enemies, to be in league with us. But if we sin against him, he can raise up evil against us out of our own bowels, houses, estates etc.[79]

Emigrants like Winthrop wanted to please the Almighty and his people. Harsh judgment would follow if they did not. So they sailed away from England with a strong compulsion to do their duty, although how to work this out in practice was unclear. New England was such a vast unknown.

IV

Susanna Bell remembered how she saw nothing but sea and sky for two months, on her voyage across the Atlantic. Many emigrants – Susanna included – had probably never been on a ship before. If they had, it would have been in coastal waters, not out on open seas. One writer tried to reassure nervous travellers by comparing the vessel to a cradle, rocked up and down by a careful mother, never turning over: 'so a ship may often be rocked ... upon the troublesome sea, yet seldom doth it sink ... because it is kept by that careful hand of Providence by which it is rocked'.[80] These were not professional sailors or itinerant merchants, but migrants who paid for a passage. The cost of the transatlantic journey was significant, and screened out those who could not afford to pay their way. A fare of five pounds for an adult, announced by the Massachusetts Bay Company in 1629, became a basic standard. A family with a cow and assorted goods might pay fifty pounds or more to reach New England – not much to a wealthy gentleman or merchant but a year's wage for a yeoman farmer or minister, and well out of the reach of a poor labourer.

The tricky question of what to pack for a New World was answered by advice put out by New England's promoters, and by letters from settlers with instructions about what to bring. For example, a sheet printed in London – *Provisions needfull for such as intend to plant themselves in New England, for one whole yeare* – included bacon, butter, cheese, vinegar and salt; stockings, six pairs of shoes, twelve handkerchiefs; a spade, a shovel, two hatchets; nails, locks; a musket and shot; two lines for fishing. Another tract, *New Englands Prospect*, recommended a long list of items for the voyage, including skillets to cook in, live poultry, prunes, and (for those who could afford it) good claret wine to cure sea-sickness.[81] Before settlers' work to tame the land produced adequate food, some advised migrants to bring basic supplies to feed their families for eighteen months, to cover two growing seasons. In an effort to encourage those daunted by the expense, poorer travellers were given hints to trim the costs – for example, they would not need to bring as much malt for brewing if they were prepared to drink water in the heat of summer, 'which is found by much experience to be as wholesome and healthful as beer'.[82] Some, though, travelled with a great deal more than the bare necessities. The Reverend Jose Glover and his wife Elizabeth, for example, brought not only a printing press – the one press in early New England, which stood idle for years in Harvard Yard – but also a substantial collection of silver that Elizabeth obviously could not bear to leave behind. The extent of the treasure is on record because of family strife over it after her death: 'a very fair and large silver basin and ewer, spoons, dishes, cups, bowls, tankards etc. ... . a fair and full cupboard of plate there was, as might ordinarily be seen in most gentlemen's houses in England'.[83]

When they got their goods and chattels to a port, emigrants often had to wait weeks to find a ship bound for New England. Most vessels could take around a hundred passengers. People competed for space with animals and cargo. The Lancashire minister Richard Mather sailed on the *James* with a hundred other travellers, twenty-three crew, twenty-three cows, three calves and eight mares. He kept a journal of his voyage, with daily entries from 23 May 1635 – when, after more than a month's wait in Bristol to find a passage, he and his family went aboard ship – to 16 August, when the ship reached Boston harbour. Just before the ship left Bristol, government bureaucracy worked as it was meant to (which often it did not). Customs searchers came aboard to check that all passengers had a certificate from their parish minister or a Justice of the Peace to attest their honesty and orthodoxy. This was the passport to sail away. Mather's entries for the first few days, when the ship danced at anchor offshore in the wind and the women and children got seasick while sailors stowed supplies, reflected passengers' frustration: 'We . . . would . . . have had anchor weighed, and sail set, that we might have . . . been gone. But the mariners would insist that they could not stir till the goods were stowed.' Three days later, when the decks were more or less clear of cargo, 'the wind turned directly against us . . . so that we were forced to cast anchor again, and sit still' – the first of many delays in a three thousand mile journey at the mercy of the wind and the waves.[84] *2 to 3 month*

The voyage usually took between eight and twelve weeks, though one ship took twenty-six, struggling on the open seas for eighteen. Vessels often sailed together, for safety. On the way, travellers heard two sermons on a Sunday and (in defiance of a government order) did not follow the Book of Common Prayer.[85] Passengers slept in hammocks and cots, separated by flimsy canvas partitions. A gentleman might get a cabin. Shipboard rations deteriorated as time went on: a predictable diet of oatmeal, buttered peas, cured beef and pork, biscuits, dried bread; enlivened by eggs and milk from animals aboard and fresh fish when passengers or crew could catch it. Richard Mather noted sights on the way: 'mighty whales spewing up water in the air like the smoke of a chimney . . . of such incredible bigness that I will never [again] wonder that the body of Jonas could be in the belly of a whale'.[86] John Winthrop recorded how skiffs (small boats that took oars or a sail) ferried people between ships in mid-Atlantic, to bring shipmasters and eminent passengers together for dinner; to fetch a midwife for a woman in labour.[87] Thomas Weld sent back to Essex an ecstatic account of God's protection on the way over, as an incentive to persuade more of his parishioners to follow him:

Yea, mercy, mercy in the Lord, inwardly outwardly, in spite of devils and storms as cheerful as ever, my wife all the voyage on the sea better than at land, and seasick but one day in eleven weeks, at sea my children never better in their lives. They went ill into the ship but well there and came forth well as ever. Myself had not one ounce of seasickness, nor one motion or inclination thereunto, not all the way. 'Stand still and behold the salvation of the Lord.'[88]

Hanserd Knollys (a minister from Lincolnshire who returned to England within three years, and became a prominent Baptist) was more realistic about his fourteen-week voyage:

> By the way my little child died with convulsion fits, our beer and water stank, our biscuit was green, yellow and blue, moulded and rotten, and our cheese also, so that we suffered much hardship . . . but God was gracious to us, and led us safe through those great deeps . . .[89]

Whatever terrors the wind and waves unleashed, migrants felt protected by Providence. John Winthrop wrote that preservation from danger was 'so frequent, to such ships as have carried those of the Lord's family between the two Englands, as would fill a perfect volume to report them all'.[90] Richard Mather testified that in the storms on his voyage, 'my fear was the less, when I considered the clearness of my calling from God this way'. He recorded in his journal how one morning the wind and rain tore the sails into shreds, like rotten rags. The *James* lurched towards a vast rock, and all aboard waited to hear and feel the crash – but God took them past it: 'On that day the Lord granted us as wonderful a deliverance as I think ever people had . . . The Lord so imprint the memory of it on our hearts, that we may be the better for it . . . I hope we shall not forget the passages of that morning until our dying day.'[91]

After two and a half months at sea, Governor Winthrop recorded the sensory delights of reaching land: 'there came a smell off the shore which was like the smell of a garden'; a wild pigeon and a small land bird flew on board; English fishing boats could be seen off the coast. At four in the morning, the *Arbella* came close to Boston harbour. Later that day, the seafarers went ashore and enjoyed venison pasties, good beer, and wild strawberries.[92]

THE CREATION OF THE NEW ENGLAND WAY

Hail holy land wherein our holy Lord
Hath planted his most true and holy Word . . .
Methinks I hear the Lamb of God thus speak:
'Come my little dear flock, who for my sake
Have left your country, dearest friends and goods
And hazarded your lives over the raging floods.
Possess this country: free from all annoy
Here I'll be with you, here you shall enjoy
My sabbaths, sacraments, my ministry
And ordinances in their purity . . .'

Thomas Tillam, 'Upon the first sight of New England, 29 June 1638'[1]

Tillam's vision of New England is a classic of early American poetry. What is not well known is that soon after Tillam first set eyes on America he left it for good. He arrived in Boston in the summer of 1638, at the high tide of immigration to New England, one of at least three thousand settlers who arrived that summer.[2] He stepped into the aftermath of the Antinomian Controversy of 1637, the dispute that split Massachusetts over how Christians received assurance of God's free gift of salvation. To judge from his later history as an exotic religious radical in England, Tillam probably had sympathies with the outlawed free grace movement; that is, with the antinomians who believed assurance could come in an instant, by an act of the Holy Spirit. He found himself out of step with orthodoxy in Massachusetts, which insisted on an intense process of self-scrutiny to prepare the heart for God. Quite quickly, Tillam – a shadowy character in the New World, apart from his poem – decided to go home.[3]

Tillam's decision to turn back to England was not exceptional. At the start, many immigrants took the first opportunity to leave. Of the thousand or so migrants who arrived in Massachusetts in the summer of 1630, on the seventeen ships in the Winthrop Fleet, two hundred went back to England within a year – a hundred within just a few weeks, seizing the chance of a passage home when the fleet set sail again; more the following spring, after a harsh New England winter carried another two hundred of their fellow-settlers to the grave.[4] Sir Richard Saltonstall, who brought over six children and a company of settlers from Yorkshire, left three of his sons in New England but took the rest of his family home in 1631. He had invested heavily in the Bay Company, but was disenchanted.[5] At the same time, Thomas and Tabitha Sharpe left for Essex – a few months after the death of their daughter, a few days after a devastating fire destroyed their home.[6] *New-Englands Plantation*, a promotional tract published in London in 1630, told settlers to expect fertile soil, thick grass, root vegetables in the soil just waiting to be dug up – 'turnips, parsnips and carrots . . . bigger and sweeter than is ordinarily to be found in England'; good dry air that would heal those who had been weak in old England – 'a sup of New England's air is better than a whole draught of old England's ale'.[7] What settlers actually found was quite different.

Conditions were tough. Newly built houses often went up in flames, a hazard of open fires and poorly protected wooden chimneys, and the practice of clearing ground by burning it. The immigrants struggled to cultivate land, which required far more hard manual labour than most had been used to.[8] They worked the ground using the farming customs they brought with them from different parts of England, and made what they could of a short growing season. Icy winters froze the ground, froze rivers and harbours, froze off fingers and toes, froze beards so that settlers had trouble taking a swig of 'strong water' to keep warm. Plagues of pigeons threatened the crops; hogs ran amok and spoiled the corn; marauding wolves carried off cattle and swine.[9] The venison pasties and strawberries enjoyed by passengers from the *Arbella* on their first day in America were an exception, not the rule. In 1631, when food ran short and settlers waited for the next ship to arrive, women in coastal communities foraged for clams 'once a day, as the tide gave way . . . with much heavenly discourse of the provisions Christ had formerly made for many thousands of his followers in the wilderness'.[10] At the beginning, everything manufactured had to be imported from England: cloth, hats, shoes, metal goods, and much more. (Industry in Massachusetts – Yorkshire settlers who wove fabric and rugs at Rowley, ironworks powered by water wheel on the Saugus River at Lynn – made a faltering start in the 1640s.)[11] John Winthrop, the Governor of Massachusetts, observed that in the winter of 1630 to 1631, many of the poorer settlers, 'who lay long in tents', were debilitated by scurvy. A ship from England brought a stock of lemon juice, which gave the scurvy sufferers some relief from too much food preserved with salt and too little fruit and vegetables. But in an early example of many bitter judgments that dropped from his pen against those who pined for home, Winthrop commented, 'it hath always been observed here, that such as fell into discontent and lingered after their former conditions in England, fell into the scurvy, and died'.[12] A colonist called John Pratt wrote home that settlers, like Jesus in the wilderness, were tempted by the devil to ask God to turn stones into bread. Pratt's letter annoyed colonial leaders, who were keen to protect recruitment, but it was near the mark. New England's soil, apart from a few rich pockets, was stony and poor. The huge influx of migrants from 1634 onwards overstretched fragile resources and made the provision of basic supplies a constant struggle.[13]

Despite the difficulties, most settlers battled on rather than return to a native country where it seemed things were going from bad to worse. As more and more people arrived from England, a 'Great Reshuffling' took place. Colonists fanned out from Boston and its surrounding towns to pioneer new settlements across Massachusetts, to the west on the Connecticut River valley and along the coast of Long Island Sound.[14] This reshuffling helped New England to accommodate the appetite of its fast-growing population for land to live off, but Governor Winthrop resented internal migration because he thought scattered settlers would threaten the viability of the Bay Colony: he wanted controlled and focused settlement, not randomly dispersed communities.[15]

In one regard, though, migration was useful to a Bay Colony magistrate like Winthrop. Forced migration – banishment – limited the damage that religious disputes could cause. Differences within the puritan movement, which had long been submerged back home by the need to keep up a common front against popery, soon broke to the surface in New England. Massachusetts expelled Roger Williams in 1636 for his separatist rejection of the Church of England. In the aftermath of the Antinomian Controversy of 1637, the Bay Colony banished or froze out advocates of free grace. Many went to Maine or Rhode Island, or (like Sir Henry Vane and Thomas Tillam) home to England. The eviction of separatists and antinomians gave the Massachusetts authorities a valuable opportunity to show the godly in England how well they could suppress heresy and promote unity.[16] To protect investment and immigration – both of which were desperately needed if the frail new settlements were to have a future – it was essential to safeguard New England's reputation for orthodoxy.

difficult farm conditions

I

How to keep settlers settled, and give structure to fragile communities? This was the question that lay behind many of the decisions that colonial leaders took in hammering out codes for religious and civic life.

On the way to Massachusetts in 1630, John Winthrop told fellow travellers they should not expect simply to replicate what they had known at home, but must go further: 'whatsoever we did or ought to have done when we lived in England, the same must we do and more also where we go'. New England must turn theory into reality: 'what most in their churches maintain as a truth in profession only, we must bring into familiar and constant practice'.[17] The detail was not worked out in advance. Before he left for America, Winthrop asked the puritan theologian William Ames for advice. Ames, a leading theorist on church reform who had lived in Rotterdam for many years, intended to join the Great Migration but did not live to make the voyage. (Massachusetts had to make do with his picture: his widow and family arrived in 1637, probably bringing over the Dutch portrait of Ames that still survives in a New England collection, a rare relic from the early days.) Ames told Winthrop he felt unable to give specific guidance for a New World: 'I have nothing to write . . . being ignorant of special difficulties'. He imagined, in general terms, 'care of safety, liberty, unity, with purity, to be in all your minds and desires'; if anything more occurred to him, he would let Winthrop know.[18]

Within a few years of the arrival of the Winthrop Fleet in 1630, settlers had translated vague principles into what became known by the 1640s as the 'New England Way', or Congregationalism. This was a new and controversial model of what a pure church should be: distinct from what settlers had known in England; distinct from the practice of other Reformed churches in Europe; distinct even from the views of William Ames, which had influenced a whole generation of zealous English Protestants.[19] The unique character of New England's churches came about because the convictions that carried settlers away from England, in the tough environment of the New World, turned pious practices into the foundations for pure churches. Old habits took new forms. Settlers' inventive use of covenants and spiritual testimony, and the local horizons that circumscribed their churches, all had deep roots in migrants' experiences back home, but led to striking innovations in the New World. What started out in England as voluntary strategies among the godly – used to express their identity as zealous Protestants – became essentials in New England, to define the identity of the Church.

To create stability in settlements that were starting from nothing, settlers used covenants – solemn agreements which bound settlers together with common rights and responsibilities – as a foundation for both religious and civic life.[20] Covenanting had its roots in the rich seams of covenant theology that ran through the Reformed tradition, drawing on God's covenant with the old Israel and the new (the Church). In practical terms, it drew on solemn religious vows the godly had long used to steady themselves in times of difficulty or to give a framework to their fellowship.[21] Many literate settlers (and those they read to) would have been familiar with a best-selling guide to Christian living written by the Elizabethan minister Richard Rogers, of Wethersfield in Essex. This recounted how Rogers and the keenest Christians in his parish entered into a covenant together in 1588, the year when England quaked in fear of a Catholic invasion by the Spanish Armada. To distinguish Wethersfield's covenant from the covenants separatists used to create illegal alternative churches, Rogers presented what they had done as a way to support individuals' growth in faith, by binding the community together. He insisted it was not a decision to found a new church. What happened at Wethersfield inspired Protestants of the next generation. In 1616, the future Governor of Massachusetts, John Winthrop, got up at dawn to read over 'the covenant of certain Christians set down in Mr Roger's book'; in the 1620s John Cotton used a covenant to gather the godly together in his parish at Boston, Lincolnshire. Long before godly migrants sailed for the New World, pious vows were part of their religious life. In New England, covenants quickly emerged as a Scripture-sanctioned innovation to brace new communities.[22]

In civic life the practice of covenanting had less of a hinterland than in piety, which meant it took a wider variety of forms in New England. But civil covenants (or their equivalent, 'articles of association' or 'town orders') usually came first, before a church covenant. To get farming underway, land had to be shared out immediately. The inhabitants of a new plantation quickly drew up agreements about land allocations and mutual obligations (for fences, control of livestock, common grazing areas and the like), using principles derived from English trading companies and land corporations. Town covenants provided an immediate framework for the difficult and expensive enterprise of launching new settlements.[23]

Settlers could take longer over the serious business of setting up a church. To make a covenant the foundation of a new church was a step beyond godly practice in England (as exemplified by the Wethersfield covenant) and hence aroused suspicions back home that colonists had turned separatist. New England's leaders argued that this was not so; that church covenants were a legitimate innovation in a New World where new churches had to start from scratch.[24] In Massachusetts, 'church-gathering', as settlers called it, required at least seven potential members, and permission from the magistrates. Once these conditions were met,

> A ... number of Christians, as allowed by the General Court to plant together, at a day prefixed come together in public manner, in some fit place, and there confess their sins and profess their faith unto one another, and being satisfied of one another's faith and repentance they solemnly enter into a covenant with God, and one another (which is called their church covenant, and held by them to constitute a church) . . . [25]

Each church composed its own covenant. Members at Boston wrote their founding vow as the first entry in the church record book:

> We whose names are hereunder written, being by [God's] most wise and good Providence brought together into this part of America in the Bay of Massachusetts . . . do hereby solemnly and religiously . . . promise and bind ourselves to walk in all our ways according to the rule of the Gospel . . . and in mutual love and respect to each other, so near as God shall give us grace. [26]

Some settlers refused to accept this innovation. A 'Master Martin', who dared to suggest that church covenant was a human invention – and produced his sword to argue the point – was fined ten pounds. He did not have the cash, so the authorities took his cow. [27]

Covenants gave settlers an obligation to watch over each other. This, in theory at least – the reality was rarely so tidy – put brakes on movement. Anyone bound up in a church covenant who wanted to live for a while in another settlement, or to visit England, was expected to ask for a 'letter of recommendation' to gain the credentials to join another church temporarily. When a move was permanent, church members were meant to be 'dismissed' to the church at their new place of residence. [28] Critics in England quickly spotted that people who joined a covenanted community could not leave without permission. An English merchant advised his son not to settle in Massachusetts for this reason. [29] But supporters of covenants presented them as a powerful means to stop settlers leaving at will, to avert the 'ruin that may fall upon the body, if every ... member should depart at his own pleasure . . . If one man may . . . depart, why not another also . . . And if one, why not two, six, ten [or] twelve?' [30]

In New England, the Church was all about closely connected believers known to each other – not a building, or a hierarchy, but a community. Each settlement was expected to centre on a meetinghouse for the town and church: usually built of wood, and 'as fair . . . as they can provide'; usually unheated – except by fiery sermons and fierce town debates – because they were also used to store munitions. In 1636, the Massachusetts General Court tried to insist that all houses must be built within half a mile of the meeting-house. An unsigned and undated 'essay on the ordering of towns' set the meeting-house at the heart of a plantation's circumference, with no house more than fifteen hundred paces away, 'orderly placed to enjoy comfortable communion'. Of more than two hundred meetinghouses built before 1700, only the Old Ship Meeting House at Hingham in Massachusetts still exists, dating from 1681.[31] It used to be thought that Henry Whitfield's stone house at Guilford, Connecticut, built in 1639 and 1640, was the earliest surviving meeting place for church and town. Whitfield and his company, who made a plantation covenant as their ship stood at anchor off New Haven in 1639, decided to build four fortified houses as community strongholds. Whitfield built in granite, with a lookout window onto Long Island Sound, and a Great Hall thirty feet by fifteen. But even at the start, Guilford's forty-five families could not have squeezed into the Great Hall. Until they built a meetinghouse on the town green in 1643, the settlers of Guilford – like their neighbours at New Haven – probably worshipped outdoors when the weather permitted, and at other times in a large barn.[32]

Guilford's godly inhabitants believed they had rediscovered the pattern of primitive purity from the New Testament. Advocates of the New England Way made a distinctive claim: Christ's visible Church on earth existed only in local gatherings of 'saints'. No infrastructure existed beyond the local congregation, except for the duty of churches to consult each other for advice, and the responsibility of magistrates to stamp out heresy. Church members voted one another in or out, and elected or ejected ministers. In a draughty meeting-house, or in a barn or the open air, the community gathered by a covenant constituted the Church.[33] These local horizons were shaped by settlers' experience in England. In the early decades of the seventeenth century, the activities of the puritan movement had been strongly focused in local communities of the godly, and in the 1630s these defined themselves ever more sharply against what they saw as a come-back of Catholicism.[34] When emigrants crossed the Atlantic, they carried over both the local horizons of their godly circles and a determination to create churches that were the antithesis of everything 'popish'. The result – the local autonomy of individual churches in New England – broke the mould in an age where national churches with a strong clerical hierarchy were the norm.

The most striking innovation of all was the decision to ask people who wanted to join the church to give a testimony of religious experience. Susanna Bell made this event the pivotal moment in her spiritual autobiography.[35] Like covenants and the local focus of puritan piety, this innovation also turned a voluntary element of English puritanism into something that defined the boundaries of the Church: who was in and who was out. For more than a generation before settlers arrived in New England, zealous English Calvinists had examined their lives for signs of God's predestinating grace, to fathom the mysteries of Providence and discover assurance of election to salvation. Once in New England, this habit found a new, communal, context.[36] First in private to the church elders, then in public to the congregation, people were invited to give a personal history of God's work in their soul. Men could speak for themselves. Women, in Boston at least, did not address the whole church: the pastor read out what had been said in private, from notes he had scribbled down at the time.[37] Sometimes, as in Susanna Bell's case, the occasion could be fraught. One jaundiced settler remembered how an old man crumpled under a torrent of questions, struggling to satisfy the church that he was a genuine believer:

> At last . . . he said, with tears in his eyes, that it was more than he could do to show his assurance for heaven and salvation . . . for he himself had been in doubt thereof above forty years and knew not when he should come to the end of his doubts and fears.

Some liked what the old man said, others muttered at it – whether he was accepted as a member or not is unknown.[38] But he seems to have found the road to heaven as rocky in the New World as in the Old. Settlers' testimonies often told a tale of dashed hopes: many expected that coming to New England would bring an end to spiritual confusion, but were disappointed. It seems to have been a comfort to confess this to each other. Golden Moore told members of the Cambridge church that he emigrated 'to enjoy more of the Lord', but found himself in worse shape than ever. Ann Errington thought one New England sermon would do her more good than a hundred back home, but did not find what she hoped for.[39] The uncertainties of the New World, where settlers from all over England lived cheek by jowl in small communities under difficult circumstances, made conversion narratives a valuable way to weld 'saints' together. The times when a church heard new arrivals tell their spiritual stories were as much about settling godly hearts in America as about gate-keeping.[40]

New England departed sharply from England, and indeed from other Reformed churches in Europe, in the decision to make a testimony of religious experience compulsory for those who wanted to join a church. (New England churches that chose not to adopt this practice were the exception, not the norm.) As the godly commonwealth of Massachusetts allowed only male church members to become freemen – and only freemen could vote, become a magistrate, or serve on a jury – this unusual spiritual test defined not only membership of the church, but also participation in the state.[41] Another highly controversial implication was that only the children of church members could be baptised. In English parishes, making sure only the 'worthy' received communion was part of the agenda for godly discipline, but ministers rarely refused to baptise a child. The decision by New England's churches to limit both baptism and communion to those who could give an acceptable account of God's work in their soul meant colonial practice was stricter, with the potential for many children to go unbaptised. In 1642 Thomas Allen, minister at Charlestown, pointed out that many in New England and back home objected to this, 'murmuring that we come to make heathens rather than convert heathens to Christians'.[42]

The tight limits on access to sacraments outraged Mary Oliver of Salem, who came over in 1637 from Thomas Allen's parish church in Norwich. She stood up in Salem meetinghouse, when the church members were about to celebrate communion, to argue that she had a right to take part. She took offence 'that she might not be admitted to the Lord's Supper without giving public satisfaction to the church of her faith, etc., and covenanting or professing to walk with them according to the rule of the gospel'. One of the magistrates threatened to get her ejected by a constable. She ended up in court for 'disturbing the peace in the church', and spent several days in prison before admitting she had been wrong to make a public nuisance of herself. However, she stuck to her conviction that 'all that dwell in the same town, and . . . profess their faith in Christ Jesus, ought to be received to the sacraments there'. Governor John Winthrop thought Mary Oliver was 'for ability of speech, and appearance of zeal and devotion' far more likely to do damage than the antinomian Anne Hutchinson – 'but that she was poor and had little acquaintance'. Mary Oliver continued to campaign against New England's innovations. In 1639 the authorities put her in prison again, for making speeches at the arrival of newcomers – conjuring up an image of her haranguing immigrants on the quayside as they stepped off the boat.[43]

New England stayed close to colonists' roots in its settlement-based sermon culture, which replicated public preaching in English parishes. Everyone was required to attend the meetinghouse to hear sermons on the Sabbath, church member or not. Morning and afternoon, preachers addressed settlers perched on hard benches.[44] Everyone was also expected to contribute to the minister's salary. (Sabbath by Sabbath, in order of social rank within the community, settlers trooped up to the deacons' seat to drop money, or papers promising money, into a wooden box. At Salem, church members gave in public, but non-members were asked to pay up privately, at a house-to-house collection. If what people turned out of their pockets voluntarily was not enough, a local tax paid the bill.)[45] Preachers went out of their way to raise the spirits of settlers who had just arrived – who, by definition, had not yet had a chance to join a church. One man remembered being revived by 'Mr Shepard speaking upon a text to encourage them that came newly to land'. In Boston, even settlers who had been voted out of the church for misbehaviour were expected to come and hear the sermon. In tougher New Haven, those who had been excommunicated had to stand outside to listen, 'in frost, snow and rain'.[46] After the sermon ended, the church began its business: admissions, dismissions, discipline, baptisms and – once a month – communion, the Lord's Supper. Often, non-members could remain as spectators, a practice which helped new immigrants to become familiar with the New England Way. Mary Oliver seized this opportunity to make her noisy protest about access to communion. Thomas Lechford, who was turned down for church membership at Boston because he refused to identify the Pope as Antichrist, noticed that most non-members went away – few stayed on. Lechford could paint a picture for his English readers of how the Boston church took communion, using a silver cup with a cover. But he had not sipped from it. As a non-member, he knew what went on because he had peeped in from outside the meetinghouse door. (The silver cup still exists: a tall 'steeple cup' nineteen inches high, made in London and donated to the church by John Winthrop.)[47] Nevertheless, New England's churches were not closed-off congregations that could not bear the presence of ungodly outsiders. The affairs of the covenanted church were usually open to public gaze, whether the wider community took advantage of this or not. And New England's culture of public preaching stuck close to the godly discipline the puritan movement had aspired to bring to English parishes. Preachers had a truth for the whole community to hear.

Sermons for all: in New England this meant far more than four to six hours in the meetinghouse on the Sabbath. On weekdays, settlers could walk to hear lectures – extra sermons given either by their own preacher or in nearby settlements – just as in England. Boston set up its market to coincide with John Cotton's lecture on Thursdays. Meetinghouse and marketplace stood close together. In 1639, a row over rebuilding the church on Boston's town green was defused when church members voted to keep it close to the market, to protect the interests of traders who had set up shop near the church on purpose.[48] Just as in England, fasts and thanksgivings (extra days of preaching and prayer, called by church or civil authority) also punctuated the calendar. Apart from the Sabbath and fast days, when work gave way to sermons, early Massachusetts had just one civil holiday: election-day in May, when male church members turned out to vote in new magistrates. The climax, even of this day, was a special sermon in Boston.[49]

Some Massachusetts magistrates thought it possible to have too much of a good thing. In 1639 they complained that 'there were so many lectures now in the country, and many poor persons would usually resort to two or three in the week, to the great neglect of their affairs, and the damage of the public'. Sometimes church meetings ran on into the night. The Massachusetts General Court managed to persuade churches to end gatherings in time for people to get home before dark, but found it hard to limit the number of meetings. This was primarily an issue in the Boston area, where the density of settlement was greatest. Outlying communities struggled to recruit and retain ministers.[50]

Away from the centres of settlement, much about New England seemed alien and mysterious. John Dane, one of Susanna Bell's neighbours at Roxbury, remembered an incident as he walked to Ipswich, thirty miles north. He followed as best he could a path made by Native Americans. Suddenly, he came across forty or fifty of them. Apprehensive, he stuttered out the first greeting that came to mind: 'What cheer'. They laughed, and imitated what he had said, again and again – 'What cheer, what cheer' – so loud the woods rang with the noise. Dane was walking to Ipswich to hear the preacher John Norton, who had been curate and schoolmaster at Bishop's Stortford in Essex, where Dane grew up. Everyday life in New England was a bewildering mixture of the familiar played out in unfamiliar surroundings.[51]

II

To prove to the godly back home, and to themselves, that the decision to leave England had been legitimate, settlers wanted to show what purity they could achieve in America. But they also wanted to continue to affirm their close connection with England. This double aim meant colonial leaders trod a fine line. They asserted the superiority of their spiritual experience in New England, while not completely disparaging or cutting themselves off from those back in their homeland. Thomas Weld wrote to his former parishioners in Essex that he mourned for the blemished purity of their meetings, but added, 'I assure you we look at our dear native country as the place where the Lord showed us mercy'. Emigrants' first experience of God's grace had been in England.[52] Ezekiel Rogers told church members at Boston, Massachusetts, that while he judged the Church of England's hierarchy 'wholly antichristian', England had such power in religion it outshone 'all the known world besides'.[53]

The difficulty about New England's commitment to purity was that making comparisons with the state of religion at home tended to backfire. The decay in understanding between the two Englands is clear from the issues that divided old allies as the 1630s progressed. Reports of New England's innovations travelled back across the Atlantic, and sparked off questions and comments from those who had stayed at home. These exchanges started in personal letters and evolved into elaborate debates, with New Englanders and their critics each defending their position. Settlers' claims about purity led to something they neither intended, nor expected – the alienation of some of New England's chief supporters in England.

Thousands of letters crossed the Atlantic between early settlers and those they left behind, of which only a tiny fraction survive.[54] 'Like as cold waters to a weary soul, so are good news from a far country, Proverbs 25:25', wrote Henry Jessey from Suffolk, who scribbled letters after midnight to a correspondent in Massachusetts.[55] Nehemiah Wallington, a London artisan, copied into his letterbook (and so preserved for posterity) messages from friends in New England, and other missives from the colonies that must have been passing from hand to hand among the godly of Essex and London.[56] Passengers and shipmasters carried bundles of letters. Like their bearers, letters risked the hazards of the journey. Edward Howes reported that a letter from New England 'was so rinsed with sea water I had much ado to read it'.[57] A traveller carrying letters to the Bay Colony from a newly arrived ship at the Isles of Shoals (off the coast of modern Maine and New Hampshire) had a close brush with death when his guide across a frozen river fell through the ice and was swept away. Winthrop attributed the traveller's survival to a special act of Providence, because 'he had about him all the letters from England . . . which surely were the occasion of God's preserving him, more than any goodness of the man'.[58] Writers often sent two copies of correspondence in case one miscarried. Official surveillance of shipping to New England also made them nervous. One took the precaution of writing under a variety of false names. Another sent over a 'casement', a piece of paper with holes cut out, to lay on top of his letters: the words visible through the holes revealed his hidden message.[59]

By the late 1630s, a chorus of critics back home voiced disquiet about what they heard from New England. Prominent members of the puritan movement who had originally supported emigration expressed unease at the direction colonial churches had taken. Local godly communities, who had sent people off to the New World with a blessing, fired off questions to call their former neighbours to account.

From the West Country, John White of Dorchester in Dorset, a pioneer of the idea of godly settlements in America, wrote to Governor Winthrop. In the months before he set sail for New England in 1630, Winthrop had looked to White as a mentor. Now White warned him that New England must not turn voluntary acts of piety like covenants and spiritual testimony – desirable, but not vital – into something quintessential for true churches. Just as 'sweetmeats' could tempt people to eat too much, White feared the sweetness of liberty would lead settlers astray.[60] A friend of White's, Richard Bernard of Batcombe in Somerset, sent letters and papers to John Cotton in Boston.

Bernard was well known in godly circles: he veered into separatism briefly in 1607, binding a hundred Christians from his flock and neighbouring parishes in a covenant, but since that time he had been an implacable opponent of separatist churches, with the fervour of one who had seen the error of his ways. His interest in New England was close and personal because two of his children had gone there, Mary and Masakiell. Mary was the wife of Roger Williams, who turned out to be New England's most notorious separatist. Williams, banished from Massachusetts for his opinions in 1636, found refuge in Rhode Island – and within a few years decided that for the sake of purity he must not worship with any congregation, but only pray with his wife. So, ironically, Cotton contended at the same time with two members of one family, divided by religious conviction as well as the Atlantic: Williams the arch-separatist, Bernard the anti-separatist. Bernard accused Cotton and his like of being tainted with the same errors as his son-in-law Williams. Settlers had not been ejected from English churches, so what right had New England's churches to shut them out? Congregations should admit all-comers: 'Take them in, if bad to make them good, if godly minded, to make them better.'[61]

Another friend turned critic was the esteemed veteran of the English puritan movement, John Dod, who wrote with twelve other ministers from the Midlands in 1637.[62] Five years earlier, Dod had encouraged John Cotton to leave for America. Now he protested that letters from New England were encouraging the godly in England to desert their parish churches and form separatist assemblies. Had settlers changed their mind and adopted opinions they once condemned? Dod hoped New England's churches had not become separatist in secret, or by self-deception (proving what opponents of the godly often alleged, that 'nonconformists in practice are separatists in heart'). To this, Cotton replied that nothing had changed in settlers' regard for godly religion in England: 'our native country and the ordinances of God therein, and our holy brethren, we have left not in affection but in place'.[63] But in Dod's view, something had changed. He was disenchanted not only by what he heard of colonial innovations for the sake of purity, but also by the sheer numbers leaving England. He now advised against emigration: 'If . . . all the godly of the land because of persecution should . . . leave . . . what do you think will become of our poor native country? . . . The Lord's arm is not shortened but that he can retrieve and save us . . . Let's wait a while upon our God.'[64]

Rumours abounded in the circles which emigrants had left, stirred up by letters from New England that disparaged the purity of English churches, and by settlers who acted 'holier than thou' when they came back to visit. An East Anglian minister had heard that colonists would not receive anyone into church fellowship until they had disowned the churches of England as 'limbs of the devil' (to which John Cotton replied 'God forbid, God forbid').[65] A lly man in the West Country confessed he scarcely knew how to pray for ew England any more.[66] One of New England's chief defenders, Richard Mather of Dorchester, Massachusetts, honed his skills as an apologist by fielding a barrage of questions from his native county of Lancashire. Before he left England in 1635, Mather had presented his reasons for leaving home to members of the godly community in his local area, to seek their advice and approval.[67] However, soon after he reached Massachusetts Mather received alarmed letters from three of his peers, and had to reassure his Lancashire interrogators on dozens of points about New England practice.[68] Later, he replied to a long list of questions from a group of ministers in the county who wanted to know (amongst other things) if they could set up a church in Massachusetts that did not conform to the New England Way. Mather's answer was no: the New England Way was 'the same which Christ appointed and therefore unalterable'. This turned into necessities – at least on New England's soil – the practices which John White of Dorchester in Dorset had argued might be valuable for Christians, but were not essential to make a church. However, Mather thought the question inappropriate, because:

> we are persuaded that if you were here you would set up and practise the very same that we do . . . or else if we be swerving from the rule . . . God would by you send more light unto us than yet we see, and make you instruments in his hand for perfecting what is here begun.[69]

Like other advocates of the New England Way, Mather trod the fine line of not only justifying the form of settlers' pure churches but also showing strong loyalty to the godly back home. In 1645 he and a fellow minister wrote to their 'dear countrymen of Lancashire' to express no regrets about their decision to go to America, but – equally – to insist that not 'all the water that in all this time hath flown in this great Atlantic Ocean between England and us . . . shall wash away the thought and remembrance of England, of God's people therein from our hearts'.[70]

Local debate about the legitimacy of colonial innovations split families and friends well before it burst onto the national stage. But as the party lines of religious politics hardened back home, New England's critics across England coalesced into the Presbyterian party. By 1643, the lines of debate were drawn up. Presbyterians argued for a national Church of England ruled by a hierarchy of synods instead of bishops, following Scotland's model of reform, but English Congregationalists rejected this and insisted that the visible Church existed only in local congregations, following New England's model.[71] After censorship melted away in the heat of civil war, manuscripts from transatlantic exchanges in the 1630s got snapped up by both sides to feed the London printing presses. To shore up New England's reputation, Hugh Peter – the minister of Salem, in London as an agent for Massachusetts – put into print an anthology of replies to English critics, from documents penned in New England in the late 1630s and sent to ministers in Lancashire, to Richard Bernard in Somerset, and to John Dod in the Midlands.[72] In response, William Rathband of Lancashire printed a ferocious attack on colonial churches, based on correspondence sent by colonists to their families and friends in his locality – an attack 'as far from truth, as old England is from New', claimed another agent for Massachusetts in London, Thomas Weld, conveniently placed to publish a swift riposte.[73] Colonial writers saw the devil at work in the black-and-white polemic, and in the difficulties of communication across the Atlantic. The Massachusetts ministers John Allin and Thomas Shepard believed that, in the year or two it took colonists to get hold of books published in England and send back answers to be printed, Satan created 'strange thoughts and distasteful affections' towards New England. To pour oil on troubled transatlantic waters, they insisted that while the godly in both Englands shared a desire to create pure churches, New England's path to reform was not a prescription to cure old England's ills. If any had been 'too clamorous to cry up the New England Way', 'they have neither patent nor pattern from us so to do'.[74]

Settlers' declarations of loyalty to the godly in England have often been seen as hollow or self-deceiving, masking the truth about how far New England's innovations in religion had really gone.[75] However – like the godly in England, who gathered within and across parish boundaries but put huge amounts of energy into arguing that they were not schismatic separatists from the national Church – colonial leaders spilt a great deal of ink defining how New England's churches stood vis-à-vis England.[76] At a distance of three thousand miles, they could have ploughed a separatist furrow regardless of English opinion. Instead, they went to elaborate lengths to acknowledge both the purity of New England's churches and their loyalty to godly Christians in parishes back home. The idea that New England steered closer and closer to separation from England as the 1630s progressed – as English critics contended – is misleading. As pressure in England built up over the decade, a broader spectrum of the puritan movement was galvanised into leaving for America. Emigrants were stirred up enough to brave the dangers of the Atlantic for a life in the New World, but this did not necessarily turn them into radical sectarians, whatever the godly at home might think.[77]

III

Emigration peaked in 1638, against a backdrop of rising suspicion among the godly in England about the direction New England was taking. As the 1630s came to an end, the reasons that had been woven together to justify the Great Migration were disintegrating. Former allies pilloried New England's 'purity' as separatism. News of religious disputes in Massachusetts – the Antinomian Controversy, above all – threatened to make it 'a kingdom divided against itself', which could not survive.[78] To English eyes, New England's errors made the hand of Providence on the venture uncertain. The question mark over settlement was confirmed by financial losses and hardship. There was a belief that if God approved, the colony would prove itself commercially sound; or, at least, not a disaster. The fact that it turned out to be so hard to make a decent living in New England raised doubts about God's blessing.

The debate about what Providence intended emerged sharply in transatlantic exchanges between Governor Winthrop of Massachusetts and William Fiennes, Viscount Saye and Sele. By the late 1630s, Fiennes and other influential backers, seeing too little profit from their New England investments, speculated about whether the Almighty might want settlers to move to the Caribbean instead. To people steeped in thinking about the ways of Providence, this was not just a cover for pursuing material interests. Would God want settlers to work against the odds for profits in a harsh wilderness, when (under the hand of God) they could move on to better opportunities elsewhere? The Providence Island Company, set up by Fiennes with Lord Brooke and others to promote godly settlements in the Caribbean, recruited John Humfrey of Salem to lead New England settlers south.[79] Winthrop – who earlier fiercely opposed movement west to Connecticut – viewed this as a betrayal. If New England was judged a mistake, settlers and investment would evaporate. Winthrop insisted 'that God had chosen this country to plant his people in', and threatened Fiennes with judgment from on high. Fiennes, irritated, pointed out that perhaps Winthrop stood more at risk of a thunderbolt from heaven, for presuming to think God had called settlers to fix in New England in the same way that he called the Israelites to the Promised Land. Fiennes rejected Winthrop's claim of God's special interest in Massachusetts: 'it is as likely that you have in Providence been cast upon that place to remove from thence . . . as to stay there'. Everyone knew the 'barrenness of the land and coldness of the air in winter'. Why should it be wrong to suggest that settlers should 'live in a warmer climate and in a more fruitful soil'? For a short time, with John Humfrey poised to sail south from Massachusetts with a party of settlers, it looked as if godly settlements in the Caribbean might threaten the viability of New England. Then Spanish troops seized Providence

Island in 1641 and renamed it Hispaniola. Winthrop must have seen this as divine intervention.[80] (Contests to claim the blessing of Providence lay behind decisions to name rival plantations: not only Providence Island in the Caribbean, but Providence, Rhode Island, named by Roger Williams after his banishment from Massachusetts in honour of 'God's merciful Providence to me in my distress'.)[81]

By the end of the 1630s, the tightly wound threads of providential reasoning used to legitimate settlement seemed to be unravelling in the minds of settlers, too. An inhabitant of Ipswich, Massachusetts (who not long after returned home to England) told Governor Winthrop that people were drawing harsh conclusions. The fact that colonists found the cost of settlement so financially devastating meant 'it was not a way of God, to forsake our country, and expose ourselves to such temptations, as we have done'. Those who made this judgment linked New England's poor fortune to the separatist path they assumed its churches had taken. God did not smile on separatists.[82]

New England's ministers had to reassure the godly on two fronts. Back home, former allies needed to hear why the changes in religion across the Atlantic did not mean a separation from the godly in England. In the mainstream puritan colonies of Massachusetts, New Haven and Connecticut, meanwhile, settlers had to be convinced that New England still had the blessing of Providence – all the more so when news from England hinted at change and reform.

To reassure the godly in England, colonial ministers put the relation between the two Englands into perspective. They leaned heavily on a distinction between churches newly 'planted' in a pure form, and churches in need of reformation – or, more precisely, re-formation. New England's churches could be built from the ground up, on the pure foundation of covenants in the blank terrain of a New World: this made the true Scriptural pattern of a church clear for all to see. But in England, although pure churches had been planted in ancient days, when the country converted to Christianity, corruption had run riot. England's churches needed to be re-formed to primitive purity: they were still real churches, but only implicitly.[83] As Richard Mather explained in a letter to Lancashire, the more plain and clear the bedrock of covenant was, the surer it was that a congregation was a true church. However, even in England where things were not yet 'plain and pure', true churches could still exist.[84] New England's critics protested that this heavily qualified affirmation of English churches damned with faint praise.[85] Despite this, defenders of the New England Way ploughed on with the argument.

The freedoms of Civil War England gave colonial writers liberty to imagine what shape the reformation of England's Church might take. Until then, the argument was normally conducted without specific reference to how congregations in English parishes were (implicitly if not explicitly) true churches. But one unusual set of proposals from New England survives, written in the 1630s 'some years before the suppressing of the bishops' – before the polarised debate about church reform in the 1640s. These proposals for 'the way of reformation in the congregations of England' tried to show exactly how New England truths were already implicit in old England's churches. The author made concessions to the circumstances of Christians in English parishes. It is surprising, then, that the author seems to have been John Cotton: Cotton, accused by Richard Bernard and John Dod of being a separatist in all but name, and of provoking people to abandon parish churches.[86] The moderate character of Cotton's proposals followed a path often taken by earlier puritan writers who wanted to affirm the truth that survived, even in a Church of England only half-reformed.[87] What was new in the arguments shipped home from America was the transatlantic application of this strategy, to show common ground between the pure congregations of New England and England's ancient churches.

Alongside these tactics to reassure the godly in England, colonial preachers tried to convince their audience in New England that God wanted them to stay put. In sermons of the late 1630s, Thomas Shepard addressed time and again the relationship between Providence and hardship. He painted a stark picture of how settlers felt, deep in debt; secretly regretting their fellowship with God's people in New England and tempted, like the Israelites in the wilderness, to return to where they had come from. 'The Israelites, brought to the wilderness, they would go back: why? They questioned whether God was with them: why? Because they wanted water, bread and a variety of blessings.' Shepard argued, however, that hardship could not discredit New England. Adversity was a sign of God's affection, to stop settlers turning complacent. In America, there were 'no enemies to hunt you to heaven, nor chains to make you cry . . . no sour herbs to make the Lamb sweet'. Hardship took the place of popery and persecution, to turn hearts from the world to the joys of heaven.[88] Like Shepard, John Cotton also tried to reassure settlers about God's purpose for New England. He took an image from colonial kitchens – making toffee. People should not be 'flittering':

If men be weary of the country and will [go] back again to England because in heart they are weary . . . I fear there is no spirit of Reformation . . . As it is with some syrups, when they are boiled up to their full consistence, they will not run where they fall, but there they will stand: so if men be boiled up . . . they will not be flittering.[89]

In sermons preached early in 1640, when settlers already scented change in England, Cotton admitted how dispiriting day-to-day life in Massachusetts could be. But he pointed out to his audience in the Boston meetinghouse – which stood perilously close to the docks and to the ships that could take them home – that if they went back to England they would return 'to that from which the Lord by his outstretched hand hath delivered you'. Settlers enjoyed freedom from England's compromises with corruption. Back home they would be entangled again in a national Church governed by bishops, marked by the 'image of the Beast' – the beast of Antichrist depicted in Revelation 13. Despite this hostile language, calculated to stop people from sailing away, Cotton held back from renouncing England. He might accuse his hearers (as Shepard did) of being like the Israelites who wanted to go back from the wilderness to Egypt, but he immediately added, 'God forbid I should count all our native country as Egypt'. His sermon-series on Revelation 13 ended with an appeal for prayer for England, and in particular for the Short Parliament called to meet in April 1640.[90]

Cotton knew that change in England made leaving New England a qualitatively different prospect. Early in 1640, a correspondent from London warned that few passengers were now likely to come over to Boston, 'and the reason I conceive to be hopes of some Reformation in England'. With a reforming Parliament in prospect (the Short Parliament), migration to New England all but dried up. In August, the Scots invaded England, and another Parliament (the Long Parliament) met in November. Late in the year, Governor John Winthrop recorded the arrival of English fishing ships at the Isles of Shoals, with fresh reports from across the Atlantic. News of all the changes at home travelled down the coast to the settlements of Massachusetts – 'whereupon some among us began to think of returning back to England'.[91]

UNSETTLED SPIRITS

In 1639 Richard Mather, the minister of Dorchester, Massachusetts, gave his son the name 'Increase', to mark the 'great Increase of every sort' with which 'God favoured the country . . . about the time of his nativity'.[1] Two years later, Mather baptised another Dorchester child with the name 'Return' – a sign of changed times in New England, 'the times of the unsettled humours of many men's spirits to return for England'. Increase and Return grew up in the same small settlement. As an adult, Return Munnings defied his name by staying on in America.[2] Increase Mather defied his name by sailing to England as soon as he could: twelve days after he turned eighteen and preached his first sermon. (He came back to New England rather unwillingly after the Restoration of Charles II, and went on to play a major role in the Salem witch trials and much more.) Looking back over New England's history in 1689, the year he turned fifty – no doubt with the irony of his given name in mind – Increase Mather observed that since 1640 'more people have gone from New England than have come hither'.[3]

Nathaniel Ward, like Increase Mather, returned to England. Ward lived for twelve years at Ipswich, Massachusetts, but went back to his native county of Essex in 1646. In a tract he wrote before he left, Nathaniel invented a quirky character, the *Simple Cobler of Aggawam in America*, who was willing to help mend an England 'tattered both in the upper-leather and sole'. Through the Simple Cobbler, he drew attention to what some settlers, at least, made part of their 'American Creed': 'no man ought to forsake his own country, but upon extraordinary cause, and when that cause ceaseth, he is bound in conscience to return if he can'. Ward wrote this not long after news of Archbishop Laud's execution reached New England.[4] Laud, as Bishop of London, had ejected Ward from his work as a minister in 1632. Now Laud was finished, so the 'extraordinary cause' for Ward's absence from his native country was over. Within a year of Laud's death, and soon after news of the end of civil war in England arrived in New England, Nathaniel took most of his family home.

Only his eldest son stayed on, as a minister in New England's Ess
Nathaniel picked up the threads of his life in old England's Essex,
Shenfield – about four miles from Stondon Massey, where he had ⌐
minister before he went to America.[5]

How unusual was Ward's decision? Hard evidence can be mustered for the godly preachers who, like him, emigrated to New England in the 1630s. Among these, it turns out that Ward's decision to return to England was far from exceptional. *One in three* of the godly preachers who emigrated in the 1630s went back to England – in fact, 24 out of the 70 who lived to hear of the changed circumstances back home in 1640. Only one minister returned to England before 1640 (and that was in the earliest days of settlement). But twelve left between 1640 and 1643, after the first news of change came from England.[6]

Equally hard evidence is available for Harvard students, but here the ratio is more dramatic. Almost *one in two* left New England: 43 of 108 who graduated with a BA in classes up to 1659, and more who went to England without staying to complete a degree.[7]

Among settlers in general, hard evidence is more difficult to find. Nevertheless, at least 600 colonists who returned to England in the 1640s and 1650s can be identified by name. Most of these people went back for good, although some did so only for a while. Of the 600, a disproportionate number (almost 450) are adult men. To arrive at a figure that includes women and children (usually a silent presence aboard ship), it seems reasonable to scale up by using the ratio of adult men to the total number of migrants on lists of passengers who sailed to New England in 1637 – the most complete set to survive. (Unfortunately, no passenger rosters exist for the return journeys back home.) Of 273 voyagers on these lists, 81 were men. If this ratio is brought into play, it gives a fairly secure figure of a minimum of 1,500 settlers who returned to England.[8]

But what was the size of the colonial population from which the travellers came? Estimates of the number of immigrants in the 1630s vary from 13,000 to 21,000. Estimates of the colonial population in 1640 vary from 13,500 to 17,600.[9] Thereafter, New England saw little growth between 1640 and 1660. From a low estimate of immigrants, 13,000, the 1,500 settlers who returned to England after 1640 represent one in nine; if the immigrants numbered 21,000, the proportion returning would still be one in fifteen.[10] These ratios are remarkably high, bearing in mind that they come only from what is known about returning settlers who can be identified by name or by household.

Of course, restricting attention to the settlers who can be named probably leads to a serious underestimate of the actual outflow. In August 1641, John Winthrop recorded that forty passengers set sail for England by way of

Newfoundland. Of these, only seven can now be named – that is, roughly one in six.[11] Of other ships' passengers, the fraction who can be named falls well short of one in six.[12] On this basis, it is plausible to suggest how many went back by multiplying the hard figure of 600 names by at least six. In other words, it is possible that at least 3,600 came back, rather than a minimum of 1,500.

If this is so, and the estimate of 1630s immigrants is set low (at 13,000), it means that perhaps as many as *one in four* settlers went back. Even with a high immigrant figure (21,000), the proportion of settlers who left is still *one in six*.[13] These figures are admittedly only tentative, because the hidden number of returning settlers has been arrived at from those whose names are known. However, the ratios gain more traction when set against the hard evidence that one in three of the original clerical emigrants left for England, along with almost one in two early Harvard students. Clergy and university graduates were, naturally, more likely to leave – they were more likely to have the resources to pay for a passage home; more likely to have good opportunities in England; more likely to feel the pinch of poverty in New England. (It is ironic that the settlers who provided New England's leadership were also the most liable to pluck up stakes and go home.)[14] But for settlers in general, in a context where so much is unknown about the number and identity of migrants, the evidence of 600 names also suggests a significant rate of return.

It is tempting to see the settlers who sailed home in one of two ways: either as ardent promoters of the New England Way who wanted to share their wisdom with England; or as individuals disenchanted with colonial life. The true picture is rarely so black and white, however. In the 1640s the relation between the two Englands was particularly complex and untidy, because of England's convulsions in civil war and New England's evolution in matters of church and state. Moreover, those who returned were quite disparate in outlook; not only because Massachusetts' drive to create a united 'orthodoxy' shook out diversity, but also (to look at the situation from a different perspective) because a great variety of people, radicalised into emigration by the particular circumstances of the 1630s, found that their commitment to the New World unravelled when circumstances in England changed. After the execution of Charles I in 1649 and the establishment of Cromwell's regime, transatlantic relations became more settled and predictable. The strongest ebb-tide of return came in the early 1650s, when many more settlers – some long unsettled in New England, others not different in outlook or fortune from colonial neighbours who stayed on in America – said their farewells and sailed away.

Increase Mather's name, bestowed with such optimism in 1639, quickly turned out to be a misnomer. From 1640 onwards, the ships that once sailed into Boston harbour full of new faces came stacked with manufactured goods but precious few people. Places on the passenger deck were more in demand for the journey home. Settlers had to get used to seeing houses in their communities sold for a song, or abandoned to the ravages of New England's climate; 'he who last year, or but three months before, was worth £1000, could not now, if he sold his whole estate, raise £200, whereby God taught us the vanity of all outward things'.[15]

I

Who left New England first, when news of change came? If migrants had been pushed out by circumstances in the 1630s, might there be a sudden rush back to England? This seems to be what preachers like John Cotton expected, to judge from their efforts to fix settlers in New England and see off the destabilising effect of reform at home and hard times in New England. In fact, no simple equation existed between the arrival of news from across the Atlantic and the numbers of people who jumped aboard an eastbound ship. Apart from the commitments to family, church and town that tied settlers down, the outbreak of civil war soon seriously inhibited return. All 'news' from war-torn England was two or three months old by the time it crossed the Atlantic: what fresh horrors might have happened in the meantime?

A quest for justice, a return from exile, dissatisfaction with religious life in New England, financial loss: these themes thread through the personal histories of the first colonists who set sail.

Samuel Eaton wanted to set the record straight, and sort out legal action taken against him in the 1630s. Eaton, the first minister to return in 1640, went back to Cheshire partly to find settlers for a new grant of land at 'Totokett' (later Branford), along the shore from New Haven. He was also keen to rescue his estate from the clutches of the Court of High Commission, which was trying to seize his assets – land which had been left with a tenant when he went away to New England. Eaton claimed that 'if the High Commission at York could have let him alone, he might probably have ended his days [in America]'. As it was, he became notorious as 'New England Mr Eaton', a 'great apostle' of the New England Way. Eaton arrived home just after the Long Parliament convened in November 1640, and quickly got caught up in local controversy.[16]

A cloud of illegality also hung over the shoemaker Ferdinando Adams. After locking the bishop's officials out of St Mary-le-Tower in Ipswich, he had defied a court order to emigrate – which John Winthrop worried would bring trouble to New England. In 1641, Ferdinando asked permission from the church at Dedham, Massachusetts, to visit England. He sailed home at the same time as the lawyer Thomas Lechford, who had acted for him in England.

Ferdinando never came back: a year later he sent for his wife and children; then, despite his distinctive name, he disappears from view.[17] What Samuel Eaton and perhaps Ferdinando Adams tried to do in person to clear their names, others tried to achieve from New England through friends and relatives at home – arguably, paving the way to go back. When the House of Commons started to gather evidence against Bishop Matthew Wren in 1640, relatives and parishioners of Robert Peck petitioned that he and his wife had been 'made exiles in their old age'; Robert Allen petitioned that his brother Thomas had been 'compelled to live in foreign parts'.[18] Charles Chauncy sent instructions to friends in England to print the manuscript he had left with them about the dangers of railing in communion tables, 'for the satisfaction of all such who either are, or justly might be, offended with his scandalous submission made before the High Commission Court, Feb. 11, Anno 1635'.[19]

Thomas Weld and Hugh Peter, as agents for Massachusetts, had a different agenda – but, like Eaton and Adams, ended up rooted in England again. Weld and Peter, ministers at Roxbury and Salem, left in August 1641 on a controversial mission: to offer advice on religious reform, to seek the lifting of restrictions that had been imposed on shipping, and to seek financial help without (to use Winthrop's words) looking for 'supply of our wants in any dishonourable way, as by begging or the like, for we were resolved to wait upon the Lord'.[20] This, it was hoped, would help to satisfy the godly in England who regretted the absence of New England's leaders, like the parliamentarian who wrote to tell John Winthrop 'now we see and feel how much we are weakened by the loss of those that are gone from us'.[21] Within New England, the wisdom of sending agents was questioned. Was it not 'somewhat preposterous to go from a place of safety provided of God, to a place of danger under the hand of God to seek relief'?[22] The Salem church and the Massachusetts authorities tried hard in later years to get Hugh Peter back. Weld and Peter often declared that they were on the brink of sailing for America – to the point where Presbyterian opponents made a running joke of this – but neither set foot in New England again. In the arguments of the 1640s about religious reform, New England's public *persona* in England chiefly consisted of its agents, and the tracts they delivered to London printers to defend the New England Way. Hugh Peter became a favourite target for the jibes of Thomas Edwards, the arch-Presbyterian campaigner against separatists: a cipher for all that was wrong with New England.[23]

Dissidents of various stripes quickly found a passage home and slipped away. At least one recalcitrant critic of New England sailed back on the same ship as the colonial agents, which (since the agents had been chosen to personify orthodoxy in Massachusetts) must have made for an interesting journey.[24] The strength and variety of dissent is not surprising: circumstances of the 1630s radicalised people into emigration, but not necessarily particular view of church government or of the theology of grace. Differences intrinsic to the English puritan movement, hidden before emigration, showed themselves in tensions and controversies that troubled New England in the 1630s.[25] Now some of the dissidents who had scattered into outlying communities, or who chafed against the ethos of Massachusetts, found their way home: antinomians and newly convinced Baptists; advocates of godly episcopacy; people who disliked New England's strict criteria for church membership.

Religious radicals were among those quick to find a passage home. Christopher Marshall, for example, had taken refuge outside Massachusetts in the aftermath of the Antinomian Controversy. He had strong ties with Anne Hutchinson and her brother-in-law John Wheelwright: his wife, Sarah, was their niece, and Christopher grew up in Anne Hutchinson's home town of Alford, Lincolnshire. He emigrated to Boston in 1634 to continue his education with the minister John Cotton – in a kind of 'household seminary' familiar from godly circles in England – but fell out with Cotton in the controversy over free grace. The Marshalls followed Wheelwright north out of Massachusetts to found what is now Exeter, New Hampshire; then one of a collection of small settlements on the fast-flowing Piscataqua River and its tributaries, which took advantage of the vast natural harbour formed by the Piscataqua tidal basin. In this watery community, Sarah drowned. Christopher Marshall left his isolated home for England in around 1642. In a career that moved between antinomian hotbeds in old England and New, he gathered a church at Woodkirk in the West Riding of Yorkshire in the late 1640s, and served as a parish preacher in the locality. Woodkirk had connections with the 'Grindletonians' of Lancashire, whose perfectionist teaching shaped English antinomianism and paved the way for the Quakers. James Nayler, later infamous for riding a donkey into Bristol (imitating Christ's entry into Jerusalem), belonged to Marshall's Woodkirk congregation before he became a Quaker. Christopher Marshall resisted the Quakers – there was no love lost between him and George Fox, who poached Nayler from the Woodkirk flock.[26]

Another radical who quickly left New England, Hanserd Knollys, came (like Marshall) from antinomian circles close to John Wheelwright in Lincolnshire. Knollys renounced his ordination in the Church of England before he left for New England, and sailed into Boston in 1638 as a marked man. As soon as he stepped ashore, the magistrates refused him permission to stay in Massachusetts – for which he judged them 'worse than the High Commission'. While he was considering where to go next, 'two strangers coming to Boston from Piscataqua, hearing of me by a mere accident, got me to go with them to that plantation, and to preach there'. Knollys' time on the Piscataqua (at what is now Dover, New Hampshire) proved turbulent, not least because of violent

antinomism
played down outward signs of grace

arguments with another minister, Thomas Larkham. In the end, Knollys left under a cloud, accused of having 'solicited the chastity of two maids in his household'. To John Winthrop, this lapse proved the error of antinomian ways, which played down the importance of visible holiness. Knollys headed west to Long Island, but, 'being sent for by my aged father', took his chance to get back to England: 'I returned with my wife and one child about three years old, and was great with another child, and came safe to London on the 24th of December 1641'. He and his wife – 'my companion in all my sufferings, travels and hardship for the gospel' – had lost their first child on the voyage over to New England. After a year or two as a schoolmaster and as a chaplain in the Parliamentary army, Knollys became leader of a Baptist church in London; another settler for whom New England was a stage in his journey, not an end in itself.[27]

A fellow Baptist, Thomas Patient, went through a quiet conversion while he lived at Salem, Massachusetts. His belief in adult baptism came to light when he failed to bring his newborn baby to be baptised. The local magistrates issued a warrant for his arrest in 1641. Thomas set off across the Atlantic with his wife and unbaptised child before the case could come to court. He became an ardent advocate of 'believer's baptism' in England and Ireland. The threat of arrest in Massachusetts, he testified later, had been 'no trouble to me, being filled with unspeakable joy, as I walked up and down in the woods in that wilderness'.[28]

Thomas Lechford dissented for different reasons, convinced by his experience in Massachusetts that 'Christians cannot live happily without Bishops . . . nor Englishmen without a King'.[29] As the London solicitor who acted for William Prynne, Lechford fled to Boston in 1638 as 'a kind of banishment' after the disaster of Prynne's trial.[30] He chose Massachusetts over Providence Island to the south, and over the offer of a post from George Rákóczy, Prince of Transylvania. But New England failed to greet Lechford as he expected. To pass the time on the Atlantic voyage he wrote a tract, and presented this to Deputy Governor Thomas Dudley when he reached Boston: 'the next news I had was, that at first dash he accused me of heresy'. The Boston church – where Dudley was a leading member – refused to admit Lechford, because he thought Antichrist had not yet come (and so could not be identified with the Pope), and because he believed in bishops as long as they were godly.[31] As he was not a church member, Lechford could not hold civil office in Massachusetts. He made a living, good enough to buy the 'best sugar' and expensive Spanish tobacco, by writing legal documents such as wills, deeds, leases, letters of attorney and formal copies – virtually all of it out-of-court work, recorded in a notebook he kept until four days before he sailed home.[32] In 1641, when the situation in England had clearly changed, he ended his voluntary exile: he took the same boat back as the colonial agents Hugh Peter and Thomas Weld, and his former client Ferdinando Adams. Lechford published an account of what he had seen in Massachusetts – a lawyerly witness against the colony, entitled _Plain Dealing or News from New-England_ – which, because of his contacts, had the potential to inflict serious damage. Thomas Weld's counterblast, _New Englands First Fruits_, was a poor match. Lechford's death in 1642 cut short his contribution to the debate, but William Prynne took up the cudgels on his behalf.[33]

The question of access to church membership and to sacraments – local arguments between those inside and outside the gathered church – sparked off disputes. A spectacular fall-out occurred at Dover, on the Piscataqua River, between Hanserd Knollys and Thomas Larkham, a minister from Northam in Devon. Known as Dover from 1637, the 'plantation of Cocheco' had been set up in 1631 by a trading company from London, to provide a fishery. In 1633 it had been bought by an English consortium that included William Fiennes, Viscount Saye and Sele – the same pool of investors that backed Providence Island in the Caribbean and the plantation of Saybrook at the mouth of the Connecticut River on Long Island Sound. The meetinghouse at Dover was short of a preacher because George Burdett, a self-appointed spy for Laud, who wrote letters to the Archbishop about what he saw in New England, had moved on.[34] Knollys gathered a church 'of such as he could get, men very raw for the most part'. When Larkham came on the scene, the church – which could not afford two ministers, unlike larger settlements – chose Larkham over Knollys. The dispute became, literally, a contest for the identity of the plantation: Dover was briefly rechristened Northam after Larkham's English parish. According to John Winthrop, Larkham caused trouble when he admitted to the church 'all who offered themselves, though men notoriously scandalous and ignorant', as long as they promised to repent. Knollys excommunicated Larkham, who then 'laid violent hands on Mr. Knollys'. A riot ensued. Knollys' party took to the streets with a Bible strapped to a pikestaff as their banner to march by, and the reverend Mr Knollys brandishing a pistol. Knollys' troop declared they were the Scots, and their opponents the English (putting the local scuffle into a bigger frame, by siding with the Scots who took on Charles I in the Bishops' Wars). Arbitrators from the Bay Colony waded in to restore peace. Knollys left. Within a year or so, Larkham also sailed to England – like Knollys, with a tarnished reputation. Winthrop noted that Larkham broke his word by deserting the community: he 'gave them his faithful promise not to go, but yet soon after he got on ship board'. Winthrop also set down the local scandal: 'it was time for him to be gone, for not long after a widow which kept in his house, being a very handsome woman . . . proved to be with child, and being examined, at first refused to confess the father, but in the end she laid it to Mr Larkham'. [35] Larkham (conveniently for the widow) was no longer there to answer the charge, but the tale followed him across the Atlantic and haunted his ministry in the 1650s. Later, for many years after he reached home, Larkham gave thanks on the anniversary of the date he sailed away from America: 'I call to mind with a humble and thankful heart that upon the 12th day of November 1642 I left my house in the morning and came down to the mouth of the River Piscataqua in New England to come for England.'[36]

In Weymouth, Massachusetts – as in Dover – a combustion broke out over how tightly the Church should be defined. Richard Bernard of Batcombe in Somerset may well have been provoked by reports from Weymouth into sending sharp questions to John Cotton about New England's churches. Joseph Hull pioneered the settlement of Weymouth with families from Devon and Somerset in 1635, including some of Bernard's parishioners and Bernard's son Masakiell.[37] By 1637 Hull's refusal to admit some inhabitants to the sacraments caused tension. When a minister from Buckinghamshire, Robert Lenthall, arrived in New England, some of Weymouth's settlers invited him to join them, 'to get such a church on foot as all baptised ones might communicate in without any further kind of trial'. Lenthall delivered what they wanted. He rejected New England's innovation of asking people to give a testimony of spiritual experience, making only baptism the door to the church. Thomas Dudley, hearing of a possible outbreak of smallpox at Weymouth, commented, 'if this be true the plague is begun in the camp for the sin of Peor' (a biblical allusion to unlawful mingling with the ungodly). Support for Lenthall led to intervention by the magistrates in 1639. Lenthall, persuaded by other ministers, accepted the General Court's ruling against him. One of his flock, James Britton, was whipped in public (in lieu of a fine, because he had nothing to pay with) for taking Lenthall's side, and for criticising the answer New England had sent to Richard Bernard in Somerset, to rebut Bernard's critique of church covenants. Lenthall became a poor schoolmaster at Newport, Rhode Island, but found himself at odds with the radical spirits of 'Rogues' Island' (as contemporaries often called it). Before long, he was a Rector in Buckinghamshire again, within a few miles of his old parish at Aston Sandford.[38]

The sour turn of New England's economy – an immediate effect of the drying up of immigrants and investment in 1640 – created a restive population. By 1642 Winthrop noted that 'the sudden fall of land and cattle, and the scarcity of foreign commodities, and money, etc., with the thin access of people from England, put many into an unsettled frame of spirit, so as they concluded there could be no subsisting here'.[39] A wealthy but discontented settler from New Haven sailed away with his goods, family, and £1,000 in his

purse – against the advice of the godly, who predicted he would be ⟨
by the Turks: 'and so it fell out, for in Spain he embarked . . . in a grea⟨ ⟨
bound for England . . . but the ship was taken'; he and his family were 'carried
to Algiers, and sold there for slaves'.[40] John Humfrey of Salem, who had hoped
to restore his fortunes by leading a party of settlers to Providence Island in
the Caribbean, left for England in 1641, shortly after this controversial venture
fell apart (because the Spanish captured the island). He had long struggled
with debt. In 1638, his minister, Hugh Peter, petitioned the General Court to
help Humfrey financially, because 'his friends fear the Gospel may suffer by
his sufferings' (in other words, his plight would make investors judge
Massachusetts unviable).[41] Humfrey's flight to England – like that of the
equally well-connected George Fenwick, who left Saybrook Plantation in 1645
– reflected the new agenda of prominent backers like Lord Brooke and
Viscount Saye and Sele. Fenwick complained in 1640 that he was more
strapped for cash than he had ever been; he grew weary of looking after land
for eminent but absent Englishmen whose interest in the New World had evaporated.[42] Humbler colonists like the Boston haberdasher Walter Blackborne
beat a retreat to safer prospects back home before ruin came. Blackborne had
left his London business in 1638, and spent long enough in Boston to acquire
land and join a church, to become a freeman and to sign up with the Artillery
Company. To cut his losses he returned to London early in 1641, and set up in
premises on Ludgate Hill, near St Paul's. His wife Elizabeth stayed on briefly
after him, to sell their 'late dwelling house and shop new built', and to appoint
attorneys to collect debts.[43] Despite the financial conditions that sent people
like Humfrey, Fenwick, and the Blackbornes away, other settlers struggled on.
Many must have found they could not afford to pay for a passage home – shoemakers, blacksmiths, carpenters, husbandmen, who had invested everything in
coming to New England.[44] The extent of debt is illuminated by the obscure
colonial career of John Sams of Roxbury, who left New England in around
1642, owing the substantial sum of fifty pounds and eighteen shillings to
Deputy Governor Dudley. By 1645, Sams had become a minister in Kent,
where his annual income was probably less than what he owed Thomas
Dudley. After he left for England his land at Roxbury had been seized in lieu of
payment.[45] Thomas Hooker, minister at Hartford, reflected on the harsh reality
of settlers ensnared by an unmanageable level of debt, in a place 'so forlorn and
helpless, that men cannot support themselves'. To wrestle with it was 'altogether
bootless and fruitless . . . to increase a man's misery, not to ease it'. Like birds
caught in a net, the more debtors struggled, the tighter they were held. In such
a situation, 'why should a man stay until the house fall on his head'?[46]

John Phillip and Robert Peck started their voyage back to England about
three months after the House of Commons voted Bishop Matthew Wren unfit

[handwritten annotation:] Economic downturn – 1640-41

for office – they set off as soon as this news crossed the Atlantic. Both left the diocese of Norwich in the late 1630s as a last resort to evade pressure from Wren's officials. In New England, John Phillip avoided commitments that would tie him down. He side-stepped invitations to act as a minister, although in 1640 he and his wife finally accepted a call to join the church at Dedham, Massachusetts. Robert Peck travelled from Hingham in Norfolk to be a minister at Hingham, Massachusetts. Before he left England in 1638, Peck had made elaborate arrangements for his property to be looked after in his absence. By the end of 1641, both he and Phillip were back in their English parishes. For both, Massachusetts turned out to be a short but remarkable interruption to fifty years of settled work in one place.[47]

So the initial leakage from New England, after 1640, came from those with most reason to return home fast: people such as Samuel Eaton and Ferdinando Adams, who wanted to rescue their name and fortune in the courts; colonial agents; settlers ill at ease with the spectrum of permitted opinions or practices; disappointed entrepreneurs and colonists, mired in debt, who could not make a decent living; and those such as Peck and Phillip, who made their way back from 'exile', after what turned out to be a brief tactical retreat to the New World. While these settlers sailed home for a variety of reasons, what catalysed their return to live in England (whether they intended to stay on at first, or not) was a change in circumstances – an end to the 'extraordinary cause' that sent them to America.

II

With the outbreak of the English Civil War in the summer of 1642, trans-atlantic traffic dried up. News was hard to come by. The disturbance of shipping meant fewer letters passed to and fro. Thomas Peter (one of the few migrants to New England after 1640, who fled the West Country to escape fighting between the forces of King and Parliament) complained that he had sent eighteen letters to his wife, but had not received one syllable in reply.[48] Colonists, naturally, were reluctant to travel to a war zone.[49] Preachers encouraged them to vent their concern for England with a spiritual ambush, 'to lie in wait in the wilderness, to come upon the backs of God's enemies with deadly fastings and prayer, murderers that will kill point-blank from one end of the world to the other'.[50]

Although many colonists restricted their participation in England's war to fasting and prayer, perhaps the most significant contribution by New Englanders to Parliament's cause was in the army – not in the Long Parliament; nor in the Westminster Assembly, a weighty committee of the Long Parliament, created to advise on religious reform. Fighting for the cause often led to a decision to stay on in England, with a ripple effect into the 1650s as families and friends followed. The Massachusetts Artillery Company – drilled and ready for combat in a frontier environment – proved a good recruiting ground. The Artillery Company had been founded in 1638 to form a cohort of the colony's best military personnel, a disciplined and covenanted band. Governor Winthrop viewed it with suspicion because he thought it caught up many antinomians. Most of those who joined came from the Bay Colony's trading community, so its members were at ease with, and had a strong interest in, transatlantic communication.[51]

Settlers' involvement in military campaigns back home began with the naval expedition mounted in 1642 by the 'Adventurers for Ireland', to suppress Irish Catholic rebels in return for land.[52] Towards the end of 1643, after summer victories in the English Civil War for the Royalists, Israel Stoughton – sergeant-major-general of the Bay Colony – led a party back to join Thomas Rainborowe's new foot regiment in the Earl of Manchester's Eastern Association army. Stoughton, who used his combat skills against Native Americans in the Pequot War of 1637, became Rainborowe's lieutenant-colonel. Rainborowe, who drew most of his officers from New England, had one sister married to Governor Winthrop of Massachusetts, and another to Winthrop's son Stephen; his brother William had also been in New England.[53] Stoughton took with him other members of the Artillery Company. Captain John Leverett's buff leather coat from the wars, made from panels of quarter-inch thick ox-hide, sewed with linen twine – and punctured and blood-stained – still survives, together with a portrait painted while he was in England (wearing the coat), possibly by a young Peter Lely.[54] William Hudson, a Boston innkeeper who served as an ensign in Leverett's troop, entrusted his family to Henry Dawson while he was away. William's wife Ann and Dawson were subsequently convicted of 'adulterous behaviour', and sentenced to stand on a ladder at the gallows with halters round their necks for an hour, and then to be whipped (the jury acquitted them of full-blown adultery, which carried the death penalty).[55] Early in 1645 – in the hiatus before the creation of the remodelled Parliamentary forces, the New Model Army – all these Massachusetts soldiers returned to New England (except for Stoughton, who died in May 1644 in the fight to recapture the city of Lincoln). Hudson forgave his wife: she had been immodest, but he was 'confident of her innocency'. Leverett and another of Stoughton's recruits, Nehemiah Bourne, began to cross the Atlantic regularly: the journey to England opened their eyes to opportunities in transatlantic trade.[56]

Later, as news of the New Model Army reached New England, more members of the Artillery Company returned to fight. Stephen Winthrop, for example, became a captain in his brother-in-law Thomas Rainborowe's regiment in 1646, and took part in the siege of Worcester; in May 1647, when he was on the verge of setting sail for Massachusetts, he accepted an invitation to serve alongside his other brother-in-law, the former colonist William Rainborowe. George Cooke of Cambridge, Massachusetts, took command of Thomas Rainborowe's regiment after Rainborowe's death in 1648.[57] Others returned to join the Parliamentary army, but remain shadowy figures: like George Dennison, 'a young soldier come lately out of the wars in England', whose experience there between 1643 and 1646 – whatever it was – persuaded the young men of Roxbury to propose him (rather than an older candidate) as captain of the town's militia.[58]

Parliament's army needed medical and spiritual support. John Winthrop noted that 'surgeons were . . . in great request . . . by occasion of the wars'. Francis Lisle, a Boston barber-surgeon, left with Stoughton in 1643 and served with the Earl of Manchester's forces. Abraham Pratt, seasoned by fourteen years as a colonial surgeon, sailed in November 1644 with Giles Firmin of Ipswich, a young 'apothecary physician'.[59] A good number of the ministers who left before 1643 served as army chaplains, preaching to troops fired up by radical religion. As the banners of parliamentary regiments proclaimed – emblazoned with biblical texts and godly mottos – the saints went to battle with the aid of the Almighty.[60]

Soldiers, surgeons and chaplains: returning to the army, like being a colonial agent, took settlers to England temporarily, but often ended in a decision to stay on. The experience of religious freedom in the army produced disquiet with the tight rein of orthodoxy in Massachusetts. A certain Oliver Cromwell almost joined the flood of migrants to New England in the mid-1630s.[61] If he had gone, he would no doubt have been among those who returned in the 1640s to sign up for Parliament's cause.

III

After early departures precipitated by the first news of change back home, and years when the hazards of civil war discouraged return, the mid-1640s saw a much more substantial exodus to England. Trade and travel started to pick up after Parliament removed restrictions on shipping in August 1643 and paved the way for a rush home when news of peace came. The heaviest homeward traffic came towards the end of 1646. The *Supply* sailed from Boston on 9 November. The *Raynbow*, with eighty passengers, left the next day. On 19 December Captain Thomas Hawkins set out from Nantasket for Malaga in Spain, where passengers could pick up another ship to London. The same day a hundred more settlers boarded a ship in Boston captained by Nehemiah Bourne. (Bourne's departure with his wife, Hannah, was recorded by John

Winthrop as an incidental detail in a sad story: Hannah's maidservant murdered her illegitimate newborn child out of shame, and hid it in a chest in their house – a discovery made after her master and mistress set sail, a crime for which she hanged.)[62]

The settlers who returned in 1646 made their decision in the context of significant and complex events. From England, settlers heard of a freshly brokered peace. News that Charles I had surrendered at Newark in the summer of 1646, ending the First Civil War, reached New England by the autumn. The end of hostilities made it easier to go home. Reports that England would have Presbyterian church government tempted settlers who were out of step with the New England Way.[63] In Massachusetts, a series of crises had come to a head. A decision by the Bay Colony magistrates in 1644 to banish Anabaptists went against the tide in favour of religious toleration among English Independents. Letters of protest came from alarmed allies back home – such as the minister Thomas Goodwin and other leading Congregationalists – and from New England merchants who wanted to stay in the good books of their London contacts.[64] In 1645 a dispute in Hingham about the town's militia inflamed a long-simmering dispute between the Massachussetts deputies (representatives of the freemen) and the magistrates, in a tense struggle for power. The deputies came out of it worst. In the aftermath, someone like Nathaniel Ward – whose arguments on behalf of the deputies did not win the day – was less inclined to stay.[65]

The Remonstrant Controversy of 1646 pulled together, in an untidy way, these threads of colonial dissent and dissatisfaction. Edward Johnson later said the protagonists in this dispute were 'of a linsey-woolsey disposition, some for prelacy, some for presbytery, and some for plebsbytery', but all agreed on one aim: 'to stir up the people to dislike of the present government'.[66] In May 1646 seven 'Remonstrants' – Robert Child, Thomas Burton, John Smith, Thomas Fowle, David Yale, Samuel Maverick and John Dand – petitioned the Massachusetts General Court for a more inclusive approach to church and state.[67] It is significant that Child had been in England from 1641 to 1645, on the English end of an attempt to make New England self-sufficient in iron: he had excellent contacts there.[68] If the General Court ignored their plea, the petitioners threatened to appeal to London, to Parliament's Commissioners for Foreign Plantations. Over the summer, the Remonstrants' petition circulated as far away as Virginia and Bermuda. In November, the General Court heard and rejected their case.[69]

What happened next turned into a Providentialist drama, and led to a classic exchange of polemic in print. Thomas Fowle intended to sail to London on the *Supply*, with another agitator, William Vassall from Scituate in Plymouth Colony. John Cotton, at his Thursday lecture in Boston, warned that any petition they carried against New England would be like the biblical prophet Jonah, whose presence meant shipwreck: better to throw the paper overboard than risk death at sea. This so alarmed one traveller, the minister Thomas Peter, that he decided to take Thomas Hawkins' ship to Spain and travel to London via Malaga, instead of sailing directly from Boston. According to Edward Winslow – a *Mayflower* Pilgrim, and the Governor of Plymouth Colony, at this point sailing back as an agent for Massachusetts – the *Supply* encountered 'the terriblest passage that ever I heard of for extremity of weather'. Remembering Cotton's sermon, godly passengers calmed the storm by casting 'New England's Jonas' overboard: 'they cut it into pieces as they thought it deserved, and gave the said pieces to a seaman who cast them into the sea'. Winslow's opponents debunked this version of events: the weather had not been bad – 'in the winter season all passages from New England are tempestuous' – and what had been thrown overboard was not the original petition, just a copy.[70]

Many signs suggest that in the mid-1640s settlers felt a new liberty to go home. The volume of traffic is reflected in the large numbers of letters of attorney which were drawn up and given to passengers in the days before ships set sail. These gave travellers authority to transact business for other colonists in England.[71] Matters left untouched in wartime could now be dealt with. Thomas Bell, Susanna's husband, set off with a letter of attorney from Barbara Weld of Roxbury, to obtain all property due to her in England following the death of her husband.[72] Joseph Longe also went, to claim a legacy of sixty pounds.[73] Matthew Boyes was sent as a 'fit messenger' from the church at Rowley, Massachusetts, to an old acquaintance, William Sykes of Hull. Sykes had written to propose trade with Rowley, which wanted to set up a cloth industry. Ezekiel Rogers, Rowley's minister, told Sykes 'your letters were brought to us as by a special hand of Providence', since the settlers had been 'in deep consultation (upon prayer) what way to take for some way of trading out of England'.[74] With the advent of peace in England, the pattern of return changed: families left together, instead of one adult returning first; or wives and children followed husbands home.[75] The outbreak of the Second Civil War (fought between May and August 1648, after Charles I signed an 'Engagement' with the Scots) interrupted the flow of return for about eighteen months – indeed, several families and traders who had already gone home came back to New England – but the rate of loss from New England picked up again after news of the King's execution on 30 January 1649 reached Massachusetts in May.[76]

Nathaniel Ward followed his Simple Cobbler's creed: he went to Essex late in 1646, after Laud's death and once news of peace had arrived. Ward had long had doubts about the strategy for settlement. In December 1635, he voiced disquiet at the number of the ungodly, idle and profane in Ipswich, Massachusetts, which 'if it be not yet remedied we and many others must not only say with grief we have made an ill change, even from the snare to the pit, but must meditate some safer refuge if God will afford it'. He was ill at ease with some of Massachusetts' religious innovations, although he supported the crackdown on antinomian dissent. In 1636 he resigned as a minister, ostensibly on grounds of ill health, but played a significant part in Massachusetts' civic life. After his return to England, he sharply criticised his fellow ex-colonist, Hugh Peter, for turning away from colonial orthodoxy to support religious toleration. Ward represented an older style of puritanism: he was somewhat out of step with developments in New England, but also at odds with the deep divisions in politics and religion (between Parliament and the New Model Army, and between Presbyterians and Congregationalists) that had opened up among the godly in England during his twelve years away in America.[77]

Many settlers like Ward made their way back between 1646 and 1648, in the interval between the First and Second Civil War. Debates about church government, with the ascendancy of England's Presbyterians in mind, occupied individual churches, and New England's ministers at the Cambridge Synod of 1646 to 1648.[78] Newbury, Massachusetts, where some leaned towards presbyterianism, lost settlers, including Thomas Rashley, John and Benjamin Woodbridge, Henry Sewall, and Stephen and Alice Dummer – an interconnected clan who made their way back to Hampshire and Berkshire.[79] Another colonist who left at this point, Richard Sadler of Lynn, later composed an eyewitness critique of New England's church practices – neatly penned as if ready for the press, though it was never printed. Sadler had abandoned his studies at Emmanuel College, Cambridge, to come to New England in 1638. He sailed back to England from Boston in November 1646 on the *Supply*, along with Thomas Fowle and his infamous petition. Sadler was not a natural ally of Fowle and his fellow Remonstrants, who petitioned for more inclusive churches: in fact, according to Edward Winslow, Sadler was one of those who cut up the petition and gave it to the sailors to throw overboard.[80] Yet his critical account of New England's churches, written after he became a minister in Shropshire, homed in on the tight boundaries of the Church in Massachusetts, which squeezed tighter 'than the Gospel does', shutting out many godly people by asking for a testimony of religious experience. Perhaps Sadler, on home turf again, wanted to clear his name from the taint of association with New England. But what he composed was not so much a fully-fledged Presbyterian attack on Congregational theory, as a condemnation of the ways in which New England went beyond what he had known in England.[81]

John Winthrop noted in 1645 that 'the scarcity of good ministers in England and want of employment for our new graduates here, occasioned some of them to look abroad'. New opportunities at home and lack of work in New England sent many Harvard students back across the Atlantic.[82] One of the first to leave, Nathaniel Rowe, was disenchanted by Harvard's shaky start and saw no future for himself in America. His father, Owen Rowe, a London silk merchant (one of those who in 1649 signed Charles I's death warrant), intended Nathaniel to stay on and take possession of property he had acquired in New Haven. Like a good number of godly parents, Rowe sent his son to Harvard but did not come to New England himself.[83] The College began in 1636 as an alternative to Oxford and Cambridge, but for the first few years was little more than a grammar school. When its first head was dismissed in 1639 for harsh treatment of students – beatings, inadequate food – Nathaniel was sent out to board with the schoolmaster at Lynn. There he learnt Latin, not so much by instruction as by bribing the schoolmaster's sons to supply all the answers. Nathaniel reckoned his father had sent him to Harvard 'very hastily', without adequate provisions. A member of the local church at Cambridge bailed him out, and afterwards tried to recover money from Rowe for providing 'clothes, diet, books and other necessaries unto his son'. Nathaniel asked permission from Governor Winthrop to return to London in 1642 – whatever his father might think – and sailed home without a degree.[84]

Harvard's first class graduated in 1642: seven out of the nine graduates in this first batch eventually went to England.[85] Ironically, Harvard began to produce graduates just after the rapid expansion of New England's settlements stopped. Pulpit vacancies became rare. Lucy Downing reported that her son George – one of the class of 1642 – intended to travel, 'his motive is his little expectation, and fears of supply here'. George Downing had an infamous career, the most notorious of all the colonists who went home: a preacher to fishermen in the West Indies, a chaplain in the Parliamentary army, and a high-ranking servant of the state under Cromwell; then a turncoat, with a meteoric career in Charles II's service after the Restoration.[86]

Nathaniel Norcrosse, though not a Harvard graduate, illustrates the dilemma of the younger generation. He settled with his parents at Watertown, Massachusetts, in 1638 – where the minister John Knowles (who had been a popular tutor at Norcrosse's Cambridge college, St Catherine's) soon became a pastor. In 1645, when Watertown's inhabitants 'outswarmed' to make a new settlement at Nashaway (Lancaster), they called Norcrosse as their minister. However, after two years they had not built three houses, so he left. Norcrosse struggled to get settled, first at Lancaster and later further north, at Exeter and in the tiny coastal settlement of York, Maine. He promised Lucy Downing that if she came to visit he would have a house with three chimneys, a boast she took with a pinch of salt: 'if two of them blow not down this winter, which may be feared, being but the parson's house'. Norcrosse feared that if he went to an isolated settlement he would not find a wife. He asked John Cotton more than once whether he should delay looking for a church until he had found a mate. Cotton replied, 'I think no place in the country, but may find way for marriage'. Cotton's letter, from the relative metropolis of Boston, went up the coast and into the wilds by boat. In the end, Norcrosse did find a wife, Mary Gilbert of Taunton, Massachusetts. He took her to England in 1649.[87]

Last in the parade of migrants from the 1640s, Nehemiah Bourne: his incremental and ambivalent detachment from New England is typical of a certain kind of colonial entrepreneur. A merchant-mariner, ship-owner and ship-builder – Bourne played a crucial part in the consortium that built the first ship in Boston, on land next to his house – he started and ended his life close to Wapping, on the Thames near the City of London, in an environment dominated by shipwrights and seafarers.[88] Between 1638 and 1650 he lived a transatlantic life. He crossed the ocean many times with goods for merchants trading between the two Englands. Early in 1640, writing from London, he said he believed 'times that are approaching threaten heavy and sad things', and wanted to make good use of 'precious liberties' in the colony: he hoped his absence from America would make him 'set a higher price upon New England than ever'.[89] But within a few years, Bourne's frequent visits to England – which included service as a major in Thomas Rainborowe's regiment in 1643, and possibly at the Battle of Turnham Green in 1642 – had made him wary of Massachusetts' opposition to religious toleration.[90] In 1645 he joined others to protest to the Massachusetts General Court against the banishment of Anabaptists, on the grounds that this caused offence to 'many godly in England'.[91] At the height of the Remonstrant Controversy in 1646, he sailed to London with his wife Hannah. Within a short time his mother-in-law Katherine Earning insisted on following them to London with their children. Bourne wrote to Governor Winthrop, defensively, to justify this removal from Boston: 'there was no design in us . . . to pluck up my stakes or to disjoint myself from you'. He plied his trade across the Atlantic until 1650, when the Admiralty Committee in London persuaded him to join Cromwell's navy. His commitment to New England waned as opportunities in England grew.[92]

IV

As the decade progressed, news of change at home undercut the reasons for staying on in America. When civil war ended, English correspondents sent word that the way was clear to come back. Hannah Dugard, for example, wrote from Warwick to her kinswoman Mary Wyllys in Hartford, Connecticut, to say that 'we have hopes of peace and reformation of our church discipline ... there is not any speech or inclination in any that I hear of towards New England, but rather an expectation of some from thence'. In the English circles that had recruited emigrants, enthusiasm for New England evaporated. Hannah – asked to find a maidservant for Mary Wyllys – simply could not find a servant willing to go.[93] By the same ship, Mary received a letter from William Bisbey, who reported 'we have excellent means in London, never the like, almost every congregation an able godly minister'.[94] With sermons galore available back home, why stay on in New England? Dr Lawrence Wright pointed out to his kinsman John Winthrop that now colonists could enjoy 'soul comfort' in England after the model of the New England Way, there was no need to risk the hardships of life in the American colonies.[95] This argument gained momentum as time went on. William Cutter of Newcastle-upon-Tyne wrote to Henry Dunster in 1654 to say that, though he often wished to see his family and friends in New England, he would not leave England again: 'truly the sad discouragements in coming by sea is enough to hinder: unless it were as formerly: that we could not enjoy the ordinances of God'.[96]

Nathaniel Ward's Simple Cobbler quoted a 'celebrated divine' for the maxim that colonists had a duty to return home when circumstances changed. The divine was William Perkins, in a commentary on Hebrews 11, published in 1607. Perkins argued that:

> as a man is not to depart out of that land where God hath appointed him to dwell, but upon good and sufficient causes: so, when those causes cease, which drew him out, he is not to stay longer from home; but to repair again to the place of his ordinary dwelling.[97]

Although fear of return to a war-torn country affected the flow back to England, it appears that a substantial number of colonists acted on the axiom of the Simple Cobbler's 'American Creed' – particularly in view of the exodus that followed news of peace, at the time Ward himself came away in 1646. Given the slow and reluctant way in which most clergy came to a decision to cross the Atlantic to America in the 1630s, the fact that plenty went home after 1640 (but scarcely any before) confirms New England's significance as a refuge in troubled times.[98] In the 1640s, changes in England – the removal of bishops, the advent of peace, the strength of the Presbyterian party, the rise of religious toleration – catalysed decisions to return home, rather than to stay put or move on within New England. Many of the first to leave were either too radical or too conservative for the 'New England Way': the sheer variety of those who went back before the English Civil War shows how stresses in

England had sent a broad spectrum of zealous Protestants to New England in the 1630s. Tensions and contradictions in the English puritan movement played out in the tough circumstances of the New World, against the background of fresh news from home. While the settlers who went home might be thought of as 'failures' because they did not see out their days in America, many actually succeeded in staying on until the 'extraordinary cause' for their absence from England had gone. Nathaniel Ward, for example – despite his caveats about New England – stayed until 1646, when he took his first chance to return to an Essex parish in peacetime, after the abolition of bishops and the death of Archbishop Laud.

A FRESH GALE TOWARDS EUROPE

When my spirit was . . . under sail, and steering with a fresh gale towards Europe,
the wise disposer of all the preparations of our hearts (in whose stretched-out
hand all our times are) . . . constrained me (by the wind which he caused to blow
upon my soul and conscience . . .) to tack about, and to turn my thoughts to
harbour in America a while longer . . .

Marmaduke Matthews[1]

In his response to an invitation in 1649 to become minister of Pequot
Plantation, on Long Island Sound, Marmaduke Matthews revealed his deliberations about whether to leave America. He first considered returning home
about a year before, around the time of the Second Civil War. At that time he
decided not to leave New England, partly because his wife refused to move
'from a land of peace to a seat of war and field of blood', and partly because
he had heard that the English Parliament had banned preachers like him, who
were not Presbyterian. He told the settlers at Pequot that his wife's 'unwilling-
ness to go beyond sea in these destructive days' was still a factor that held him
in New England. The invitation from Pequot also made him think God
wanted him to 'tack about, and . . . harbour in America a while longer'.[2]

Matthews did indeed make America his harbour for a few more years
(although in the end he turned down Pequot in favour of the new town of
Malden, Massachusetts). But by 1655 he tacked about no more. He hoisted the
sails of his spirit and let the Atlantic winds carry him to Swansea, after sixteen
years in New England.[3] He attributed his return to repeated invitations
from Philip, Lord Jones, the Governor of Swansea, a Commissioner for the
Propagation of the Gospel in Wales, and a member of Cromwell's Council of
State. Jones and Matthews grew up in the same parish, Llangyfelach,
Glamorgan.[4] Matthews had sent Jones copies of his sermons from New
England. Later, he dedicated a tract to Jones as one 'eminently instrumental to

the well-being of me and mine, whilst I yet lived in the midst of wild men, and wild beasts, amongst the Lord's exiles in America'.[5]

Although New England's communities were more settled by the 1650s, the 'Lord's exiles' in places like Pequot and Malden still had to work hard to make ends meet. Only a handful of entrepreneurs and traders had grown rich. The ironworks at Saugus struggled; New England's cloth industry had not taken off. Colonists continued to rely on imports from England. Younger settlers, born and reared in New England, were now of an age to find work. New England's communities put a high premium on education, not only to turn children into Bible-readers, but also to train up the next generation of magistrates and ministers. In 1647 the General Court of Massachusetts passed its 'Old Deluder Satan Law' (named for its reference to the 'one chief project of that old deluder, Satan, to keep men from the knowledge of the scriptures'). Under the new law, every town of fifty householders had to employ a schoolmaster, and every town of a hundred families must set up a grammar school. Harvard College gained its charter in 1650.[6] But the children reared in New England found it easier to make a living on the land than by the pen or in the pulpit. After the great expectations of the 1630s died away, and attention turned to England in the 1640s, New England looked like a backwater.

In the 1650s, a fresh gale blew towards Europe. Opportunities abounded for colonists to resume life on the English side of the Atlantic, among old friends and neighbours, and in the context of new Cromwellian ventures. Within the borders of England and Wales there was peace and stability, and a regime committed to promoting free and plentiful access to preaching and pure churches. The suppression of Royalist and Catholic forces in Ireland in 1649, and the defeat of the Scots at Dunbar in September 1650 after they declared support for Charles II, brought a clear agenda for Cromwell's policy in Ireland and Scotland.[7] Settlers heard about all this by letter, and from packets of newsbooks that arrived on ships. A hundred and fifty eyewitnesses of Dunbar soon reached New England: Cromwell transported over Scots prisoners captured in the battle and its aftermath, to serve time as labourers. Fifty were put to work at the Saugus ironworks and the rest were scattered to communities across the colonies.[8]

When John Cotton preached a thanksgiving sermon in 1651 for Cromwell's victory over the Scots, he presented a new vision of the homeland. In 1640, Cotton had told his congregation that a return to England would take them away from New England's purity, back to the corruptions of a national Church. Now, he declared, the saints in England had conquered the antichristian Beast (foretold in Revelation 13 and 15:2), which he interpreted as the 'visible Catholic Roman Church', and also the Beast's image, 'national, provincial,

diocesan and cathedral churches'. A vast sum of forty thousand pounds a year
– soon to be augmented to an even more extravagant eighty thousand – had
been confiscated from the property of bishops and cathedral chapters, to pay
for preachers in poor and dark corners of the land: 'Out of the eater cometh
meat. They that devoured the people of God . . . shall nourish God's ministers
and his churches.' Places without godly ministers now had 'liberty to enjoy as
many as they can procure'.[9] This was the kind of news to make a minister like
Marmaduke Matthews pack his bags. The years from 1650 to 1656 – the first
years of the English Republic – saw the highest concentration of settlers
travelling home.

religious intolerance persisted into 50s

I

England was attractive to settlers who chafed against the demands of New
England's orthodoxy. Under Cromwell, their native country allowed freedom
of conscience in matters of religion. Massachusetts, Connecticut and New
Haven did not. Some settlers who had been forced out of these colonies to
distant settlements now looked to England. Others, who had managed to
express their dissent in local communities within the orthodox colonies – but
not comfortably – also chose to find greater freedom by crossing the Atlantic.

Marmaduke Matthews was one of those who found it more appealing to set
a course for home than to find room for his views in New England. Six
months before he considered the invitation to become minister at Pequot,
the Massachusetts General Court rebuked him for erroneous opinions.[10]
When he wrote to the people at Pequot, he was out of a job. His appointment
at Malden immediately proved contentious: although thirty-six women from
Malden and Charlestown signed a petition in his favour, the churches at
Charlestown and Roxbury lodged objections to him, along with one or two
Malden church members. The General Court's enquiries into Matthews'
beliefs – his idiosyncratic and faintly antinomian ideas on justifying faith and
Christian righteousness – rumbled on, mixed up with questions about
whether the Malden church should have asked the advice of its neighbour
churches before it chose Matthews as its minister. In the end Malden's church
members were fined fifty pounds (a fine waived after the majority of male
church members repented of ordaining Matthews without wider consultation
– the court records failed to mention what his female supporters thought of
this capitulation). Matthews was also fined, but the authorities dropped the
penalty when he claimed he could only pay with his books.[11] Within a few
years, Matthews resolved his uneasy truce with the authorities by acting on the
invitations that came from Philip, Lord Jones: he took his sons out of Harvard,
detached himself from Malden, and went back to Wales.[12]

Ministers like Matthews could easily become rolling stones, with a sequence of moves to different communities in New England. Preachers were particularly vulnerable to being moved on because of a peculiarity of the New England Way – the contract between minister and flock, which rested in the congregation's right to vote a minister in or out. Congregations could and did fall out with their ministers and decide to vote them out of office: this might mean ejection from house and home, as well as from the pulpit.[13] In addition, the magistrates' duty to protect religion meant that when other churches saw a minister as unfit, even if his own congregation had no objections, the civil authorities could send him away. Joseph Hull, by far the most unsettled of all the ministers who came over from England, moved eight times in eleven years before he returned to the West Country. (Surprisingly, Hull settled well as a parish minister in Cornwall. Perhaps his wanderings in New England arose more from a failure to get matched with a congenial community than from unorthodox opinions. The main concern in Cornwall was not his theology but the size of his family: ''Tis hoped the man is godly. He has a very great charge of children, near twenty. Some say more.')[14] John Wheelwright, banished from Massachusetts in the Antinomian Controversy of the 1630s, chose to live outside the borders of the Bay Colony even when his sentence of banishment was lifted in 1644. In the 1650s, when his reputation had been dragged through the mud in pamphlets printed in London, Wheelwright wanted to go home to clear his name. After wringing a subdued apology from Massachusetts, he became a parish minister in his native county of Lincolnshire.[15] After the Restoration of Charles II, he came back to New England again, unable to accept the prospect of a return to episcopacy in the Church of England. For dissenters like Wheelwright, migration and ministry went hand in hand.

Settlers who had long-simmering differences with their neighbours over the New England Way found the religious freedom of England could provide a way out. Nathaniel Biscoe, a wealthy tanner from Watertown, Massachusetts, had Baptist sympathies. His conscience would not allow him to join the Watertown church. Until 1647, this meant he could attend town meetings, but not vote. Without a vote, Biscoe objected to paying taxes – particularly to support Watertown's ministers. He made frequent and noisy use of his right to address fellow townsmen: 'it is a very common thing with the said Mr Biscoe to affront the town in public meetings with high words and to much disturbance'. He drew up a handwritten pamphlet objecting to New England's ways in church and state, which circulated hand to hand. As soon as the non-freemen of Watertown got a town vote, Biscoe was elected to a leading role. But he left in 1651 to find freedom to express his Baptist convictions in England. He would have preferred to stay in Watertown: he wrote back the following year, 'if you in Massachusetts had liberty of conscience, I had rather be there.'[16] Like Biscoe, Ann Eaton lived for many years as a dissenter in a small community. She finally returned to England in 1658 after the death of her husband, Governor Theophilus Eaton of New Haven. The New Haven church had excommunicated Ann in 1645, for her belief in adult baptism. Her seat in the meetinghouse was kept vacant for years, in the hope that she would return to the fold. She never did.[17]

Boston lost members of its church to radical religious movements in the 1650s. William Aspinwall, the notary who recorded transactions for so many travellers before they set off for England, sailed away from Massachusetts himself in 1652, after twenty-two years in America. Although the immediate cause was his suspension for a legal offence, Aspinwall had sympathised with antinomian ideas of free grace since the 1630s. Back in England, his interest in millenarianism led him to the Fifth Monarchy movement, which expected the imminent arrival of God's kingdom on earth. He became a leading pamphleteer for the cause.[18] One of Aspinwall's fellow church members, Thomas Venner, took his family to England in 1651 and became a Fifth Monarchist of a far more militant stripe. Venner, a cooper, believed that the kingdom of God would only arrive with violence, by force of arms. In 1655 he lost his job as a master cooper at the Tower of London for plotting to blow up that vast garrison and its stock of munitions. Undeterred, Venner plotted on: a more extensive scheme to overthrow the government came to light in 1657, which resulted in his imprisonment (without trial) in the Tower for two years. In January 1661 he led a revolt against the newly restored Charles II: for this he was hung, drawn and quartered.[19] In the summer of 1651, the Boston church threw out two recalcitrant settlers who soon became known in England as Quakers. Richard Lippincott, a barber, had withdrawn from communion with the church and could not be persuaded back again. By 1653 he had joined Quaker circles in Plymouth, Devon. With his wife Abigail and their memorably named children (Remember, Restore, Freedom, Increase and Preserve), the Lippincotts began a formidable Quaker dynasty that in later generations stretched between old England and America.[20] Ann Burden, a long-time member at Boston, deserted 'the fellowship of the church at the Lord's table' after fifteen years as part of the covenanted community, and 'would give no reason of it, save only she was commanded silence from the Lord'. She sailed for Bristol in England with her children, followed by her husband George, a tanner and shoemaker. When Ann came back to Boston in 1657 to settle George Burden's estate, the authorities refused to let her set foot ashore. As a known Quaker, she had to take the next boat home.[21]

In William Pynchon's case, a short sharp controversy uprooted a clump of well established colonists. Pynchon sailed over in the Winthrop Fleet of 1630 from Springfield, Essex and became a wealthy trader in furs at Springfield,

Massachusetts, a settlement he pioneered in 1636. As the most westerly town in the Bay Colony, Springfield was relatively isolated from outside intervention, and Pynchon dominated civic life. He also took to the pulpit when Springfield's minister, George Moxon, was absent.[22] Pynchon's deviation from Reformed orthodoxy became only too public in 1650, when – on a visit to England – he published a tract that challenged the conventional Calvinist interpretation of the atonement. His book, *The Meritorious Price of our Redemption*, argued that Christ secured redemption not solely by the obedience to God that took him to the cross, but also by his 'mediatorial obedience' throughout his life. On the title page it described Pynchon as a 'New English Gentleman', which infuriated the controllers of orthodoxy in Massachusetts.[23] When Pynchon returned to New England, the magistrates judged his book heretical, and had it burned in Boston marketplace by the common executioner.[24] In 1652, after twenty-two years in America, Pynchon retreated from Massachusetts to the more tolerant climate of England. His son John stayed on to manage his father's substantial business interests, but other members of the family – and Springfield's minister, George Moxon – followed Pynchon's lead.[25]

The correlation between dissent and setting sail for the godly republic back home was a symptom of the rupture between the two Englands over the question of religious toleration. Even English allies of the New England Way – including the leading Congregationalists Thomas Goodwin, John Owen and Philip Nye – had found it necessary in 1645 to protest at Massachusetts' treatment of Anabaptists. Sir Henry Vane and others appealed against the condemnation of Pynchon for heresy.[26] By the 1650s, New England was well out of step with the drumbeat back home. For those of a radical temper, England looked a better prospect than a war of attrition with colonial orthodoxy, or life in an outlying settlement.

II

It would be a mistake to assume that all settlers who left for England had been marked out from their colonial neighbours by dissent. The histories of those who left suggest that, in advance, it would not have been easy to predict who would leave and who would stay.

Of the families who returned to England, around 250 households can be traced from their arrival in New England until they sailed home. The majority lived in the same community throughout their time in America, putting down good roots where they first planted themselves. Around a quarter of the households moved once, usually within a short time of arriving in the New World – this fits into the pattern of the 'Great Reshuffling' in the late 1630s and early 1640s. Only a fraction moved more than twice within

New England before returning home: over half of these were ministers, whose conditions of employment increased the chances of having to move on. In broad terms, it seems that most of those who left for England went after many years in particular communities, and were not noticeably rootless or restive.[27]

A good indicator of how far the idea of return penetrated the minds of well established settlers comes from New England's response to England's appetite for preachers. The lively market for ministers in England tempted many to think of a return home: not only young and upwardly mobile Harvard graduates, but also prominent colonial clergy and older laymen who switched to a clerical career. Colonists gravitated to preaching posts at the frontiers of the Cromwellian regime in Ireland and Scotland, as well as to parishes across England.[28]

Many of New England's leading ministers seriously considered a return to England, even if, in the end, most decided to stay on in America. Successful pastors had a strong bond with their flock, not easily broken. (Their long loyalty to particular communities contrasts with the roving ministries of less successful peers.) John Cotton of Boston received many encouragements from the corporation and church of Boston in Lincolnshire. Ever since he arrived in New England, when 'the strong hand of the Lord, and the malignancy of the times ... set this vast distance of place, and great gulf of seas between us', Cotton's former parishioners had sent over each year a 'token' of their love – perhaps a package of scarce goods. After the mid-1640s, 'when the Lord ... had dispelled the storm of malignant church government', the Bostonians of old England invited Cotton 'again and again to return to the place and work wherein I had walked'. Although Cotton judged it his duty to stay with his church at Boston in New England, he could envisage his wife and child returning to old England's Boston after his death: he made allowance for this in his will.[29] Others received similar invitations from old friends and parishioners. For a large part of the 1650s, John Davenport, the founding minister of New Haven, teetered on the brink of setting off for London. In 1654 he started to plan the journey: 'now I see my call to be clear, to hasten, with the consent of the church, for my native land'.[30] Richard Mather of Dorchester had 'serious thoughts' about returning to Lancashire, 'by reason that his old people at Toxteth, after ... the hierarchy was deposed in England, sent to him, desiring his return to them'. Charles Chauncy was on his way to Boston, ready to set sail for his former parish at Ware in Hertfordshire, when he was diverted by a summons to be President of Harvard. First generation ministers like Mather and Chauncy, who decided not to desert New England, often saw their Harvard-trained offspring cross the Atlantic instead. In the 1650s, three of Mather's four adult sons looked to a future in old England not New. Chauncy's son Ichabod – named by his father in 1635 for the glory that departed from old England while Archbishop Laud steered religious policy – decided the outlook was brighter back home after all.[31]

While the likes of Cotton and Davenport stayed on, other established pastors left in the 1650s.[32] All had been deprived or harassed for nonconformity in England in the 1630s; all now had years of experience in New England's gathered churches. Henry Whitfield's fortified house at Guilford was designed for permanence – built from granite. But after eleven years in New England, Whitfield asked his neighbours for permission to return to England. His reasons included the sharpness of New England's air; 'the toughness of those employments wherein his livelihood was sought, he having been tenderly and delicately brought up'; the decay of his fortunes; and – especially – invitations from people who wanted his help in England. When Whitfield left Guilford, 'the whole town accompanied him to the shore and took their farewell of their beloved pastor with tears and lamentations' (an echo of the elders of Ephesus bidding farewell to the Apostle Paul).[33]

Thomas Allen, like Whitfield, left a New England community in which he had lived in since the late 1630s. He deserted Charlestown for his native Norwich. In January 1651 the corporation of the city, of which his brother Robert was by now a leading light, sent two letters to New England, to invite Allen to become preacher to the mayor and aldermen. With painstaking formality and care, they sent one letter to Allen and one to the Charlestown church, with second copies sent on another ship, 'lest the first should miscarry'. By the following autumn the corporation had heard that Allen intended to come back to Norwich. After he arrived, they voted ten pounds 'to Mr Thomas Allen who at the city's call came from New England'.[34] Other ministers, like Whitfield and Allen, left after many years in New England communities.[35]

The emptying of Harvard's halls shows what temptations England presented in the 1650s. By 1660, half the students had crossed the Atlantic to find better paid work. In 1651, soon after he reached England, Samuel Mather wrote to his friend Jonathan Mitchell an account of Harvard students' circumstances in England. His letter gave a line or two about each student – working through the Harvard class lists from memory, year by year, from the start in 1642. He omitted those who (like him) had just arrived back, who would 'write I suppose every one of himself'. Samuel insisted that England had 'great need of good ministers and faithful men for places of trust'. His brother Nathaniel, who travelled back with him, wrote to another friend 'if you find any thing worth minding, make all convenient speed over'; 'I had rather see yourself here than your handwriting'.[36] Increase Mather followed his brothers to England as soon as he could: his father Richard, 'as I took my leave of him, laid his hands over my shoulders, and wept over me abundantly (and so did I pour out tears on him) and solemnly blessed me ... so we parted, not expecting to see one another again in this world'.[37]

Jonathan Mitchell turned out to be the only member of the Harvard class of 1647 who stayed in New England. The exodus reached its zenith between 1650 and 1654, when so many left without taking a degree that graduating classes were thin in subsequent years. Seventeen scholars in the class of 1651 left because Harvard increased the period of study for the Bachelor's degree from three to four years (probably to make Harvard students better qualified to transfer to the English universities, Oxford and Cambridge).[38] Marmaduke Matthews' sons joined the throng: 'Matthews senior', Mordecai, graduated from Harvard with a BA in 1655 and in 1657 became parish minister at Llancarfan, Glamorgan; 'Matthews Junior', Manasseh, left without taking a degree and entered Jesus College, Oxford, in 1658.[39] In one sense, the departure of students fulfilled settlers' hopes for Harvard as a centre of Reformed learning, which could send graduates out into the wider world and be seen as a partner for the Reformed academies in Leiden, Saumur, Geneva and Heidelberg. But the authorities recognised a need to stop talent draining out of America. On three occasions between March 1652 and March 1653, fast days in Massachusetts included prayer for 'lack of meet persons for public service' and 'want of officers in church and commonwealth'. In 1652 the Massachusetts General Court proposed a minimum salary of fifty pounds a year for ministers in New England, and Harvard fellowships of forty pounds. This was too little, too late. Nathaniel Mather had already sent word of much more lavish salaries in England: one hundred and forty pounds a year for a preacher, sixty pounds for a Fellow at an Oxford college.[40]

The demand for preachers in England also attracted settlers from other walks of life: cutlers and coopers, tanners and traders. The wealth of new opportunities in England coincided with a decision by Massachusetts – not unconnected with the need to find work to keep Harvard graduates in New England – to put a stop to preaching by anyone who lacked a university education.[41] Edward Fletcher, a Boston cutler, sold his house and shop in 1654 and left for England. Within three years he was installed in a rectory in Gloucestershire. Another member of the Boston church, Edward Bendall, seems to have followed a similar path. Bendall had been an important player in the development of the port of Boston, with wharves at 'Bendall's Dock' (now filled in, the site of Faneuil Hall); he also invented a diving bell to recover wrecks. Around 1652, Bendall returned to London, and in 1654 probably became Rector of a parish in Nottinghamshire.[42] From communities across Massachusetts and Connecticut, people who sometimes had experience as lay preachers in New England (perhaps as an elder of their church, in the absence of a minister) turned up in parishes close to their roots in England, or in posts sponsored by the Cromwellian regime across Scotland and Ireland: the Boston notary William Aspinwall, and his fellow townsman John Milam, a cooper;[43] John Clement of Haverhill, Massachusetts;[44] John Hoadley of Guilford and Thomas Thornton of Stratford, on Long Island Sound;[45] Clement Chaplin, a church elder at Hartford;[46] William Horsford, an elder at Windsor, Connecticut,[47] and Zephaniah Smith, a tanner from the same town.[48]

III

The attractions of England cut deep enough to tempt many well settled colonists back to their native country in the 1650s. Across the map, New England's towns lost inhabitants to England. However, some communities experienced far more loss than others: New Haven and Guilford on Long Island Sound, Rowley and Ipswich in northern Massachusetts, and the commercial centres of Boston and Salem. Why?

The settlements on Long Island Sound, already struggling to survive economically, took a hard hit when Anglo-Dutch hostilities threatened to spread to the New World. A war between England and the Netherlands – the first to be conducted entirely at sea – began in 1652, steeped in commercial rivalry.[49] The Dutch territories of New Netherland adjoined English settlements. The lookout window Henry Whitfield built into his house at Guilford, to keep watch over Long Island Sound, had the Dutch in mind as much as any potential threat from Native Americans. In June 1652, the Guilford settlers dismissed talk of establishing a college at New Haven, 'in light of the unsettled state of New Haven town, being publicly declared from the deliberate judgment of the most understanding men to be a place of no comfortable subsistence for the present inhabitants there'.[50] Even when peace came in 1654, the truce was uneasy, and the erosion of morale continued to take a toll. New Haven lost prominent citizens like John Evance – once a London merchant and a member of John Davenport's congregation at St Stephen's, Coleman Street. In 1654 his house and farm were said to be unlikely to fetch twenty pounds, 'and many more are so lowly esteemed at New Haven'. In the 1660s, the town, with its 'stately and costly houses', was said to be 'not so glorious as once it was', its merchants 'either dead or come away, the rest gotten to their farms'.[51] Evance and a good number of others like him left for England in the early 1650s, in the first flush of Cromwell's Commonwealth and Protectorate.[52] John Davenport's indecisive attempts to leave for London coincided with an exodus from the town. To the west of New Haven, Roger Ludlow left Fairfield in 1654: one-time deputy-governor of Connecticut and the founder of both Fairfield and Stratford, Ludlow had been angered by Massachusetts' refusal to support the coastal settlements against the Dutch.[53]

To the east of New Haven, Guilford lost many of its principal inhabitants in the first part of the 1650s. Henry Whitfield found it hard to sell off his land there. Even though he set a particularly low price, his fellow townsmen took only a fraction of what was on offer – partly out of poverty, and partly because they reckoned they too might desert Guilford for England.[54] William Leete (who looked after Samuel Desborough's property in the town after Desborough left with Whitfield, his father-in-law) felt he had to insist to his neighbours that Desborough had not tried to tempt him back home: 'I told them over and over that you had wrote nothing to invite or give a call.' Watching land values plummet, Leete judged it would have been better 'if many had knocked . . . lesser stakes into the rocky sandy parts of this wilderness'. Leete saw how the settlers who stayed resented the deserters: they had 'an aptness to have harsh thoughts on almost all men that go for England'.[55]

The settlements of Ipswich and Rowley, in northern Massachusetts, lost important movers and shakers. Ipswich – which had tried with little success to establish merchant activity, including a trade in furs – lost several 'men of good rank and quality'.[56] Nathaniel Ward and his family deserted the town in the mid-1640s. Richard Saltonstall, a force to be reckoned with in Bay Colony politics, left in September 1649, four months after news of Charles I's execution reached Massachusetts. Saltonstall had taken his wife to England in 1646, for her health's sake, and now went to join her. He had the connections to find a role in the new republic. In March 1650 he was appointed, together with his father Sir Richard Saltonstall, to the High Court of Justice commissioned by the Rump Parliament to try the crimes of the Commonwealth's enemies – a successor to the court that tried and condemned Charles I.[57] Another inhabitant of Ipswich, John Tuttle, responded to an invitation to support Cromwell's regime in Ireland. Tuttle became a receiver of revenue at Carrickfergus. He kept property in Ipswich, partly because some of his family stayed on and perhaps also because he thought he might return, or because it was not worth selling at a loss. His widow Joanna Tuttle later wrote from Ireland to complain at the dilapidated state of her possessions: 'if I should come to New England I fear I should go a-begging . . . I hear the house goes to ruin, the land spends itself, the cattle die, the horses eat themselves out in keeping'.[58]

Rowley, which struggled to establish a cloth industry, lost four leading citizens, all with roots in Yorkshire, all active in town politics and all representatives for Rowley at the Massachusetts General Court. Matthew Boyes was one. His permanent return to England in the early 1650s was paved by a visit home in 1646, when he went as a messenger from the Rowley church to discuss trade in cloth with William Sykes, a clothworker from Hull.[59] Boyes returned to his native town of Leeds for good a few years later, with his wife Elizabeth and a brood of ten children, settling close to her father Elkanah Wales, minister at

Pudsey. Boyes tried to tempt more settlers back. One of his associates wrote to Massachusetts to say that 'if the Lord should incline any of your hearts to make a return back to our European England we should be glad of it'. The writer passed on Boyes' assurances that 'our climate would better agree with your constitution than New England doth'. A minister from Massachusetts could certainly expect to find a preaching position, and make a comfortable living, 'even in these parts of Yorkshire about Leeds, if you would come'.[60]

Merchants and artisans from Boston and Salem, equipped with trading contacts, and with high hopes of better profits back home, headed east across the Atlantic. John Harwood of Boston moved to the City of London in 1657, after a long trading partnership with Thomas Bell, who left Roxbury for London in the late 1640s. Another Boston merchant, David Yale (son of Ann Eaton of New Haven, and originally from Davenport's church in Coleman Street, London) sailed home in 1651. Ralph Fogg of Salem left for London in 1656, perhaps frustrated at being refused permission by the Massachusetts authorities to act as an agent between employers and servants, buyers and sellers. Emmanuel Downing – lawyer, adventurer, builder of an admirable distillery at Salem (New England's first) and father of the Harvard graduate George Downing – went back to ride on the coat-tails of his son's rapid rise to power and influence in Cromwell's service.[61]

The 1650s show many signs that traffic to England had become a familiar part of New England's life. Families sailed back together. Rebecca Lord and Martha Thurston, sisters who shared a house in Boston inherited from their mother, travelled back with their husbands and children. The Lords and Thurstons cropped up again in the records of Stepney church in Middlesex, all living in 'New Gravel Lane', probably crammed into a single house, just as they had been in Boston.[62] Vulnerable travellers – widows and orphans – also took the decision to move back across the Atlantic. Joan Nelson of Rowley took her two young children back to live near relatives in Hampshire (Stephen and Alice Dummer, who had left Newbury, Massachusetts, in the mid-1640s).[63] Sarah Astwood of Boston went to England after her husband died and left huge debts (accompanied by her brother-in-law John Astwood, who was on a futile mission to secure Cromwell's help for the New Haven Colony against the Dutch).[64] Anna Palgrave of Charlestown, widow of the physician Richard Palgrave, went to join her daughter at Stepney near London, and from there sent word about the care of her houses, lands, 'cattles and chattels' in New England.[65] Mary Lowle of Newbury, an orphan, petitioned the Massachusetts General Court for the release of a legacy of ten pounds, so she could pay for a passage home to be with her friends in England.[66] Many settlers made provision in their wills in case relatives returned to England. Peter Bulkeley, minister at Concord, left one of his sons some theological tomes but – not wanting to deplete New England of its all too meagre stock of scholarly texts – stipulated that 'if he should remove from this country to England then (instead of the books) . . . I give unto him five pounds of English money to be paid there in England by my son John'.[67]

Of many settlers who returned to England, little is known except that they stayed in America for ten or twenty years, and then went home. Mark Vermace, a member of the church at Salem, had emigrated in 1638 from Yarmouth in Norfolk; by 1652 he was back in Yarmouth, where he joined a congregational church 'by dismission from the church in New England'.[68] Thomas and Mary Parish went to Nayland in Suffolk after twenty years at Cambridge, Massachusetts, leaving Mary's brother with power of attorney to sell off their 'mansion place', 'lately burnt down'.[69] Occasionally a settler whose nearest and dearest had gone back to England betrayed the wistful hope that one day they might return. John Busby went back to England some time before his father Nicholas wrote his will in 1657. Nicholas, a worsted weaver who emigrated to Massachusetts from Norwich in 1637, left instructions to send seventy pounds' worth of goods, physic books and 'my black stuff cloak' to John in England, but he also left John his weaving loom, if 'he come over to New England'.[70]

IV

What patterns run through the histories of the hundreds of settlers who left for England in the 1640s and 1650s? For the colonial elite, wealth and connections gave them a greater ability to pull out of New England, and more incentives to do so. People like John Humfrey and George Fenwick – whatever their losses in the colonies – had excellent prospects in England. For younger people, the end of New England's rapid growth meant stunted prospects: Harvard graduates could not find professional opportunities, except perhaps in isolated new settlements – which, though they offered youngsters a chance of leadership, had limited appeal. For some ministers, the New England Way meant a deep obligation to their flock; this kept several prominent individuals in America (such as John Cotton) who might otherwise have gone home. Other clerics experienced a restless cycle of deteriorating relations with different local communities – for ministers like Marmaduke Matthews or Joseph Hull, a return to England came at the end of a chain of moves within New England. For merchants and mariners, operating in the Atlantic world, trade and toleration spurred them to relocate to London.[71] For settlers in plantations that struggled because of poor land (like Guilford's 'rocky sandy parts') or difficulties with trade (like Rowley's cloth industry), a return to their roots across the Atlantic seemed a better option than a move into Boston, or elsewhere in New England. Of all the colonists, yeomen and husbandmen probably had most to gain by staying on. Although almost every settler worked the land, these working farmers had skills which gave them a comparative advantage. Generous land grants meant most were doing well enough, better than in England. More than a few had close ties to New England ministers, but stayed on to farm after the minister went home. The yeoman Henry Chickering, for example, had in 1638 followed John Phillip to Dedham, Massachusetts, from Wrentham in Suffolk. He remained in Dedham after Phillip returned to Wrentham in 1641, although he may have teetered on the brink of a decision to leave – he delayed his decision to become a church deacon because of his 'affections to Mr Phillip in England'.[72]

Were settlers from certain parts of England more likely to return than others? The evidence is impossible to quantify, but it is hard to avoid the impression that many of those who went back came from areas where pressure had been high in the 1630s: East Anglia, Yorkshire, Cheshire and Lancashire, Hertfordshire, Kent and London. Those who had been most uprooted from England by events in the 1630s were also the most likely to go back. West Country settlers played a smaller role in the return movement, perhaps because their migration had been inspired in part by earlier aspirations to create godly settlements abroad for fishing or trade, along the lines pioneered by the Dorchester Company of Adventurers – or possibly because they had, relatively, worse prospects back in England.[73] Of the six West Country ministers who emigrated from the diocese of Exeter, three had been recruited early in the 1630s under the aegis of the Dorchester Company; the other three, who emigrated later in the decade, claimed harassment by the church authorities. Who came back to England? Only the three who claimed to have been uprooted under pressure.[74]

The histories of the settlers who returned to England show neither simple dissent against the New England Way, nor a wish to broadcast it as gospel. Something more complex was afoot, which had to do with how changed circumstances in England altered the balance of opportunities between colony and homeland. In that context, the debate about return – which drew in many who stayed on in America but hankered to go home, as well as those who left – uncovers strains and disappointments that are often masked by the relative stability of New England's early communities. Was Marmaduke Matthews typical? Not really: his unsettledness as a minister, and his idiosyncratic religious convictions, make him stand out from the crowd. Many who had been far more firmly anchored in New England than Matthews unfurled the sails of their spirit and plotted a course for home.

PARTING FROM AMERICA

In the times of the unsettled humours of many men's spirits to return for England, you to settle your own thoughts, made a vow to God not to leave the country, whilst the ordinances of God continued here in purity . . .

John Cotton to Richard Saltonstall[1]

I will (the Lord not letting or hindering) return again into New England to this place to my . . . father to settle mine abode and dwelling as my father shall advise . . . this to the best of my skill I promise and swear to perform without fraud, deceit or reservation; so help me God through Jesus Christ.

George Wyllys[2]

Two small scraps of paper convey the extraordinary measures some settlers took to ward off the temptation to abandon America: a reply drafted by John Cotton, minister of Boston – full of crossings out and corrections – to a dilemma put to him by Richard Saltonstall of Ipswich, Massachusetts; and an oath signed by George Wyllys, son of the Governor of Connecticut, before he sailed to England.

Richard Saltonstall took a solemn vow early in the 1640s, to stop himself leaving America. As Cotton summed it up, at a time when many were unsettled and ready to go home, Saltonstall vowed to stay on in Massachusetts come what may, as long as the purity of New England's religious life continued. A Yorkshire gentleman with entrepreneurial interests, Saltonstall had much in common with people like John Humfrey, who left (deep in debt) in 1641. Saltonstall's father and sisters had gone back to England in 1631. So to prevent himself from deserting New England, he made his vow. Then a difficulty arose: his wife fell ill. Saltonstall took her across the Atlantic in 1645 to her family – the Gurdons of Assington in Suffolk – then went back to his responsibilities in Massachusetts.[3] His wife's health improved, but physicians and friends advised her not to return to America. What should Saltonstall do? Cotton's letter summed up his quandary: 'whether notwithstanding your vow of continuance here, you may lawfully remove your family to England to cohabit there with your wife'. In Cotton's opinion, Saltonstall's vow had been excessive: it should have carried a condition, 'a reservation of liberty always to follow God's call'. Although Saltonstall had made the vow seriously, from the best of pious intentions, 'a Christian man may be called of God (upon sundry just grounds) to remove from one country to another, even whilst the ordinances of God remain in purity'. Cotton judged that Saltonstall's marriage vow took precedence over his commitment to New England's purity – he should go to his wife. However, Saltonstall should keep faith with his promise to stay in America by coming back when he could. Saltonstall's return to New England in the 1660s, and his transatlantic travels on into the 1690s, suggest he followed Cotton's advice.[4] But in the autumn of 1649 – free for the moment to override his vow of loyalty to New England – Saltonstall sailed home.[5]

George Wyllys of Hartford, Connecticut, set off for Fenny Compton in Warwickshire late in 1639, travelling back to his birthplace to find a wife and to sell land for his father, Governor George Wyllys. His father drew up an oath for him to sign before he sailed away. George Junior bound himself to come back and settle in Connecticut, as his father wished, invoking God as a witness to his sincerity.[6] Governor Wyllys proved unable to hold his son to this promise. In 1644, after his expectations of seeing his son return to Connecticut had been dashed several times, he wrote a long letter to argue with George about the reasons for his failure to honour the oath. He dismissed his son's complaints about lack of funds, and even the dangers of travel in wartime – 'never any ship ever miscarried coming into New England (so merciful and good hath God been in his Providence for the good of his people coming hither and abiding here)'. It was harder to answer his son's claim that he need not cross the Atlantic to New England again because England now had 'many churches gathered ... and the purity of God's ordinances may there be enjoyed'. But Wyllys Senior tried. He composed a vigorous defence of New England's church-fellowship as purer still: in England, 'such as are gathered dwell not together and so cannot watch over one another as they should'; 'with us none are admitted to partake of the seals of the covenant, but such ... as in the judgment of charity have truth of grace'. In any case, many of 'God's servants' at Fenny Compton had died, so it was not likely that George could enjoy church fellowship there.[7] If his son needed to move within England to find church fellowship, he might as well come back to New England. God would compensate for any financial loss with spiritual gain – 'as he usually doth'. Wyllys sent his son the oath he had signed, 'that you may seriously consider of it'. He invoked the Almighty: 'I see not yet how I can quit you from your engagement as you desire . . . the nature of the engagement being such (as I conceive) that God is become a third party in it'.[8] Governor Wyllys' will, written soon afterwards, referred to this letter to his son. He left him substantial property at Wethersfield, Connecticut, but only if 'he do come over into New England and settle himself and his family here according as I have wrote him by letter . . . it being my will that he attend the terms propounded in the letter'. After his father's death, George fiercely disputed the conditions of his inheritance, and never came back.[9] The row in the Wyllys family may have led Thomas Hooker, the minister at Hartford, to specify in his own will that his eldest son must return from Oxford: 'I do not forbid my son John from seeking and taking a wife in England, yet I do forbid him from . . . tarrying there'. Despite his father's wishes, John Hooker stayed on in Oxford.[10]

Saltonstall's vow and George Wyllys' broken promise introduce the grand ideas and untidy reality that surrounded decisions to return to England. In practice, high-flown thoughts about Providence and the vows and covenants that bound settlers to New England were typically accompanied by partings from church, settlement and family that were much less clear-cut.

I

Like Richard Saltonstall, many saw the purity of New England's religion as compensation for the difficulties of colonial life. Samuel Mather and the English congregationalist William Greenhill declared that 'one of the sweetest refreshing mercies of God, to his New England people, amidst all their wilderness trials . . . hath been their Sanctuary enjoyments'.[11] But, as George Wyllys and many English correspondents pointed out, when the same spiritual riches could be enjoyed in England, what need was there to live in a wilderness? In the 1640s and 1650s the drift of settlers back home tested the arguments that carried emigrants to New England in the first place. How could convictions about God's providential purpose in bringing settlers to New England be unpicked, without damage to the future of the American colonies? How could godly migrants put the logic that had taken them to New England into reverse, and come home?[12] Penalties for defying the Almighty were high – this was the implicit threat in Governor Wyllys' invocation of God as party to his son's oath. Colonists like Saltonstall took seriously the need to determine where their calling lay. In the same way that the decision to leave England had been a corporate, social process, with wide consultation among 'the godly', so too was a decision to return to England. 'Just grounds' for sailing home had to be weighed up with friends and mentors, and debated in church and town meetings, to fulfil the mutual obligations of New England's covenanted societies – in theory, at least.

Manoeuvres by the New England authorities, and in the writings of individuals, betray settlers' faltering confidence in what Providence intended for New England: the habit of collecting details of 'remarkable providences' to bolster evidence of God's blessing on New England, for example; or of delivering rhetorical flourishes to insist that they had never had second thoughts about coming over. Around the time immigration dried up, Connecticut appointed a small committee to record 'passages of God's providence which have been remarkable since our first undertaking these plantations'. No trace remains of the committee's work, but no doubt the intention was to muster evidence of dramatic deliverances from danger – at sea and on land – and of judgments that struck the ungodly (like those John Winthrop recorded in his *Journal*).[13] Early in 1647, after an autumn that saw record numbers sailing home, Samuel Symonds of Ipswich, Massachusetts, sent John Winthrop a list of reasons why God still wanted settlers in New England. He believed God intended New England to stir up England and Scotland to reform religion. The 'richer sort' in America had opportunities for godly government and virtuous belt-tightening amid hardship, while the poor could enjoy more prosperity than in England. During the English Civil War, New England had been 'a hiding place for some of his people that stood for truth while the nation was exercised unto blood'; a place to train up godly soldiers and (what he thought of as a rare breed) godly sailors, for the fight against Antichrist. Last but not least, Symonds adduced the conversion of Native Americans, 'which mercy if attained in any measure will make us go singing to our graves'. In sum, Symonds judged, 'God's providences . . . at this time seem plainly to tend to settle his people here'. What had rattled him was the determination of some settlers to leave despite the protests of their peers. This caused 'a deeper search of heart' about why God had brought his people to America.[14] It became a point of virtue in New England never to have doubted the wisdom of emigration. Governor Theophilus Eaton of New Haven was heard to say 'that he never had a repenting . . . thought about his coming to New England'.[15] Roger Clap of Dorchester, looking back from the 1680s to early hardships, wrote:

I do not remember that ever I did wish in my heart that I had not come into this country . . . The Lord Jesus Christ was so plainly held out in the preaching of the gospel . . . that our hearts were taken off from old England and set upon heaven. The discourse, not only of the aged, but of the youth also, was not, 'How shall we go to England?'. . . but 'How shall we go to heaven?'[16]

Ironically, migration back to England often shadowed expressions of faith in New England's future. Two members of the Connecticut committee to count up Providences towards New England found Providence led them away across the Atlantic in the 1650s. Theophilus Eaton proved to be almost the only member of his extended family who did not return to England before 1660.[17] Roger Clap's comments about the faithfulness of young and old to New England contradicts the flood of younger people who deserted America though their parents stayed on. Governor John Winthrop's sons John and Stephen crossed the Atlantic often in the 1640s (Winthrop did not live to see Stephen settle in England permanently in the 1650s). In a letter to John, sent to him just after he returned from England, Governor Winthrop argued the value of New England. Was this to persuade his son to stay in America? Life as a settler might not make him rich: 'thy prosperity depends not on my care, nor on thine own, but upon the blessing of our heavenly father'. And God's blessing could 'make our lives happy and comfortable in a mean estate, as in a great abundance'. But, putting 'all the turnings of divine Providence together', Governor Winthrop saw the hand of God in the settlement of New England: 'The Lord hath brought us to a good land; a land, where we enjoy outward peace and liberty, and above all, the blessings of the gospel, without the burden of impositions in matters of religion. Many thousands there are who would give great estates to enjoy our condition.'[18]

Winthrop's devotion to New England made him a fierce critic of people who left: his *Journal* is peppered with hostile comments against deserters. In the case of John Humfrey, who wanted to take settlers away to the Caribbean, Winthrop followed his sour account of Humfrey's betrayal with a diatribe against those who deserted New England in pursuit of material gain. Winthrop defended the covenant ideal: 'such as come together into a wilderness, where are nothing but wild beasts and beastlike men, and there confederate together in civil and church estate ... do, implicitly at least, bind themselves to support each other'. How could settlers desert New England?

Ask thy conscience, if thou wouldst have plucked up stakes, and brought thy family 3000 miles, if thou hadst expected that all, or most, would have forsaken thee there. Ask again, what liberty thou hast towards others, which thou likest not to allow others towards thyself; for if one may go, another may, and so the greater part, and so church and commonwealth may be left destitute in a wilderness, exposed to misery and reproach, and all for thy ease and pleasure ...

Winthrop followed this outburst with a record of a happy event: the first graduation at Harvard College, in September 1642. He was unaware that seven of the nine graduates would within a few years take a passage to England.[19]

Others beside Winthrop saw migration to England as a threat to New England's viability, and – implicitly or explicitly – as a questioning of why Providence had brought settlers to America. In 1641, John Endecott opposed sending colonial agents to England on the grounds that this would admit weakness, and divert settlers and investment elsewhere instead of attracting more.[20] In the autumn of 1646, William Morton lamented the possible departure of Thomas Peter, minister of Saybrook: 'If Mr Peter go for old England it will much dash our beginnings, our plantation being in the infancy, many being discouraged.'[21] William Pynchon, founder of Springfield, wrote, 'Mr Haynes is going for England and so I hear is Mr Pelham and many others: which the land can ill spare without a shaking ague: the pillars of the land seem to tremble.'[22] When Hugh Peter wrote from England in 1646 to invite John Winthrop to come and help Parliament's cause, people feared Winthrop would be elected into Parliament and so be detained back home. Also 'many were upon the wing', and the Governor's departure would stir up worries of a greater exodus to England.[23] In the changed climate of the 1650s (and with the loss of Winthrop's voice – he died in 1649), the attitude to departures was more resigned, but the concerns stayed the same. A public day of humiliation in Connecticut, in 1654, mourned not only the death of Governor John Haynes but also 'some eminent removals'. Connecticut settlers elected Edward Hopkins as their Governor, even though he had gone to England. They hoped Providence would bring him back, and prayed this would be so: 'Lord, if we may win him in heaven, we shall yet have him on earth.'[24]

Debate over 'liberty of moving for outward advantage' was profound, sharpened by the fresh opportunities in England, and by the fact that colonists often had an interest in property back home (owned from before emigration, or inherited since arriving in America).[25] William Leete reported that his neighbours in Guilford accused those who left of forgetting New England, 'as if they regard not Christ's poor people here, having ... obtained great things for themselves there'.[26] The charge of fortune-hunting tarred the reputations of former colonists in England. Thomas Edwards, the Presbyterian propagandist, threw this charge at Hugh Peter in the 1640s. Peter had criticised Presbyterians as gold-diggers for preaching in parishes that paid two or three hundred pounds a year, but Edwards made a counter-claim:

> I believe it would be found upon search, that Mr Peter ... hath had two or three hundred pounds a year, and better some years, since he came over into England; he hath had the Archbishop's Library given him ... he bought apparel, hangings and such like at one time, as he could not get [for] less than two or three hundred pounds.

The accusation that Hugh Peter was on the make was revived with force and wry humour in the 1650s, when he moved into what had once been Archbishop Laud's lodgings in Whitehall.[27] In another case, a Wiltshire minister alleged that his new neighbour, John Woodbridge, had deserted Andover in Massachusetts for richer pickings: 'It is likely Barford in old England is (if not a purer church) yet a better parsonage than Andover in the New. We are not much beholden to New England for such reformers.' Benjamin Woodbridge tried, not very convincingly, to throw off this slur on behalf of his brother: 'I could name many ministers, that . . . have returned from thence hither and have gained ten times more by their return than my brother . . . is ever like to do; were they all deserters of their churches for fatter morsels?'[28] William Perkins, a distinguished English puritan of an earlier generation, had rejected 'attainment of greater wealth, pleasure and prefer-ment' as a reason for making a move.[29] The *Cambridge Platform* took up this theme in its landmark statement about New England's churches, drawn up by colonial ministers between 1646 and 1648 at a time when migration back to England was gathering momentum. The *Platform* devoted a remarkable amount of space to the question of when members could legitimately leave a church. Covenant fellowship meant 'members may not remove or depart from the church, and so from one another, as they please . . . they who are joined with consent, should not depart without consent'. Only real hardship – not a 'pretended want of competent subsistence' – could justify a settler's detach-ment from the community (and then only if God had opened a door to better opportunities elsewhere, in a place with spiritual support).[30] In the 1630s, the tight bonds of covenant had helped to prevent uncontrolled migration to western parts of New England. By the late 1640s, the divines who drew up the *Cambridge Platform* probably had as much in mind the allure of England.

II

Colonists who wanted to return, and who took obligations of calling and covenant seriously, had to resolve with their neighbours whether their voca-tion lay in New England or old. This could be tricky. On the one hand, all godly settlers were expected to show support for the hand of Providence in reform back home, and to stand behind those who returned to England after proper consultation. On the other hand, settlers still wanted to affirm the blessing of Providence on New England, to protect their own interests and the interests of church and town. So a particular person's reasons for leaving America might be greeted with deep suspicion by the community – despite general approval for religious change back home. Settlers had to decide whether their neighbour's wish to leave savoured of 'self will, inordinate love of gain, rash precipitancy'; or were there genuine (godly) reasons for making a move?[31]

To determine the right course of action required weighing up general circumstances (the intentions of Providence towards New England or England) with the particular intentions of Providence for an individual.[32] Such deliberations had a public face at the gathering of the covenanted church and also (where there was a plantation covenant or its equivalent) at the town meeting. Six months before Henry Whitfield left for England, Guilford's General Court recorded that 'Mr Whitfield's reasons, tendered to the church here for his removal, were read in public'.[33] Behind the formal debates of church and town lay a thicket of private conversations – with friends, neighbours, ministers, church elders and magistrates. A small weekday prayer meeting might be the right time for a church member to risk giving a first airing to a call to go to England.[34] If a prominent citizen declared an interest in leaving, this set off a flurry of consultations and letters. Edward Hopkins of Hartford had hoped to return to England in 1648, just after news of the Second Civil War reached New England, but decided 'I dare not, having such a stream of advice to the contrary ... until more of the mind of the Lord appear that way'.[35] Thomas Allen of Charlestown preached a sermon on 'callings' in the autumn of 1650 – probably as part of a campaign to soften up his church to allow him to leave for England. The sermon closed with a question: 'How shall we come to know when a minister is called to remove from one place to another?' Allen's answer: 'the necessity of a people, the importunity of a people, the greatest probability of being most serviceable to Christ'. A short time after this, Norwich corporation shipped letters to Allen and his church with a formal call for Allen to return to be preacher to the mayor and aldermen.[36] In the summer of 1654, John Davenport canvassed many friends and colleagues about whether he should leave New Haven for London. He built his case – strangely, at first sight – on the commandment 'Thou shalt not kill', which he interpreted in terms of his duty to preserve his life for ministry. He wanted to leave New England's harsh climate to get medical treatment from Cromwell's physician, Lawrence Wright. Of course, if God provided the means to cure him in New England, he would stay – at least until he had 'made further trial of the issues of God's providence towards this place'. In the event, the Governor of New Haven asked for a medical opinion from another colonist, and Davenport agreed to persevere when told that he could survive another New England winter.[37] (While Davenport saw ill health as a reason to leave New England, both John Cotton and John Winthrop cited frailty as a reason to refuse invitations to return. Cotton thought the journey would put him out of action, his 'infirm body ill brooking the seas'. Winthrop, at '59 years of age wanting one month', declared himself willing to go – 'but he was very glad when he saw the mind of the Lord to be otherwise'.)[38]

New England's formal mechanism to show that a congregation had agreed to release a member was 'letters testimonial': either 'letters of dismission', which paved the way for admission to a new church elsewhere; or 'letters of recommendation', used to cover a temporary absence, which put the individual under the watch of a distant church. Giving people letters to carry, as a guarantee of good standing, seems to have been peculiar to New England. England's equivalent of the *Cambridge Platform* – the *Savoy Declaration* of 1658 – made no mention of letters.[39] The drive to 'put it in writing' probably reflects the high level of literacy in New England, as well as the need to prove good character in a context where many started out as strangers to each other; colonists relied on paperwork to communicate between distant settlements and across the Atlantic. In line with the theory, Ferdinando Adams of Dedham, 'having a purpose to sail into England and there to remain for a [time] out of the watch of the church', presented his case to fellow church members: 'if his reasons were not weighty and his course warrantable he was willing to hear the advice of the church about the same'. But the members accepted his arguments, so he left for England with 'a testimony of his unblameable conversation amongst us'. John Phillip, hoping to return to his parish at Wrentham in Suffolk, had a rougher ride: 'divers were unsatisfied in his reasons yet yielded consent to his departure'. The church book mentions notes on Phillip's case, but these have long been lost.[40] John Fiske kept a record of similar discussions at his church, where members usually gave grudging consent to those who wanted to move (if it seemed they would go anyway). On one occasion, three people who had 'some thoughts and inclinations' to go to another settlement asked 'the church's loving leave . . . and their prayers for them or a blessing of God upon their undertakings'. The brethren seemed not to like this. Fiske asked if they wanted to hear more. The muttering from the benches was audible: 'scarce a man in the church, but presently said "the grounds, the grounds"'.[41]

The covenant bond meant those who departed without consent could be judged harshly by the community they left. One of New England's critics, William Rathband, alleged that if a member wished to leave against the church's wishes, he or she went away 'tacitly accused, slandered, yea, virtually cast out and cursed'. Thomas Weld insisted this was not so, though he defended the right of New England's churches to condemn members' actions: 'must they needs act against light and conscience, and say they are satisfied, when they are not, especially when they see a brother . . . running into evil or danger by such a removal?' But in such a case a church would usually suspend its vote and let a member go, 'abhorring to make our churches places of restraint and imprisonment'.[42] The *Cambridge Platform*, likewise, suggested that 'if the case be doubtful and the person not to be persuaded, it seemeth best to leave the matter to God and not forcibly to detain him'.[43]

Acts of God against deserters were to be expected, however. Thomas Weld believed that when people left against advice, 'God follows them with the cross, till they are driven to repent . . . and desire to return to the place which they left'.[44] John Winthrop remembered how in 1641 a ship had a 'fair and speedy voyage' almost all the way home, but three ministers and a school-master kept up a torrent of complaints against New England. Close to England's shores, the ship ran into such a tempest that it could carry no sail. The passengers fell to prayer, and attributed the storm to the hand of God as a punishment for speaking evil of New England and its people. One man – John Phillip, on his way home to Wrentham in Suffolk – had spoken up for New England. For Phillip's sake, God spared the ship, 'when they expected every moment to have been dashed upon the rocks'. Winthrop noted, though, that God's wrath pursued the complainers ashore:

> One had a daughter that presently ran mad, and two other of his daughters, being under ten years of age, were discovered to have been often abused by . . . lewd persons . . . The schoolmaster had no sooner hired a house, and gotten in some scholars, but the plague set in, and took away two of his own children.[45]

A decade later, a jocular complaint by Nathaniel Mather – when his fellow Harvard students sent no letters to him and his brother in England – reflected the same shared belief that Providence would act to punish those who left New England without good reason: 'did they so much question our call . . . that they also question God's blessing on us, and therefore conclude we are either drowned or, if got to England, such despised afflicted creatures as are not worthy the bestowing a few lines upon?' (Alternatively, Mather speculated, perhaps his friends had forgotten to write because the meagreness of the food at Harvard had 'shrunk up their guts and made their brains to perish'.)[46] Fear of divine wrath deterred migration, both within New England and back home. John Stansby, in the spiritual testimony he gave to the Cambridge church, said he thought he could not leave, 'for then I must go with God's arrows in my heart'. Nicholas Wyeth admitted that he had been 'much drawn away unto new plantations', but could never see his way clear to go, 'for I saw so much of love of God's people here that I thought I should bring much evil on me if I did remove'.[47]

III

Colonists' desire to reach a common mind about Providence imposed clarity on situations which in practice were far from tidy. When it actually came to plucking up stakes, a fair degree of chaos reigned. Church members behaved in ways that defied the neat lines of congregationalist theory about the ties of church covenant. Settlers held onto American property long after they sailed away, unwilling to sell at a loss or unable to find a buyer. Parents left children behind in New England, husbands and wives were parted by the Atlantic – a separation that was welcomed by some, but was for most a cause of sorrow. Poor and debt-laden citizens scrabbled around to find enough money to pay for a passage home.

A requirement more honoured in the breach than in the observance was the *Cambridge Platform*'s stipulation that 'order requires, that a member ... removing, have letters testimonial'. Thomas Weld admitted that it was 'a constant and usual thing (especially if any of the church knows them) to accept members of other churches upon their desire, without any letters testimonial'.[48] Giles Firmin claimed that many settlers relied on the weaker letters of recommendation, rather than securing a full letter of dismissal from one church to another where they now lived: 'members lived many miles, twenty or sixty from their own churches, and . . . would partake of the sacraments six or eight years together in another congregation'. A pastor might find himself with members of five or six churches in his meetinghouse, which had the potential to create a 'confusion of churches, contrary to Scripture' – it went against the local definition of the Church in the New England Way.[49] Perhaps this reflected the determination of church members not to be corralled by their ministers.[50] Or perhaps, given that fellow members – and Providence – might condemn a false move, it seemed safer to keep up the tie with their original church. Possibly a tacit conservatism led settlers to assume that (as in England's parish churches) membership of one church qualified a Christian to receive sacraments in all.[51]

The untidiness of these arrangements spilled over into settlers' behaviour when they went to England. Some asked for letters of recommendation or dismission before they left; others wrote back years later; some never sought release at all. Scant trace survives of the documents that went to and fro – they were ephemeral, perhaps tucked inside the church book for a while, but now lost.[52] 'Sister Edwards', a member at Salem from 1639, was just marked down in the church records as 'removed'. In fact, she returned to England and joined the congregational church at Yarmouth in Norfolk, where the records noted her formal dismission from Salem.[53] John Westgate of Boston, Massachusetts, must have been the colonist mentioned in a query sent between churches in

Norfolk about 'whether a member of a church in New England should join here by confession of faith or without any dismission, in case that his dismission miscarry, or is not sent to him'. The Boston church records show that in 1647 Westgate was dismissed from Boston to 'the church of Pulham Mary in Norfolk . . . with the consent of the church by their silence'.[54] Some former settlers waited years before severing ties with the covenanted community of their New England church. Thomas and Susanna Bell returned to live in London in 1647, but only asked for letters of dismission from Roxbury in 1654. Hannah and Nehemiah Bourne, who were based in England from 1648, were still counted by the Boston church as members after 1687, 'in London'.[55]

In terms of property, the reality was also far less tidy than the certainty of a call from Providence to go to England would suggest. People often kept a stake in New England after they had left. Thomas Allen took his entire family back to Norwich in 1651, but still had property in Charlestown, Massachusetts, at his death in 1673. The town allowed him grazing rights in his absence, and he kept the house he had occupied as teacher of the church – near the meeting-house and marketplace, next to that of pastor Zechariah Symmes – until 1659, when he sold it to his newly arrived successor. This makes Allen's return to England look more provisional than it might appear with the benefit of hindsight.[56] Many took a similar path, and did not make a clean break. William and Jane Horsford held onto land in Windsor, Connecticut, for two years after they left for England, then gave it to their children and the Windsor church.[57] John Phillip and Robert Peck, who went back to their English parishes in 1641, both kept houses and land in New England for almost a decade afterwards – perhaps to see how things went in England, or possibly to provide for younger relatives who stayed on in America.[58] Some who returned home may have delayed the sale of their New England assets in the hope that they would not have to sell at a loss. Some just had to sell up and leave. Samuel Bellingham and two of his neighbours in Rowley disposed of property at a low price in around 1650, when 'many were unsettled and sold their land cheap'.[59] Often, people were unable to wind up their affairs before they went aboard ship, and had to entrust others with the disposal of goods and chattels. John Davenport of New Haven (who in the end never went back to England) complained that he would be forced 'to commit what I leave unto others, to sell away for me, as they can, and return the price to me'.[60] For a landed gentleman like Herbert Pelham, property in New England was part of a portfolio that included lands in England and Ireland. In 1648 Pelham was said to be 'now for the present in England resident'. In 1673 he bequeathed lands and tenements, with 'all other brass, bedding, and linen with all my books and other utensils and movables which I have in Massachusetts Bay'. He and his brother William (who had also gone to England) kept land in Sudbury, Massachusetts, where their agent caused a stir by casting their votes by proxy, raising the question of non-residents' rights.[61] Of course, there were colonists who had nothing, and so came away with nothing – like Adam Ottley, 'turning every stone to get something, for he is poor'.[62] All in all, few were as brisk and clear-cut in disposing of property as John Trotman, who sent word from London to his wife Katherine to sell their house, land, and virtually everything else, and follow him home: 'I pray wife make sale of all your goods, bedding, pewter, brass, iron pots, and all your wearing clothes, saving the bed you lie on, and the clothes that you bring on your back.'[63]

The Atlantic separated kith and kin. Some took advantage of this. A colonial soldier in the Parliamentary army deserted his spouse, and received a letter from his minister in New England: 'your wife is yet alive, and never received word, nor penny from you; and which is most sad, we are informed by two letters, that you have been sometimes ready to marry again'.[64] Richard Bidgood, a clothworker who had been in Ipswich, Massachusetts, sent word from England that he could not maintain his wife, and did not want her to follow him across the Atlantic. Mary Bidgood appeared before the Ipswich Quarterly Court for living apart from her husband: at first the Court took no action, just to see 'what the providence of God may lead unto', but later it despatched her to England.[65] In contrast, Rosamund Saltonstall wrote from London to her brother in Massachusetts about their scattered family: 'the Lord give us all a gathering in Christ, and there we shall meet without separations to all eternity'.[66] The poet Ann Bradstreet composed verses to mark the departure of her son Samuel for England, and his safe return four years later.[67] Edward Winslow had his portrait painted in London, holding a letter from his wife – whom he had left in New England and would not see again – showing the words 'from your loving wife Susanna'.[68] Some settlers may have divided their family deliberately, to show they intended to return. Richard Saltonstall (because of his vow to stay in New England as long as worship there stayed pure) probably felt an obligation to come back. He took all his family home in 1649 except for his son Nathaniel, aged ten, and gave church officers power of attorney over him.[69] Stephen Winthrop may have had a similar arrangement in mind when he broke the news to his father that he would not be returning to Boston immediately, 'Providence opening a way of employment in the army'. He thought it his duty to send for his wife, but 'I desire one of my children may stay with you; and I am confident that God will either dispose of things so as I shall come to you again, or else that you and many others will have a call hither'.[70] In a different kind of case, Christopher Youngs' children were kept in New England despite his clear wish that they should go to England after his death. Youngs specified in his will that his son should be cared for by John Phillip, minister of Wrentham in Suffolk, 'as his own'; his daughters should go to their grandparents in Great Yarmouth. He even provided for each child to have two 'suits of apparel' made up, to take with them. His executors petitioned the Salem Quarterly Court, successfully, 'to place them in this country and not to send them to old England'.[71]

The final hurdle to clear before setting sail for England was to pay for the passage. For many, cost ruled out return. Edward Carleton of Rowley wrote to John Winthrop in August 1640, hard pressed to find the money he needed for an urgent journey home: 'truly . . . I was never put into such a strait in all my days'. Winthrop's delay in repaying a debt of twenty-three pounds meant Carleton (literally) missed the boat. He hoped to sail a week later, and nagged Winthrop again: 'my necessity is such in regard of my journey that I cannot be silent for the want of the money'.[72] The lawyer Thomas Lechford, about to set sail in 1641, heard that fellow settlers 'supposed Mr Prynne had sent me money for my passage'.[73] Occasionally a town paid to be rid of a settler. The town of Salem tried to find employment for Margaret Page, 'a lazy idle and loitering person', but in the end levied a rate of five pounds in 1647 to transport her to England.[74] Invitations in the 1650s – to find preachers for the 'dark corners' of the north of England, or for Ireland – invariably came with a promise of removal expenses.[75] Some settlers took out loans to get home. Rodolphus Elmes of Scitutate promised to pay back six pounds, 'for my passage and moneys lent', probably secured against a legacy of ten pounds from his mother, a widow of St Saviour's, Southwark.[76] Robert Clements took his brother's family to Ireland, 'aiding and assisting his wife and children which otherwise could not have undertaken the voyage'. The cost – travelling up to Piscataqua to find an England-bound ship, the passage to London and on to Ireland, Robert's fares back to New England again – amounted to a vast sum of over one hundred pounds, which he later claimed from his brother's estate. He asked nothing for 'the loss of my time which was a whole year'.[77]

Sea raids from pirates and privateers were a risk for Atlantic travellers. Robert Clements' largest single expense on his journey was twenty pounds – all he had with him – which was taken when the ship was seized by Spaniards and he and his brother's family were 'carried captive to Spain and with very great hardship got to England'. Abraham Browne, a Boston sailor who had been home to the West Country, set off back to New England by way of Madeira and Barbados in 1655. But he fell into the hands of a 'Sallee Rover' – a Moorish pirate ship – off the coast of Africa. After months in a dark dungeon, Browne was ransomed and found his way back to Massachusetts. He set down his captivity story in 'A book of remembrances of God's Providences towards me, A.B. . . . written for my own meditation in New England'.[78]

IV

Providence, of course, could be inscrutable, and smite the righteous as well as the ungodly. In January 1646 a small ship set out from New Haven for London in the depth of winter – 'the harbour there being so frozen ... they were forced to hew her through the ice near three miles'. On board were seventy passengers, including Francis Austin of Guilford. Austin borrowed two pounds and ten shillings before he left, to buy a handsome coat and sword to wear when he presented himself to his father in England. Sadly, 'the ship never went on a voyage before, and was very cranksided, so ... she was overset in a great tempest'.[79] The shipwreck cost all seventy lives, a valuable cargo, and a manuscript by Thomas Hooker which was on its way to the London press. (Hooker's *Survey of the Summe of Church-Discipline*, a vast answer to *The Due Right of Presbyteries* by the Scot Samuel Rutherford, was 'buried in the rude waves of the vast Ocean'. What providential meaning might that have? John Winthrop recorded that 'while Mr Hooker lived, he could not be persuaded to let another copy go over'.)[80]

Godly settlers' instinct for looking to Providence, and for observing ties of covenant, brought order and discipline to discussions about return. The reality usually turned out to be far more messy and ragged. As on the way to New England, putting everything within a providential framework provided a way to link together and sanction different motives, sacred and secular, public and personal. As in the shaky early years of settlement, the combination of a belief in the purposes of Providence for New England, and the binding of a covenant – expressed intimately in Richard Saltonstall's private vow – helped to secure commitment to America. Although, as Saltonstall found out, and as George Wyllys proved by his broken oath, the strategy did not always succeed.

A TALE OF THREE NATIONS

Leaving America was a rite of passage that took many forms. When Samuel Mather gave his last lecture at Harvard, his students wept, and pinned tokens of mourning to their clothes when he went away.[1] As Thomas Larkham came down to the mouth of the river Piscataqua one Saturday in November 1642, to start his journey to England, he rejoiced; and for many years afterwards observed the anniversary of that day with thanksgiving.[2] Young Josiah Winslow, about to go to London to get married, was told to beware of bringing disgrace on his family by drunken farewells, 'lest by occasion of many taking their leave, he should be too often at the wine'.[3] With tearful farewells, delight, or as much of a rowdy send-off as a godly citizen of New England dared to enjoy, settlers sailed home.

England-bound travellers found the return journey much quicker than their outward journey because of the prevailing westerly winds on the Atlantic, and because the Gulf Stream could add a hundred and thirty miles a day to the speed of ships.[4] The outward voyage to Boston could take two or three months, but an English correspondent reported that a traveller on his way back from New England had come 'safely from your coasts to ours . . . in 3 weeks and 3 days'.[5] Colonists faced longer at sea if they went north from Boston to Newfoundland and took a passage in a West Country fishing vessel. In 1641 John Winthrop Jr took nine weeks to reach England this way, with 'very foul weather, continual storms'.[6] Another indirect route took a southerly course, by way of the West Indies and the Canary Islands or Spain.[7] Shipping had a seasonal pattern. English fishing boats crossed the Atlantic to Newfoundland early in the year (when easterly winds were strongest), to catch the cod that appeared off the Grand Banks in May – dried it over two or three months, or salted it, often at fishing stations onshore in New England – and sailed back to England in the late summer. Ships carrying manufactured goods to Boston started out from England in the spring, and made the return journey in the autumn, carrying fish, furs and timber.[8] So most passengers from New England to England sailed in the second half of the year. John Davenport of New Haven thought October or November the best time to travel, as 'the Michaelmas storms will be over, and the cold of the winter avoided'. Unpleasant memories of the journey to New England stayed strong. Davenport loathed the prospect of the voyage; 'my wife is very weak at sea, not well able to bear the smells and troubles in the vessel'.[9] As on the way over, ships often made the Atlantic crossing together for safety, but disaster could still strike. In 1644 the *Sea Fort* – named for its size and strength – set out from Boston in company with a London ship. Both ships ran aground off the coast of Spain and broke up. Nineteen people died. Survivors came ashore 'naked and barefoot as they went frighted out of their cabins'.[10]

When settlers reached their native country, how did they pick up the threads of a life left behind in the 1630s? Travellers came back to a rich landscape of local and family connections, and to a changed climate in politics and religion. New arteries of power existed under Parliament and the army, and in Cromwell's regime. The old structures of the Church of England had been swept away – bishops were no more – and in parish pulpits and out on the streets a variety of preachers, radical and not-so-radical, jostled for influence. Some settlers came back to find opportunities they would not have dreamt of when they left for America, in far-flung parts of Ireland and Scotland as servants of Cromwell's administration – soldiers, government officials, state-sponsored preachers.[11] Others made their way home to familiar places in England. Many – who have only left a trace in the historical record because they emigrated to New England in the 1630s – vanished once again into the thick of local communities, to become as unknown and unknowable as they were before they set out for America.

I

The journey ashore starts with merchants and mariners in London. Susanna Bell remembered how 'God showed much of his goodness to me' when she stepped back onto English soil. Thomas and Susanna settled into the London merchant community. Their children grew up in the City and became merchants and merchants' wives. Thomas Bell traded with the Bay Colony and Barbados from Seething Lane and later Tower Street, close to the heart of merchant activity at Cheapside and Cornhill. The main street in Boston had been named Cornhill from the start, a sign of the Bay Colony's close connections with London. A Boston bookseller turned merchant, Hezekiah Usher, and his brother-in-law John Harwood, acted as Bell's contacts in Massachusetts.[12]

Merchants like Thomas Bell slipped easily into a London community with dense transatlantic connections.[13] The City supplied the colonies, with Boston merchants as smaller stakeholders in the enterprise.[14] Major players like Joshua Foote and Edward Shrimpton shipped over all manner of goods: iron pots, nails, brass and pewter, gunpowder, lead shot, scissors and knives, shoes and boots, window glass, tobacco pipes. Shrimpton's brother Henry sent New England produce back from Boston. Henry's ability to ask his brother in London for credit was typical of the kind of arrangement that, early on, supported New England's fragile economy.[15] Ironmongers such as Foote branched out to meet the demand for cloth, alongside drapers like Henry Ashurst, John Pocock and William Peake: they shipped fabric to make settlers' clothes – Kentish linens; 'northern kerseys' (a homely kind of ribbed woollen material); 'linsey-woolsey' (a linen-wool mixture); 'taffaty' (taffeta, a shiny cloth).[16] One of Governor John Winthrop's English correspondents expressed concern about requests from New England for luxuries. What did settlers want with 'cutwork coifs', close-fitting caps for women, decorated with openwork embroidery? Or 'deep stammell dyes', cheap dark red dye used to brighten up linsey-woolsey? Or lace? The writer drew some comfort from the fact that at least the lace would be virtuously narrow, 'for we hear that you prohibit them any other'.[17]

Thousands of transactions written down by William Aspinwall, the Boston notary, show how colonists made good use of kinship and old acquaintance with City traders. Business had a human face. John Rucke of Boston, in London to act for his father, for example, dealt with his father's namesake and relative Thomas Rucke, a haberdasher of London Bridge.[18] Robert Keayne, one of the most affluent Boston merchants, appointed his son Benjamin and William Gray as attorneys in London. Gray was from Birchin Lane – where Robert Keayne traded before he left for New England in 1635. Benjamin Keayne established himself in Birchin Lane, too. He had gone back to fight in the Parliamentary army, and stayed on to trade. Robert Keayne hoped to lure him back to New England by bequeathing him land, not goods, 'because my desire is that he would resolve to live in this country . . . so long as he can enjoy his peace and keep a good conscience . . . which I think he may do as well, if not better than in any other part of the world'. But Benjamin would not come back from London.[19] (His wife Sarah did return to America, notorious in both Englands because she had become a 'great preacher'. The Boston church reprimanded her for continuing to preach in New England, and later excommunicated her for 'odious, lewd and scandalous behaviour'. The Massachusetts General Court granted Benjamin a divorce: he sent word from London that Sarah had 'unwived herself'.)[20]

London drew New England merchants back to their roots. A significant number – led to the New World by Theophilus Eaton and John Davenport in the late 1630s – had originally come from the City parish of St Stephen's Coleman Street. In the 1650s Eaton, New Haven's chief magistrate, refused to admit to a shred of regret about emigration, but Davenport, New Haven's leading minister, almost returned to London. Davenport's decision to stay on in New Haven was distinctly lukewarm – he agreed to remain a little longer, to test what Providence intended for the settlement.[21] Among the merchants who set up shop in London's streets again – last encountered on the shores of Long Island Sound – were Robert Newman and John Evance, both significant in New Haven's civic and religious life.[22] (Another merchant, Thomas Gregson, was lost at sea: he carried to his watery grave many of John Davenport's sermon notes, which he had requested to take with him on the voyage, perhaps to publish in London.)[23] David Yale of Boston, Governor Eaton's stepson, and Edward Hopkins of Hartford, Eaton's stepson-in-law, also returned to London. Hopkins admired Theophilus Eaton's unwavering faith in New England, but could not match it: 'surely in this matter he hath a grace far outshining mine . . . I cannot say as he can, I have had hard work with my own heart about it'.[24] Differences of opinion and divided loyalties cut deep in New England circles with close ties to the City of London.

First generation colonial merchants brought back their children – a gener- ation born or raised in New England, who became part of the backbone of Atlantic trade. Edmund Bendall, the entrepreneur and trader who operated wharves in the port of Boston, originally came from Southwark on the south bank of the Thames, across the river from the City. Edmund returned to London with his wife Jane and at least some of their children, whom they had named – with more than a dash of godly zeal – Freegrace, Reform, Hoptfor, More Mercy, Ephraim and Restore. Edmund seems to have changed direction, from counting-house to pulpit. But for many years to come, Freegrace and Hoptfor made a living as transatlantic traders: like others who grew up in New England, they had a competitive edge in the Atlantic world because of their colonial experience.[25]

Merchants' premises provided a contact point for transatlantic news and business. Settlers who came to London knew places like Joshua Foote's shop at the Golden Cock in Gracechurch Street; or the Golden Key, Cannon Street, where William Peake and Edward Shrimpton traded. Nathaniel Mather sent a message back to New England that, until he gave further instructions, his letters should go to 'the 3 Kings in Watling Street, with Mr Henry Ashurst, to be conveyed to me'.[26] Sometimes documents needed to be witnessed by people known in the colonies, or by transatlantic travellers. Merchants could oblige. In 1656 Thomas and Alice Venner sold their house in Boston (five years after they left it, and a year after the militant Fifth Monarchist Venner lost his job for plotting to blow up the Tower of London). Visiting New England merchants witnessed the sale, and later testified in Boston that they had seen the Venners in London.[27] London merchants provided a vital clearing house for financial transactions. Bills of exchange – promissory notes, a precursor of paper money, cheques and credit cards – criss-crossed the Atlantic.[28] At the premises of a merchant who traded often with New England, a colonist in London could make payments to clear debts on the other side of the Atlantic. New England citizens could send money to be collected at the trader's address – or send saleable goods instead, if cash was in short supply.[29] (Settlers were cash-poor, not just because they lacked liquid assets but because coins themselves were scarce. Any coins that reached New England in travellers' purses soon went back to England to pay for imported goods. Settlers used 'wampum' – bead strings made from clamshells – to trade with Native Americans for furs. But the value of wampum slumped in the 1640s when furs became harder to find, and salted cod and timber became more important to New England's economy. Merchants engaged in Atlantic trade wanted 'proper' money. Massachusetts minted its own silver shillings from 1652. A Massachusetts shilling was deliberately made three-quarters the weight of an English one. Underweight coins, not acceptable abroad, would stay in the country. Not only settlers, but shillings, too, had to be prevented from draining back to England.)[30]

Until the Great Fire destroyed it in 1666, the Exchange (built for the City by Sir Thomas Gresham in 1566 as a gathering place for merchants) was a good place to track down people with transatlantic interests. In 1660 John Winthrop Jr advised an enquirer to go to the 'New England Walk' at the Exchange to get information from colonial merchants who now lived in London, and from a Boston sea-captain.[31] Enemies of the minister Thomas Larkham at Tavistock in Devon cited 'New England corner' as the place to hear rumours that he had fathered an illegitimate child in America.[32] Francis Willoughby of Charlestown, visiting the Exchange on a trip to London in the 1640s, almost had a punch-up with another former colonist, Dr Robert Child. Child's expertise had been crucial to the development of ironworks in Massachusetts, but his relationship with the authorities went sour after he became a leader in the Remonstrant faction, who petitioned in 1646 for changes to Massachusetts' style of government. Willoughby had been one of the magistrates at the time. Falling into conversation with Willoughby at the Exchange, Dr Child started to disparage the people of New England as nothing better than rogues and knaves. Willoughby answered 'that he who spake so . . . was a knave'. At this, 'the Doctor gave him a box on the ear'. Willoughby was more than ready to return the blow, but friends of Child stepped in to break up the fight. To bring peace, Child agreed to compensate for his insult to colonists' honour with five pounds for New England's poor.[33]

Child had his arm twisted to give five pounds, but many in the London merchant community – some with experience of the New World, others without – joined initiatives to support New England. A fund to transport poor children to Massachusetts raised donations from Joshua Foote and the linen-draper Thomas Andrewes. Schemes to boost colonial populations usually relied on forced transportation. This pious alternative, marginally kinder (it at least promised the children a godly upbringing), was organised by the colonial agents Thomas Weld and Hugh Peter.[34] Foote and others who traded with New England also invested in the Saugus ironworks.[35] The Corporation for the Propagation of the Gospel in New England – the 'New England Company', which promoted mission to Native Americans – was packed with London merchants and ex-colonists.[36]

What kind of religious life did former settlers seek out in London? The church at Roxbury, Massachusetts, sent letters of dismission to England for Susanna Bell and her husband Thomas, but failed to note which congregation they joined.[37] Colonists probably gravitated to City churches that followed the 'New England Way', like St Dunstan-in-the-East, St Stephen's Coleman Street, St Margaret's Fish Street and St Giles, Cripplegate. But in general, church records both in New England and London yield little.[38] Exceptionally, the original church book of a gathered church at Stepney in Middlesex survives.[39] The Stepney church had a remarkable number of New Englanders in its orbit – more mariners than merchants, because Stepney lay just to the east of the City, close to the Port of London. The church was gathered in 1644, New England style, by William Greenhill, who had already made his mark at the Westminster Assembly (which advised the Long Parliament on church reform) as part of a small but determined band of Congregationalists.[40] Stepney members who had been in New England included mariners like John Pierce, Freeborn Balch and Robert Lord; and Samuel Higginson, son of the New England minister Francis Higginson, who commanded a vessel in the Protectorate navy.[41] More colonists (not listed as members, but accepted because of church membership elsewhere) presented children for baptism: 'Mr Pellam of New England'; Captain Edward Witheredge 'of Boston church in New England'.[42] Theophilus and Ann Hutchinson, baptised in 1648 and 1654 as children of Richard Hutchinson of Mile End, may have been grandchildren of the antinomian Anne Hutchinson.[43] Nehemiah Bourne, the parliamentary soldier and New England sea-captain, came from Wapping near Stepney: he may be the 'Major Bourne' who took part in a debate in 1650; his brother and brother-in-law were church members.[44] John Knowles – minister at Watertown, Massachusetts, from 1639 until 1651 – had one daughter baptised and another married at Stepney; he also witnessed William Greenhill's will in 1671. (Knowles was in Bristol, England, in the 1650s and became a nonconformist preacher in London after 1660.)[45] Late in life,

John Harwood, Thomas Bell's trading partner, joined the Stepney church. Harwood left Massachusetts in 1658 but continued to be a member at Boston for fifteen years after his return to London.[46]

Susanna Bell had at least a small connection with Stepney, through not only John Harwood but also John Knowles. She remembered Knowles in her will with a generous bequest – twenty shillings a year for life – probably because he had the courage to stay on and preach in the City of London throughout the Great Plague, to people like her.[47] (Samuel Pepys, who lived near Susanna, noted with disgust that his minister at St Olave's Hart Lane was first to leave town and the last to come back.)[48] Susanna's account of her spiritual experiences – which says nothing about trade – actually provides the most direct voice of a New Englander from London's merchant community, sweeping from the 1630s to the 1670s and to the New World and back.[49]

II

In 1651 Samuel Desborough, fresh off the boat after more than ten years in America, presented himself by letter to Cromwell. Long connected with Cromwell by the marriage of his brother John to Oliver's sister Jane, Samuel hoped to find a place in the regime:

> My Lord, it having pleased God by his divine providence, through many difficulties and dangers, to bring me once again to see my native country, where I have an inclination to abide . . . and was I in any way capable of doing your Lordship any service, I hope I have a heart ready pressed . . .[50]

England bristled with invitations and opportunities for the colonial elite. New England settlers' involvement in the British 'War of Three Kingdoms' started with the Forbes expedition to Ireland in 1642, and ran through the English civil wars to Cromwell's campaigns in Ireland and Scotland in the 1650s. Soldiers and army chaplains who joined up to fight for Parliament in the 1640s moved on to other positions, opened up by their return to England. Although some went back to New England when the fighting in England stopped, more were attracted by what their native country offered – military and civilian posts, work as state-sponsored preachers. The English background of people like Desborough had much in common with the obscurity and bitterness of Cromwell's career in the 1620s and 1630s. Most had family or friends who rose with Cromwell. Those with experience of office in New England had a taste for government (Francis Willoughby of Charlestown set off for England with a legally attested statement to prove he had been a Bay Colony magistrate).[51]

What is striking, though, is how few settlers found roles at the heart of the English regime. The exceptions were Sir Henry Vane Jr, Hugh Peter and George Downing. Vane, who served as Governor of Massachusetts in 1636, had left in the heat of the Antinomian Controversy in 1637. He played a crucial role in the Long Parliament and in the early years of the Interregnum as an advocate of religious liberty, steering the management of religious radicalism.[52] Hugh Peter, sent over as an agent for Massachusetts in 1641, never returned to America and became infamous as an army preacher and chaplain to the Protector.[53] Downing, one of the first class of Harvard graduates, moved on from work as an army chaplain to be Scoutmaster General of the English army in Scotland, in charge of intelligence and surveillance. His swift rise continued in work for the Council of State; as a Member of Parliament; as an envoy of the Protectorate to The Hague; and in the Exchequer as a financial reformer (where a young Samuel Pepys worked as one of his clerks).[54] But Vane, Peter and Downing were not typical. Most former colonists remained at the frontiers of Cromwellian government, in Ireland, Scotland, or further away; or in the middle ranks of 'the State's servants' in England. To find out why requires a look at what purposes the godly at home had in mind for talent from New England.

The effort to harness the energy of the Protestant godly to Irish causes, which began with the Forbes expedition in 1642, reached massive new proportions with Cromwell's occupation of Ireland in the 1650s.[55] The Irish Catholic Rebellion of 1641 led many to support an expedition in 1642 led by Alexander, Lord Forbes. Its intention (not achieved) was to suppress the revolt, which claimed to have approval from Charles I. Investors who had put money into New England helped to finance the expedition and several former settlers volunteered their military skills. John Humfrey, newly returned from Salem in Massachusetts, acted as sergeant major of land forces. He tried to tempt John Winthrop Jr (in England on a visit to secure expertise and investment for New England's ironworks) to join him: 'You are a thousand times welcome home, and should be 1000000000000000 times . . . if you would go along with me.'[56] Winthrop was not to be diverted, but his brother-in-law William Rainborowe signed up. Hugh Peter, who had been Humfrey's minister at Salem, served as a chaplain.[57] George Cooke, commander of the Massachusetts Artillery Company in 1643, joined Parliamentary troops in Ireland in 1646 and was in Cromwell's army, twenty thousand strong, during the notorious campaign of 1649 to 1650. Cromwell's black reputation for vicious treatment of Royalist troops and Irish civilians arose principally from ferocious assaults on Drogheda and Wexford. Cooke took part in the sack of Wexford, where thousands died. Any rebel soldiers who lived were sent as slaves to Barbados. Cooke stayed as military governor of the town when

Cromwell moved on, and battled hard against resistance. He died in combat in 1652.[58]

Cromwell hoped New England would provide godly settlers for Ireland, as well as soldiers to subdue it. However, efforts to attract civilians fell flat. Few came, and those who did took relatively humble positions in the administration. The talents of Roger Ludlow – a lawyer who had served as Connecticut's deputy governor, and who had framed the colony's constitution and legal code – were distinctly under-employed in his work as a commissioner for forfeited lands.[59] The Council of Ireland was assiduous – and more successful – in recruiting preachers. Fourteen New England ministers received personal invitations (though in the end none accepted). John Cotton of Boston circulated a general call.[60] Several skilled laypeople – including a couple of tanners and a cooper – took up the handsome salaries on offer, and set off to join the ranks of Protestant preachers who lent support to the regime. William Aspinwall, the Boston notary and Fifth Monarchist, became minister at Kilcullen, County Kildare.[61] The Council of Ireland also contacted settlers already in England, such as Samuel Eaton, an experienced military chaplain in Cheshire and Scotland.[62] An invitation sent to Norfolk ministers attracted Thomas Jenner, Rector of Horstead, who had at one time been at Weymouth, Massachusetts. Jenner complained of poverty after his return home, and sold two hundred books to the Corporation for the Propagation of the Gospel in New England to supplement his Norfolk stipend of sixty-five pounds.[63] Jenner did better in Ireland, where government preachers could expect at least ninety pounds a year. He preached for a time at Drogheda, where a few years earlier Cromwell's troops had massacred thousands of soldiers and civilians.[64] Three former colonists joined an elite paid two hundred pounds or more: Thomas Harrison, a personal chaplain to the Lord Deputy of Ireland, Henry Cromwell; the Harvard graduate Samuel Mather; and another Harvard student, Nathaniel Brewster, who, like Jenner, was recruited for Ireland from a parish in Norfolk.[65] These three, with the Baptist Thomas Patient – as ardent as he had been when he left New England in 1641 with a warrant out for his arrest – were among the leading preachers to the 'godly regime' in Dublin.[66]

A letter to Oliver Cromwell in December 1650 from a number of Massachusetts ministers and laymen shows settlers' caution about moving to Ireland. In a separate paper, the writers listed strict terms for coming over. They wanted freedom to run their churches New England style, and free choice of the military governor of their garrison – one of their own number, if possible. The site for settlement must be healthy, and 'no Irish may inhabit amongst us, but such as we shall like of'. In a move that suggests they anticipated criticism when they came back, the writers asked Cromwell to ensure that the authorities publicly exonerated them for leaving England: to 'intimate our sufferings under the tyranny of episcopacy, which forced us into exile (to our great hazard and loss) for no other offence but professing that truth which . . . is now acknowledged'. Of those who signed the letter, only John Tuttle of Ipswich went to Ireland. He and his wife Joanna settled in north-east Ireland, at Carrickfergus in County Antrim, where John collected taxes. Joanna told her daughter, who was still in New England, that – remarkably – she had a neighbour from England, known to her before she emigrated in 1635: 'the apothecary's wife that lived in Saint Albans she dwells next house to me'. Joanna asked her daughter to report to her minister in Massachusetts that 'I enjoy the ordinances of God in New England Way; we want nothing but more good company'.[67]

If settlers were reluctant to transplant to Ireland, Cromwell's assault on the Presbyterian Scots and their Kirk was quite a different matter. The army that marched across the border to invade Scotland on 22 July 1650 required troops willing to fight a fellow nation that practised 'rightly reformed religion'. Supporters of the New England Way shared Cromwell's antipathy to the Scots' efforts to bring Presbyterianism to England. (English Presbyterians preferred to leave this particular military campaign to Independents and Baptists.)[68] New Englanders played a key part in the invasion and subsequent occupation of Scotland. George Fenwick was to become Governor of Edinburgh and Leith; Thomas Reade, Governor of Stirling.[69] A massive propaganda campaign accompanied the army's march north into Scotland, in sermons and in print.[70] Samuel Eaton, an early advocate of the New England Way in England, acted as chaplain to Cromwell's regiment of foot. George Burdett, in another twist of his maverick transatlantic career – in New England he had turned informer against the godly and sent hostile reports back to Archbishop Laud – served as chaplain to Robert Lilburne's regiment of horse.[71] Nehemiah Bourne abandoned New England trade to captain the newly built frigate *Speaker* as commander-in-chief off Scotland's coast, from 1650 to 1652. All supplies arrived by sea, as did – vitally – money for soldiers' pay: the huge sum of 140,000 pounds came north early in 1652, carried on two ships. Bourne's vessel took Scotland's public records, seized when the English entered Stirling Castle, to the security of the Tower of London – for this he received a medal. In one of the more bizarre moments of the Scottish campaign, Bourne's naval colleague Captain William Pestell ordered a sixty-ton vessel to be lugged six miles over land to operate as a floating garrison on Loch Ness.[72]

New England held a day of thanksgiving in 1651 to celebrate Cromwell's victory over the Scots at the Battle of Dunbar on 3 September 1650. At Boston, John Cotton gave thanks for 'a great and wonderful deliverance of the English army, in that great battle, when they was so weather beaten with rain and cold, and charged upon . . . by a double number to their own'.[73] Presbyterians in

NEVVES
FROM
IPSWICH:

Diſcovering certaine late deteſtable practices of ſome
dominiering Lordly Prelates, to undermine the
eſtabliſhed Doctrine and Diſcipline of our Church,
extirpate all Oxthodox ſincere Preachers and preaching of Gods Word, uſher in Popery,
Superſtition and Idolatry.

*Voe be unto the Paſtors that deſtroy and ſcatter the ſheep of my Flocke, ſaith the
Lord.* Ierem.23.1.

Firſt printed at Ipſwich, and now reprinted for *T. Bates.* 1641.

1 The title page of William Prynne's tract, *Newes from Ipswich*, (London, 1641). The first
edition, in 1636, launched a furious attack on the religious policies of Matthew Wren,
Bishop of Norwich.

The South part of New-England, as it is Planted this yeare, 1634.

2 Massachusetts Bay, in the year Susanna Bell arrived. A map from WilliamWood, *New Englands Prospect* (London, 1634).

3 'The Saltonstall Family', *c.*1637, by David Des Granges. A strange representation across time of Sir Richard Saltonstall, with his wife Grace, who died in 1625, and two of their six children, Rosamund and Grace; along with his new wife, Elizabeth (whom he married in 1632), and her baby. Sir Richard sailed to New England as a widower in 1630 with five of his six young children. He returned to England in 1631, leaving a son in Massachusetts. All his sons later lived in New England, but not his daughters. Rosamund, who last saw her brother Samuel in 1631, wrote to him in 1644, 'The Lord give us a gathering in Christ, and there we shall meet without separations to all eternity … only remember me and I shall never forget you' (*The Saltonstall Papers*, I, p. 137).

4 George Wyllys' 'Promise and Oath' to return to New England after a visit to England. This copy, unsigned and undated, is among the papers of his father, Governor George Wyllys of Connecticut. Governor Wyllys sent the original to his son in England, with a reminder that God would judge him if he failed to honour his oath.

5 The Henry Whitfield House, Guilford, Connecticut. Whitfield, who pioneered the settlement of Guilford in 1639, built a fortified house with granite walls three feet thick, and a lookout window (cut into the stone, at an angle, near the chimney) to watch for trouble from Long Island Sound. He returned to England in 1651, and became a preacher at Winchester Cathedral. The Whitfield house is now the oldest house in Connecticut, and the oldest stone house in New England.

6 John Leverett, painted in England in the 1640s, possibly by a young Sir Peter Lely. After a decade in New England, Leverett had come back to fight in the Parliamentary army, as a captain in Colonel Thomas Rainborowe's regiment. At the end of his life he became Governor of Massachusetts (1673–1679).

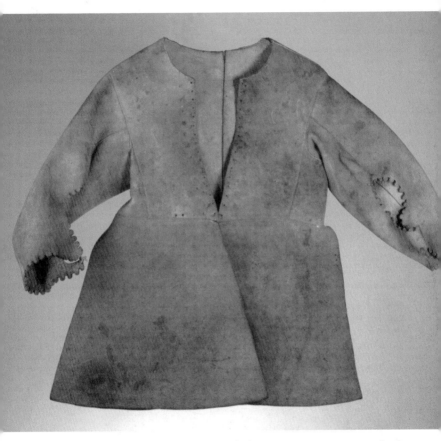

7 The buff leather coat Leverett wore when he sat for his portrait survives – punctured and blood-stained – in the collections of the Massachusetts Historical Society, Boston.

8 An engraving of Dukinfield Hall, Cheshire. Samuel Eaton, who left for his native Cheshire from what is now Branford, Connecticut, late in 1640 – and later became a chaplain in the Parliamentary army – gathered the first church in England modelled on New England practice. This met in the domestic chapel of Dukinfield Hall (on the right of the picture), which was home to Colonel Robert Duckenfield. The main Hall was demolished in 1950, but the 'Old Hall Chapel' survived intact until arsonists set it alight in 1978. Today the ruins are in poor condition, and on the English Heritage list of Buildings at Risk. There is talk of repair and restoration.

9 Edward Winslow, painted in London to mark his son Josiah's marriage to Penelope Pelham. Winslow, a *Mayflower* Pilgrim in 1620, returned to England as an agent for Massachusetts in 1646. His wife stayed in New England. In the portrait, Winslow holds a letter from her. The only words legible are 'From yr loving wife Susanna'. He died before he could return to New England. This is the only known portrait of a *Mayflower* Pilgrim.

10 A wedding portrait of Penelope Pelham, who returned to England with her family in the 1640s, painted in London to mark her wedding in 1651 to Josiah Winslow. Josiah sailed back across the Atlantic for the wedding, and in 1655 the couple returned to New England.

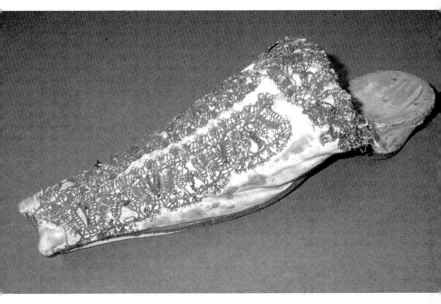

11 An embroidered shoe, thought to have been worn by Penelope Pelham at her wedding. Made in England or France, of pigskin, silk and galoon (silk-covered thread).

12 Susanna Bell's London: a detail from Richard Newcourt's *An Exact Delineation of the Cities of London and Westminster*, 1658. Seething Lane, with the tower of All Hallows Barking at its foot (marked 2), is immediately west of Tower Hill.

Byrsa Londinensis *vulgo* the Royal Exchange.

13 The Exchange, City of London, where the 'New England Walk' was a place to hear news from merchants trading across the Atlantic and from settlers visiting the City. Dr Robert Child and Francis Willoughby nearly came to blows here over the reputation of New England and its people.

14 Thomas Larkham: a portrait he commissioned as a frontispiece for a collection of his sermons, *The Wedding-Supper* (London, 1652), which – as his diary records – he had printed at his own expense and distributed to his patrons and allies in Tavistock.

15 St George Tombland, Norwich, where Thomas Allen became Rector and pastor to a gathered church. He returned to the city after thirteen years at Charlestown, Massachusetts. The church stands close to Norwich Cathedral (the cathedral spire is visible on the right), where Allen's sentence of excommunication had been publicly announced on Bishop Matthew Wren's authority in 1636.

16 A cartoon of Hugh Peter from the title page of *Hugh Peters Figaries: Or, his Merry Tales and Witty Jests*, which was published anonymously by his detractors, around the time of Peter's execution as a traitor in 1660.

England refused to mount similar celebrations of victory.[74] Henry Dunster, the President of Harvard, wrote a long letter to his 'Christian friends in and about Bury in Lancashire' late in 1650, fortified with news of the campaign up to 20 September, 'whitherto our intelligence by the last ship . . . reacheth'. Dunster's letter praised the works of God for his people, 'whereof no nation under heaven hath larger experience (if their eyes were open to see it) than now the English nation'. New England fasted and prayed, feasted and rejoiced, for England's godly Parliament and army.[75] Dunster had a personal stake in events because his stepson Roger Glover, who grew up in his household in Massachusetts, had joined the campaign. Glover died shortly after the battle of Dunbar in the fight to seize Edinburgh Castle; this news had not yet crossed the Atlantic to Dunster.[76]

The Cromwellian occupation of Scotland from 1651 to 1660 attracted a New England elite drawn to opportunities for government.[77] Unlike Ireland, the work did not involve planting new settlements; and, after Cromwell's second decisive victory against the Scots at Worcester in September 1651, Scotland held less danger. George Fenwick, Governor of Edinburgh and Leith from December 1650, became a Commissioner for Scotland. Stephen Winthrop served as colonel to a regiment, part of a force that staffed dozens of English garrisons across Scotland, from Jedburgh in the Borders to Scalloway Castle in Shetland, from St Andrews in the east to Duart Castle on Mull in the west.[78] Sir Henry Vane Jr spent the winter of 1651/2 in Scotland, as one of eight Parliamentary commissioners sent north to negotiate for a union of the two nations.[79] Cromwell's regime in Scotland attracted more ex-colonists to its middle ranks. George Downing, the Scoutmaster General, brought over his family: his brother Joshua found a position in customs and excise; his father Emmanuel became clerk to the newly formed Council of Scotland in 1655.[80] Fitz John Winthrop, grandson of Governor John Winthrop of Massachusetts, came to Scotland in 1658 to join his uncles Stephen Winthrop and Thomas Reade. He took a commission in the army with Reade at Stirling.[81] Richard Saltonstall – who had consulted John Cotton about his vow to stay in New England – came to Scotland as a trustee for confiscated estates in 1651, and later worked as a Commissioner for customs and excise. In 1652, Fenwick, Saltonstall and Desborough became Commissioners for Scottish universities and for matters relating to the ministry. (It was said the Commissioners treated the University of St Andrews particularly well because of a friendship between Fenwick and the minister Robert Blair of St Andrews, who had met in London.)[82] The Harvard graduate Nathaniel Mather thought Scotland a likely place to find employment when he arrived in London three months after Cromwell's victory at Dunbar: 'which way I am intending by the first opportunity'.[83] Samuel Mather was invited to preach to English soldiers serving in Cromwell's forces, and left his post as chaplain at Magdalen College, Oxford, for the citadel at Leith, near Edinburgh. This opportunity paved the way to his high position as a preacher in Dublin.[84] Four ex-colonists – Samuel Desborough, George Downing, Thomas Reade and Stephen Winthrop – sat as Members of Parliament for Scottish constituencies at Westminster, after Cromwell created the first ever Parliament of three nations for England, Scotland and Ireland, in 1654.[85] Of all the colonists in Scotland, Samuel Desborough rose highest: he became a founder member of the Council of Scotland in 1655 and Keeper of the Great Seal in 1657. In 1660, he cooperated with the forces that restored Charles II to the throne, and as a result received a full pardon from the king for his role in Cromwell's republican regime. The strength of Desborough's influence led more than one of his Guilford townsmen to follow him to Scotland, which no doubt explains why William Leete wanted to insist to his beleaguered neighbours on Long Island Sound that Desborough had not tried to tempt him away.[86]

Cromwell's navy took New Englanders into the heart of its administration, and capitalised on the skills and interests of Atlantic merchants and mariners. Sir Henry Vane Jr, Treasurer to the Navy from 1642, sought out colonial contacts. It was he who persuaded Nehemiah Bourne to sign up: 'we will use our endeavours to take him off from his merchant affairs'; 'the man is without exception, and will do the state . . . both service and honour'. Bourne's professional skill as a sailor (and shipbuilder) and his impeccable godly connections made him exemplary officer material for the new regime.[87] Vane, as the most prominent Admiralty Commissioner, played a crucial role in the expansion of the navy after 1649 to help England to face out the hostility of Europe after the execution of Charles I. Even though Vane left abruptly at the end of 1652, criticised by Cromwell and opposed to war with the Dutch (he questioned the wisdom of attacking fellow Protestants), his influence at a critical time placed people with ties to New England in key roles. Vane's work was reinforced by the Rump Parliament's appointment of sixteen 'Regulators' to assist the Admiralty Commissioners to supervise naval administration. London merchants who traded with the colonies dominated this group. The 'Committee of Merchants' (as it soon became known) appointed many relatives and associates to naval posts – and so played into the hands of cynics, who accused it of nepotism.[88]

The patronage of Vane and the merchants resulted in New England colonists filling the ranks of Navy Commissioners. Francis Willoughby, Robert Thomson, Nehemiah Bourne and Edward Hopkins, with the Navy Treasurer Richard Hutchinson (the son or brother-in-law of the antinomian Anne Hutchinson), looked after day-to-day administration – supplies and pay, staff and shipbuilding – at a time when the navy's size and role expanded dramatically, particularly during the Anglo-Dutch War, which was entirely fought at sea.[89] Francis Willoughby followed in the footsteps of his father, William Willoughby, and Robert Moulton (who had close American ties), as Naval Commissioner for Portsmouth. Nehemiah Bourne moved from ship to shore, to develop the naval base at Harwich. As a sideline he kept up his father's shipyard in Wapping, and – seizing a lucrative opportunity – supplied New England timber for masts when the navy's supply from the Baltic dried up. Edward Hopkins of Hartford, who served alternate years with John Haynes as Governor of Connecticut, was recruited by the navy when he came to London in 1652.[90] (Ann Hopkins, his wife – sister to David and Thomas Yale – followed him back, probably with Thomas in 1656. She suffered from 'distempered melancholy ... an incurable distraction, with ... ill-shaped ideas in her brain'. John Winthrop thought she had lost her reason through 'giving her self wholly to reading and writing'. If she had stuck to household affairs, 'and not gone out of her way and calling, to meddle in such things as are proper for men, whose minds are stronger ... she had kept her wits'.)[91] Connecticut elected Hopkins as Governor in his absence, and prayed for his return, but he was inclined to think Providence wanted to fix him forever in England: at least, that was the conclusion he was tempted to draw from the 'dreadful terrors' of his Atlantic voyage when he sailed away from New England. Hopkins stayed on in London as an Admiralty Commissioner, Warden of the Fleet Prison, and Keeper of the Palace of Westminster. Both he and Willoughby entered Parliament as members for the constituencies that held the naval bases for which they were responsible, Portsmouth and Dartmouth.[92] By 1660 Willoughby had a house within the Navy Office buildings on Seething Lane in London, and Bourne and Hopkins probably lived there too. They may well have worshipped at St Olave's, Hart Lane, which in Samuel Pepys' day had a special gallery set apart for members of the Navy Office.[93] Edward Hopkins died in the parish of St Olave's, a stone's throw from St Stephen's Coleman Street, where he had worshipped as a London merchant in the 1630s. (After Edward's death, David Yale cared for his sister Ann Hopkins. Despite her melancholy, she outlived him, too, and died in London in 1698.)[94]

In the Cromwellian navy, religious zeal became a qualification equal to experience at sea. To ensure loyalty, the Admiralty and Navy Commissioners tried to recruit like minds: colonial captains like Nehemiah Bourne and Samuel Higginson met the criteria. Early in 1653 some documents listed nominees for promotion as either 'godly' or 'civil'. Naval chaplains had less status and less pay than their equivalent in the army, but this work attracted a few colonial ministers in transit to better prospects. Nathaniel Norcrosse, fresh from the isolation of a tiny settlement in Maine, served at sea before he became Vicar of St Mary's at the port of Dover in Kent.[95]

Just as Cromwell hoped to attract settlers to Ireland, he hoped New Englanders would support his Western Design: a plan to send a fleet to conquer Spanish territories in the Caribbean, at the same time as negotiating for peace with Spain in Europe. Inspiration for the project may have come partly from John Cotton in Boston. A letter from Cotton to Cromwell, now lost, apparently suggested that 'to take from the Spaniards in America would be to dry up the Euphrates' (a reference to a verse in Revelation 16). This helped to prompt Cromwell's poorly planned Hispaniola expedition.[96] At an audience with Cromwell, John Astwood of Milford realised the Protector wanted settlers to move south, away from New England – lock, stock and barrel. Astwood had come to England to ask for help to defend English settlers against the Dutch of New Netherland. But Cromwell more than hinted that he thought settlers would be better off in the Caribbean: would it not 'be better that New England were removed to some place where they might have cities ready builded and land ready tilled'?[97] A fleet of thirty-eight ships left England for the Caribbean in December 1654. Edward Winslow, who had been in London as an agent for Massachusetts since 1646, was one of three Commissioners appointed to accompany the expedition. Winslow died at sea before it was completed, bringing an end to his remarkable Atlantic travels, which began as a pilgrim on the *Mayflower* in 1620. By the time Robert Sedgwick and John Leverett took troops and supplies from Massachusetts to reinforce the expedition, it was clear the Western Design had failed to meet its aims, except for the capture of Jamaica.[98] When Cromwell heard the news he shut himself in his room for a day, to find out what 'accursed thing' had provoked God's wrath.[99] But he remained earnest about transplanting New Englanders south. He asked Daniel Gookin of Boston, who was in England at the time, to advertise prospects in Jamaica to New England settlers. Gookin took his mission to Boston, but met with little success. He came back across the Atlantic on family business, and was appointed by the Council of State as a collector of customs at Dunkirk.[100]

Colonists clustered in Ireland, Scotland and the navy (and earlier, to an extent, in the army) – but were few and far between in central and regional government.[101] Only two New Englanders sat in the Long Parliament in the 1640s: George Fenwick and Sir Henry Vane Jr. The majority of the select number who became Members of Parliament in the 1650s had special interests related to government work – in Scotland, or the navy – rather than local connections.[102] The only former colonist to join the Council of State, which carried general executive power from 1649 after the end of the monarchy, was Sir Henry Vane.[103] Of the major-generals Cromwell appointed to govern English regions, only Hezekiah Haynes (son of Governor John Haynes of Connecticut) had been in New England.[104] New Englanders took middling roles: as Registrar-Accountant, for example, or Commissioner for Customs.[105]

Herbert Pelham, a long-time resident of Bures, Essex, is the only settler known to have served as a Justice of the Peace.[106] William Hooke, minister at New Haven, was related to Oliver Cromwell by marriage and became one of his chaplains: in this respect, he and Hugh Peter were the colonists who got closest to the Lord Protector. Hooke was also Master of the Savoy Palace, on the north bank of the Thames between Westminster and the City of London, where Cromwell housed officers of his court. The Savoy Conference met there (a meeting of congregational churches from across England, to draft a statement of church order). Its outcome was undermined by the death of Cromwell on 3 September 1658, just before the Conference started.[107]

For Cromwell, who barely mentioned New England unless it was to suggest its settlers should transplant elsewhere, the puritan colonies were a resource to fill strategic gaps. Talent from New England supported key aims of Cromwellian policy at the frontiers: to bring godly order to Ireland; to take a loyal occupying force into Scotland; to provide the navy with the ethos and expertise it needed at a critical time. Although colonists resisted Cromwell's attempts to pluck up their communities from New England, many individuals – usually with family ties to each other and to important players in England – responded to the opportunity to take part in government, or to become state-sponsored preachers. The lack of colonists in central and local government suggests they were less well placed to shape politics at the centre, and locally, because they had been away during crucial years in the 1640s when the trajectory of the careers of those who stayed on (rather than emigrated) was established. The careers of John and Samuel Desborough make an interesting contrast. John – who married Jane Cromwell when Oliver was still an obscure East Anglian gentleman – stayed in England, rose in the army alongside Cromwell, and took a pivotal role as a major-general and member of the Council of State. He refused to accept a posting as general of the army in Scotland. Samuel lived in New England from 1639 to 1651; his opportunity for government came only in Scotland.[108] To put this displacement from the centre in a more positive light, the godly in power believed that colonists had special skills for work at the frontier. Contemporaries saw parallels between settlers' work in subduing the wilderness of a New World and the task of bringing godly order to what they saw as 'dark corners' at the edge of the civilised nation.

III

Unsurprisingly (though it has not often been remarked upon) many settlers returned to their roots. Familiarity and contacts predisposed them that way, whether or not they still had property in England. Even an adventurer like Nehemiah Bourne came back close to his origins as a shipbuilder and mariner of Wapping, through his work at the Navy Office in Seething Lane.[109] Samuel Desborough, at the height of his power in Cromwellian Scotland, bought property in Cambridgeshire three miles from his birthplace, to which he retired after the Restoration of Charles II.[110]

Evidence about local resettlement is patchy. Very often, either a settler's whereabouts in England before emigration are known, or it is known where he or she came back to – but not both. And unless a paper trail exists to make a link to the colonies, many settlers disappear (lost in a mass of people with similar names) soon after they return to England. Occasionally, however, a source is extremely clear. The will of John Caffinch, 'now of Tenterden, Kent, and late of New Haven in New England', bequeathed to his wife and three young daughters 'my house and land in Tenterden which I lived in before I went to New England'. Caffinch returned in the late 1650s to a home he left in 1639. (He arrived ahead of his family, and had been waiting anxiously for their arrival: his will said they 'were coming to England about a year since', and made provision in case they never reached Tenterden.)[111] Like Caffinch, Herbert Pelham stayed close to his roots. He lived in Cambridge, Massachusetts, from 1638 to 1646, but before and after this was in the Stour Valley at his manor at Bures Hamlet in Essex – which accounts for his credibility as a local Justice of the Peace. William Cutter left Newcastle-upon-Tyne for Massachusetts in the 1630s. At the time, a friend of his thanked God for those who got away to New England, 'those that he has plucked like firebrands from the burning'. Cutter was back in Newcastle by the 1650s.[112] Edmund and Mary Munnings returned to the Essex coastal community of Tillingham. Their sons Hopestill and Takeheed, born in Dorchester, Massachusetts, also came back – but not Return Munnings, named in 1641, at a time when many thought of returning to England. Return stayed on in New England and married a minister's daughter.[113]

The attraction of familiar haunts is clear in the choices made by preachers who came back from New England. In the 1640s and 1650s, seventy-nine left the mainstream puritan colonies for English parishes and government-funded preaching posts. (By coincidence, this matches almost exactly the seventy-six preachers who left England for America in the 1630s: New England gave as good as it got.) One in three ministers who emigrated before 1640 returned to England by 1660. The rest who came back were young graduates (mostly from Harvard) and a sprinkling of people with no university education.[114]

Local ties stayed important, and survived the settlers' time away – even for young Harvard graduates, born in New England or raised there from childhood. The older generation of ministers returned to the localities they left in the 1630s: with a few exceptions, they resettled not many miles from their roots, rarely across a county boundary or outside their old diocese. Three went back to their original parishes in the 1640s, with New England a brief interlude in a long career: Robert Peck of Hingham in Norfolk; John Phillip of Wrentham, Suffolk; Thomas Peter of Mylor, Cornwall. Others settled in a new parish close by, like Nathaniel Ward, who ended up four miles away from old haunts in Essex, or John Wheelwright in Lincolnshire in the 1650s, who settled six miles from where he had preached before emigration. Thomas Allen returned to Norwich and, instead of a parish on the outskirts, took a prestigious role as corporation preacher.[115] Younger men – graduates from English universities who had not been able to launch careers as ministers before emigration – still showed strong local preferences. Giles Firmin went back to Essex, into the godly circles he had come from.[116] Harvard students, who left England as young children or were born in America, were more likely to sign up as preachers for far-flung parts, but still often chose where to go on the basis of local family ties. Samuel Mather's comment that his fellow students John Birden and Abraham Walver were 'preachers in their own county' reflects this.[117] John Bulkeley, born in Odell, Bedfordshire, moved across to Essex when he came back, but married Ann Try of Odell. Comfort Starr, the only Harvard graduate to take up the invitation to preach in the 'dark corners of the North', moved back from Carlisle to his childhood roots in Kent when he lost his post at the Restoration. Increase Mather (born in New England) visited his father's home county of Lancashire soon after he first set foot on English soil, and was 'very kindly entertained by my father's old friends and Christian acquaintance'.[118]

As preachers went back to the localities from which settlers had originally come, they found themselves in the company of people with connections in New England. Even where a minister went to an English parish distant from his roots, it was likely to be a place that had sent migrants to New England in the 1630s – sympathetic to New England ways, happy to receive someone with a transatlantic history. Christopher Marshall originated in Lincolnshire but came back to Yorkshire, to a parish from which two ministers in succession left for New England in the 1630s.[119] If a settler had neighbours in America who came from another part of England (in the 1630s colonial towns had often attracted waves of immigrants from different areas), then he or she might be led to return to the neighbours' part of the country. Henry Butler's parents, for example, came from Kent. He grew up in Dorchester, Massachusetts, a community with strong links to its namesake, Dorchester in Dorset. When Butler went to England, he became a West Country preacher at Yeovil in Somerset – with support from a well known minister from old England's Dorchester.[120]

To get settled in England again, colonists used a rich mixture of local and transatlantic connections. Nowhere is this clearer than in a set of records from

Cromwell's time – now in Lambeth Palace Library, their pages not much turned in 350 years. By the 1650s, all the old bureaucracy of the Church of England had vanished. Although Cromwell's policy of religious toleration meant almost a free-for-all in belief and practice, the state still administered the revenues of the English Church, and the state believed it had an obligation to install well qualified public preachers in parish pulpits. Traditionally, the bishops had licensed preachers. Under Cromwell, the Commissioners for Approbation of Public Preachers introduced a system of certificates to vet ministers. From 1653, every applicant to be a public preacher had to find at least three people willing to testify to their worth. The Commissioners' records uncover the contacts ministers looked to.[121]

When settlers presented certificates, some brought baggage from the New World; others built from the start on local connections in England. Some presented a full slate of certificates from people who favoured the New England Way, Congregationalism; a surprising number ran on a mixed ticket, looking for support from local godly ministers (whatever their views on church order). John Wheelwright sought admission to the role of public preacher at Belleau, Lincolnshire, in 1655. This was not only close to Bilsby, where he had been Rector for a decade from 1623, but also near the country seat of Sir Henry Vane Jr. Vane and Wheelwright had been close allies in Massachusetts' Antinomian Controversy of 1637: the controversy that sent Vane back to England and banished Wheelwright to outlying settlements in New England.[122] Perhaps because Wheelwright was jaundiced by his treatment at the hands of Massachusetts ministers and magistrates, his certificates in 1655 came only from London merchants with strong New England connections: Thomas Bell, once of Roxbury; David Yale, once of Boston; John Hill, brother of the Boston merchant Valentine Hill; and Richard Hutchinson, the son (or brother-in-law) of Anne Hutchinson – the kind of people who had supported him in Boston.[123] Wheelwright's decision to go to Belleau, and his certificates, drew on a personal history that dated back twenty years in New England, and thirty or more in England. The certificates presented by Edward Bendall of London had less of a history, but show how he used connections with New Englanders in England to get placed. This Boston entrepreneur and inventor, for admission as Rector of Cotgrave in Nottinghamshire, brought certificates from the colonists Thomas Harrison and Edward Winslow: Harrison was by this time pastor to the gathered church at St Dunstan-in-the-East, London, where Bendall may have been a member; Winslow – a *Mayflower* Pilgrim and an agent for Massachusetts – was also in London. For good measure, Bendall also presented a certificate from Edward Whalley, the major-general for Nottinghamshire (who in 1660 fled to New England). So

Bendall, a Londoner born and bred, may have been recommended to Whalley by New Englanders in the City.[124] In contrast to Wheelwright and Bendall, George Moxon looked locally for certificates. To support his application to be a public preacher at Newbold Astbury in Cheshire, he approached Sir William Brereton, the leading Independent in the county. In the distant past, long before he went to New England, Moxon had been Brereton's chaplain. Although Moxon secured most of his certificates from fellow travellers in the New England Way, he shared the rectory and pulpit at Astbury with John Machin, an ardent preacher with Presbyterian views on church order.[125] In fact, many settlers who became preachers in England brought a variety of certificates from godly ministers with strong local connections, rather than from a network of Congregationalists or ex-colonists. When Joseph Hull applied for a preaching post in Cornwall, he produced certificates from two ministers with good local ties but very different outlooks: George Hughes of Plymouth, the leading Presbyterian in the south-west, who in the 1630s decided against emigration to New England; and Hugh Peter, hawkish Independent, Cornishman and colonist.[126]

For most travellers from New England – unlike ministers – only traces of their stories survive. What of Robert Mascall, released in 1646 from the church at Boston, Massachusetts, 'unto the church of Christ in Dover'? In Boston, Mascall lived with the family of the godly sea-captain William Pierce. From Dover in Kent, a 'Mr Mascall' found his way into the pages of Thomas Edwards' *Gangraena*. Edwards pilloried Mascall as a customs collector turned radical preacher, who 'in private meetings persuades people that they will fall into most miserable slavery if they have a Presbytery', and threatened to 'stand and laugh at them' in their troubles. Mascall denied Edwards' ripest charges, but his assault on the power of the presbytery tallied with experience of the New England Way. 'Bro. Mascall of Dover' appeared in the church book of the Canterbury gathered church in 1647; in the 1650s, 'Rob. Mascall' recommended a divinity lecturer for Canterbury Cathedral; after the Restoration of Charles II, 'Capt. Mascall' was in trouble for belonging to an illegal church in Canterbury. Scraps are all that remain of Mascall's journey.[127] Another traveller's tale comes from the testimony of Raphael Swinfield, given to a congregation organised on New England lines that met at Christ Church, Dublin. Swinfield, a seafarer, had crossed the Atlantic to Massachusetts, 'and had much comfort from them, and their ministers, and was much affected with their way'. Swinfield could not bring his family over to join him in New England, and so came back to his wife and children, 'whom I found (I thank God) all well and living'. The Dublin church provided a home for Swinfield, who was nostalgic for New England church fellowship: ever since he left America he had been 'walking alone, and very disconsolate for want of such a society as this'.[128] In characters like Mascall and Swinfield, individual voices ring out with an authentic note, although most of their story is lost.

IV

From New England to all corners of England, Scotland and Ireland, and beyond: settlers ended up in many contexts that they could not have imagined when they left England in the 1630s, although their long absence from home meant few made headway at the heart of government. Persistent attachment to familiar places and people ran through their choices when they came back. Even adventurers at the frontiers of Cromwell's regime showed an interest in returning home, eventually. And the recruitment of colonists for far-flung parts, particularly in Scotland, worked almost exclusively through old godly connections of kith and kin. Merchants and mariners, like ministers, looked to local roots in spite of years away in New England. Once all the exceptional reasons to move away from home – to New England, to Ireland, to Scotland – had gone, many settlers wanted to turn full circle and come back (as best they could) to where they were before they left for America.

THE NEW ENGLAND WAY
IN ENGLAND

On 1 February 1650 John Phillip, Rector of Wrentham in Suffolk, called on his congregation to make a covenant: 'for as timber and stones are not a house unless they be joined and compacted together, so saints are not a visible church and house of God unless joined and united together'. Phillip read aloud a paper, to give a clear rationale for what they were about to do, 'to prevent misconstructions of meddling with or censuring' other churches. Wrentham's covenant should be understood simply as 'the reforming of ourselves according to that church estate the pattern whereof is set before us in the words of Christ . . . as all right reforming must be, by reducing things to the primitive and first institution'. Twelve men entered into covenant that first day (a suitably apostolic number), led by John Phillip and watched by fifty-two others.[1] Anthony Baker was among the twelve, his wife Elizabeth an onlooker. Years later, their son claimed that in Wrentham 'religion has . . . flourished longer, and . . . the gospel and grace of it have been much more clearly and powerfully preached, and more generally received . . . than I think in any village of the like capacity in England'.[2]

John Phillip had an unusually long stint as Rector of Wrentham: more than half a century, from 1609 until his death in 1660, apart from three years in Massachusetts, from 1638 to 1641. He emigrated after trying to evade demands to conform from Bishop Matthew Wren; he returned as soon as news of Wren's impeachment reached New England. In the late 1640s his nephew William Ames joined him at Wrentham, fresh from Harvard. Phillip and Ames exercised ministry together to the church gathered by covenant – Phillip as pastor, Ames as teacher – and a public ministry as parish preachers.[3] Both had personal experience of covenanted churches in Massachusetts; Phillip had been admitted to covenant at Dedham, Ames at Cambridge.[4] During the 1640s John Phillip attended the Westminster Assembly, the Parliamentary committee appointed to guide religious reform. Parliament had invited the colonial ministers John Cotton, John Davenport and Thomas

Hooker to cross the Atlantic to join the Assembly. When they declined (on grounds of distance and colonial commitments), this left Phillip as the only Westminster divine with first-hand knowledge of New England.[5]

The record of Wrentham's covenant-making in 1650 is an uncommon survival. Not much exists to show how colonists adapted their experience of New England's churches to life in English parishes – although around sixty colonists took parish appointments.[6] The unusual circumstances of the 1640s and 1650s opened the doors to new possibilities for realising the vision of pure churches, and placed 'parish reformation' in the hands of local clergy. Unfortunately, what actually happened is hard to discover. Diocesan record-keeping stopped early in the 1640s, and after the Restoration of Charles II in 1660 the church authorities wanted to kick over traces of unconventional activity.[7] Where a church gathered within a parish, as at Wrentham, its records probably took the form of notes kept alongside the parish register and vestry minutes. After 1660, when Wrentham's gathered congregation had to find a new identity outside the parish church, John Phillip's paper about the Wrentham covenant took pride of place, copied into the first pages of a new church book.[8]

The reformation John Phillip brought to Wrentham is intriguing. It suggests that the New England Way, as worked out in the flesh-and-blood histories of colonists who came back, was far less clear-cut than the version that appeared in print. Phillip's career was altogether more ambiguous and less dramatic than the 'battle of books' that divided Congregationalists from Presbyterians in the 1640s. He waited almost a decade to gather a church by covenant after his return from Massachusetts. He did not stand out at the Westminster Assembly as a strident activist for the New England Way. Also, his decision to work within a parish context, right up to his death in 1660, suggests how strong the gravitational pull of the old puritan commitment to public preaching could be – even for someone with experience of, and who was sympathetic to, New England's gathered churches. Phillip kept up a ministry to church and parish – to those who appeared to be genuine Christians, and to the community at large. This contradicted what New England's opponents alleged: that the New England Way was incompatible with parish religion.

So how typical was Phillip? What happened in the 1640s and 1650s, at a local level, when people carried home the New England Way?

I

Thomas Edwards, arch-polemicist for the Presbyterian party, liked to pillory colonists who came back to England as militant campaigners for the New England Way – or, worse, religious rebels whose unorthodoxy was so sour that not even New England could stomach it. He was quick to dub Hugh Peter, agent for Massachusetts, 'solicitor general for the sectaries'; George Downing, newly returned to England as an army chaplain, was 'Peter junior'. Edwards went out of his way to make New England responsible for a radicalism it could no longer contain: 'how many cast out of New England for their Antinomianism, Anabaptism . . . have come over . . . so that poor England must lick up such persons, who like vomit have been cast out of the mouth of other churches'. Edwards' *Gangraena* presented New England as seditious and disruptive. While earlier critics had restricted themselves to raising the alarm about what was happening on American soil, Edwards brought the threat of New England close to home, with lurid reports about the antics of ex-colonists – fierce apostles of radical religious ideas, often with lives tainted by scandal – up and down England.[9]

Ironically, the most powerful advocates of the New England Way in England were not those who had been to America and come back (contrary to Edwards' propaganda), but those whose knowledge of New England came indirectly, from books or letters. This was true of John Owen, England's leading Congregationalist in the 1650s and beyond:

> Of the congregational way I was not acquainted with any one person, minister or other . . . but sundry books being published . . . I perused, and compared them with the Scripture, and with one another . . . I fixed on one to take under peculiar consideration . . . which seemed most methodically and strongly to maintain that which was contrary, as I thought, to my present persuasion. This was Mr Cotton's book of the *Keyes*.

John Cotton's *Keyes of the Kingdom of Heaven* convinced Owen to accept beliefs about the Church he thought he opposed – indeed, Cotton's book made him realise how close he had been to the New England Way without knowing it.[10] Thomas Goodwin and Philip Nye, two of the 'Dissenting Brethren' who lobbied hard for the congregational way at the Westminster Assembly, gave Cotton's *Keyes* a puff by writing a preface.[11]

Like John Owen, the Dissenting Brethren – Goodwin, Nye, Jeremiah Burroughes, Sidrach Simpson and William Bridge – learned the New England Way not by going to America, but from arguments on paper. In the 1630s, all took refuge in the Netherlands rather than in New England, and so refined their understanding of the Church in a different kind of exile.[12] (English congregations in the Netherlands had a long history as quasi-independent churches in a foreign state, like their counterpart, the Dutch church in London.) Early in 1644 the Dissenting Brethren made their first pitch for reform in print, *An Apologeticall Narration*, presenting themselves as dispassionate appraisers of the best way forward. Exile in Holland had made them 'unengaged spectators', with 'no new commonwealths to rear' (unlike Massachusetts).[13] They had freedom to weigh up rival theories of the Church – from home and abroad, from 'good old nonconformists' and the 'fatal miscarriages and shipwrecks' of the separatists. New England settlers took a special place: 'those multitudes of godly men of our own nation, almost to the number of another nation', who transplanted themselves 'many thousands miles distance, and that by sea, into a wilderness, merely to worship God more purely'.[14] The Dissenting Brethren argued (as did New England's leaders) that their absence from England had let critics leap to false conclusions about their opinions – 'a cloud of mistakes and misapprehensions' – but, although provoked, they had not fired back answers to justify themselves.[15] To an extent this was true: a coalition of leading preachers had agreed to stop arguing against each other in public, in order to focus on the common task of opposing both the bishops and radical sectarians.[16] But by the time the *Apologeticall Narration* came out, the Dissenting Brethren and others who wanted to resist the influence of Presbyterians were more than happy to see manuscripts from New England run off on London presses. Pamphlets from Massachusetts became a convenient stalking-horse.[17] The Dissenting Brethren chose a striking metaphor from the publishing trade to describe New England: colonists had 'improved to a better edition' earlier attempts to create a pure Church.[18] In the crucial debates of the 1640s, printed books, not New Englanders in England, articulated the New England Way.[19]

Print gave a black and white picture of what happened when settlers came home, which – as colonists complained – could be misleading. Thomas Edwards painted Giles Firmin as an Independent preacher, unqualified and unordained: 'one out of New England, one Mr F', 'an apothecary physician' who had only preached 'on shipboard as he came over'.[20] Firmin hated 'being branded by Mr Edwards for an Independent', but would not admit to being Presbyterian either.[21] His career after he left Massachusetts in 1644 shows him engaged not in the kind of sectarian activity Edwards depicted, but in a more complex task: to translate a vision of reform shaped by New England into a parish in his native Essex.

The journey home from New England, for people like Firmin and John Phillip, led back to parish life as it existed in revolutionary England, not to the chaotic sectarian circles caricatured by Edwards. Admittedly, a small and noisy minority of ex-colonists found their way to radical sects, and some took state-sponsored posts in Ireland or Scotland. But the vast majority who came home from New England's mainstream colonies as preachers found their way to parish pulpits: over half the original clerical emigrants from the 1630s and the older colonial laymen who turned preacher; all the young graduates from English universities, whose aspirations to ministry in England had originally been thwarted under the Laudian regime; and virtually all the Harvard students who entered the ministry. All in all, around sixty out of seventy-nine went to parish pulpits.[22] Preachers from New England voted with their feet.

Perhaps this was an obvious move to make. A parish living offered a stable income. By 1649, Parliament's Commissioners for Scandalous and Malignant Clergy had ejected about a third of parish clergy (something like 2,300, mostly from the puritan heartland of East Anglia, which probably reveals more about the religious zeal of the decision-makers than about the calibre of clergy).[23] The demand for godly preachers far outstripped supply, and in the right circles New Englanders had a strong reputation. As Nathaniel Mather reported to a fellow Harvard graduate in Massachusetts, 'the naked truth is, here is great encouragement for any to come over, especially such as design themselves for the ministry . . . I think they need not much to question a living here, for it is with the honestest on both sides a matter of high account to have been a New-English man'.[24] A decision to join the ranks of parish clergy was pragmatic, especially as ministers could take advantage of the new freedom to define the relation between the parish population at large and the saints within it.

On the other hand, why should colonial preachers return to parishes, rather than to Independent gathered churches? Critics of New England claimed that the colonial churches had cast off parish churches, or at least damned them with faint praise. Presbyterians argued that the New England Way had whipped up the growth of autonomous separatist churches in England. From this point of view, New Englanders' stampede to English parish pulpits is surprising.

In another twist to the story, the preachers who came back across the Atlantic had opinions that defied the neat lines of the print debate between old England and New. Many were presbyterian in a broad and undogmatic sense, ill at ease with the innovations of the New England Way – following an older style of puritanism, rather than the sharper Presbyterianism that was emerging in England.[25] Nathaniel Ward, like his son-in-law Giles Firmin, claimed to be neither a party-Presbyterian nor a card-carrying Congregationalist. As Ward put it, through his character the *Simple Cobler*,

for Church work, I am neither Presbyterian, nor plebsbyterian, but an Interpendent. My task is to sit and study how shapeable the Independent way will be to the body of England – then my head aches on one side. And how suitable the Presbyterian way . . . will be to the mind of Christ – then my head aches on the other side.

Ward (famous for his use of new and odd words) had confidence that Parliament could 'commoderate' a way between the extremes, to end the headache.[26] Another settler who sailed home late in 1646, like Ward, was Richard Sadler. Sadler accused New England's churches of being 'dissonant to peace and truth'. His attack came not from the high ground of Presbyterian theory, but from a thicket of pastoral concern: when New England churches made a testimony of spiritual experience the door to church membership, this shut out many plain godly folk who were not good at speaking out about their faith.[27]

Unlikely though it might seem, some preachers from New England accepted the authority of bishops after the Restoration of Charles II. Those most likely to take this path, no doubt to the great dismay of their parents, were sons of well known New England clergy, puritan-reared and Harvard-educated. Most were young and had come back to England after 1655. Not all gave in without qualms: William Hooke reported that Joseph Swinnock, 'yielding to put on the surplice, but with reluctancy, read the service with a disturbed spirit, and was so smitten with it, that he took to his bed and died . . . within two or three days following'. Hooke's own son signed up to the new order on St Bartholomew's Day, 24 August 1662, the last day for ministers to comply with the new regime or lose their jobs.[28]

Alongside the old-fashioned presbyterians and would-be episcopalians, around half the sixty or so colonists who occupied parish pulpits were, like John Phillip, known to favour covenanted churches in New England style, but also to favour preaching to the whole parish.[29] Such people were a rare breed. Even in the exceptional circumstances in England at the time, this was unusual. Leading congregationalists such as Thomas Goodwin and John Owen left parish pulpits to work with gathered churches.[30] So New Englanders punched well above their weight in a small band of preachers who took the view that it was possible to combine ministry to gathered church and parish.[31]

Thus instead of the clarity of Thomas Edwards' picture of New England as a nursery that raised sectarians, or the colonial vision of the New England Way as a revival of pure New Testament practice, the waters are muddied by a migration of New England preachers back to the ambiguities of parish life. To explore how far and how fast these American migrants went with the New England Way in England, and with what results, requires a closer look at the experiences of John Phillip and some of his fellow-travellers.

II

Why did John Phillip wait until 1650 before he gathered a church in his parish at Wrentham, even though he set sail from Massachusetts in 1641? Phillip's interest in the congregational way was clear in the 1640s, but more apparent in principle than in parish practice. Local Independents regarded him highly. Members of the Yarmouth gathered church who lived in Norwich asked him for advice about starting their own church, and invited him to its formation in 1644; Yarmouth gave one of its members a letter of recommendation to Wrentham in 1646.[32] Yet although Robert Baillie (an observer for Scotland at the Westminster Assembly and an ardent Presbyterian) quickly identified Phillip as one of ten or so 'Independent men' at the Assembly, he was not one of the Dissenting Brethren. In fact, Phillip rarely spoke – like the majority at the Assembly, he was a silent member. His few speeches recorded in the Assembly Minutes made no mention of New England.[33] He made brief interventions to temper the Assembly's crackdown on antinomian opinion, which tallied with a paper he signed in 1640 in Massachusetts, on 'propositions concerning evidence of God's love'.[34] He spoke up for 'the divine institution of a doctor [teaching elder] in every congregation, as well as a pastor', a reflection of the Reformed ministry he had seen in New England.[35] Phillip did not sign a pro-Presbyterian petition from Suffolk and Essex ministers to the House of Lords in 1646, but after Parliament voted to make England Presbyterian he was nominated to a local division of the Suffolk classis (presbytery).[36] However, by the time he drew up a covenant for Wrentham in 1650, the idea of a Presbyterian national church was a spent force, and Congregationalism had been sanctioned as part of a spectrum of practice, in an ethos of religious toleration. Phillip waited for nine years before he invited the people of Wrentham in whom 'God hath begun a good and saving work' – some no doubt known to him since his arrival in the parish in 1609 – to enter into covenant.[37] He made the move only when it was in step with what the state would allow – a cautious reformer, willing to work with the godly magistrate and bide his time before he brought the New England Way to Wrentham.

Phillip had a clear perception of what the covenant meant. He told the parishioners who witnessed the first twelve members enter into covenant that this was merely a 'reforming', to take Wrentham back to primitive purity.[38] Phillip echoed John Cotton's view: since the apostolic origins of English churches (set out in Foxe's *Book of Martyrs*) were plain, 'we cannot but conceive the churches in England were rightly gathered and planted according to the Gospel', rooted in covenant. But centuries of corruption had barnacled the ship of the Church. So the task for Wrentham and other parish communities was 'not to make them churches which were none before', but to strip away the accretions to restore purity.[39] John Phillip's actions followed a course recommended by John Allin (minister at Dedham, Massachusetts, where Phillip had been a church member) and Thomas Shepard (minister of the church at Cambridge, which the young William Ames had joined while at Harvard). In a letter written in 1645, Allin and Shepard drew a contrast between colony and homeland. In New England, settlers began new churches from scratch. But in England, where old corrupt churches had to be reformed, it was different: 'such congregations should be called by able ministers unto repentance . . . and renew a solemn covenant with God to reform themselves, and to submit unto the discipline of Christ'.[40] In other words, New England churches could follow the pattern of primitive purity from their first beginnings, but in England corrupted churches had to renew their covenant – as at Wrentham. These arguments, first used by settlers in the 1630s to defend New England's innovations against English critics, now justified Wrentham's reformation: by 1650 Phillip judged the time was right to make the implicit covenant explicit.

The slow pace of reform at Wrentham raises questions about how far and how fast other colonists moved to bring New England ways to English parishes. The picture is complicated. Not all 'congregational' parish clergy would have gathered churches in the 1650s as Phillip did, however clearly their Congregationalist convictions shone out after 1660. No doubt some carried out their duties as public preachers but never found enough 'fit material' in their flock – parishioners both godly and willing – to form a covenanted church. In parishes where a Congregational church emerged soon after the watershed of 1662 – as at Wrentham – it is more likely that the minister had re-formed his church by covenant in the 1650s. Up and down England, in developments like this, New Englanders are implicated: Nathaniel Mather at Barnstaple, Devon; Nathaniel Brewster at Alby in Norfolk; George Moxon at Astbury, Cheshire; Christopher Marshall at Woodkirk in the West Riding of Yorkshire. Some stepped into the pulpits of English converts to the New England Way who moved out of parish ministry – John Sams followed John Owen at Coggeshall in Essex and Thomas Harrison followed Thomas Goodwin at St Dunstan-in-the-East in London. John Knowles and Henry Whitfield combined office as public preachers with ministry to gathered churches in the former cathedrals of Bristol and Winchester.[41] What John Phillip's case suggests is that the process of reform could be quite tentative: even advocates of congregationalism with experience of New England might rely for a time on the argument that parish churches were true churches (implicitly) before they took the step of re-forming their church by covenant. In Wrentham, Phillip seems to have managed this reformation without a hint of controversy – but that would not be the case elsewhere.

III

Thomas Weld and Thomas Larkham each gathered churches in their parishes, with spectacularly explosive results. Weld – minister of Terling in Essex, and later of Roxbury in Massachusetts – was Rector of St Mary's, Gateshead from 1650 to 1660. He had made a name for himself as a promoter of New England, through his work as a London agent for the Bay Colony in the 1640s.[42] Larkham – minister of Northam, Devon, then Northam, New England (the settlers of Dover briefly renamed their town in his honour) – was Vicar of Tavistock in Devon from around 1648 until 1660, apart from nine months as a preacher in north-west England, in the area around Cockermouth in Cumberland. Larkham seems at first sight an unlikely advocate of the New England Way, since he usually noted with relish the anniversary of the day he sailed away from America. But he introduced a church covenant not only in Tavistock, where it was extremely divisive, but also far to the north in Cumberland, where it became a successful model for the county.[43]

Conflict broke out in Tavistock not long after Larkham's arrival. His opinions made him unpopular with the 'profane ones', who 'gnash their teeth to see Christ's ordinances on foot in public, and themselves laid by as reprobate silver'; they began 'to quarrel at my preaching and to join shoulder to shoulder against the new Church (as they were pleased to call us . . .)'.[44] Larkham had at least tightened up access to the sacraments, and had perhaps already drawn up a covenant. He first came to Tavistock with his regiment, as a chaplain in the Parliamentary army. During the civil wars the town had been occupied in turn by the forces of King and Parliament. Tavistock's previous Vicar, George Hughes (who took John Dod's advice not to emigrate to New England, and in the 1650s was Devon's leading Presbyterian) fled in 1643 to escape the conflict.[45] So by the time Parliament won the day and Larkham arrived, the townspeople were eager to recruit a new minister.[46] But things turned sour over Larkham's wish to separate 'God's people' and 'reprobate silver', and also because of an ugly dispute about tithes. Frustrated, Larkham shook the dust of Tavistock off his feet in 1651. He and his son George (newly graduated from Oxford) went north to Cumberland – at first sight, this was an unlikely voyage up the west coast of England, but in fact the Larkhams followed an old tradition among the godly of the south-west, who had long provided preachers for 'dark corners of the North'.[47]

At Cockermouth in Cumberland, Thomas Larkham was hailed as a 'blessed instrument of God'. He led local people to form a gathered church in the autumn of 1651, with George Larkham (curate of the parish), and George Benson (Vicar of Bridekirk) as founding members. The two Georges acted as pastor and teaching elder to the new church, but continued to preach in their parish pulpits, where the Commissioners for the Propagation of the Gospel in the Four Northern Counties ratified their role as public preachers. Members of the Cockermouth gathered church attended sermons on Sundays with their neighbours, but met in private on other days to admit members, to share the sacraments, and to resolve matters of faith and discipline.[48] The pattern at Cockermouth was repeated across the county. An exceptionally high proportion of parish clergy in Cumberland took this path.[49] 'For Reformation of our people, more ought to be done by us than bare preaching', wrote Richard Gilpin and other Cumbrian ministers in 1653.[50] Larkham's initiative at Cockermouth convinced ministers like Gilpin that gathered churches could build up local religious life, but also that preaching to the whole community must continue, to prevent Christian life in the area disintegrating into sectarian fragments. (The scale of local conversions to the Quaker movement made the Cockermouth church fear for its survival.)[51] Gilpin formed an Association of Ministers in Cumberland and Westmorland in 1653, to pursue a common pattern of preaching and pastoral care, despite differences about the ideal form of church order.[52] George Larkham joined – a sign that his gathered chuch at Cockermouth was a pragmatic step to advance reformation, rather than a decision to withdraw into closed circles of the godly and end ministry to the people at large. He shared the Association's vision for the county: a godly preacher in every place, to turn a corner of the north that had been a byword for ignorance and profanity into 'a blessing and praise', so that people would say 'behold in the wilderness waters have broken out, and streams in the desert'.[53]

George Larkham stayed on in Cumberland, but Thomas Larkham received a letter from more than sixty people in Tavistock, imploring him to come back.[54] He returned to Devon in 1652, but when he reached the town he found his enemies had locked the church to keep him out. He took an iron bar and broke in. A riot followed.[55] Larkham's enemies included parish officers, disenchanted members of the gathered church, and ministers of nearby villages who had been excluded by him from Tavistock's pulpit. His opponents – with no old-fashioned church courts in existence to turn to – pursued complaints against Larkham with various Whitehall Commissioners. A great outcry came when he told members of the gathered church, after it had been in existence five years, that he intended to dissolve it and start afresh. When Larkham asked them to sign a paper before they could be admitted to communion, about twenty refused to cooperate.[56] According to his accusers, he threatened to make public the sins of the dissenters, from the record he kept in the church book – 'let them go to what church they will, we shall find dirt enough to cast after them'.[57] They interpreted his acts as a device to shut out a faction who preferred his predecessor, the Presbyterian George Hughes: 'he hath often said there were two parties in the Church, the Hugonites and the Larkamites'.[58] Larkham managed to secure the support of Interregnum Commissioners against his critics, but the 'Hugonites' eventually scored a point. They set up a pulpit contest – a rival lecture day on Thursdays, to compete with Larkham's Wednesday sermon. Early in 1660, in a snub to Larkham that showed which way the wind was blowing, the Council of State ordered that the new lecture should continue, despite his protests.[59] Six months later, after the Restoration of Charles II heralded a change in religious policy, he left Tavistock parish church at the request of the patron, the Earl of Bedford.

Larkham drew a clear distinction between his duties as public preacher in Tavistock and his duties to the gathered church there: 'I teach all in the public meetinghouse, but do only baptise the children of such as are received and allowed members of the church, and admitted to the Lord's table'.[60] He preached for the parish as a whole on Sundays, at the Wednesday lecture, on fast days and at funerals.[61] For the church, he celebrated communion at least once a quarter.[62] The records of Tavistock baptisms are too unsystematic to give an exact picture, but Larkham seems to have let a large cohort of children go unbaptised. He had strong views on the matter: 'how . . . are they deceived, that think it enough to be born in Christian lands . . . and to buy for their babies twelve pennyworth of water to sprinkle in their faces . . . I tremble to think how this sealing ordinance is abused, profaned . . . every week almost'.[63] By 1658 the Tavistock gathered church had acquired a strong identity. Entries in his diary show that the church paid ten shillings a quarter to use a 'meeting chamber' in his house.[64] What may have begun in Tavistock as an attempt to restrict the sacraments to the visibly worthy became a church defined ever more tightly by written covenant and pastoral inquiry, an increasingly separate entity within the parish.

Thomas Weld's time in Gateshead ended with not so much parish reformation as parish revolution. Gateshead had chosen an anti-puritan Rector in 1647; Weld's arrival in 1650 gave a boost to the godly party in Newcastle. He had a strong reputation as an advocate of the New England Way – albeit slightly tarnished by accusations that he had siphoned off some of the money donated to send poor children to Massachusetts.[65] Until he left the north-east for London in 1660, after he had been ejected as Rector, Weld cooperated with local Presbyterians against Quakers and Baptists (most successfully in the strange case of the 'False Jew of Hexham', claimed as a convert to Christianity by the Baptist preacher Thomas Tillam, who, like Weld, had been in New England).[66] He had the support of significant local figures.[67] But in Gateshead he was massively controversial.

Before he agreed to become Rector, Weld announced from the pulpit – so there could be no misunderstanding – that if he took office it would be on condition that he would only 'preach the gospel unto them, and visit the sick, and that they should expect no other work from him than this'. Within a short time, a hundred and fifty parishioners had signed a petition to call him as their preacher – they would not presume to ask him to celebrate the sacraments, 'till you shall know us better and find us fit'.[68]

The trouble was, Weld found very few fit. His first step towards gathering a church was to preach a sermon series on the pure primitive church (Acts 2:41–7) – 'publicly in Gateshead meeting place' – in which he set out the congregational way. Then he waited: 'wonder not at it', argued a supporter, 'churches of Christ are not made up of the rubbish of parishes; he would take time to know what stones were to be laid up in the building'.[69] In 1631, soon after he arrived in Massachusetts, Weld had written back to his former parishioners in Terling, Essex, to extol New England's purity: 'here the greater part are the better part'.[70] Not in Gateshead. His opponents claimed that he had admitted only ten people into his gathered church, out of a thousand. Weld insisted that eighteen people from the parish had joined, and twice that number from elsewhere. He saw nothing wrong with such small numbers: 'Christ himself did administer the Lord's Supper but to twelve'.[71] His opponents retorted that he had, effectively, excommunicated a thousand souls without any formal trial. Weld saw it otherwise. 'No, no . . . being parishioners of Gateshead hath no Scripture warrant to make you members of a church of Christ': he could not be accused of excommunicating them from the church because they had never belonged to it.[72] Weld's critics argued that there were above a thousand godly people in Gateshead, who all ought to receive the sacraments from their parish minister.[73] The parish officials were said to be 'spitting their rage against him, because he will not baptise their children, and give them the Lord's supper'.[74] They called the gathered church 'Mr Weld's new church, a seminary of schism, contention, division and separation'.[75] As Larkham had also discovered in Tavistock, those who fell out with the minister refused to pay his wage: Weld's enemies withheld revenue – which is perhaps why he decided to sell around two hundred books to the Corporation for the Propagation of the Gospel in New England.[76] Like Larkham, Weld faced a campaign to provide an alternate minister. In 1657 the churchwardens led a petition to hire a lecturer to preach once a fortnight and to celebrate the Lord's Supper once a month. Weld initially agreed, but changed his mind when he heard the terms: he was not to interfere with the choice of lecturer, nor to dismiss him without general consent. This, Weld argued, gave him 'not so much power . . . as the poorest pit-man in the parish'.[77] Weld sent word to London, and called on the Council of State to adjudicate the complaints against him. He managed to secure a parish *coup d'état*: at his request, the Council ejected all the parish officers as 'known oppressors of godliness', and replaced them with Weld's nominees.[78] Weld had the Council's order copied into the Gateshead vestry book. Throughout the dispute, he argued that his conduct in relation to the parish had been entirely legal. The Whitehall Commissioners who appointed him 'do not send men to give the sacraments, but only to preach'.[79]

Arguably, such experiments in parish reform – as in many other varieties of Reformation – succeeded best where they changed things least. Much of what John Phillip formalised by covenant had long been pious practice in Wrentham. What Thomas Larkham initiated in Cumberland was a good fit with older patterns of preaching and godly association in a sparsely populated county, and contributed to a coherent pattern of ministry under the aegis of the Northern Commissioners. However, the parishioners of Tavistock and Gateshead collided with their New England preachers. Larkham fought against firmly established parish interests in Tavistock, in a context where the character of reform had already been defined for many by the Presbyterian George Hughes. Gateshead's earlier appointment of an anti-puritan Rector suggests Weld stepped into a minefield. Both Weld and Larkham stirred up factions by stubbornly holding together a call to preach to the parish, and a wish to gather saints into a pure church. The dissimilar results of Larkham's initiative to gather churches in Cockermouth and Tavistock, and the contrast between the experience of Thomas Weld and that of John Phillip, suggest how the struggle to work out these objectives in practice could have a very different outcome in different contexts.

IV

Giles Firmin and Samuel Eaton adapted New England practice to the English context in dissimilar ways. Firmin, Vicar of Shalford in Essex from around 1648 until 1662, wanted to redeem New England from its divisive role in the English godly community: to show Presbyterians that colonial practice was not what propagandists like Thomas Edwards made it out to be, and to shame Congregationalists who hijacked 'New-England principles' in a such a way that 'men should now say, and our posterity hereafter believe it, that Independency ruined the Church of England'.[80] Samuel Eaton drew the fire of Edwards' *Gangraena* as the 'great apostle' of the Independents: the first minister to return from New England after 1640, the first to gather a church in England in light of his experience. Yet Eaton attended a parish church in the 1660s.[81] The ambiguities in the careers of Firmin and Eaton – their willingness to adapt to circumstance in working out the relationship between church and parish – is striking.

Firmin grounded his perspective within the community of what he liked to call 'old Essex Christians'.[82] His horizons had been set, early in life, by godly activity in Dedham, Felsted, Sudbury, and Bishop's Stortford – that is, in northern Essex, shading over into Suffolk and Hertfordshire. This community, divided by emigration in the 1630s – not only by the Atlantic, but also by disputes about whether it was legitimate to leave – stretched in

Firmin's mind from old England to New, and across the generations from Elizabethan puritans to Restoration nonconformists.[83] He hated the breakdown of understanding between colony and homeland, and among the godly in his home county. In the 1650s, this made him a natural ally of Richard Baxter of Kidderminster: Firmin promoted a common statement on pastoral ministry for divided Essex clergy to sign, following the model Baxter had put forward in Worcestershire.[84] His interest in overcoming division showed through even in the first report of him after he returned from New England in 1644. Thomas Edwards – a hostile witness – reported that Firmin 'exhorted to peace', saying 'how near the Independents and Presbyterians were come'.[85]

Firmin's constant refrain was 'had I not lived in New England, and seen the churches there . . . I should have been convinced that Independent (as it is here called) government was never of Christ's institution'.[86] He brought absent New Englanders into the print and pulpit controversies of Interregnum Essex, by anecdote and allusion – particularly Thomas Hooker and John Norton, who came from the locality. How scandalised 'Holy Hooker' would have been, if he had lived to hear of disruptions in Essex churches near his old parish. Firmin wished 'we had a few . . . Mr Nortons in England', who could keep 'the people's liberty' in order; 'if our congregational churches . . . are gone beyond New England, I only say, farewell'.[87] In a region that sent many settlers to New England in the 1630s, he tried to persuade two distinct audiences to recognise New England as an example of orderly reform: those who believed colonists had shattered godly unity (if not by emigration, then by strange innovations when they got there); and those who, in Firmin's opinion, misused the New England Way to justify a quest for purity that set true church against true church.

Firmin admired the 'order and comeliness' New England achieved by church covenants – 'if ever I can attain it I will' – but he was prepared to argue that the form of the churches in New England might be appropriate 'over there', but not in England. He considered it too divisive to implement a covenant in Shalford, for the moment. Although 'the strongest party in the town is religious', some in the parish 'come not to hear me . . . nor will own the church in this time of reforming'.[88] To justify the lack of a covenant in Shalford, he reiterated colonial claims that New England had not cast off England's parish churches. Like John Phillip, he supported Cotton's maxim that 'all the work now, is not to make them churches which were none before, but to reduce and restore them to their primitive institution'. To put the principle into practice, Firmin argued:

You must put a difference between churches new erecting and these in England, which have been churches for so long; when I raise a house from new from the ground, I may then do as I please, but if I be mending of an old house, I must do as well as I can, repair by degrees.[89]

Firmin's distinction between 'newbuild' and 'restoration' meant he looked to implicit signs of a true church within his parish – albeit an old house of God, much in need of repair. Knowledge of faith, good conduct, and a promise to submit to discipline, was all the covenant he required in order to admit parishioners to sacraments. For those who wanted more, he recommended they imitate the covenant of piety made by Richard Rogers' parishioners in Elizabethan Wethersfield (just up the road from Shalford): 'excel those Christians if you can'.[90]

In Shalford, Firmin worked out ways to apply as much as he dared of New England church order. He restricted admission to baptism, as well as to communion. He thought it absurd that Presbyterians would exclude half the parish from communion, yet felt it their duty to baptise all children.[91] (He said of his own parishioners who requested baptism for their children, 'when I came to enquire but a little about Christ and sin, I could find as good among our Indians'.) However, despite his strict policy on sacraments, he endorsed the value of parish ministry. He thought it schismatic to gather Christians from different parishes into a new church. New England experience showed each community should have a single church.[92] Firmin looked on certain people as church elders (in all but name) and worked with them on matters of discipline.[93] To stoke up his local credibility, he invoked a prominent neighbour (and erstwhile critic of New England) as his closest collaborator: his cooperation with Daniel Rogers of Wethersfield was similar to mutual help between churches in Massachusetts.[94] In his belief that the Church had wider boundaries than the local congregation, Firmin stood with the Presbyterians – but 'that I am a Presbyterian, is more than I knew before, or know now'.[95] Firmin held onto what he valued in colonial practice, but nipped and tucked the New England Way to accommodate to his context in an English parish.

Firmin's argument, like John Phillip's, relied on the principle that true but implicit churches existed in English parishes – an argument with a long history in the puritan movement, given a new twist and impetus in the debate over New England's innovations. Firmin's identification of implicit equivalents to New England's practice followed the same line of argument as the proposals for 'the way of reformation in the congregations of England', probably written by John Cotton in the late 1630s.[96] By the time the 1650s arrived, Cotton had been convinced by the activities of radical sects that England was not yet 'capable of fellowship in Independent churches'. In a document printed by the ex-colonist Thomas Allen, Cotton gave grist to Firmin's mill by affirming an old formula: church government 'gives not being but well-being to churches'. 'New-churching', New England style, was not essential.[97]

Like Firmin, Samuel Eaton accommodated to his context, but in a completely different way. Unlike most other New England preachers, Eaton held no parish living after he returned from America.[98] However, he managed to progress from parish ministry in the 1630s to a separate gathered church in the 1640s and 1650s; and back to attendance at a parish church in the 1660s. Eaton's Independent church was the first to be gathered in England by someone with direct experience of New England. He returned to Cheshire late in 1640 and quickly made a name as an enemy of episcopacy and as an advocate of churches organised in New England fashion. His opponents claimed he preached at Chester and Knutsford, early in 1641, that 'every particular congregation' is an 'absolute church', and that 'the members of it must be only saints; these must enter covenant among themselves, and without such a covenant no church'.[99] He became chaplain to the Chester garrison and was well known to the county's leading parliamentarian, Sir William Brereton. Military campaigns later took Eaton to Ireland, and to Scotland.[100] From an early stage, his ties with the army allowed him to voice Independent convictions, though 'the New England Mr Eaton' was reported not to be as radical as others in Lancashire and Cheshire. He made the main focus of his ministry a gathered church, which met from around 1644 in the chapel at Dukinfield Hall, the home of the military commander of the Chester garrison, Colonel Robert Duckenfield.[101]

This 'great apostle' of the New England Way gathered saints out of various parishes to form a church. He argued that circumstance made this legitimate. When the Lancashire Presbyterian Richard Hollingworth attacked Eaton and his colleague Timothy Taylor for gathering a church illegally, they argued that the church that met at Dukinfield Hall only took in people from parishes where reform was desperately needed. If and when change came, the church would dissolve its covenant and members would rejoin local congregations, gravitating back to where they had come from. (Some of Eaton and Taylor's adherents, perhaps with this in mind, kept up payments for pew-rent in their own parish churches.) In any case, Eaton and Taylor contended, what had happened at Dukinfield was nothing new:

at least fourteen years since, such a church was extant in Wirral in Cheshire (the vocal covenant being only wanting) which consisted of the choicest Christians of many parishes ... Mr John Angier's church at Denton in Lancashire, hath of long time been such, and many other such have there been besides.

In other words, their church had merely added an explicit covenant to what had long gone on.[102] Despite the dispute with Hollingworth, Eaton worked closely with local Presbyterians, including John Angier of Denton. A neighbour minister noted in 1646 – when Presbyterians and Congregationalists competed fiercely, 'like Jacob and Esau struggling in the womb' – that Angier, although a Presbyterian, 'was very moderate towards all that he judged godly of the congregational way', and had great respect for Eaton and Taylor.[103] (The respect was mutual. Angier had a troublesome son, ejected for some misdemeanour from Emmanuel College, Cambridge, who was then sent to Harvard: Eaton may have come up with the plan.)[104] In the 1660s Eaton had a clear commitment to nonconformity. His will included legacies to twenty-one Independent and Presbyterian preachers who had lost their parish livings after the Restoration of Charles II, and more 'to all such poor ministers as are . . . in a distressed condition'. His friend John Angier stayed on as minister to the chapelry at Denton, under the authority of the bishops of Chester, without too much interference – using the Book of Common Prayer from time to time.[105] The nonconformist Eaton attended Angier's church until his death in 1665 – at first sight a surprising gesture from 'the New England Mr Eaton', but a sign of his conviction that there was a fundamental continuity in the long godly struggle to balance the needs of Church and parish.

V

Individual histories tell a story different from the hard and fast certainties of the 1640s print debate, but put flesh and bones on New England's claim that its godly settlers had not cast off the godly in English parishes back home.

The crucial issue at the local level turned out to be the old question – as old as the puritan movement – of how to relate the godly and the wider community. The presence in parish pulpits of ministers who had been ministers and members of New England's gathered churches underlines the tenacity of the parish ideal. Let loose on English soil, they still wanted to preach to the community at large, as well as to gather saints for closer fellowship. Relations between the godly and the rest always had the potential to be tense: an interest in separating the 'precious' from the 'vile' was not a good start for neighbourliness; the godly's pursuit of piety drew them apart, within and across parish boundaries. But the twin imperatives of public preaching and a pure church had deep roots in English puritanism, way back before emigration in the 1630s. Former colonists' loyalty to these essentials is not surprising, given the religious motives threading through their reasons for emigration: on the one hand, the threat to public preaching they perceived in Laudian policy; on the other hand, a desire to shake off the threat of popery at home by seeking purity abroad. But in revolutionary England, preaching and purity could be pursued at home. In general, those who came back from New England with congregationalist sympathies were less willing than English Independents to cut ties with parish preaching, but more willing than their Presbyterian neighbours to separate the precious from the vile. Paradoxically, restricting access to the sacraments may have meant a stronger sacramental life in parishes, at least for the select few. Thomas Larkham celebrated communion regularly with the gathered church in Tavistock, whereas the Essex minister Ralph Josselin was so uncertain about whom to admit to communion that he did not celebrate the sacrament for nine years.[106] Despite the strict discipline surrounding sacraments, the persistence of these ministers in parish duties (preaching on Sundays and lecture days, giving funeral sermons, visiting the sick) suggests that they should not be labelled 'sectarian' too soon. Even Samuel Eaton, who stayed outside the parish system in the 1640s and 1650s, attended a Church of England chapelry in the 1660s – to all intents and purposes, a parish church.

Working out the relationship of church and parish was fraught with difficulty. Pragmatic compromises often worked where rigid policy did not. So Giles Firmin did not press an explicit church covenant on his parish, although he would have liked to. Instead, he controlled access to the sacraments strictly: to baptism as much as to communion – unusual in England, closer to New England's practice.

Ironically, while former colonists tried to work towards the New England Way in English parishes in the 1650s, New England churches were inching their way through the long discussions that led to the 'Half-Way Covenant' of 1657. This stretched the tight ties of covenant to include more settlers in the rituals of local churches, and shifted New England some way towards a broader, parish-based religion.[107] Well before 1657 it was clear that many settlers who had been baptised in New England's churches as infants had grown up without a conversion experience, and so could not meet the requirement of a testimony to enter church covenant. In 1642 Thomas Allen had been one of the first to identify this as a possible pitfall: 'if grown to some years but expressing no truth of grace, what is the church to do in such a case?'[108] The Boston Synod of 1657 proposed to allow people who had been baptised as youngsters to present their own children for baptism without having to jump the hurdle of giving a narrative of their religious experience. This would not bring them into 'full communion' with the church. It created a half-way house, a Half-Way Covenant.[109] Nathaniel Mather recommended New England's pragmatic compromise to England: indeed, people back home were already thinking of it, 'so the hearts of the saints in both Englands . . . being touched with the same spirit, have moved together towards the same enquiries'.[110]

In different ways, the Half-Way Covenant and Firmin arrived at a compromise to meet the needs of both the godly and the wider community. New England's churches relaxed the covenant by softening baptismal policy, to welcome a wider number of settlers at least half-way into fellowship. In Shalford, Giles Firmin never drew an inner circle of parishioners into a covenanted community, but effectively marked out the circle by taking a stricter than usual line on which of his parishioners' children he would baptise. The Restoration of Charles II meant nonconformists like Firmin lost their parish ministry, so in England the heat went out of the debate about how to cater for parish and church. In New England the older imperatives of supporting both public preaching and pure church continued, arguably fulfilling the ideal of godly parish-based religion for much longer.[111]

In another respect, New England continued to fulfil the ideal of a reformed parish in a way often compromised by ex-colonists in England – by limiting geographically the boundaries of gathered church membership. Giles Firmin advocated the New England model of a single gathered church in each community. He felt so strongly about this that he thought any Christian who wanted to enjoy the life of a church in another place should 'remove his dwelling into that town . . . if you think it will hinder you a little in your estate . . . friend, they who went to New England for true liberty of conscience paid dearer for it than you do here'.[112] Samuel Eaton and others argued that it was legitimate to gather Christians together across parish boundaries in extenuating circumstances, 'if they have no minister at all, or have one that is scandalous, or one that hath not competent abilities'; otherwise, Christians had a duty to join 'the nearest congregation, where a godly and able minister is settled'.[113] Wrentham's gathered church drew the godly together across parish boundaries, but perhaps not from other preachers' flocks – rather, from a cluster of parishes William Ames and John Phillip together served as public preachers.[114] Thomas Weld was more radical, and had no qualms about admitting to his gathered church as many from outside the parish of Gateshead as from within it.[115] Thomas Allen also believed it was legitimate to gather people from different parishes into a church. But he insisted they should still contribute in their own parish to funds for the poor, and for preaching, 'that the word may be dispensed all the land over'. Significantly, Allen recognised he could not cite New England as a precedent. Instead, he looked to the 'strangers' churches' formed by foreigners in Norwich and other cities to show that the arrangement could work without disorder. New England's example was not apposite: each town (except Boston) still had only one church, like a gathered church drawn from a single parish.[116]

In all this, context was crucial: what could happen in a parish would be different from what might happen at the heart of Cromwell's regime in

London, or at a Scottish garrison, or in the government circles of occupied Dublin. Ministers like John Phillip and Giles Firmin provide a perspective different from that of the career of Hugh Peter (always a chaplain in England, never in pastoral charge of a parish) or a young and mobile Harvard graduate like Samuel Mather (in his ministry to a gathered church of soldiers from Leith Citadel, or at Christ Church in Dublin).[117] Even John Cotton, master theorist of New England's church order, conceded that what was appropriate in Massachusetts could not necessarily be transported back to England. Building churches of 'primitive purity' from the ground up, as New England had a special opportunity to do, required a different approach from restoring the ancient churches of England.[118]

8

JOURNEY'S END

In July 1660 Samuel Pepys turned up at the door of Major Francis Willoughby's house with a pair of bedsheets, and asked to stay the night. Willoughby agreed. Pepys had his eye on Willoughby's house, part of a complex of Navy Board houses in Seething Lane, close to Tower Hill in London. In the new administration of Charles II, Pepys was on his way up in the Navy Office, Willoughby on his way out. Within two days Pepys laid claim to the house, and within a fortnight his household took possession. In an untidy handover, Willoughby had to send for his goods nine days later.[1] He had come to England in 1650; he moved back to New England in 1662 to a career that included a spell as Deputy Governor of Massachusetts.[2]

With the Restoration of Charles II, migration from New England to England stopped. Rumours ran high that a new wave of emigrants would leave England for America. Massachusetts held five solemn fast days in just over a year for the 'dark prospect' in religion and politics on the other side of the Atlantic.[3] Colonists received letters from anxious enquirers wanting advice by return about what the prospects for settlement would be, 'if times press them to transport their families into New England'.[4] John Davenport predicted that the new Act of Uniformity (which reintroduced bishops and the Book of Common Prayer) would make many set sail for New England. In June 1662 he recorded the arrival of several hundred passengers. One was a messenger sent over by the English Congregationalist Thomas Goodwin – who would have come himself if his wife had not stopped him – on behalf of various churches and 'many men of considerable quality and estate who have a desire to come into this country'. There was 'great talk of many ministers coming over with their congregations . . . if room can be found for them'.[5]

In the end, far fewer came than expected. First-time emigrants were scarce. The hunted regicides William Goffe, John Dixwell and Edmund Whalley found a refuge in New England – and a place in American mythology – hiding in the 'Judges Cave' above New Haven.[6] Henry Hatsell, another first-time settler, had worked with Francis Willoughby in Cromwell's navy. He came over with his wife Susanna, widow of the former New Haven merchant John Evance. Susanna was one of a number of New Haven's settlers to return.[7] But only a few of the colonists who left New England in the 1640s and 1650s came back.[8] Those who made the Atlantic journey again tended to be younger members of prominent colonial families, with good connections and prospects in New England. Several, like Francis Willoughby, had a strong future ahead in colonial government. John Leverett was a Governor of Massachusetts, Fitz John Winthrop a Governor of Connecticut.[9] Less than a dozen ministers came back, over the 1660s and 1670s, but this small band had cachet. Nathaniel Brewster, for example, became minister at Boston's First Church. Leonard Hoar and Urian Oakes returned to be Presidents of Harvard. William Stoughton was Chief Justice in the Salem Witch Trials.[10] Increase Mather played a leading part in New England's civic and religious life. When he returned in 1661, the sight of his father Richard moved him to tears. Neither had expected to see the other again: 'it was the first, and I think the only time that I ever wept for joy'.[11]

What of those who stayed on in England? The migrants who had travelled to New England in the 1630s, and later came home, were elderly by the 1660s. Like Samuel Desborough, who retreated to his roots in Cambridgeshire, they were inclined to retire and lie low in Restoration England. Although plenty of former colonists kept or inherited property in America, this was not enough to tempt them back. Thomas Allen saw out his days in Norwich, and left his children to inherit and dispose of property at Charlestown, Massachusetts.[12] Allen and many others abandoned parish pulpits at the Restoration, because they could not accept the fixed liturgy of the Book of Common Prayer and the authority of bishops.[13] Thomas Larkham ran an apothecary's shop in Tavistock until the Five Mile Act of 1665 (which prohibited ejected ministers from going near their old parishes) made it illegal for him to stay in the town. John Allin – ejected from his parish at Rye in Sussex – was another who turned to medicine. He sent a remarkable series of letters from London to his friend in Rye, Dr Philip Frith, with an almost day-by-day account of the horrors of the Great Plague in 1665.[14] Ministers found themselves hauled before the authorities, accused of nonconformity.[15] One or two deployed the time-honoured strategy of a tactical retreat to the Netherlands.[16] Giles Firmin preached at nonconformist gatherings – 'conventicles' – three Sundays in the month, but attended his parish church on the fourth, satisfying the authorities with his 'occasional conformity'.[17] Conventicling and compromise sustained most former settlers, although Thomas Venner – the militant Fifth Monarchist – tried violent resistance to the new order, and lost his life for it.

The Baptist Hanserd Knollys was implicated in the uprising, and imprisoned, but few others rallied to 'Venner's Rebellion'.[18] As nonconformity found its way in late seventeenth-century England, godly friends and London merchants kept up connections between the Old World and the New, by letters and by trade.[19] Freegrace Bendall eventually went back to live in Boston. Nehemiah and Hannah Bourne briefly returned to New England in 1662, with mixed feelings. For someone like Bourne, with experience of religious toleration in England, the intolerance of Massachusetts marred the beauty of its churches, like the 'prickles that are near the rose'. He complained of a 'severe and narrow spirit amongst them who have had a large and plentiful experience of the grace of God'.[20] Susanna Bell, long gone from Massachusetts, bequeathed to Ann Eliot of Roxbury her black cloth gown, with a petticoat; no doubt knowing how precious and useful a good gown from the metropolis of London would be.[21]

The characters who spring to mind as the best known former colonists in England – Sir Henry Vane, Hugh Peter and George Downing – took a different path from the rest. Vane and Peter met death at the executioner's block in 1662, the only people sentenced to die for treason who had not signed Charles I's death warrant, and the only two who had spent time in New England.[22] George Downing, in contrast, turned Royalist in 1660. He rose high in Charles II's service, rewarded with a knighthood, a baronetcy, and land in Westminster on which to build a house (now famous as Downing Street). Notoriously, Sir George betrayed his former army commander, the regicide Colonel John Okey. He stage-managed Okey's extradition from Holland to face execution for treason. On the scaffold Okey forgave his army chaplain Downing, 'who pursued my life to the death'.[23]

෯ ෯ ෯ ෯ ෯

These New World settlers travelled across a sweep of time and territory, to New England and back, over thirty turbulent years. Their story is one of displacement within the Atlantic world: of what happened when pressure (real or threatened) drove people to leave their native country, and of what happened when the pressure eased.

Their stories speak powerfully of how strong local loyalties remained, in communities parted by the Atlantic. Many felt tempted, or even duty-bound, to return to England. The numbers who left are significant: perhaps as many as one in four of those who came over in the Great Migration went back to England before 1660; certainly, one in three of the ministers who emigrated in the 1630s deserted their flocks, and one in two Harvard students. The return of a third of the clergy after 1640 (and scarcely any before) underlines the significance of the religious climate in England in the 1630s: many emigrants came from parts of the country where conflict over religion was fiercest. They found New England a safe haven, but left as soon as they could.

Settlers who abandoned America were not noticeably more unsettled than their neighbours who stayed on. More than a few were pillars of their community. The very people who had encouraged other emigrants to leave England were often those who could afford to pay for a passage home, had contacts to get well placed there, and still owned property in England. Humbler colonists found it harder to reverse their journey – but still many sold up, borrowed, fled their debts, or went back to live off an inheritance that allowed them to make the move. How near many of the remaining settlers came to giving up on New England might seem odd in light of America's future, but the call of home exerted a strong pull, even on those who ended their days far away on the other side of the Atlantic; a sign of the stresses and disappointments of a New World, and of a persistent attachment to their roots.

The transatlantic horizons of settlers' histories bring together the 'puritanisms' of old and New England. Migration to New England needs to be seen in a long perspective: a history of debate (back to the time of Marian Protestants in the 1550s) about whether to conform to what church authorities required; when and how to resist; and the wisdom, sometimes, of tactical compromise or retreat. In the heat of the 1630s, emigration to New England was a drastic move to sidestep pressure, which resulted in a reformation by evasion. The flight from popery that carried migrants across the Atlantic, combined with the tough conditions of the New World, precipitated the choices settlers made to recreate primitive purity. Voluntary practices like covenants and soul-searching for signs of grace became compulsory, a means of defining the Church. To justify their decision to leave England to the godly left behind, New England's settlers had to show what purity they could achieve – or divine judgment would follow. The 'city on a hill' was not so much a world-redeeming beacon as an exposed and vulnerable outpost.

No simple connection existed between a desire to return to England and a wish to spread the New England Way (or, for that matter, between religious discontent and remigration). New England's leaders envisaged that colonial principles could be trimmed to fit the constraints of the English context, if need be, since the task back home was not to plant new churches (as in America) but to reform old ones. Settlers' protestations of loyalty to the godly in England have often been judged insincere, but the conduct of preachers who came back from New England suggests that this was not a sham or self-deception. Most still wanted to preach to the parish community at large as well as to a gathered circle of the godly – concerns which shaped puritan identity long before emigration, and which moulded religious life in New England.

Print, not people, brought the New England Way to England. The debate between New England and its godly critics in the late 1630s is significant, not only because of the energy colonial apologists put into refuting charges of schism and separation, but also because these manuscript exchanges, printed up, became the first salvos in a battle of books in the 1640s, amid the tumult of civil war. In the complex and polarising print culture of that time, arguments that started out as a defence of New England's innovations were used as a model for England to follow. English Independents found a blueprint in books, rather than from settlers fresh off the boat. Granted, one or two colonists, as agents for Massachusetts, were instrumental in bringing manuscripts to the press to defend New England's reputation. But real-life motives and behaviour proved much more complicated than the certainties expressed in print.

Last but not least, the migrants' story is about the power and ambiguities of their belief in Providence. To determine whether God called them to New England, emigrants amassed proofs to make the case. For Susanna Bell, the death of a child tipped the balance and gave her the courage to cross the Atlantic. Habits of Providentialist thinking encouraged migrants to bind together many different kinds of motive, sacred and secular. Once in America, Providence could be invoked to press them to stay – even if God's reasons for planting settlements had to be reviewed and reinvented as time went on. The use of covenant bonds, with the judgment of the Almighty as a sanction, proved a powerful means to steady new settlements. But settlers also found ways to put the logic that brought them to America into reverse, to allow many of their number to return home with God's blessing, while the rest stayed on. The mindset of these godly migrants turned the untidy chaos of their lives, lived out within narrow bounds of time and circumstance, into a journey under the hand of Providence.

Appendix 1 PILGRIMS, PURITANS, MIGRANTS

'Pilgrims', as a name for early English migrants to New England, came into fashion in the 1800s. It harks back to Hebrews 11:13, where the patriarchs of Israel were said to have thought of themselves as 'strangers and pilgrims' on the earth. William Bradford, a *Mayflower* passenger who became Governor of Plymouth Plantation, chose the word to describe the settlers who crossed the Atlantic with him from Holland in 1620: 'they knew they were but pilgrims, and . . . lift[ed] up their eyes to the heavens, their dearest country'. Bradford, like the few other seventeenth-century writers who called settlers 'pilgrims', had in mind exiled citizens of heaven (following Hebrews), not migrant saints who founded a new nation. However, in the nineteenth century the word became popular for early colonists of New England in general, and for the inhabitants of Plymouth Plantation in particular. The phrase 'Pilgrim Fathers' fused together the Hebrews text and reverence for heroic 'founding fathers'. In recent times, Pilgrim Fathers has silently given way to the more inclusive Pilgrims.[1]

'Pilgrim' also has a general meaning pertinent to the lives of the people who appear in this book, New England settlers of the Great Migration in the 1630s who later returned to England: literally, a person on a journey, a traveller, a wanderer, an itinerant, a foreigner, an alien, a stranger; figuratively, someone travelling through life, on a spiritual journey.[2] The use of 'pilgrims' for those who went to New England *and back* is gently subversive, because it under-mines the common assumption that migrants only ever took a one-way passage to America. A picture of migration to New England as a huge fat arrow labelled 'Puritans', pointing westward across the Atlantic from England, features on at least one university website, with not a trace to show that a single settler went back.

Debate about the meaning of the word 'puritan' has generated heat (and some light) in historical circles. It originated as a term of abuse early in the reign of Elizabeth I, hurled at those who wanted more reform in the Church of England. The puritan movement depicted in recent scholarship is far from monolithic: constantly changing, showing new faces in different settings and circumstances. A good introduction to the debate can be found in Peter Lake, 'Defining Puritanism – Again?', in Francis J. Bremer, ed., *Puritanism: Transatlantic Perspectives on a Seventeenth-Century Anglo-American Faith* (Boston: Massachusetts Historical Society, 1993), pp. 3–29. See also Patrick Collinson, 'A Comment: Concerning the Name Puritan', *Journal of Ecclesiastical History* 31 (1980), pp. 483–8; John Morrill, 'A Liberation Theology? Aspects of Puritanism in the English Revolution', and Dwight Brautigam, 'Prelates and Politics: Uses of "Puritan", 1625–40', in Laura Lunger Knoppers, ed., *Puritanism and its Discontents* (Newark, N.J. and London: University of Delaware Press, 2003), pp. 27–48, 49–66; Tom Webster, 'The Piety of Practice and the Practice of Piety', in Francis J. Bremer and Lynn A. Botelho, eds, *The World of John Winthrop: Essays on England and New England 1588–1649* (Boston, Mass.: Massachusetts Historical Society, 2005), pp. 111–46; David D. Hall, 'Narrating Puritanism', in Harry S. Stout and D.G. Hart, eds, *New Directions in American Religious History* (New York: Oxford University Press, 1997), pp. 51–83.

The settlers who went to New England but did not stay have attracted attention in studies of Atlantic history, and from scholars intrigued by the relation between the 'puritanisms' of old and New England: see Philip F. Gura, *A Glimpse of Sion's Glory: Puritan Radicalism in New England, 1620–1660* (Middletown, Conn.: Wesleyan University Press, 1984), pp. 136–43, 222–4; David Cressy, *Coming Over: Migration and Communication between England and New England in the Seventeenth Century* (Cambridge: Cambridge University Press, 1987), pp. 191–205; Francis J. Bremer, *Puritan Crisis: New England and the English Civil Wars, 1630–1670* (New York & London: Garland, 1989), pp. 234–44, 262–4; Francis J. Bremer, *Congregational Communion: Clerical Friendship in the Anglo-American Puritan Community, 1610–1692* (Boston, Mass.: Northeastern University Press, 1994), pp. 120–1, 145–6, 150–1, 179–90; Norman Pettit, 'God's Englishman in New England: His Enduring Ties to the Motherland', *Proceedings of the Massachusetts Historical Society*, 101 (1989), pp. 56–70; Andrew Delbanco, *The Puritan Ordeal* (Cambridge, Mass.: Harvard University Press, 1989), pp. 184–214; Stephen Fender, *Sea Changes: British Emigration and American Literature* (Cambridge: Cambridge University Press, 1992), pp. 141–7 and passim; Alison Games, *Migration and the Origins of the English Atlantic World* (Cambridge, Mass., and London: Harvard University Press, 2001), pp. 193–206, 236–8; Louise A. Breen, *Transgressing the Bounds: Subversive Enterprises among the Puritan Elite in Massachusetts, 1630–1692* (Oxford & New York: Oxford University Press, 2001), pp. 97–143; Carla Gardina Pestana, *The English Atlantic in an Age of Revolution, 1640–1661*

(Cambridge, Mass., and London: Harvard University Press 2004), pp. 56–63, 185. Virginia DeJohn Anderson and Roger Thompson have suggested that the number of colonists who left New England was too small to undermine the general settledness of the early communities: Anderson, *New England's Generation: The Great Migration and the Formation of Society and Culture in the Seventeenth Century* (Cambridge: Cambridge University Press, 1991), p. 122n.; Thompson, *Mobility and Migration: East Anglian Founders of New England, 1629–1640* (Amherst, Mass.: The University of Massachusetts Press, 1994), p. 223. For a review of the relatively new and burgeoning field of Atlantic history, see Bernard Bailyn, *Atlantic History: Concept and Contours* (Cambridge, Mass.: Harvard University Press, 2005).

Despite fresh interest in these Atlantic migrants, the recent literature focuses on New England settlers who loom large in the surviving sources, but are not particularly representative, such as religious radicals, social or political misfits and the educated elite. William Sachse's sketches, written more than half a century ago, still tend to define the boundaries of the evidence: 'Harvard Men in England 1642–1714', Colonial Society of Massachusetts, *Publications*, 35 (1942–1946), pp. 120–31; 'The Migration of New Englanders to England, 1640–1660', *American Historical Review*, 53 (1947–1948), pp. 251–78; *The Colonial American in Britain* (Madison, Wisconsin: University of Wisconsin Press, 1956). Harry Stout took up Sachse's comments on the striking exodus of university-educated settlers: 'The Morphology of Remigration: New England University Men and their Return to England, 1640–1660', *Journal of American Studies*, 10 (1976), pp. 151–72. Frank Bremer explored the material further, initially within the framework of Perry Miller's pivotal essay of the 1950s, 'Errand into the Wilderness'. Although he changed his emphasis in view of the critique of Miller's 'Errand' by Theodore Dwight Bozeman and others, Bremer's later work still homed in on a tightly defined network of Congregationalist ministers: Bremer, *Puritan Crisis*; Bremer, *Congregational Communion*.

While studies that follow the best known colonists can create a lively impression of connections between individuals, the landscape they paint is rather flat: they are less good at capturing how New England's 'deserters' expose tensions and nuances in the drive to settle in America. As for identifying the number of settlers who went back, only David Cressy has made a stab at quantifying this. He makes some brief and bold suggestions based on broad demographic evidence, but admits that this is tricky because estimates of New England's population vary considerably: Cressy, *Coming Over*, p. 192.

The settlers who people the pages of this book take the discussion beyond faceless demographics, and beyond the prominent or notorious characters who have dominated the debate so far. Well known migrants like Sir Henry Vane the younger, Hugh Peter, George Downing, and Increase Mather and his brothers, appear only in passing. Instead, the story starts with the emblematic tale of Susanna Bell, an obscure inhabitant of Roxbury, Massachusetts.

Appendix 2 NEW ENGLAND SETTLERS WHO RETURNED HOME, 1640 – 1660

This is not an exhaustive list. For the most part, only those who left from the colonies of Massachusetts Bay, Connecticut and New Haven are included, and only those who returned home after 1640, for good – or at least until times changed in 1660, with the Restoration of Charles II.

NAME	NE settlement	OE origins	To NE	Left NE	OE resettlement [* To NE again 1660+]	Occupation / Publications [P]
Adams Ferdinando & Ann	Dedham	Ipswich	1637	1641 1642		Shoemaker
Adams John	Concord		1634?	1649		
Allen Thomas & Ann [Harvard]	Charlestown	Norwich Patcham, Sussex	1638 1637	1651	Norwich	Minister [P]
Allin John	Dedham; Harvard BA 1643	Wrentham, Suffolk	1637 with parents	by March 1650	Rye, Sussex; London *To NE 1674	Minister

Ambrose Joshua	Harvard BA 1653	Toxteth, Lancs.	1650	1654	Oxford; Walton, Childwall, Lancs.	Student at Pembroke College, Oxford; minister [conformed]
Ambrose Nehemiah	Harvard BA 1653, MA 1656, Fellow 1654-7	Toxteth, Lancs.	1650	1657	Kirby, Lancs.	Minister
Ames John	Salem; Harvard, class of 1647 but took no degree	[Netherlands]	1637	by 1645	Wrentham, Suffolk	
Ames William	Salem; Harvard BA 1645	[Netherlands]	1637	by 1645	Wrentham, Suffolk	Minister [P]
Andrewes Samuel	New Haven			1654		
Angier John & Hannah [Aspinwall]	Harvard BA 1653, MA 1655	Denton, Lancs. Hannah b. NE	1650	1656 1656	Ringley chapel, Lancs.	Minister [conformed]
Angier Samuel	York	Lezant, Cornwall	by 1640	before 1652	Lezant, Cornwall	
Aspinwall William & Elizabeth	Charlestown; Boston; Portsmouth RI; Boston	Manchester	1630	1652	Ireland; Chester	Merchant, notary, surveyor, minister [P]
Astwood John	Roxbury; Milford	Abbotsley, Hunts.	1635	1653	London	Merchant/farmer; colonial agent
Astwood Sarah	Roxbury; Boston		1638	1653		Widow of James, sister-in-law of John
Austin ? & family	New Haven		1638	c.1640	Captured by Turks	Merchant
Austin Francis	Guilford	London?		1646	Lost at sea	
Bachiler Stephen	Lynn; Ipswich; Yarmouth; Newbury; Hampton; Portsmouth	Newton Stacey; Hampshire	1632	by autumn 1651	Buried at All Hallows Staining, London, 1656	Minister

NAME	NE settlement	OE origins	To NE	Left NE	OE resettlement [* To NE again 1660+]	Occupation / Publications [P]
Baker John	Boston; Newbury; York; Dover; Wells [some conflation of identities?]		1630	1653?	Army; took part in Venner's rebellion, 1662	Grocer? Tailor? Lay preacher; said to have been one of Cromwell's halberdiers
Balch Freeborn				by 1656	Wapping, Middlesex; admitted to Stepney church, 'late of New England'	Mariner
Barnard Tobias	Harvard, BA 1642		1639	by 1651		
Bartholomew Richard	Salem		1637	early 1646	Died at sea? Visited OE 1645	Merchant
Beales John	Hingham			late 1657	Died at sea?	
Bell Thomas (1) & Susanna	Roxbury	London / Bury St Edmunds	1634	1647	London	Merchant
Bell Thomas (2)	Boston	b. NE, son of Thomas & Ann; sister Deborah		by 1667	London	Tailor
Bellingham Samuel	Rowley; Harvard, MA 1642	Boston, Lincolnshire	with parents	c.1650?	D.Med, University of Leiden; London	Doctor
Bendall Edward & Jane	Boston	Kersey, Suffolk; Southwark	1630	in OE 1646; left NE 1652? OE by 1654	London; Cotgrave, Nottinghamshire?	Merchant, wharf owner, inventor; minister?
Bendall Freegrace	Boston	b. NE 1635		1652?	London *NE by 1666	Merchant [m. Mary Lisle]
Bendall Hoptfor	Boston	b. NE 1641		1652?	London, Antigua	Merchant
Betscomb Richard	Hingham	Bridport, Dorset	by 1640	autumn 1647	[Appointed attorney to enquire in Oxfordshire]	

Name	New England	Origin in England	Arrival	Return	Destination	Occupation
Betts William, Alice & son Hope	Scituate; Barnstable; Dorchester	Suffolk? *Winthrop Papers* III 364	by 1635	sold house and land 1652		Dish-turner
Bidgood [Betgood] Richard & Mary	Boston; Ipswich	Romsey, Hampshire; London	1638	R. by 1650 M. 1653		Clothworker, merchant
Birden John	Harvard BA 1647			by 1651	'His own county'	Minister
Biscoe [Briscoe] Nathaniel	Watertown	Buckinghamshire	late 1630s	1651	London	'A rich tanner'; a Baptist
Blackborne Walter & Elizabeth	Roxbury	London	1638	W. 1640 E. 1641		Milliner & shopkeeper
Blackwood Christopher	Scituate	Kent; Rye, Sussex	1640	1642	Kent, Sussex; Ireland	Minister (Baptist) [P]
Blinman Richard & Mary	Marshfield; Gloucester; New London; New Haven	Chepstow, Monmouthshire; Herefordshire	1640	summer 1659	Chepstow; Bristol	Minister [P]
Bourne Nehemiah & Hannah	Charlestown; Dorchester; Boston	Wapping	1638	N & H 1646, children 1648	London (Wapping)	Atlantic mariner, shipbuilder, naval official
Boyes Matthew & Elizabeth	Roxbury; soon to Rowley	Leeds, Yorkshire	before 1639	1656	Leeds, Edstone & Welburn, Yorks.	Clothworker
Bradstreet Samuel	Harvard BA 1653, MA 1656, tutor 1656–57	Lincolnshire	1630 with parents	1657	Studied medicine *To Boston 1661	Doctor
Brecy [Brasie] Mr (John?) & Mrs (Phoebe?)	New Haven (and Branford?)	Bedfordshire / London? 'Mrs Brasie', servant of Lady Mary Vere	before 1644	Nov. 1647, with children	Wrote from England to John Davenport & Susanna Evance	Minister?

NAME	NE settlement	OE origins	To NE	Left NE	OE resettlement [* To NE again 1660+]	Occupation / Publications [P]
Brewster Francis	New Haven, father of Nathaniel	London	1640	Jan. 1645/6	Died at sea	Merchant
Brewster Nathaniel	Harvard BA 1642	London	1640	by Oct. 1649	Walberswick, Suffolk; Alby, Norfolk; Ireland *To NE 1663	Minister
Brigham Sebastian	Rowley	Holme, Yorkshire	by 1643	by 1652	Died by July 1646	Mariner
Buckmaster Laurence	Scituate; Boston	with father (Thomas)?	soon after Nov. 1645			
Bulkeley John	Concord; Harvard MA 1642, tutor 1644	Odell, Bedfordshire	1635	late 1645	Fordham, Essex, 1650; Wapping 1660–89	Minister
Bullock Edward	Dorchester	Barkham, Berkshire	1635	1649, to claim inheritance	Probably to Berkshire, died by Jan. 1656/7	Husbandman
Burden [**Burdin**] George & Ann	Boston	London	by 1636	A. late 1651, G. 1652	Bristol	Shoemaker, tanner
Burdett George	Salem; Dover; York	Dublin and Cambridge; Silkstone, Yorks; Yarmouth, Norfolk	1635	1641	Army chaplain, Scotland and Ireland	Minister [conformist cleric in Ireland after 1660]
Bury William	Boston	London		late 1647	London	'Gentleman'
Busby John	Newbury; Watertown; Boston	Norwich	1637 with parents	before 1657	Norwich?	Weaver?
Butler Henry (& Ann, m. 1655)	Dorchester; Harvard BA 1651, MA 1654	Ashford, Kent	1635 or 1637 with parents	1655 or 1656	Bridport, Dorset; Yeovil, Somerset	Schoolmaster at Dorchester; Minister
Caffinch John	Guilford; New Haven	Tenterden, Kent	1639	by 1658	Tenterden, Kent	

Name	New England	Origin in England	Arrived	Returned	Place returned to	Occupation / notes
Carleton Edward & Ellen	Rowley	Hornsea, Yorkshire	1639	Edw. 1650, Ellen followed before 1660		
Carter Joseph	Newbury	London?	by 1635	by 1656	Thetford, Norfolk	Chandler; minister after return to OE
Chaplin Clement & Sarah	Cambridge; Hartford (elder to church)	Semer & Bury St Edmunds, Suffolk				
Chauncy Ichabod	Scituate; Harvard BA 1651, MA 1654	Ware, Hertfordshire	1635 with parents	by 1656	Compton, Dorset; Coggeshall, Essex; Dunkirk; Bristol 1666–91	Army chaplain, physician [P]
Chauncy Isaac	Scituate; Harvard BA 1651, MA 1654	Ware, Hertfordshire	1635 with parents	by 1656	Woodborough Wilts.; Hampshire; London	Minister, physician [P]
Child Robert	Saugus; Boston 1638–41, 1645–47	Northfleet, Kent	1638	1647	Kent; London; Ireland from 1651 [Close to George Starkey]	Physician, alchemist, agriculturalist; ran the Saugus ironworks
Clarke John	Boston; Newport, RI	Westhorpe, Suffolk	1637	1651 as colonial agent	London *To Newport, 1663	Medicine; colonial agent; Baptist preacher [P]
Clements John & Sarah	Haverhill		by 1649	by 1659	Castledermot, Co. Kildare, Ireland	Minister after left NE
Cockram William	Hingham	Southwold, Suffolk	1635	1642	Went to fetch his family	Mercer / mariner
Cogan Henry & daughter Abigail	Dorchester; Barnstable	Dorchester, Dorset?	1637/8	by 1648 died 1649	Rotterdam, 1648? Winthrop Papers, V, p. 243	
Coggswell John Jr	Ipswich	London	1652		London died on the voyage back to NE	Widower; hoped to find a wife for his motherless children' in 'OE

NAME	NE settlement	OE origins	To NE	Left NE	OE resettlement [* To NE again 1660+]	Occupation / Publications [P]
Collins John	Harvard BA 1649, MA 1652, Fellow, 1651–1653	Wethersfield, Dedham, Essex; London	1638 with parents	1653	Cambridge; Scotland; London	Fellow, Pembroke College; army chaplain; minister [P]
Cooke George	Cambridge	Pebmarsh, Essex (cousin of Joseph)	1635	autumn 1645	Parliamentary army in England & Ireland	Military governor, Wexford
Cooke Joseph & Mary [Haynes]	Cambridge	Yeldham, Essex	1635	1658	Stanway, Essex (1665)	Gentleman
Corbet John and his father	relatives of Thomas Cobbet of Lynn?			by 1650	Ireland (Nathaniel Mather met him there)	
Coytmore Thomas	Charlestown		by 1640	1644	Died in shipwreck off Spanish coast	Sea-captain
Cutter William	Cambridge	Newcastle-upon-Tyne	by 1638	by 1653	Newcastle-upon-Tyne	
Davis John	Harvard BA 1651, MA 1654			Nov. 1657	Died at sea	Teacher in Connecticut
Day Wentworth	Boston; Cambridge		by 1640	by 1647?	Perhaps the WD who served as a cornet under William Rainborowe in Thomas Harrison's regiment, 1647?	Soldier, later notorious as a Fifth Monarchist?
Denton Richard	Wethersfield; Stamford; Hempstead LI	Halifax, Yorkshire	1638	1659	Essex	Minister
Desborough [Disbrowe] Samuel & Dorothy	Guilford	Eltisley, Cambridgeshire	1639	autumn 1650	Scotland; 1660–90, Elsworth, Cambridgeshire	Politician and administrator; Keeper of the Great Seal of Scotland

Downing, Emmanuel, Lucy & Martha	Salem	Dublin; London	1638	E. late 1654, L. & M. by 1658	Scotland	Merchant entrepreneur
Downing George	Salem; Harvard BA 1642	Dublin; London	1638	1645, as ship's chaplain; reached OE 1646	Parliamentary army; Scotland; The Hague; London; Cambridgeshire	Army chaplain; diplomat and financial reformer [P]
Downing Joshua	Salem			by 1652/3	Scotland	Mariner; customs officer in Scotland
Dummer Stephen & Alice	Newbury	Bishopstoke, Hampshire	1638	winter 1646/7	Bishopstoke, Hampshire	[related to Joan Nelson]
Earning Katherine	Dorchester, Boston	Wapping, Middlesex	by 1639	by 1648	Wapping, Middlesex	Widowed mother of Hannah Bourne
Eaton Ann m. (1) Thomas Yale; (2) Theophilus Eaton	New Haven	Chester; London	1637	1658, after death of Theophilus	London, died 1659	
Eaton Hannah	New Haven	London	1637 with parents	1658 with mother, Ann	London *To NE 1660	
Eaton Nathaniel	Cambridge	Great Budworth; Cheshire; Franeker; Essex	1637	Left for Virginia 1639, to OE 1646	University of Padua 1647; Vicar of Bishop's Castle, Shropshire, 1661; Bideford, Devon	Minister [conformed 1661]
Eaton Samuel	'Totoket' (Branford)	Great Budworth & West Kirby, Cheshire	1637	late 1640	Dukinfield, Cheshire	Minister, army chaplain [P]
Eaton Theophilus Jr	New Haven	London	1637 with parents	1658 with mother, Ann	London, later Dublin	
Edwards Thomas & Elizabeth	Salem		1637	T. late 1646, E. late 1649	Yarmouth, Norfolk	Shoemaker
Eldred Rebecca	New Haven			before 1647	London?	Estate of £1,000
Elmes Rodolphus	Scituate	Southwark	1635	autumn 1656	Southwark	'A servant'

NAME	NE settlement	OE origins	To NE	Left NE	OE resettlement [* To NE again 1660+]	Occupation / Publications [P]
Evance John & Susanna	New Haven	London	1639	J. by 1653 S. in 1655	London	Merchant
Eyton Sampson	Studied at Harvard for eight years, but not a graduate		by 1642	1651	Oxford; Gray's Inn, London, 1658	Fellow of University College, Oxford; lawyer
Fairfield Daniel	Salem; convicted of child abuse 1642		by 1639	autumn 1652		[Told that if he came back to NE he would be imprisoned]
Farnworth Joseph	Dorchester; Harvard, but left without a degree		by 1638 with parents	by April 1655	South Hanningfield, Essex; later London	Minister
Farwell John	Taunton, son of Thomas		1639	?	?	
Feke [Feake] Robert	Watertown; 1636 to CT; 1640-7, Greenwich	London	1630	autumn 1647	London? Returned to Watertown; d. 1663	Goldsmith
Fenwick George	Saybrook	Northumberland, London	1636 briefly; 1639	1645	Colonel; Governor of Berwick, and later Edinburgh	Army officer; politician
Fenwick Mary	Saybrook, sister of George	Northumberland, London	1639	late 1646, with GF's children		
Firmin Giles	Boston; Ipswich	Ipswich	1632	Nov. 1644	Colchester, Shalford & Ridgewell, Essex	Minister, physician [P]
Firmin, Susan, Nathaniel, Giles	Ipswich	wife of GF, daughter of Nathaniel Ward		late 1646	Colchester, Shalford & Ridgewell, Essex	
Fletcher Edward & Mary	Boston		by 1639/40	late 1654	1657 Bagendon, Gloucestershire	Cutler NE Minister OE

Name	New England	English origin	Arrival	Return	Destination in OE	Occupation/notes
Fletcher William	Oyster River Plantation [Dover]	Leicestershire; Aston, Yorkshire, 1631–51	1656	? perhaps confused with Edward	To OE late 1650s? *To NE, d. Saco 1668	Minister
Floyd [Lloyd] Richard	Boston		by 1642	by July 1649	London	Merchant?
Fogg John	Plymouth; Salem	London b. 1628	with parents, 1633	1648?	Barnstaple, Devon, 1665	
Fogg Ralph & Susanna	Plymouth; Salem	London	1633	visited OE 1647–9, returned for good after 1652	London; Plymouth, Devon	Skinner; disciplined by Salem church 1650 & excommunicated
Foulsham Adam	Hingham	Hingham, Norfolk	1639	before 1660		Yeoman
Fowle Thomas & Margaret	Boston		before 1635	Nov. 1646	London?	Merchant
Franklin William	Boston; Newbury	Hampshire/Wiltshire 1634	after 1638	between 1653 & 1658	London	Blacksmith, merchant
Freeman Samuel	Watertown	Blackfriars, London; Devon	1630	after 1638		
Fugill Thomas	New Haven	Rowley, Yorkshire	1638	c.1645	Northern England	Notary, surveyor
Garnsey Elizabeth	York	Devon	?	after 1652	Pinhoe, Devon	
Gibbons Margaret	Charlestown; Boston	Plymouth, Devon	1623 with Edward?	after 1654; died 1656	Plymouth, Devon	Widow of Edward Gibbons, merchant and soldier
Gibson Richard & Mary	West Country fishing plantation, Richmond Island	Emmanuel, Cambridge	1637	1642		Minister
Gilbert Thomas & Jane	Dorchester; Taunton		with parents by 1636	1653, after a visit in 1650		Daughter Mary m. N. Norcrosse

NAME	NE settlement	OE origins	To NE	Left NE	OE resettlement [* To NE again 1660+]	Occupation / Publications [P]
Gill Arthur	Dorchester; Boston	probably Devon		1650, with F. Willoughby		'Ship carpenter' *Aspinwall NR*, p. 306
Gill Thomas	b. NE 1644, son of Thomas			before 1656		Went to OE to settle father's estate
Glover John	Cambridge; Harvard BA 1650	Sutton, Surrey	with parents 1638	by Dec. 1650	MD Aberdeen 1654; Scotland, London	Physician
Glover Roger	Cambridge	Sutton, Surrey	with parents 1638	by July 1649	Scotland	Soldier; died at siege of Edinburgh Castle, Dec. 1650
Godfrey Edward	Piscataqua; York	Wilmington, Kent; London	1630	visited OE 1638; resettled autumn 1655	London	Agent for Sir Ferdinando Gorges
Godfrey Oliver	York	Kent; London	1642	1645?	Married before Jan. 1648/9, at Seal, Kent	
Goodyear Mrs	New Haven	London	1638?	Jan. 1645/6		Died at sea
Goodyear Stephen	New Haven	London	1638?	late 1657	Died OE 1658	Merchant; wanted to attract investors for the East Haven ironworks
Gookin Daniel	Virginia; Boston; Roxbury; Cambridge	Kent	1644 from Virginia	Nov. 1657	Dunkirk 1659 * To NE 1660	Merchant; customs collector at Dunkirk [P]
Gould Jeremiah	Weymouth; Rhode Island		before 1644	sailed from Boston 1652	The Raven, New Fish Street, London (with his son Simon)	
Gregson Thomas	New Haven	Derbyshire, London c.1637		1645/6	Died at sea	Merchant. Two of his children later went to England; his wife stayed in NE

Name						
Hadden [Hawden] George	Harvard, BA 164?. Son of Garrett Hadden? Cambridge		1630 with parents?	by May 1654	MA Cambridge; Vicar of Stannington, Northumberland, then Nazing, Essex?	Minister? [1 so, conformed 1662]
Hall Samuel	Explored Connecticut river, 1633; Ipswich, Salisbury	Essex?	by 1633	frequent visitor to OE, resettled there after 1662	Langford, near Maldon, Essex; London	Merchant
Harding Robert (1)	Boston; Portsmouth & Newport RI; Boston	Boreham, Essex?	1630	resettled in OE by 1651	London	Merchant; transatlantic and coastal trader
Harding Robert (2)		?	1633?	by 1653	Dublin, Ireland	CSPC, p. 466
Harlakenden Elizabeth & Mary	Cambridge		b. NE 1636, 1638	late 1646 / early 1647	Bures, Essex	Daughters of Elizabeth Pelham
Harrison Thomas	Virginia 1640, Boston 1648	Hull, Yorkshire	1648	winter 1649/50	London; Dublin	Minister [P]
Harwood John & Elizabeth [Usher]	Boston		by 1645	1657	London; Bethnal Green & Stepney, Middlesex	Merchant tailor
Haynes Hezekiah	Son of John Haynes, Governor of Connecticut	Essex	In NE c.1633–7. Also to NE in 1648 (according to Josselin, Diary)	1657	Copford Hall, Essex	Parliamentarian army officer & deputy major-general
Haynes John	Half-brother of Hezekiah & Mary [Cooke]; Hartford; Harvard, BA 1656		b. NE 1635		1657 Pembroke College, Cambridge; MA 1660. 1658 minister at Hemingstone, Suffolk	Minister. Conformed 1666: parish minister at Stanway, Essex, near Copford Hall
Haynes Roger	brother of John; Harvard class of 1658, no degree	b. NE		1655 or later		Died at sea?

NAME	NE settlement	OE origins	To NE	Left NE	OE resettlement [*To NE again 1660+]	Occupation / Publications [P]
Hefford [Heyford] Samuel	Ipswich			Dec. 1651		
Higginson Francis	Salem; Charlestown; New Haven	Claybrook, Leicestershire	1629 with parents	1639? Leiden by 1648 OE	Yorkshire; Kirkby Stephen, Westmorland	Minister [conformed] [P]
Higginson Samuel	brother to Francis & Theophilus	Claybrook, Leicestershire	1629 with parents	1652 or 1653?	Admitted a member of church at Stepney, Middlesex, 1654	Cromwell's navy
Higginson Theophilus	brother to Francis & Samuel	Claybrook, Leicestershire	1629 with parents	1652/3, with Mark Pierce?	London	Died by 1654
Hoadley John	Guilford	Rolvenden, Kent?	1639	autumn 1653; family 1654	Scotland; Rolvenden, Kent, 1662	Chaplain to Edinburgh Castle
Hoar Leonard	Harvard BA 1650, MA 1653	Gloucester	1638 with mother & siblings	1653	MA, Cambridge, 1654; Wanstead, Essex; London. *To NE 1672	Minister; President of Harvard, 1672–5 [P]
Hobart Joshua	Hingham; Harvard BA 1650			[1650?] 1656	[Scotland, see Hubbard] London; New Ross, Co. Wexford, Ireland	Minister
Holland Jeremiah	Harvard BA 1645			in or soon after 1645	London; Northamptonshire	Minister
Hooke Ebenezer	Taunton; New Haven	b. NE c.1643, son of William & Jane		1654 with mother	London?	*To NE 1663, to serve John Winthrop Jr
Hooke Jane [Whalley] m. William	Taunton; New Haven	Nottinghamshire; cousin of Cromwell	c.1637	1654	[Her brother, the regicide Edward Whalley, fled to NE in 1660 with his son-in-law William Goffe]	
Hooke John	Taunton; New Haven; Harvard, class of 1655	b. Axmouth, son of William & Jane	c.1637 with parents	1652 matric. Magdalen Oxford	1658 Rector of Kings Worthy, Hampshire; Savoy Chapel, London; later in Berkshire	Minister [conformed 1662 at the Savoy Chapel]

Name	New England	English origin	Arrived	English destination	Returned	Notes
Hooke Walter	Taunton; New Haven	b. Axmouth, son of William & Jane	c.1637 with parents	BA 1657, Pembroke, Cambridge	1654	Student, minister. Chaplain to East India Company, 1668–9 [P]
Hooke William m. Jane	Taunton; New Haven	Hook, Hampshire; Axmouth, Devon	c.1637	Axmouth briefly, then London	1656	Minister
Hooker John	Cambridge; Hartford; son of Thomas	Essex	1633	University of Oxford	by 1645	Minister
Hopkins Ann [Yale]	Hartford, wife of Edward	Denbighshire	1637	London	1656	Brought to OE by her brother Thomas Yale
Hopkins Edward	Hartford Deputy Governor, Connecticut	Herefordshire? London	1637	London	1652	Merchant, Admiralty Commissioner, Warden of the Fleet Prison, MP
Horsford [Hosford] William & Jane	Dorchester; Windsor 1635 (ruling elder); Springfield 1653?	Beaminster and/or Dorchester, Dorset	1633	Parliamentary army; minister at Calverleigh, Devon, ejected 1660; Jane in Tiverton, 1671	1640s army; 1654 returned for good	Husbandman? Preached in Springfield, 1653? Minister in OE
Hubbard ⸺	Harvard graduate, known to N. Mather			Scotland	1650	See Joshua Hobart
Hubbard Benjamin & Alice	Charlestown		by 1633	London	1644; Alice after 1645	Inventor of navigation aids; mathematician; surveyor
Hudson William	Charlestown; Boston	1630	autumn 1647	London; Chatham, Kent by 1656 visited NE 1650		Baker

NAME	NE settlement	OE origins	To NE	Left NE	OE resettlement [* To NE again 1660+]	Occupation / Publications [P]
Hudson William Jr	Boston		1630	in OE 1643–5	Temporarily, to serve in the Parliamentary army	Innkeeper
Hull Joseph, Agnes & many children	Multiple moves (eight) including Weymouth; Barnstable; Yarmouth; York	Northleigh, Devon	1635	by 1648	Launceston, then St Buryan, Cornwall *To NE 1662	Minister
Humfrey John	Lynn; Salem	Dorchester, Dorset & Lincoln's Inn, London	1634	Oct. 1641	Lawyer; colonial adventurer; colonel in the Parliamentary army; sword-bearer to Lord President Bradshaw at the trial of Charles I	
Humfrey John Jr	Lynn; Salem; son of John		1634	after 1642	Parliamentary army; commanded troops in Ireland, 1649, and in the Western Design (to the Caribbean) 1655–6	
Humfrey Joseph	Lynn; Salem; son of John		1634	by 1644?		See also Ann Ottley [Humfrey]
Hutchin George	Cambridge	County Durham?		autumn 1647	Given power of attorney to enquire about legacies in Whickham, County Durham	Wheelwright
Hutchinson Richard	Boston; son of William & Anne	Alford, Lincolnshire	1634	by 1645	Dismissed to Thomas Goodwin's church in London; children baptised at Stepney, Middlesex?	Nephew of his namesake, a powerful London merchant; he or his uncle became Navy Treasurer
Ince Jonathan	Hartford; Boston; New Haven. Harvard BA 1650, MA 1653				1657	Died at sea

Name	New England	Origin	Emigrated	Returned	Destination	Occupation
James Abraham	Harvard, known to Samuel Mather			by 1651	Norfolk	Minister
James Thomas, Elizabeth & family	Boston; Charlestown; Providence RI; New Haven 1639	Boston, Lincolnshire	1632	c.1648	Needham Market, Suffolk, 1650–83	Schoolmaster; later town preacher at Needham Market
Jeffreys Robert	Boston		by 1637	after 1646; in OE by 1649	London	Merchant; Registrar-Accountant, 1649–52
Jenner Thomas	Roxbury; Weymouth; Saco; Charlestown	Fordham, Essex; Northumberland	1635	late 1649	Coltishall, Norfolk; Ireland – Drogheda, Limerick, Dublin	Minister [P]
Jennison William	Charlestown; Watertown		1630	1648	Colchester, Essex	
Jones Thomas	Guilford	Kent / Surrey?	1639	c.1652	Scotland, with S. Desborough?	
Jordan Thomas	Guilford	probably Lenham, Kent	1639	c.1654	Lenham, Kent	Lawyer
Jupe Benjamin	Boston; lived in the household of his uncle, the wealthy merchant Robert Keayne	London		c.1654 with his sister, Mary Morse [Mosse]	London	Inherited two houses in parish of St Botolph, Aldgate, London
Keayne Benjamin	Boston, son of Robert Keayne; Lynn 1640	London	1635	c.1645	London	Parliamentarian soldier; merchant
Kerman [Carman]	Roxbury; New Haven?		1633?	died at sea Dec. 1644		Shipmaster
Knight Francis & John	Salem, sons of William Knight (who died in NE)		by 1637		John fought in Parliamentary army?	

NAME	NE settlement	OE origins	To NE	Left NE	OE resettlement [* To NE again 1660+]	Occupation / Publications [P]
Knight William	Ipswich; Topsfield 1641–55?	Emmanuel, Cambridge; half-brother of Israel Stoughton?	1637	1643 with Stoughton? 1655?	1655 Rector of St Matthew, Ipswich?	Minister [conformed after 1660?]
Knollys Hanserd	Piscataqua	Lincolnshire	1638	1641	London	Army chaplain; Baptist preacher
Knowles John & Elizabeth [Willis]	Boston briefly; Watertown	Fellow of St Catherine's, Cambridge	by 1639	1651	Twickenham, Middlesex, 1652; Bristol 1653; London after 1662	Minister; brother-in-law to Thomas Willis Jr
Lamberton George	New Haven		c.1638	1645/6, died at sea		Merchant
Larkham George	son of Thomas & Patience, perhaps in NE	Northam, Devon	1639	by 1647	University of Oxford; Cockermouth, Cumberland	Student, minister
Larkham Jane	daughter of Thomas & Patience	Northam, Devon	1639	by 1650	Tavistock, Devon	
Larkham Patience	daughter of Thomas & Patience	Northam, Devon	1639	by 1654	Ireland by 1654; Rossgarland Castle, Co. Wexford, 1656	m. Joseph Miller, a lieutenant, by June 1654
Larkham Thomas & Patience	Dover [Northam]	Northam, Devon	1639	Nov. 1642 (T.) Patience later	Kent; Tavistock, Devon; Cockermouth, Cumberland	Army chaplain; parish minister [P]
Larkham Thomas Jr	eldest son of Thomas & Patience	Northam, Devon	1639	1642 with father		Died in the West Indies, 1648/9
Latham William	Plymouth; Duxbury	Sherbourne, Dorset	1620 on the *Mayflower*, a servant	1651?	To England and then the Bahamas; died there of starvation	'Planter'

Name						
Lechford Thomas	Boston	London	1638	August 1641	London	Solicitor, notary [P]
Lenthall Robert	Weymouth; Newport, RI	Aston Sandford, Buckinghamshire	1637/8	1642	1643 Great Hampden, Buckinghamshire; Barnes, Surrey, 1658	Minister
Leverett John	Boston	Boston, Lincolnshire	c.1633 with father	1643–4 1646–7 1655–61	London *To NE 1661	Parliamentary army; trade; agent for Massachusetts
Leverett Sarah [Sedgwick]	Charlestown; Boston; wife of John	Southwark	1635?	1657	London *To NE 1661	
Ling Benjamin & Joanna	Charlestown; New Haven 1637–55	North Petherton, Somerset	1636	1655	London? *To New Haven 1662	Merchant, died 1673
Lippincott Richard & Abigail	Dorchester, then Boston		by 1644	1651 or 1652	By 1653 Plymouth, Devon; *to Rhode Island 1660	Barber
Lisle Francis & Alice	Boston		1637	late 1643–summer 1645; soon took family back	Surgeon in Earl of Manchester's forces	Barber-surgeon; daughter Mary m. Freegrace Bendall
Longe Joseph				c.1647	Died soon after he reached England?	Nothing heard from him: in 1651 his wife petitioned to remarry
Lord Robert & Rebecca	Boston; Rebecca sister to Martha Thurston			by 1657	New Gravel Lane, Stepney, Middlesex	Mariner
Lowle Mary	Newbury	b. c.1633, Portbury, near Bristol	by 1642, with father	1650	Orphaned; went to 'friends' in OE	Legacy of £21 released early to pay for her passage home

NAME	NE settlement	OE origins	To NE	Left NE	OE resettlement [* To NE again 1660+]	Occupation / Publications [P]
Ludlow Roger & Mary	Dorchester; Windsor; Stratford; Fairfield	Maiden Bradley, Wiltshire; Inner Temple, London	March 1629/30	1654	Ireland 1654-? Mary died in Dublin 1664	Lawyer; Deputy-Governor, Connecticut; administrator, Ireland
Lyon Richard	Harvard, tutor to William Mildmay	Sent over by Sir Henry Mildmay	1644	probably 1651, with William		
Malbon Richard	New Haven	London	1637	autumn 1650	London	Merchant
Malbon Samuel	Son of Richard; Harvard, but no degree – took a certificate of residence	London	1637 with father	Dec. 1650	BA New Inn Hall, Oxford, 1651; Henham, Essex; Blofield, Norfolk.	Student; minister, ejected 1660; Amsterdam 1662–9, Norwich, London [P]
Marshall Christopher	Boston; Exeter	Alford, Lincolnshire	1634 to join John Cotton	c.1642	Woodkirk/West Ardsley, Yorkshire	Army chaplain, parish minister
Marshall James	Dorchester			by 1645	Exeter, Devon	
Martin Isaac	Hingham	Norfolk / Suffolk		Dec. 1646	Norfolk? attorney for business there	
Martin [Martyn] Samuel & Phoebe	Wethersfield	London? Connected with the Wyllys family of Fenny Compton, Warwickshire		1646	William Bisbey (Phoebe's father, in London) reported they intended to return	
Mascall [Maskall] Robert	Boston		by 1640	by 1646	Dover and Canterbury, Kent	Customs collector

Name						
Mather Increase		Dorchester; Harvard, BA 1656	b. NE 1639	July 1657	MA Trinity College, Dublin; Torrington, Devon; Guernsey; Gloucester; Weymouth; Dorchester, Dorset	Student; minister *To NE 1661; President of Harvard, 1685–1701 [P]
Mather Nathaniel	Much Woolton, Lancashire	Dorchester; Harvard, BA 1647, MA 1650	1635 with parents	autumn 1650	1651–5 West Country? 1655 Sandwich, Kent; Harberton then Barnstaple, Devon	Minister. After 1660 Rotterdam; Suffolk; Dublin; London [P]
Mather Samuel	Much Woolton, Lancashire	Dorchester; Harvard, BA 1643; Fellow, 1650	1635 with parents	autumn 1650	Chaplain, Magdalen College Oxford; Leith, Scotland; Dublin, Ireland	Minister: college chaplain, army chaplain, government preacher; nonconformist [P]
Matthews Lemuel		Yarmouth; Hull; Malden	b. NE 1644	probably 1655	Swansea; Lincoln College Oxford 1661	Conformist minister, Ireland
Matthews Manasseh		Yarmouth; Hull; Malden; Harvard 1651–5, no degree	b. NE 1640/1	1655	1658 to Jesus College, Oxford	Conformist; Vicar of Swansea 1670
Matthews Marmaduke & Katherine	Llangyfelach, Glamorgan	Yarmouth; Hull; Malden	1638	1654 or 55	Swansea	Minister [P]
Matthews Mordecai		Yarmouth; Hull; Malden Harvard BA 1655	b. NE	1655	Llancarfan 1657, Reynoldston 1661	Minister; lost his living at the Restoration, conformed 1661
Mayhew Thomas Jr	Watertown; Nantucket, Martha's Vineyard			Nov. 1657	Died at sea	Minister
Milam [Millard] John	Boston?			probably 1654	Waterford, Ireland	Cooper? Minister in Ireland

NAME	NE settlement	OE origins	To NE	Left NE	OE resettlement [* To NE again 1660+]	Occupation / Publications [P]
Mildmay William	at Harvard from 1644; BA 1647, 1650	Wanstead, Essex; son of Sir Henry Mildmay	1644	1651		
Morse [Mosse] John & Mary [Jupe]	Boston, in the household of Robert Keayne	London?		c.1654 with Benjamin Jupe	London	Mary inherited houses with her brother Jupe
Moxon George & Ann	Dorchester briefly; Springfield 1636–52	Wakefield, Yorks.; St Helen's, Lancashire	1636	1652	Astbury, Cheshire	Naval chaplain? Parish minister
Moxon George Jr	perhaps in NE	Lancashire		1652?	Haverhill, Suffolk; Radwinter, Essex; in Shropshire after 1660	Naval chaplain? Parish minister
Munnings Edmund	Dorchester	Dengie, Essex	1635	1651 / 1653	Dengie/Tillingham, Essex	
Munnings Hopestill	Dorchester		b. NE 1637	1651 / 1653	Dengie/Tillingham, Essex	
Munnings Takeheed	Dorchester		b. NE 1640	1651 / 1653	Dengie/Tillingham, Essex	
Nelson Joan, Mercy, Samuel [Dummer]	Rowley	Badgeworth, Gloucestershire		before 1654	Stoneham, Hampshire, close to her relative Stephen Dummer	Widow of Thomas Nelson; took her young family to OE
Nelson Thomas	Boston briefly; prominent in Rowley	Cottingham then Rowley, Yorkshire	1637	1645	Died 1648, perhaps on the return voyage to NE	
Newgate Nathaniel	Boston	London and Bury St Edmunds, Suffolk		OE 1649–53? 1668	London?	Merchant

Name	New England	Origin	Arrived	Left	English destination	Notes
Newman Robert	Boston; New Haven	London	arrived March 1633/4	late 1649 / early 1650	London	'Citizen and vintner' of London, 1654
Nicholson, Francis & son Robert	Marblehead		there 1648	by 1656	Ipswich, Suffolk	
Norcrosse Jeremiah	Watertown	London	1638	1654	Kent / Norfolk, with Nathaniel	
Norcrosse Nathaniel & Mary	Watertown, son of Jeremiah; Lancaster; Exeter then York	London; St Catherine's Cambridge	1638 / 39	late 1649	Dover, Kent; Little Walsingham, Egmere and Waterden in Norfolk; London	Minister: naval chaplain, then parish minister
Norton Henry	York	Sharpenhoe, Bedfordshire		Oct. 1657		
Oakes Urian	Cambridge; Harvard, BA 1649, MA, Fellow		1642, with parents	by July 1656	Titchfield, Hampshire *To NE 1671	Minister; President of Harvard, 1675–81 [P]
Oliver Mary & children	Salem	Norwich	1637	1651	Norwich	Ordered to go to her husband, Thomas
Oliver Thomas	Salem	Norwich	1637	before 1648	Norwich *To NE 1663	Clothworker
Ottley Adam & Ann [Humfrey]	Lynn			1644	Ann later m. Particular Baptist minister John Miles of Wales	*Ann returned to NE mid-1660s, with John Miles
Page Margaret	Salem: a 'lazy, idle and loitering person'		before 1644	autumn 1647		Salem paid £5 to send her to England
Palgrave Anna	Charlestown		1630	by 1655	Stepney, Middlesex, to join a daughter; to Roxbury NE, 1660s, to rejoin another daughter	Widow of Richard Palgrave, physician

NAME	NE settlement	OE origins	To NE	Left NE	OE resettlement [* To NE again 1660+]	Occupation / Publications [P]
Pardon William	Weymouth			Dec. 1645	Attorney for business in Broadway, Somerset, & Plymouth, Devon	Labourer
Parish Thomas & Mary [Danforth]	Watertown; Cambridge 1637–55	Nayland, Suffolk?	1635	1655	Nayland, Suffolk	Clothier; physician?
Parish Thomas Jr	Cambridge; Harvard BA 1659		b. NE, son of the above	1659	Incorporated BA at Cambridge, 1660	In trouble at Harvard for town/gown fights
Parrat Francis	Rowley: town clerk & deacon of church	Sutterton, Lincolnshire	by 1638?	Nov. 1655	Died at sea or in England, by 1656	
Parsons William & Ruth	Boston		1635	late 1654	London *To NE, died in Boston	Joiner; also said to be a tailor. Supported Venner's Rebellion, 1661
Patient Thomas & Sarah	Salem		by 1641	1642	London; Dublin; Bristol	A Baptist minister after he left NE [P]
Payne Edward	Lynn; Charlestown; Dover		1638	1649		
Peck Robert & Ann (or Martha?) & son Joseph	Hingham	Hingham, Norfolk	1638	1641 [daughter Ann stayed]	Hingham, Norfolk	Minister
Pelham Elizabeth	Cambridge; m. (2) Herbert Pelham	b. Yorkshire; m. (1) Richard Harlakenden of Essex	1635 with Harlakenden	late 1646 / early 1647	Bures, Essex	
Pelham Frances & Mary	daughters of Elizabeth & Herbert		b. NE	late 1646 /early 1647	Bures, Essex	

Pelham Herbert	Cambridge	Bures, Essex	1638	late 1646/early 1647	Bures, Essex; child baptised Stepney, Middlesex, 1647	Gentleman; Essex JP, 1650s
Pelham Jemima, Katherine, Penelope, Waldegrave	Cambridge, children of Herbert	Bures, Essex	1638 with father	late 1646/early 1647	Bures, Essex	Penelope m. Josiah Winslow & returned to NE in 1655
Pelham John	brother of Herbert		1635	1635?		
Pelham Nathaniel	son of Herbert; Harvard BA 1651		1638	1657	Died at sea on voyage home	
Pelham William	Watertown 1630–1; Sudbury	brother of Herbert	(1) 1630 (2) by 1645	(1) 1631? (2) 1647		Gentleman
Pemberton John	Boston; Newbury 1638	Essex?	1632	between 1647 and 1653	Lawford, Essex	Weaver
Pester William	Salem		1637	c.1642		His wife petitioned in 1652 for permission to remarry; nothing had been heard of William
Peter Deliverance, wife of Hugh	Boston; Salem		1638	(1) 1643–6; (2) 1649	London	
Peter Elizabeth	Salem		b. NE	probably 1649	London, with her father Hugh	
Peter Hugh	Salem	b. Cornwall; Essex, London, Rotterdam	1635	1641	Army chaplain; later a chaplain to Cromwell	Minister; agent for Massachusetts [P]
Peter Thomas	Saybrook	Mylor, Cornwall	1644	Dec. 1646	Mylor, Cornwall	Minister [P]
Phillip John & Elizabeth [Ames]	Salem; Cambridge; Dedham	Wrentham, Suffolk	1638	Oct. 1641	Wrentham, Suffolk	Minister [P]

NAME	NE settlement	OE origins	To NE	Left NE	OE resettlement [* To NE again 1660+]	Occupation / Publications [P]
Pierce [Pearse] John				by 1656	Wapping; admitted to Stepney church, Middlesex, 1656	A mariner 'late of New England'
Pierce Mark	New Haven		by 1639	1650? by 1654	London	New Haven surveyor, schoolteacher
Pierce [Peirce] William	Boston		1632	by 1660 living in OE	London	Sea-captain, to OE every year
Pratt Abraham & Joanna	Cambridge	Wood Ditton, Cambridgeshire	1629	1644	Died at sea	Bay Company surgeon, 1629
Prichard Hugh	Gloucester; Roxbury, a leading citizen	Denbighshire?	1640 with R. Blinman?	c.1650	1657 in Broughton, Denbighshire	
Pynchon William, Frances, Joseph	Roxbury; Springfield	Springfield, Essex	1630	Sept. 1652	Wraisbury, Buckinghamshire	Merchant, entrepreneur [P]
Rainborowe [Rainsborough] William	Charlestown; Watertown 1640		1639	by 1642	Northamptonshire and London	Parliamentarian army officer; originally a mariner
Rashley [Henry?]	Boston			to OE several years before 1651?		His wife Susanna petitioned for permission to remarry
Rashley Jonathan	Son of Thomas, baptised at Boston, 1645		b. NE	1646?	Wiltshire; later a conformist minister	[His younger brother Nathaniel, b. OE, also conformed]
Rashley Thomas & wife	Cape Ann; Exeter; Boston	Charterhouse; Trinity College, Cambridge	late 1630s	1646?	Barford St Martin, Wiltshire, by 1648; chaplain of St Cross, Winchester; preacher at Salisbury cathedral	Minister

Name	New England	English origin	Arrived	Returned	English destination	Notes
Rawson Edward	Newbury, Boston; Harvard, BA 1653	Gillingham, Dorset	1637, with parents	1654	Horsmonden, Kent 1655–61; Wooburn, Bucks.	Minister [conformed 1661]
Reade Thomas	Salem	Wickford, Essex	1635?	by 1645	Parliamentary army in England, Scotland	Yeoman
Reed William & Mabel	Dorchester; Rehoboth; Woburn	Newcastle-upon-Tyne?	1635	soon after 1652	Newcastle-upon-Tyne *Mabel to NE 1661	
Richards John	Weymouth			in OE 1650		
Ridge William				1643? with Garret Trout	'Soldier to Capt. William Jackson'	Parliamentary soldier? Died 25 Oct. 1643
Roberts John	New Haven			early 1654	London	
Roberts William	Charlestown			by 1646	Middlesex	Wine cooper
Rowe Nathaniel	Cambridge; Lynn; Harvard, but boarded out after N. Eaton dismissed	London; son of the merchant & regicide Owen Rowe	1637 with Davenport & T. Eaton	c.1642	London	
Sadler John, wife & son Robert	Marshfield 1640; Gloucester 1642	Wales, Gloucestershire?	1640 with R. Blinman	1650? with wife & Robert 1651	Whixall then Ludlow, Shropshire	Minister
Sadler Richard	Lynn; Reading	b. Worcester; Emmanuel, Cambridge	1638	Nov. 1646		
Saltonstall Abigail, Elizabeth, Gurdon, Muriel, Richard	Watertown	children of Richard & Muriel	b. NE except Muriel	autumn 1649	Richard and Gurdon in London	Richard: merchant tailor
Saltonstall Henry	Watertown; Harvard, BA 1643	brother of Richard	1638	early 1644	Leiden; MD Padua, 1649; Fellow, New College, Oxford	Doctor of Physic
Saltonstall Muriel [Gurdon]	Watertown	Assington, Suffolk	1635	autumn 1645	Died Didsbury, Cheshire 1667	

NAME	NE settlement	OE origins	To NE	Left NE	OE resettlement [* To NE again 1660+]	Occupation / Publications [P]
Saltonstall Richard	Watertown	Wragby, Yorkshire	1630, 1635	autumn 1645 autumn 1649	London; Scotland; Cheshire; Shropshire	Commissioner for Customs and Excise
Sampson Robert	Boston?	Kersey, near Groton, Suffolk	1630			
Sams John	Roxbury	Langford, Essex	1640?	in or soon after 1640	West Farleigh, Kent; Kelvedon & later Coggeshall, Essex	Minister
Sanborn Stephen	Hampton		1632	by autumn 1651	London? with grandfather Stephen Bachiler	
Saunders John, Esther & family	Newbury; Salisbury	Whiteparish, Wiltshire	1635		Wiltshire	
Saunderson Edward	Watertown; Cambridge			after 1646?		
Saxton Peter	Scituate; Boston	b. Yorkshire; Leeds Grammar School; Edlington, Yorkshire	1640	August 1641	Vicar of Leeds, 1646–51	Minister
Scott Thomas	Ipswich	Rattlesden, Suffolk	1634 with father	before 1656		Son of Thomas Scott, glover
Sedgwick Hannah, Robert, Samuel, Sarah [Leverett], William	Charlestown; children of Robert & Joanna		b. NE	1655–7	London? Robert & William later to NE	Samuel: London, clothworker
Sedgwick Joanna	Charlestown	Southwark	1635?	by Nov. 1655	1657 at Stepney; later at Norwich	m. in OE Thomas Allen of Norwich, once of Charlestown
Sedgwick Robert	Charlestown	Woburn, Bedfordshire; Southwark	1635?	1653, 1654	Commanded fleets against the Dutch & French in NE, and the Spanish in Caribbean	Merchant; his son-in-law was John Leverett

Seely Robert	Watertown; Wethersfield; New Haven; later Saybrook, Stratford	London, St Stephen's Coleman Street		1646 (visited); 1659–61	*To NE 1661	Surveyor, shoemaker
Sewall Henry Jr	Ipswich; Newbury	Coventry; Warwick	1634	winter 1646	Warwick; North Baddesley, Hampshire	Minister; to NE 1658 to settle father's estate
Sewall Jane [Dummer] & children	Newbury	Bishopstoke, Hampshire	1638 with parents	winter 1646	As Henry *To NE 1661	
Sheafe Edmund	Boston			by 1647	1647 made will in London; died 1649	
Shepard Hannah & Hannah Jr	Cambridge		1635	1649/50?	In Ireland 1658	
Shepard Samuel	Cambridge	Northamptonshire	1635	1641? late 1645	England, Ireland	Major, Parliamentary army
Sherman Edmund	Boston; Watertown	Dedham, Essex	by 1632	after 1636		Clothier
Smith Henry, Ann (Pynchon) & children	Dorchester; Springfield		1630	1652; Ann & children 1654	Wraisbury, Buckinghamshire	
Smith Nathaniel	Malden			early 1649	To reclaim 'plundered estate' in OE	
Smith Richard	Ipswich	Shropham, Norfolk	by 1641	autumn 1647?	Shropham, Norfolk	
Smith Robert & Ann		London	c.1637, with Robert's sister Mary	by 1648	Kept the Golden Lion Tavern, Fetter Lane, London	Wine cooper; wanted Mary to send a nephew home from NE, to adopt
Smith Zephaniah	Windsor			Dec. 1648	Ireland by 1656	Tanner; minister
Stansby John	Cambridge	Lavenham, Suffolk	1636	1640s		Clothier, farmer

NAME	NE settlement	OE origins	To NE	Left NE	OE resettlement [* To NE again 1660+]	Occupation / Publications [P]
Starkey [Stirk] George	Harvard, BA 1646, MA	Bermuda, son of Rev. George Stirk	1639	after 1648, by late 1656	London; said to have died in the Plague, 1665	Doctor; published medical tracts [P]
Starr Comfort	Cambridge; Harvard, BA 1647, Fellow 1650	Ashford, Kent	1635, with parents	late 1650	Cumberland, 1651–60; to Kent	Minister; inherited his father's Ashford house
Stollyon [Stolion] Abraham	New Haven	London, lands in Sussex	by 1640, with mother	c.1645, again 1646	London, Sussex?	
Stone John	Hartford; Harvard, BA 1653		b. NE, son of Samuel Stone	1653	1654–60 Pembroke College, Cambridge	Fellow, died 1660
Storer Richard	Boston, related to John Hull, master of the mint		1635	after 1639, by 1643		
Stoughton Israel	Dorchester	Coggeshall, Essex; Rotherhithe, Surrey	1632	1643	London; Lieut. Col. to Thomas Rainborowe; died at Lincoln, 1644	Merchant; Parliamentarian army officer
Stoughton William	Dorchester; Harvard, BA 1650. Dorchester 1662–1701	Rotherhithe, Surrey	1632	soon after August 1651	MA 1653, New College, Oxford; Scotland; Sussex *To NE 1662	Fellow, minister, ejected 1660; colonial official and preacher
Swinfield Raphael		Ireland		by 1653	Dublin, Ireland	Probably a mariner
Swinnock Joseph	Harvard, but not a graduate			by autumn 1648?	Chaplain, New College Oxford; London	Minister [conformed]
Tare Richard & Jane	Boston			Jane followed Richard 1656		Jane took her sons: Noah, Thomas Parker
Thompson Edmund & Martha	Salem	Framlingham, Suffolk	1637 or 1638	Dec. 1647	Yarmouth, Norfolk	Mariner

Name	New England	English origin	Arrived	Left	Destination	Notes
Thomson Robert	Boston		1639, 'late of London'	by 1642	London	Merchant; parliamentarian army officer; navy commissioner
Thornton Thomas	Dorchester; Windsor; Stratford; Yarmouth, 1663; d. Boston 1700	Hertfordshire	1633	after 1653	Ireland by 1654 *To NE 1663	Tanner; minister in Ireland
Thurston Richard & Martha	Boston; Martha sister of Rebecca Lord			by Jan. 1656/7 with the Lords	New Gravel Lane, Stepney, Middlesex	Mariner
Tillam Thomas		born a Catholic, by his own account	1638	early 1640s	London; Hexham, Northumberland; Essex; the Netherlands; the Palatinate	Baptist minister, Fifth Monarchist, Seventh Day Sabbatarian
Tracy Stephen		Yarmouth, Norfolk	1623	1655		Weaver
Travers Henry	Newbury	Wiltshire or Hampshire	1634	1648		His wife said he had deserted her
Trotman John & Katherine	Roxbury, then Boston			J. 1644? K. summer 1645	London	With William Ridge?
Trout Garret				1643?	Parliamentary army?	
Trowbridge Thomas	Boston; New Haven		by 1639	left by 1647	London?	In debt to Robert Keayne of Boston
Turner Nathaniel	New Haven			Jan. 1645/6	Died at sea	
Tuttle Joanna	Ipswich; Boston	St Alban's, Hertfordshire	1635	probably autumn 1655	Carrickfergus, Ireland	Daughter Hannah (b. NE) went to Ireland
Tuttle John	Ipswich; Boston	St Alban's, Hertfordshire	1635, with Joanna & 8 children	late 1650	Carrickfergus, Ireland, by 1654	Mercer OE; Treasury official in Ireland
Vassall William	Boston; Roxbury; Scituate	Stepney, Middlesex; Prittlewell, Essex	1630	1646	London; 1650 to Barbados	Merchant

NAME	NE settlement	OE origins	To NE	Left NE	OE resettlement [*To NE again 1660+]	Occupation / Publications [P]
Venner Thomas & Alice	Salem; Boston			autumn 1651 1656 [Alice]	London	Cooper; Fifth Monarchist
Vermace Mark	Salem	Yarmouth, Norfolk?	by 1638	by Jan. 1651/2	Yarmouth, Norfolk	
Wade Joan	Dorchester; Hartford		1635	c.1642	Deserted her husband	Robert Wade granted a divorce 1657
Waldron [**Waldern**] Edward	Ipswich			after 1642	Alcester, Warwickshire in 1650?	
Walver Abraham	Harvard, BA 1647; left before MA	?	1644, to study at Harvard?	by March 1651	Preacher 'in his own county'; in Ireland from 1654	Minister
Ward James	Ipswich; Harvard, BA 1645, certificate 1646		1634	late 1646	Incorp. BA Oxford 1648; 1649 B. of Physic	Physician
Ward Nathaniel	Ipswich	Haverhill, Suffolk; Stondon Massey, Essex	1634	late 1646	Shenfield, Essex	Minister [P]
Waterhouse Thomas, Ann [& Anna, b. NE]	Dorchester	London; Coddenham, Suffolk	by 1639	by June 1643; inherited land in Coddenham	Colchester; preacher & parish minister, Essex/ Suffolk border	Colchester Grammar School, 1643–7; minister 1652–62
Wathen Thomas	Gloucester	St Stephen's, Bristol; son of Edward Wathen, baptised 1629	with parents	with 'Robert Gray', during the Civil War	Soldier in 'Capt. Wal's service'; with Prince Rupert' (i.e. Royalist?)	Died by 1652
Weld Edmund	Roxbury; Harvard, BA 1650	Terling, Essex; son of Thomas & Judith	1632	probably 1650	Ireland, 1654– ?	Minister
Weld John	Roxbury; Harvard, no degree	Terling, Essex; brother of Edmund	1632	1643? by 1645	Leicestershire, 1645; Sunderland 1651; Co. Durham 1655	Minister [conformed 1666, ordained at Durham 1669]

Weld Thomas & Judith	Roxbury	Terling, Essex	1632	1641 as agent Judith by 1643	London; Leicestershire; Gateshead	Minister; agent for Massachusetts	[P]
Westgate John	Boston (lived in John Cotton's household)		by 1640	before 1646	Pulham St Mary and Harleston, Norfolk		[P]
Wheelwright John	Boston; Exeter; Wells	Saleby & Bilsby, Lincolnshire	1636	1655	Belleau, Aby & Swaby, Lincs. *To NE 1662	Minister	
White Nathaniel	Harvard, BA 1646, MA 1649	[Bermuda, son of Rev. Nathaniel White]	1643?	1653	In OE 1668		
Whitfield Henry & Dorothy	Guilford	Ockley, Surrey	1639	1650	Winchester; Hampshire	Minister; d. 1657	[P]
Whitfield John, Mary	Guilford	Ockley, Surrey	1639 with parents	1650 with parents?	Mary in Winchester 1657		
Whitfield Nathaniel	Guilford, New Haven	Ockley, Surrey	1639	1654	Winchester; London		
Whiting John & Sybil [Collins]	Lynn; Harvard, BA 1657	father (Samuel) came from Skirbeck, Lincs.	b. NE?	1657?	Lincolnshire	Conformist minister	
Wilkes Thomas	Salem			before 1662		Haberdasher	
Willis Thomas	Lynn	Isleworth, Middlesex	by 1633	1641 or 1642	Isleworth, Middlesex	Schoolmaster	
Willis Thomas Jr	Lynn	Isleworth, Middlesex	by 1633	1641 or 1642	Vicar of Twickenham, Middlesex, 1646–60	Minister; brother-in-law to John Knowles	
Willoughby Francis & Sarah	Charlestown	Wapping	1638	visited OE 1640s, resettled 1650	Portsmouth, London *To NE 1662	Shipwright; navy commissioner; MP	
Winslow Edward	Plymouth	Droitwich; Leiden	Mayflower, 1620	1646	London; died 1655, on expedition to Caribbean	Gentleman	[P]

NAME	NE settlement	OE origins	To NE	Left NE	OE resettlement [* To NE again 1660+]	Occupation / Publications [P]
Winslow Gilbert	Plymouth, brother of Edward	Droitwich	*Mayflower*, 1620	'after some years'		
Winslow Josiah	Plymouth; Harvard, 1640s, but no degree	b. NE	b. NE	1651	London & Bures, Essex; to NE again 1655	m. Penelope Pelham in London; later, Gov. of Plymouth Colony
Winthrop Fitz John	Ipswich, eldest son of John Winthrop Jr		b. NE	by late 1657	Scotland; England 1660 *To NE 1663	Army officer; later, Gov. of Connecticut
Winthrop Stephen & Judith [Rainborowe]	Boston, son of Governor John Winthrop	Groton, Suffolk	1630	1644–5, 1646; Judith by March 1648	Parliamentary army, 1640s; Scotland 1650s	Colonel; d. 1658
Witheredge Edward	Boston			by 1651	1651 daughter baptised at Stepney, Middlesex	Mariner
Woodbridge Benjamin	Newbury; Harvard, BA 1642	Stanton Fitzwarren, Wiltshire; Magdalen Hall, Oxford, 1638	1639	1647?	MA Magdalen Hall, Oxford, 1648; Newbury, Berkshire	Minister; at the Restoration offered a canonry at Windsor but would not conform [P]
Woodbridge John & Mercy	Newbury	Stanton Fitzwarren, Wiltshire	1634	1647	Barford St Martin, Wiltshire, 1650–60 *To NE 1663	Minister; chaplain to Parliamentary leaders negotiating with Charles I, 1648
Wyllys George Jr	Massachusetts; Hartford 1638	Fenny Compton, Warwickshire	early 1630s 1639	1638? by March 1639/40	Fenny Compton, Warwickshire	Gentleman
Yale David, Ursula; David, Elihu, Theophilus	Boston	Denbighshire; London	1637 [b. NE 1645, 1649, 1651]	1652	Denbighshire; London	Merchant
Yale Thomas	New Haven	Denbighshire; London	1637	1656	London; returned to NE 1659 and stayed on	Merchant

SOURCES Early records, and recent works which include: Susan Hardman, 'Return Migration from New England to England, 1640–1660' (PhD diss., University of Kent at Canterbury, 1986); *The New England Historical and Genealogical Register* (online database: www.NewEnglandAncestors.org, New England Historic Genealogical Society, 2001–), orig. pub. New England Historic Genealogical Society, *The New England Historical and Genealogical Register*, Boston, Mass., 1847–); *The Great Migration Begins: Immigrants to New England 1620–1633, Volumes I–III* (online database: www.NewEnglandAncestors.org, New England Historic Genealogical Society, 2002), orig. pub. Robert Charles Anderson, ed., *The Great Migration Begins: Immigrants to New England 1620–1633, Volumes I–III*, 3 vols, New England Historic Genealogical Society, 1995; Robert Charles Anderson, ed., *The Great Migration: Immigrants to New England* (Boston: Great Migration Study Project, New England Historic Genealogical Society, 1999–); Annie Haven Thwing, 'Inhabitants and Estates of the Town of Boston, 1630–1800' [electronic resource] and *The Crooked and Narrow Streets of the Town of Boston, 1630–1822* (CD ROM, Boston: Massachusetts Historical Society and New England Historic Genealogical Society, 2001); David Cressy, *Coming Over: Migration and Communication between England and New England in the Seventeenth Century* (Cambridge: Cambridge University Press, 1987); Alison Games, *Migration and the Origins of the English Atlantic World* (Cambridge, Mass., and London: Harvard University Press, 2001); Roger Thompson, *Mobility and Migration: East Anglian Founders of New England* (Amherst: University of Massachusetts Press, 1994); *ANB; CR; ODNB;* Sibley.

Appendix 3 NEW ENGLAND'S MINISTERS: THE FIRST GENERATION

Listed alphabetically by diocese of origin.

*   *Returned to England (includes those who returned to America after 1660).*
[*] *Visited England.*
{ } *Schoolmaster (required a license from the bishop; not necessarily ordained, though some ministers chose to be schoolmasters to avoid pressure for conformity).*

Canterbury

Partridge, Ralph (1579–1658), baptised at Sutton Valence, Kent. Trinity, Cambridge, BA 1600, MA 1603. Curate of Sutton-by-Dover, Kent, 1607–34. Emigrated 1636. 'A hunted partridge . . . being distressed by the ecclesiastical setters, had no defence, neither of beak nor claw, but a flight over the ocean.'[1] Duxbury, Massachusetts, 1637–58. 'Radulphus Partrich', CCEd Person ID 39021.

{**Witherell** [**Witherall**], **William** (1600–1684), schoolmaster, Boughton Monchelsea parish school, 1625; later of Maidstone, Kent. Accused of teaching only the catechism of William Perkins and the writings of Thomas Wilson. Emigrated 1635. 'William Witherall', CCEd Person 1D 39152.}[2]

Chester

{**Dunster, Henry** (bap. 1609, d. 1659), schoolmaster and Curate at Bury, Lancashire, 1634. Emigrated 1640. The first President of Harvard, 1640–54; Scituate 1654–9. *ODNB, ANB*; 'Henry Dunster', CCEd Person ID 33264.}

***Eaton, Samuel** (d. 1665), Rector of West Kirby, in the Wirral, 1625; suspended and ejected, 1632. To the Netherlands 1634, where he met John Davenport; returned to England, still under censure; emigrated 1637 with his brother Theophilus Eaton and Davenport. Began a settlement at Totoket (Branford, Connecticut). Left for England late in 1640. *ODNB, CR.*

Mather, Richard (1596–1669), minister at Toxteth Park, Lancashire; suspended August 1633; sailed for New England 1635. Dorchester, Massachusetts, 1635–69. *ODNB, ANB.*

*Moxon, George (1602–1687), Curate of St Helen's, Lancashire, in 1628; emigrated 1636; cited for nonconformity after his departure. Springfield, Massachusetts, 1636–52. Returned to England 1652. *ODNB, CR*; 'Georgius Moxon', CCEd Person ID 35220.

Thompson [Tompson], William (1598–1666), Curate of the chapelry of Newton, in the parish of Winwick, Lancashire; in New England by August 1637, and initially joined Richard Mather's church. York, Maine, 1637–9; Quincy, Massachusetts, 1639–59. Mather and Thompson drew up a statement of regret about their conformity in England 'though what we did, we bless God, it was ignorantly'. Thompson regretted a great deal more besides: 'maypoles and horse races and bowling alleys . . . football . . . He fears Lancashire fares worse for his sins'.[3] 'William Tompson', CCEd Person ID 34721.

Chichester

*Blackwood, Christopher (1607/8–1670), Vicar of Stockbury, Kent, 1631; Curate of Rye, Sussex, 1632–5. Accused of keeping the communion table in the wrong place. Left Rye at the time of Sir Nathanael Brent's visitation as Laud's Vicar-General.[4] Emigrated 1640. Scituate, Plymouth Colony, 1641–2. Returned to England 1642. A Baptist. *ODNB.*

Coventry and Lichfield

Blakeman, Adam (1599–1665), matriculated at Oxford, 1617; preached in Leicestershire, then Derbyshire. Emigrated 1638, 'from the storm that began to look black upon him'. Initially settled at Guilford; Stratford, 1640–65.[5]

Exeter

*Hooke, William (1601–1678), Rector of Upper Clatford, Hampshire, 1627–31; Vicar of Axmouth, Devon, 1632. Emigrated to New England *c.*1637. His wife was Jane Whalley, niece to Lady Joan Barrington, and a cousin of Oliver Cromwell. Taunton, 1640/1–4; New Haven 1644–56. Returned to England. *ODNB, CR.*

*Hull, Joseph (1595–1665), Rector of Northleigh, Devon, 1621–35. Emigrated in 1635 from Weymouth, Dorset, to Weymouth, Massachusetts, with twenty-one Somerset families, including a son of Richard Bernard (*ODNB*). Moved frequently in New England: Hingham, Barnstable, Yarmouth, York (Maine), Isles of Shoals. Returned to England by 1648. *CR.*

*Larkham, Thomas (1602–1669), Vicar of Northam, Devon, from 1626 until deprived for absence and negligence, 1640. Claimed he had been cited before High Commission and Star Chamber (but no evidence survives to prove or disprove this). Emigrated 1639. To Dover [Northam], in what is now New Hampshire, 1640; in conflict with Hanserd Knollys. To England 1642. *ODNB, CR.*

Maverick, John (1578–1636), Rector of Beaworthy, Devon, 1615–29; came on the *Mary and John*, 1630, with John Warham and others. Dorchester, Massachusetts, 1630–6.

Walton, William (d. 1668), Vicar or Curate of Seaton, Devon; married a niece of John White, minister of Dorchester, Dorset. Emigrated 1635. Marblehead 1637–68, as minister to the fishermen's church.

Warham, John (1595–1670), as minister at Crewkerne, Somerset, he was pressed to conform during Laud's tenure as Bishop of Bath and Wells; moved to a living at St Sidwell's, Exeter. Emigrated in 1630, with John Maverick and others. Dorchester, Massachusetts, 1630–5; Windsor, Connecticut, 1636–70.

Hereford

*Blinman, Richard (1608–1687), ordained 1636; reported in 1639 to have been recently put out of a living, but preaching in Herefordshire. This followed pressure for conformity from Bishop George Coke and his Archdeacon Morgan Godwyn in Shropshire.[6] Emigrated 1640. Gloucester, Massachusetts, 1642–50; New London 1650–8; New Haven 1658–9. Returned to England 1659. *CR.*

Lincoln[7]

Archdeaconry of Bedford

*Brecy, possibly John Brecy, son of Edmund of Malden or Wolton, Bedfordshire; probably ordained before emigration, but no record survives of this or of his holding office in New England. Took oath of fidelity at New Haven, 1644; children Susanna and John baptised there; sold land 1647. Mrs

'Bressey', a member of the church at New Haven, returned to England 1647, carrying a letter from John Davenport to Lady Mary Vere.[8]

Bulkeley, Peter (1583–1659), Rector of Odell, Bedfordshire, 1610–35 (in succession to his father). Laud reported in 1634 that 'Buckley' had been 'sent to the High Commission for inconformity'. Emigrated 1635. Both he and Zechariah Symmes left at a time of increased pressure for conformity coinciding with the visitation by Sir Nathanael Brent as Laud's Vicar-General.[9] Minister at Concord, Massachusetts, 1635–59. *ODNB, ANB.*

Symmes, Zechariah/Zachary (1599–1671), Vicar of Dunstable, Bedfordshire, 1625–32. Resigned under pressure. Emigrated 1634. Charlestown, Massachusetts, 1634–71.

Archdeaconry of Buckingham[10]

Lenthall, Robert (d. 1658), Rector of Aston Sandford, Buckinghamshire, 1627–38; 1638 to Weymouth, Massachusetts, at the invitation of his former parishioners; schoolmaster at Newport, Rhode Island, 1640. Returned to England by 1643.

Worcester, William (1595–1662), Vicar of Olney, Buckinghamshire, 1624–36. Salisbury, Massachusetts, 1636–62.

Archdeaconry of Huntingdon

Fordham, Robert (d. 1674), Vicar of Flamstead, Hertfordshire. Emigrated 1638. Initially at Cambridge, Massachusetts; Sudbury, 1643–4, then Hempstead, Long Island; minister at Southampton, Long Island, c.1650–74.

Jones, John (c.1592–1665), probably Rector of Abbots Ripton, Huntingdonshire, 1619–30. Deprived, 1630. Sailed to New England on the *Defence*, 1635, with Thomas Shepard. In Concord with Peter Bulkeley, 1635–44; Fairfield, Connecticut, 1644–65.

Archdeaconry of Leicester

Higginson, Francis (1586–1630), minister at Claybrooke, Leicestershire; deprived of his licence to preach in 1627. The Court of High Commission began proceedings against him in 1628. He offered himself as a chaplain to the New England Company. Salem, Massachusetts, 1629–30. *ODNB, ANB.*

Archdeaconry of Lincoln

Cobbett, Thomas (1608–1685), b. Newbury, Berkshire; St Mary's Hall, Oxford, BA 1628, MA 1632. Studied with William Twisse (*ODNB*) at Newbury. A preacher in Lincolnshire 'from whence being driven by a storm of persecution upon the reforming and puritan part of the nation, he came over unto New England in the same vessel as Mr [John] Davenport', in 1637.[11] Lynn, Massachusetts, 1637–55 as assistant to Samuel Whiting, known to him from Lincolnshire. Ipswich, Massachusetts, 1655–86.

Cotton, John (1585–1652), Vicar of Boston, 1612. Resigned in 1633, under threat of action from the Court of High Commission. Boston, Massachusetts, 1633–52. *ODNB, ANB.*

{*James, Thomas (1595–1682/3), baptised in Boston, Lincolnshire, son of the Rector of Skirbeck. Schoolmaster at Boston, 1619. Emigrated 1632. Charlestown 1632–6; New Haven 1636–42; Virginia 1642–3. Returned to England c.1648. *CR.*}

[Johnson, Isaac (c.1600–1630), Emmanuel; Grays Inn, 1620/1; ordained 1625 but never held a living; practised as a lawyer. 1625 married a daughter of the Earl of Lincoln. Emigrated 1630: he and his wife died that summer. Not a minister in New England. *ODNB.*]

*Knollys, Hanserd (1598–1691), Vicar of Humberston, Lincolnshire, 1629–34. Resigned, probably c.1634. Schoolmaster and preacher, with the knowledge of Bishop John Williams. Renounced his ordination c.1636, probably under the influence of John Wheelwright. Arrested by the Court of High Commission in 1636 but secured release. In London until 1638, when he emigrated. Returned to England 1641, and became a Baptist. *ODNB.*

Skelton, Samuel (1584–1634), Curate then Rector of Sempringham, Lincolnshire, 1615–20; domestic chaplain to the Earl of Lincoln, c.1622–9. Emigrated 1629. Salem, Massachusetts, 1629–34.

*Wheelwright, John (1592?–1679), Vicar of Bilsby, Lincolnshire, 1623–32. Convicted of simony, 1632, for selling his living back to his patron. Preacher in Lincolnshire, with the tacit permission of Bishop Williams. Emigrated 1636. Joined the church at Boston. A key figure in the Antinomian Controversy, 1636–7. Banished. Minister at Exeter, 1638–42; Wells, 1643–4; Hampton 1647–55. In England 1655–62. Returned to New England, 1662. *ODNB, ANB.*

Whiting, Samuel (1597–1679), domestic chaplain at Stiffkey, Norfolk, 1621; Curate of Lynn, Norfolk, 1624; Rector of Skirbeck, Lincolnshire, 1625–36. Originally from Boston, Lincolnshire: the Earl of Lincoln intervened when his case came to the Court of High Commission. Emigrated 1636. Lynn, Massachusetts, 1636–79.

London

*Bright, Francis (c. 1603–?), Curate of Rayleigh, Essex, 1625–9. Signed a contract to work in New England for three years. Emigrated 1629, to Salem, Massachusetts; returned to England, 1630.

[Chauncy, Charles: see Peterborough]

Davenport, John (1597–1670), Vicar of St Stephen's, Coleman Street, London, 1625. Retreated to Amsterdam, late 1633. In 1636 he returned to England secretly, to prepare for emigration. Arrived in Boston June 1637. New Haven, 1638–67; Boston 1667–70. *ODNB, ANB.*

{*Eaton, Nathaniel (bap. *c.*1610, d. 1674), schoolmaster, Salcott and Great Wigborough, Essex; ordained. To New England 1637. The first head of Harvard College, but left in disgrace, 1639; a Rector in Virginia. University of Padua, doctorates in philosophy and medicine, 1647. 1661 Rector of Bishop's Castle, Shropshire. *ODNB, ANB.*}

{Eliot, John (1604–1690), schoolmaster: Thomas Hooker's assistant at the 'puritan academy' in Little Baddow, Essex; emigrated 1631 after Hooker's flight to Holland ended his employment. Not ordained in England. Minister at Roxbury, 1632. ODNB, ANB.}

Hooker, Thomas (1586–1647), Lecturer at Chelmsford from 1625; schoolmaster 1629–30 at Little Baddow, Essex; to Holland 1631, New England 1633. 'Newtown' (Cambridge), Massachusetts, 1633–6; Hartford, Connecticut, 1636–47. *ODNB, ANB.*

*Knowles, John (*c.*1606–1685), Fellow, St Catherine's, Cambridge, 1625–35. Town lecturer, Colchester, Essex, 1635–7. To New England 1639. Watertown, Massachusetts, 1639–51. Returned to England 1651. *ODNB, CR.*

Lothropp, John (1584–1653), from 1625 pastor to a London separatist church, in succession to Henry Jacob. Imprisoned 1632; released and emigrated 1634. Minister in Plymouth Colony: Scituate, 1634–9; Barnstable, 1639–53. *ODNB, ANB.*

Norton, John (1606–1663), Curate and schoolmaster, Bishops Stortford, 1624–31; 1631–5, domestic chaplain to Sir William Masham at High Laver, Essex, succeeding Roger Williams, who had just emigrated. To New England 1635. Ipswich, Massachusetts, 1636–53 (minister from 1638); Boston, 1656–63. *ODNB, ANB.*

*Peter, Hugh (1599–1660), Lecturer at St Sepulchre's, London; suspended 1627; to Holland 1629 and again 1632–5; to New England 1635. Minister at Salem, Massachusetts. Returned to England 1641. *ODNB, ANB*.

Phillips, George (d. 1644), Vicar of Boxted, Essex, 1615–30; Watertown, Massachusetts, 1630–44. *ODNB*.

Prudden, Peter (1600–1656), a minister in Hertfordshire and the Welsh borders. To Boston and New Haven with Theophilus Eaton and John Davenport, 1637–8; later, minister at Milford, Connecticut.

[Rogers, Nathaniel – see Norwich]

Shepard, Thomas (1605–1649), Lecturer at Earls Colne, Essex, suspended 1630; a domestic chaplain in Yorkshire; then to Heddon, near Newcastle. To New England 1635. Cambridge, Massachusetts, 1636–49. *ODNB, ANB*.

[Stone, Samuel – see Peterborough]

Ward, John (1606–1693), Rector of Hadleigh, Essex, 1633–9. To New England 1639. Haverhill, Massachusetts, 1645–93.

*Ward, Nathaniel (1578–1652), Curate of St James', Piccadilly, London, 1626; Rector of Stondon Massey, Essex, 1628. Suspended at Laud's visitation, 1631; excommunicated and deprived, 1632. To New England 1634. Minister at Ipswich, Massachusetts, until 1636, when John Norton took over; continued to live at Ipswich. Returned to England 1646. *ODNB, ANB*.

*Weld, Thomas (1595–1661), Curate of Haverhill, Suffolk, 1619; Vicar of Terling, Essex, 1624–31. Deprived and excommunicated September 1631. To New England 1632, after a brief time in the Netherlands. Settled at Roxbury, Massachusetts. Returned to England 1641. *ODNB, ANB, CR*.

[*]Williams, Roger (1603–1683), chaplain to Sir William Masham, High Laver, Essex, 1629; reached Boston, Massachusetts, in February 1630/1. Minister at Salem, 1633–5; Providence, Rhode Island, 1636–83. *ODNB, ANB*.

{*Willis, Thomas (1582/3–1666), schoolmaster, Isleworth, Middlesex, c.1610–c.1633. A cousin of Governor Wyllys of Connecticut. In Lynn, Massachusetts, by 1633. Schoolmaster. In 1641 or 1642 he returned to his school at Isleworth. His son Thomas went back to be a minister in England, as did his son-in-law John Knowles (for both, see *ODNB, CR*). *ODNB*.

Norwich

*Allen, Thomas (1608–1673), Rector of St Edmund's, Norwich; suspended, excommunicated and deprived 1636; cited to High Commission; in the Netherlands for a time, then in hiding in Norwich. In New England by 1638; minister at Charlestown, Massachusetts. Returned to England 1651. *ODNB, CR*.

Allin, John (*c*.1596–1671), Curate of Wrentham, Suffolk, alongside John Phillip; in 1624 Curate and then Rector of Saxlingham, Norfolk; resigned under pressure from Wren, 1636. Emigrated 1637, with John Fiske and a company from north-east Suffolk and south Norfolk. Dedham, Massachusetts, 1637–71. *ODNB* [Allen, John].

Brown, Edmund (1606–1678), domestic chaplain at Great Bromley, Essex; Curate at Sudbury, Suffolk. Emigrated 1638. Sudbury, Massachusetts, 1640–78.

*Burdett, George (*fl.* 1624–1666), town preacher in Great Yarmouth; suspended 5 February 1634/5; appeared before the Court of High Commission, accused of schism and blasphemy for his views that access to communion should be restricted to the elect; evaded his sentence by emigrating, 1635. Salem, Massachusetts, 1635–7; then at Dover and York. He appointed himself an informant to Laud about New England. Left for England 1641.

Burr, Jonathan (1605–1641), Curate of Horringer, Suffolk; Rector of Rickinghall Superior, Suffolk, 1627–39. To New England 1639. Dorchester, Massachusetts, 1640.

Dalton, Timothy (1588–1661), Vicar of Wolverstone, Suffolk, 1616–36; in 1634 reported as a promoter of emigration, along with Samuel Ward of Ipswich; suspended by Wren, 1636. Emigrated 1636. A petition from his parishioners in later Parliamentary proceedings against Wren described him as 'forced to flee' (Tyack, 'Migration', p.100). After a short time in Massachusetts, he served as minister at the northerly settlement of Hampton, 1639–61.

{Fiske, John (1601–1677), Peterhouse BA 1629; entered the ministry; schoolmaster at his birthplace, South Elmham St James, Suffolk; practised medicine until he left for New England. Emigrated 1637. He emigrated with his wife Anne: for this, Anne's parents disinherited her. Salem. Massachusetts, 1637–40: schoolmaster, physician, part-time assistant to Hugh Peter; moved to the new settlement of Wenham in 1640; Chelmsford, Massachusetts, 1655–76.}

Hobart, Peter (1604–1678), Curate of Haverhill, Suffolk. Followed his father to NE, from his native town of Hingham, Norfolk, in 1635. Hingham, Massachusetts, 1635–78.

Leveritch, William (1603–1677), Rector of Great Livermere, near Bury St Edmunds, 1631. To New England 1633. In Dover, 1633–5. Joined the Boston church, 1635. Minister at Duxbury 1637–9; Sandwich, 1639–53; Oyster Bay, 1653–8; missionary to the Indians on Long Island, 1658–69; minister at Newton, Long Island, 1669–73, and at Greenwich, Connecticut, 1673–7.

Norris [Norice], Edward (1583/84–1659), b. Tetbury, Gloucestershire; Magdalen Hall, Oxford, BA 1607, MA 1609; early ministry at Tetbury and Horsley, Gloucestershire. Rector of Anmer, Norfolk, 1624. Opposed the antinomianism of Rice Boye and John Traske. Emigrated *c.*1639. Joined the church at Boston, 1640; Salem, Massachusetts, 1640–59. *ODNB, ANB.*

*Peck, Robert (1580–1656), Rector of Hingham, Norfolk, 1605–38; suspended and excommunicated 1636; threatened with action by the Court of High Commission; deprived 1638 for nonresidence. Hingham, Massachusetts, 1638–41. Returned to Hingham, Norfolk, 1641.

*Phillip, John (*c.*1582–1660), Rector of Wrentham, Suffolk, 1609; excommunicated for non-appearance 1636; said to be in Holland; went to New England in 1638 at the invitation of John Allin. Settled at Dedham, Massachusetts. Returned to Wrentham, 1641. *CR.*

Rogers, Nathaniel (1598–1655), Curate at Bocking, Essex, 1619–31, with Dr John Barkham, a friend of Laud. Refused to wear his surplice at a funeral; Barkham encouraged him to move to become Rector of Assington, Suffolk, 1631–6, in the diocese of Norwich, where he again came under pressure to conform. Emigrated with a company, 1636. Ipswich, Massachusetts, 1638–55. *ODNB.*

*Walker, Thomas (1603–1684), succeeded Nathaniel Rogers at Assington, Suffolk. Said to have been in New England [Matthew Reynolds, *Godly Reformers and their Opponents in Early Modern England: Religion in Norwich c. 1560–1643* (Woodbridge, Suffolk: Boydell Press, 2005), p. 173n.], but no trace survives in colonial records. *CR.*

[***Waterhouse, Thomas**, assistant to Matthias Candler of Coddenham, Suffolk. See below, graduates' section.]

[***]Wilson, John** (1591–1667), town lecturer at Sudbury, Suffolk, 1620–30; suspended in 1627 for seditious speeches and imprisoned, but restored after the intervention of the Earl of Warwick. Came under pressure again; resigned. Emigrated 1630. Boston, Massachusetts, 1630–67. Wilson returned to Suffolk in 1631 to fetch his wife, and again in 1634 to recruit emigrants. *ANB.*

Youngs, John (1598–?), Vicar of Covehithe, Suffolk; emigrated with a company from Southwold, 1637. Son of the Vicar of Southwold, Christopher Youngs. Associated with John Phillip of Wrentham. Founded Southold, Long Island.

Peterborough

Chauncy, Charles (bap. 1592, d. 1672), Vicar of Ware, Hertfordshire, 1627–33. Vicar of Marston St Lawrence, Northamptonshire, 1633. Suspended by the Court of High Commission. Scituate, Plymouth Colony, 1638–54; President of Harvard, 1654–72. *ODNB, ANB.*

Stone, Samuel (bap. 1602?, d. 1663), Curate of Stisted, Essex, 1627–30; suspended, 1630. Recommended to preach as a lecturer in Towcester, Northamptonshire, 1630; suspended, 1633. Emigrated in 1633 with Thomas Hooker and John Cotton. Cambridge, Massachusetts, 1633–6; Hartford, Connecticut, 1636–63. *ODNB, ANB.*

St David's

*****Matthews, Marmaduke** (*c.*1606–*c.*1683), Vicar of Penmaen, Gower Peninsula. Mentioned by Laud in his annual report to Charles I, 1636.[12] Suspended and called before the Court of High Commission. Emigrated 1638. Returned to Wales in 1654 or 1655. *ODNB, CR.*

Salisbury

{**Noyes, James** (1608–1656), assisted Thomas Parker with the Free School at Newbury. Emigrated with Parker, March 1634. Newbury, Massachusetts.}

{**Parker, Thomas** (1595–1677), schoolmaster, Newbury, Berkshire, 1620–34. Emigrated in 1634 at the time of Laud's metropolitical visitation. His mentor William Twisse stayed in England.[13] Minister at Newbury, Massachusetts, 1635–77. *ODNB, ANB.*}

Winchester

Avery, John (*c.*1600–1635), Vicar of Romsey, Hampshire, 1626. Emigrated 1635. Called to be minister at Marblehead, but he and his family drowned on the journey (a vivid account survives in the letterbook of the London artisan Nehemiah Wallington).[14]

*Bachiler, Stephen (1561–1660), Vicar of Holy Cross and St Peter, Wherwell, Hampshire, 1587–1605. Deprived 1605 for 'Calvinistic opinions'. Perhaps in the Netherlands for a time; at Newton Stacey, near Wherwell, 1622–32. He was the only still-nonconforming veteran of the 1605 campaign for conformity to emigrate. Unsettled in New England. Returned to England 1651.[15]

Glover, Jose [Joseph] (d. 1638), Rector of Sutton, Surrey, 1628–36; suspended, 1634, for refusing to read the Book of Sports; resigned c.1636. Died on the voyage to America.

*Whitfield [Whitfeld], Henry (1590/1–1657), Rector of Ockley, Surrey, 1618–38. Came under the scrutiny of the Court of High Commission for not reading the Book of Sports and for neglect of ceremonies.[16] Emigrated 1639. Guilford, 1639–50. Returned to England 1650. *ODNB*.

Worcester

Huitt, Ephraim (d. 1644), held the parish of Wroxall, Warwickshire, from the 1620s without controversy. Silenced by John Thornborough, Bishop of Worcester, 1638: Laud reported that he had 'condemned the decent ceremonies commanded by the Church'.[17] Emigrated 1639. Windsor, Connecticut, 1639–44.

York

*Denton, Richard (1603–1662), Curate of Coley chapel in Halifax, Yorkshire. In New England by 1638. Stamford, Connecticut, 1641–4; Hempstead, Long Island, 1644–59. Returned to England 1659. *ODNB*.

{Maude, Daniel (1586–1655), of Wakefield, Yorkshire. In 1614 he tried to adjust the oath of subscription he was required to take at ordination, but Archbishop Toby Matthew would not permit this, so he remained unordained. Possibly a schoolmaster. Emigrated in 1635; schoolmaster at Boston, 1636–43; minister at Dover, 1643–55.}[18]

Newman, Samuel (1602–1663), Curate of Woodkirk [West Ardsley], Yorkshire, 1636; in New England by 1638; Weymouth, Massachusetts. *ODNB*.

Pierson, Abraham (bap. 1611?–1678), BA Trinity, Cambridge, 1632; in 1632 he was found to be an unlicensed Curate at All Saints, Pavement, York. Summoned to the Court of High Commission, 19 March 1639/40, as of 'Ardsley': did not attend; fined £20. Emigrated early 1640: Lynn, Massachusetts, late 1640; Southampton, Long Island, 1640–4; Branford, Connecticut, 1645–65; founded Newark, New Jersey, 1666. *ODNB, ANB*.

Rayner, John (*c.*1600–1669), born Gildersome, near Batley, Yorkshire. Married an heiress named Boyes (sister to Peter Prudden's wife). To New England 1635. Minister at Plymouth, 1636–54; Dover, 1655–69.

Rogers, Ezekiel (1588–1660), Rector of Rowley, East Riding, Yorkshire, 1621–38. 1634 charged with nonconformity. Decreed to have lapsed into suspension when did not appear to answer charges against him. Emigrated 1638. Minister at Rowley, Massachusetts, 1639–60. *ODNB*.

***Saxton, Peter** (d. 1651), Rector of Edlington, West Riding, Yorkshire, 1614–40. Ordered to conform at the 1636 visitation, but absent, and so suspended; someone else put in his place, 1640. To New England, 1640: Scituate, 1640–1. Returned to England, 1641. Vicar of Leeds, 1646–51.

Shove, Edward (d. 1638), assistant to Ezekiel Rogers at Rowley, Yorkshire; emigrated with him, 1638; died on the voyage.

Occupation/residence on eve of emigration not known

Doughty, Francis (1602–1658), of Hempstead, Gloucestershire. Preacher at Taunton, Massachusetts,1637; planter at Dorchester, 1639. 1642 to New York and gathered a church; 1648 to Virginia.

***Gibson, Richard** (d. 1645), graduate of Emmanuel College, Cambridge; preacher to fishermen at Richmond Island, 1637; 1639 to Piscataqua. In trouble with the Massachusetts authorities for episcopalian convictions and criticism of colonial government. To England, 1642.

***Jenner, Thomas** (1605–1676), born Fordham, Essex; matriculated at Christ's College, Cambridge, 1624; probably a minister in East Anglia; said to be a preacher at Heddon, Northumberland, where Thomas Shepard took refuge. Emigrated 1635: Roxbury, Weymouth, Saco, Charlestown; not active as a minister. To England in 1649; took a parish living in Norfolk. *ODNB*, within 'Jenner, Thomas (d. 1673) printseller and writer'; *CR*.

Mayo, John (1598–1676), born Northamptonshire; matriculated Magdalen Hall, Oxford, 1615; took no degree. Not ordained in England. To New England 1638. Ordained at Barnstable 1640; 1646–49 Eastham; Boston Second Church, 1655–73. d. Yarmouth, Massachusetts.

Smith, Henry (1588–1648), born Norwich; Magdalene, Cambridge, BA 1622, MA 1625; ordained, Peterborough, 1623; OE career unknown. Watertown 1636/7. Wethersfield 1641–8.

Smith, Ralph (d. 1660/1), Christ's College, Cambridge, matriculated 1610, BA 1614. Nothing more is known of his English background. Emigrated 1629. The first regularly ordained minister in the Plymouth Colony. Resigned 1636. Preached at Manchester, Massachusetts, 1645.

Wheelock, Ralph (1600–1683/4), born Shropshire; Clare Hall, Cambridge, BA 1627, MA 1631; ordained deacon, Peterborough, 1629. No record of his having held a living. To New England 1637. Watertown; later preached at Dedham and Medfield.

Emigrated before 1629

Blackstone, William (1595/6–1675), Emmanuel, Cambridge, BA 1617/18; MA 1621. To New England in 1623, with Robert Gorges' company. Weymouth 1623–35; lived near Boston as a recluse; *c.*1650–75 on Blackstone River.

*****Morrell, William**, Weymouth 1623–4. Returned to England.

Emigrated between 1640 and 1660

{**Corlet, Elijah** (d. 1688), studied at Oxford and Cambridge; MA 1638. Ordained deacon, 1633. Schoolmaster at Framlingham, Suffolk; Master of Halstead Grammar School, Essex. Date of emigration uncertain, but he was Master of the grammar school at Cambridge, Massachusetts, 1642–88.}

[*]**Fletcher, William**, Rector of Aston, Yorkshire, 1621–51; minister at the northerly settlement of Oyster River, 1656. Returned to England? Perhaps ejected in 1662. Returned to New England.

*****Harrison, Thomas** (1617/18–1682), to Virginia by 1640; in Boston 1648–50, then to England. *ODNB, CR.*

*****Peter, Thomas** (1597–1654/5), Vicar of Mylor, Cornwall, by 1628. Arrived in New England 1644, driven out of the West Country by the activity of Royalist troops. Returned to Mylor 1646. *ODNB.*

Students/recent graduates
who became ministers in New England

All from the University of Cambridge unless otherwise stated.

			Date of emigration
Baker, Nicholas	BA 1632, MA 1635	St John's	1635
Bishop, John	BA 1632, MA 1635	Balliol, Oxford	by 1640
Bulkeley, Edward	mc 1629	St Catherine's	1635
Carter, Thomas	BA 1630, MA 1633	St John's	1637
Dane, Francis	mc 1633	King's	1636
Dudley, Samuel	mc 1626	Emmanuel	1630
Fitch, James	educated by Thomas Hooker		1638
Flynt, Henry	BA 1635, MA 1638	?	1635
Greene, Henry	mc 1635	Emmanuel	1640
Harvard, John	BA 1632, MA 1635	Emmanuel	1637
*Knight, William	BA 1631, MA 1634	Emmanuel	1637
Miller, John	BA 1628	Gonville & Caius	1634
Newton, Roger	mc 1636	King's	1638
*Norcrosse, Nathaniel	BA 1637	St Catherine's	1638/9 *CR* [OE 1649]
*Rashley, Thomas	BA 1632, MA 1636	Trinity	1640 *CR* [OE 1646?]
*Sadler, Richard	mc 1637	Emmanuel	1638 *CR* [OE 1646]

Sherman, John (1613–85), b. Dedham, Essex; grew up under the ministry of John Rogers; mc Emmanuel, Cambridge 1631, but left without a degree because he refused to subscribe. Emigrated 1634.

Street, Nicholas	BA 1625, MA	Emmanuel	1636?

*Waterhouse, Thomas (d. 1680), assistant to Matthias Candler of Coddenham, Suffolk (*CR*), who was admonished for 'inconformitie' in Wren's 1636 Visitation; emigrated by 1639. Schoolmaster, Dorchester, 1639–42. To England by 1643. *CR*.

*Woodbridge, John (1613–95), entered Oxford but left because he refused to take the oath of conformity; continued his studies privately. Emigrated 1634 with uncles Thomas Parker and James Noyes, and settled at Newbury. Minister, Andover, 1645. To England 1647. *ODNB* (within the entry for his brother, Benjamin); *CR*.

Students/recent graduates of English universities who were not
ministers in New England but later became ministers in England

With the exception of Benjamin Woodbridge, this does not include Harvard
graduates who returned to ministry in England: see Appendix 4.

			Date of emigration
*Firmin, Giles	mc 1629	Emmanuel	1632 CR, ODNB [OE 1644]
*Jennings, Richard	BA 1636 MA 1639	Catherine Hall	1636 CR [OE 1638]
*Marshall, Christopher	mc 1632	Magdalene	1634 CR [OE c.1642]

*Willis, Thomas Jr (b. in or before 1618, d. in or after 1673), son of Thomas
Willis, schoolmaster at Lynn, Massachusetts. Said to have attended St
John's College, Oxford, but did not graduate. Emigrated 1633? If so, in
New England at least until his father returned in 1641 or 1642; probably
finished his education there. Perhaps a chaplain in the Parliamentary
army. Vicar of Twickenham, 1646–60. *ODNB, CR.*

*Woodbridge, Benjamin (1622–84), mc Magdalen Hall, Oxford, 1638, but did
not graduate. Emigrated 1639. BA Harvard 1642 (the first graduate in
Harvard's first class). Probably the 'Mr Woodbridge' paid £8 in 1644 by
the town of Boston for work as a schoolmaster the previous year.
Returned to England 1647? Re-entered Magdalen Hall: MA 1648. Rector
of Newbury, Berkshire, 1648–62. *ODNB, CR.*

SOURCES *ANB; CR; ODNB;* William Laud, *A History of the Troubles and Tryal of . . . William Laud* (London, 1695); Thomas Lechford, *Plain Dealing: or, Newes from New-England* (London, 1642); *Magnalia;* Samuel Eliot Morison, *The Founding of Harvard College* (Cambridge, Mass.: Harvard University Press, 1935), Appendix B; Roger Thompson, *Mobility and Migration: East Anglian Founders of New England* (Amherst: University of Massachusetts Press, 1994); Norman C.P. Tyack, 'The Humbler Puritans of East Anglia and the New England Movement: Evidence from the Court Records of the 1630s', *NEHGR,* 139 (1984), pp. 79–106; Norman C.P. Tyack, 'Migration from East Anglia to New England before 1660', (PhD diss., University of London, 1951); Richard Waterhouse, 'Reluctant Emigrants: the English Background of the First Generation of the New England Clergy', *Historical Magazine of the Protestant Episcopal Church,* 44 (1975), pp. 473–88; Frederick L. Weis, *The Colonial Clergy and the Colonial Churches of New England* (Lancaster, Mass., 1936). Last but not least, *The Clergy of the Church of England Database 1540–1835,* http://www.theclergydatabase.org.uk (only a few emigrant clergy appear on *CCEd* at present, but this will change as the project proceeds).

Appendix 4   PREACHERS FROM NEW ENGLAND

Twenty-five colonists who had held English parish livings before emigration returned in the 1640s or 1650s. Fifteen returned to parish livings: Thomas Allen, Joseph Hull, Thomas Jenner, John Knowles, Thomas Larkham, Robert Lenthall, Marmaduke Matthews, George Moxon, Robert Peck, Thomas Peter, John Phillip, Peter Saxton, Nathaniel Ward, Thomas Weld, John Wheelwright. Ten did not: Stephen Bachiler, Christopher Blackwood, Richard Blinman, Richard Denton, Samuel Eaton, William Hooke, Thomas James, Hanserd Knollys, Hugh Peter, Henry Whitfield. (Thomas Patient, whose ordination is only attested by his own account, is not included in the figures.) Knollys renounced orders before emigration. His fellow Baptists Blackwood and Patient took government posts in Ireland; Blackwood may have been in a Kent parish after his return from New England, before his conversion to Baptist doctrines. Of the others, Hugh Peter made it clear at the end of his life that he had never held cure of souls in England, which may have to do with the attachment he still had to his church at Salem, Massachusetts. William Hooke was Master of the Savoy and chaplain to Cromwell. Henry Whitfield took office as public preacher and pastor to a congregation at Winchester Cathedral. Thomas James was town preacher at Needham Market, Suffolk. Richard Blinman and Richard Denton returned to England late, in 1659. Stephen Bachiler was over ninety when he came back. Samuel Eaton's history is discussed in chapter 7. Allen, Bachiler, Blinman, Eaton, Hooke, James, Jenner, Knowles, Larkham, Matthews, Moxon, Hugh Peter, Phillip, Weld, Wheelwright and Whitfield were known as followers of the 'New England Way', Congregationalism. The views of Peck, Thomas Peter, and Saxton (who died before 1660, and so are not in *CR*) are not known. Ward and probably Hull and Denton were broadly Presbyterian; Lenthall rejected Massachusetts' strict criteria for church membership.

Ten younger colonists who had studied at Oxford and Cambridge (some of whom migrated to New England in the 1630s without completing their degrees) came back to England and took parish livings: Giles Firmin, Thomas Harrison, Christopher Marshall, Nathaniel Norcrosse, Thomas Rashley, Richard Sadler, John Sams, Thomas Waterhouse, Thomas Willis Jr, John Woodbridge. Harrison later went to Ireland as a highly paid government preacher. Harrison, Marshall, Norcrosse, Sams and probably Waterhouse and Willis were Congregationalist. Woodbridge, Sadler and probably Rashley were broadly Presbyterian. Firmin tried to take an 'interpendent' position: see chapter 7.

Thirty-four Harvard students crossed the Atlantic and entered some sort of ministry. Thirty took parish appointments, at least for a time: John Allin, William Ames, Joshua and Nehemiah Ambrose, John Angier Jr, Nathaniel Brewster, John Bulkeley, Henry Butler, Isaac Chauncy, Joseph Farnworth, George Hadden, John Haynes, Leonard Hoar, Jeremiah Holland, John Hooke, Samuel Malbon, Increase, Nathaniel and Samuel Mather, Mordecai Matthews, Urian Oakes, Edward Rawson, Comfort Starr, William Stoughton, Joseph Swinnock, John Weld, Benjamin Woodbridge; with (according to Samuel Mather) John Birden and Abraham Walver, 'preachers in their own county', and Abraham James in Norfolk. William Stoughton and John Haynes held livings and university fellowships; Nathaniel Brewster and Samuel Mather worked in Ireland; Mather also preached in Scotland. Of the four who did not hold parish appointments, Edmund Weld and Joshua Hobart seem only to have preached in Ireland; John Collins went to Scotland. George Downing's work as an army chaplain led him into civilian work. *CR* names as Congregationalists Butler, Isaac Chauncy, Hoar, Malbon, Nathaniel and Samuel Mather, Starr and Stoughton (and Increase Mather, who was not in a parish living at the Restoration). To these can be added Ames, Bulkeley, Brewster, Oakes, and probably Farnworth. Those who conformed to the Church of England at the Restoration were Joshua Ambrose, John Angier Jr, Hadden[?], John Haynes, Mordecai Matthews, Joseph Swinnock, Edward Rawson. John Whiting, and Manasseh and Lemuel Matthews, entered the ministry of the Church of England in the 1660s. Benjamin Woodbridge, who turned down a canonry at Windsor in 1662 and was ejected as Rector of Newbury, Berkshire, took holy orders from the bishop of Salisbury in 1665. However – accused of taking a step inconsistent with his principles – Woodbridge returned to his nonconformist ministry at Newbury.

Ten colonial laymen who seem not to be university graduates became preachers. Five took office as parish clergy: Clement Chaplin, Edward Fletcher, William Horsford, Henry Sewall and probably Edward Bendall. Fletcher was known as a Congregationalist; Bendall and Horsford presented certificates from Congregationalists. John Clement, John Millard, Thomas Thornton and Zephaniah Smith became government-sponsored preachers in

Ireland, and John Hoadley served as chaplain to the garrison in Edinburgh. Of all these, Sewall (with links to Thomas Rashley and to the church at Newbury, Massachusetts) is the most likely to have favoured Presbyterianism.

A small handful of people have been left out of the count, either because they went back across the Atlantic just before 1640 (perhaps disappointed at Harvard's slow start) or because their careers are too shadowy to include in the picture. Francis Higginson (*CR*) and Richard Jennings (*CR*) left New England before 1640: Higginson pursued his education at Leiden; Jennings became a domestic chaplain. George Moxon Jr (*CR*) may have accompanied his parents to New England, but this is not certain. The careers of Francis Bright, 'Mr Brecy', Richard Gibson, William Knight and William Morrell are obscure. Also left out are the mavericks George Burdett and Nathaniel Eaton who, after some dramatic twists and turns, ended their days in the 1660s as conformist episcopalians.

ABBREVIATIONS

ANB
American National Biography (24 vols). Oxford and New York: Oxford University Press, 1999. [*ANB Online* at http://www.anb.org, 2005–.]

Aspinwall NR
A Volume Relating to the Early History of Boston, Containing the Aspinwall Notarial Records from 1644 to 1651. Boston, Mass.: Report of the Record Commissioners, 32, Municipal Printing Office, 1903.

BDBR
Richard L. Greaves and Robert Zaller, eds *Biographical Dictionary of British Radicals in the Seventeenth Century* (3 vols). Brighton: Harvester Press, 1982–84.

BL
British Library, London.

Bodleian
Bodleian Library, University of Oxford.

Boston CR
Richard D. Pierce, ed. *The Records of the First Church in Boston 1630–1868, I*. Boston: Colonial Society of Massachusetts, *Publications*, 39, 1961.

CR
A.G. Matthews, ed. *Calamy Revised*. Oxford: Clarendon Press, 1934, reissued 1988.

CSPC
Calendar of State Papers: Colonial Series, 1574–1660. London: Longman, Green, Longman & Roberts, 1860.

CSPD
Calendar of State Papers: Domestic Series, of the Reign of Charles I (23 vols). London: Longman, 1858–97.
Calendar of State Papers: Domestic Series, of the Commonwealth (13 vols). London: Longman, 1875–86.

GMB
Robert C. Anderson, ed. *The Great Migration Begins: Immigrants to New England, 1620–1633* (3 vols). Boston, Mass.: Great Migration Study Project, New England Historic Genealogical Society, 1995. [Online at http://www.greatmigration.org]

GM 1634–1635   Robert C. Anderson, G.F. Sanborn and M.L. Sanborn, eds *The Great Migration: Immigrants to New England, 1634–1635*. Boston, Mass.: Great Migration Study Project, New England Historic Genealogical Society, 1999 –.

Magnalia   Cotton Mather. *Magnalia Christi Americana; or, the Ecclesiastical History of New England*, ed. T. Robbins (2 vols). Hartford: Silas Andrus & Son, 1853.

NEHGR   *New England Historical and Genealogical Register*. Boston, Mass.: New England Historic Genealogical Society, 1847–. [Online at http://www.NewEnglandAncestors.org, New England Historic Genealogical Society, 2001–.]

ODNB   *Oxford Dictionary of National Biography* (61 vols). Oxford: Oxford University Press, 2004. [*Oxford DNB Online* at http://www.oxforddnb.com, 2004 –.]

PRO   The National Archives [Public Record Office], Kew, London.

Sibley   J.L. Sibley, *Biographical Sketches of Graduates of Harvard University . . . 1642 –1689* (3 vols). Cambridge, Mass.: C.W. Sever, 1873–85.

Winthrop Papers   Allyn B. Forbes et al., eds *The Winthrop Papers, 1498–1654* (6 vols). Boston, Mass.: Massachusetts Historical Society, 1929–.

NOTES

Prologue

1. Susanna Bell, *The Legacy of a Dying Mother to her Mourning Children, Being the Experiences of Mrs. Susanna Bell* (London, 1673), pp. 44–62; A.B. Grosart, ed., *The Complete Works of Thomas Brooks* (Edinburgh, London and Dublin: James Nichol, 1867), VI, p. 436. *CR*, 'Brooks, Thomas' (d. 1680). Susanna's narrative is reprinted in Susan C. Staub, ed., *Mothers' Advice Books* (Aldershot: Ashgate 2002). For the context, see Ralph Houlbrooke, 'The Puritan Death-Bed, *c*.1560–*c*.1660', in Christopher Durston and Jacqueline Eales, eds, *The Culture of English Puritanism, 1560–1700* (London: Macmillan, 1996), pp. 122–44.
2. Carla Gardina Pestana, *The English Atlantic in an Age of Revolution, 1640–1661* (Cambridge, Mass., and London: Harvard University Press, 2004), pp. 229–32, discusses population figures in 1640. In contrast, the population of Plymouth Plantation – founded by the 'Pilgrim Fathers' who arrived on the *Mayflower* in 1620, and which was not part of Massachusetts until 1692 – stood at only 2,300 by 1640.
3. 'Since the year 1640 more people have gone from New England than have come hither': Increase Mather, *A Brief Relation of the State of New England, from the Beginning of that Plantation to this Present Year, 1689* (London, 1689), p. 5.
4. Bell, *Legacy*, pp. 45–6. Thomas and Susanna [née Brydon] Bell: *GM 1634–1635*, 1, pp. 237–43. On providentialism: David D. Hall, *Worlds of Wonder, Days of Judgment: Popular Religious Belief in Early New England* (Cambridge, Mass.: Harvard University Press, 1990), pp. 71–116; Alexandra Walsham, *Providence in Early Modern England* (Oxford: Oxford University Press, 1999); Michael P. Winship, *Seers of God: Puritan Providentialism in the Restoration and Early Enlightenment* (Baltimore, Maryland: Johns Hopkins University Press, 1996); Nicholas Guyatt, '"The Peculiar Smiles of Heaven": Providence and the Invention of the United States, 1607–1865' (Ph.D. diss., Princeton University, 2003). Although belief in Providence went far wider than the puritan movement, the habit of searching for 'providences' suited puritan piety and Calvinist theology.
5. Clement Corbet to Matthew Wren, 17 Feb. 1636/7, Bodleian, MS. Tanner 68, fol. 189r–v.
6. Peter Lake, 'Defining Puritanism – Again?', in Francis J. Bremer, ed., *Puritanism: Transatlantic Perspectives on a Seventeenth-Century Anglo-American Faith* (Boston: Massachusetts Historical Society, 1993), pp. 3–29; and see appendix 1.
7. David Cressy, *Coming Over: Migration and Communication between England and New England in the Seventeenth Century* (Cambridge: Cambridge University Press, 1987), pp. 74–106, argues that 'the primacy of puritan concerns in the bulk of the movement' is unproven. Virginia DeJohn Anderson, *New England's Generation: The Great Migration and the Formation of Society and Culture in the Seventeenth Century* (Cambridge:

Cambridge University Press, 1991), pp. 37–46, makes the case that 'puritanism
... played an essential part in convincing otherwise ordinary English men and women
to take the otherwise extraordinary step of separating themselves from their society
and embarking for New England'.

8. Kevin Sharpe, *The Personal Rule of Charles I* (New Haven and London: Yale University
Press, 1992), pp. 731–8, 751–7; G.W. Bernard, 'The Church of England
c.1529–c.1642', *History*, 75 (1990), p. 199; Avihu Zakai, *Exile and Kingdom: History and
Apocalypse in the Puritan Migration to America* (Cambridge: Cambridge University
Press, 1992), pp. 207–30.

9. Perry Miller, *Errand into the Wilderness* (Cambridge, Mass.: Harvard University Press,
1956), p. 11. See also Sacvan Bercovitch, *The American Jeremiad* (Madison: University
of Wisconsin Press, 1978); Zakai, *Exile and Kingdom*.

10. Kenneth Fincham, 'The Restoration of Altars in the 1630s', *Historical Journal*, 44
(2001), pp. 919–40; Peter Lake, 'Moving the Goal Posts? Modified Subscription and the
Construction of Conformity in the Early Stuart Church', in Peter Lake and Michael
Questier, eds, *Conformity and Orthodoxy in the English Church, c.1560–1660*
(Woodbridge, Suffolk: Boydell Press, 2000), pp. 179–205; Nicholas Tyacke, *Anti-
Calvinists: The Rise of English Arminianism c.1590–1640* (Oxford: Clarendon Press,
1987), pp. 181–247; Tom Webster, *Godly Clergy in Early Stuart England: The Caroline
Puritan Movement c.1620–1643* (Cambridge: Cambridge University Press, 1997),
pp. 149–251, 268–85.

11. Theodore Dwight Bozeman, *To Live Ancient Lives: The Primitivist Dimension in
Puritanism* (Chapel Hill and London: University of North Carolina Press, 1988),
pp. 81–119. See also Nicholas Guyatt, '"An Instrument of National Policy": Perry Miller
and the Cold War', *Journal of American Studies*, 36 (2002), pp. 107–49; Andrew
Delbanco, 'The Puritan Errand Re-Viewed', *Journal of American Studies*, 18 (1984),
pp. 343–60; Joseph A. Conforti, *Imagining New England: Explorations of Regional
Identity from the Pilgrims to the Mid-Twentieth Century* (Chapel Hill: University of
North Carolina Press, 2001), pp. 11–34; Donald Weber, 'Historicizing the Errand',
American Literary History, 2 (1990), pp. 101–18.

12. Cressy, *Coming Over*, pp. 74–106, examines a dozen or more motives; Webster, *Godly
Clergy*, highlights the importance of social networks. On fishing, see Mark Kurlansky,
Cod: A Biography of the Fish that Changed the World (London: Vintage, 1999),
pp. 65–70; David Underdown, *Fire from Heaven: Life in an English Town in the
Seventeenth Century* (London: Fontana, 1993), pp. 131–4. Bell, *Legacy*, p. 45–6.
Katherine Meakins: *GMB*, 'Thomas Meakins'.

13. Barbara Donagan, 'Godly Choice: Puritan Decision-Making in Seventeenth-Century
England', *Harvard Theological Review*, 76 (1983), pp. 307–34.

14. See chapter 1.

15. Bell, *Legacy*, pp. 46–7. See Plate 2 for a map of New England settlements in 1634, the
year Susanna arrived.

16. Bell, *Legacy*, pp. 47–55. *ODNB*: Francis J. Bremer, 'Cotton, John (1585–1652)'; Michael
Jinkins, 'Shepard, Thomas (1605–1649)'; J. Frederick Fausz, 'Eliot, John (1604–1690)'.

17. For more on 'conversion narratives' (as these tests of spiritual experience were known),
and the emergence of the 'New England Way', Congregationalism, see chapter 2.

18. For the Bells' admission to Roxbury, see *Roxbury Land and Church Records*, Sixth
Report of the Boston Record Commissioners (Boston: Rockwell and Churchill, 1884),
pp. 80, 81. No precise dates are given. Thomas is 122nd on John Eliot's list of church
members, admitted among settlers who arrived in 1634. Susanna is 143rd, admitted
with settlers who came in 1635–6. *GM 1634–1635*, 1, p. 237, dates her admission to late
1635. According to her *Experiences*, she joined the church after Thomas Shepard
started to preach on the Parable of the Ten Virgins: that is, after June 1636, according
to the date assigned by Theodore Dwight Bozeman, *The Precisianist Strain:*

Disciplinary Religion and Antinomian Backlash in Puritanism to 1638 (Chapel Hill and London: University of North Carolina Press, 2004), p. 310. The date of Susanna's initial rebuff is uncertain, but quite probably it happened around the time Thomas became a member – it would not have been unusual for them to apply together, and her narrative implies her first approach to the church came soon after the Bells reached New England. Stephen Foster points out that Susanna's narrative is unique among the surviving narratives because it speaks of an initial rejection by the church. He uses this rejection to illustrate the introduction of stricter criteria for admission to New England's churches in 1636. However, the value of Susanna's case for making this point is weakened if her admission happened in 1636, but the initial rebuff actually occurred some time earlier, in 1634 or 1635. Stephen Foster, *The Long Argument: English Puritanism and the Shaping of New England Culture* (Chapel Hill and London: University of North Carolina Press, 1991), pp. 172–3; see also pp. 161–2.

19. Michael P. Winship, *Making Heretics: Militant Protestantism and Free Grace in Massachusetts, 1636–1641* (Princeton and Oxford: Princeton University Press, 2002); Janice Knight, *Orthodoxies in Massachusetts: Rereading American Puritanism* (Cambridge, Mass., and London: Harvard University Press, 1994); Bozeman, *The Precisianist Strain*; David R. Como, *Blown by the Spirit. Puritanism and the Emergence of an Antinomian Underground in Pre-Civil-War England* (Stanford: Stanford University Press, 2004). *ODNB*: Michael P. Winship, 'Hutchinson [*née* Marbury], Anne (*bap.* 1591, *d.* 1643)'; Michael P. Winship, 'Wheelwright, John (1592?–1679)'; Ruth E. Mayers, 'Vane, Sir Henry, the younger (1613–1662)'.

20. Shepard 'cuts so desperately that men know not how to bear him; he makes them all afraid that they are all hypocrites': Michael McGiffert, ed., *God's Plot: Puritan Spirituality in Thomas Shepard's Cambridge* (Amherst, Mass.: University of Massachusetts Press, revised and expanded edn, 1994), p. 18, citing Shepard's contemporary, Nathaniel Ward.

21. John Winthrop, *The Journal of John Winthrop*, ed. Richard S. Dunn, James Savage and Laetitia Yeandle (Cambridge, Mass., and London: Harvard University Press, 1996), p. 244; Winship, *Making Heretics*, pp. 182–3, 195–6. *ODNB*, Michael P. Winship, 'Weld, Thomas (*bap.* 1595, *d.* 1661)'.

22. Winship, *Making Heretics*, pp. 143–4, 186, 235–46.

23. Winthrop, *Journal*, p. 208 (Cotton and Wilson preached to passengers bound for England in February 1636/7). John Dod and twelve other ministers in England to New England 'Brethren', [*c.* June 1637], in Sargent Bush Jr, ed., *The Correspondence of John Cotton* (Chapel Hill and London: University of North Carolina Press, 2001), p. 266.

24. McGiffert, ed., *God's Plot*, pp. 142–8.

25. Pestana, *English Atlantic*, pp. 235–40; Hugh Amory, 'Printing and Bookselling in New England, 1638–1713', in Hugh Amory and David D. Hall, eds, *The Colonial Book in the Atlantic World* (Cambridge: Cambridge University Press, 2000), pp. 86–9. On print culture in the period: Ann Hughes, *Gangraena and the Struggle for the English Revolution* (Oxford: Oxford University Press, 2004); Ian Green, *Print and Protestantism in Early Modern England* (Oxford: Oxford University Press, 2000); David D. Hall and Alexandra Walsham, '"Justification by Print Alone?": Protestantism, Literacy and Communications in the Anglo-American World of John Winthrop', in Francis J. Bremer and Lynn A. Botelho, eds, *The World of John Winthrop: Essays on England and New England 1588–1649* (Boston, Mass.: Massachusetts Historical Society, 2005), pp. 334–85.

26. Bell, *Legacy*, pp. 55–6. Thomas and Susanna had Thomas, b. *c.*1633 (taken to New England as an infant); the child b. 1634, who died before they left England; Susan (born just after their arrival in America); Sarah, b. 1640; John, b. April 1643, d. June 1643; Mary, b. 1645. See *GM 1634–1635*, 1, p. 241.

27. *Roxbury Book of Possessions*, Sixth Report of the Boston Record Commissioners (Boston: Rockwell and Churchill, 1884), p. 5. *GM 1634–1635*, 1, p. 237, dates Bell's Atlantic journeys to *c.*1640 and 1645: they can be more precisely dated to 1642 and 1646 by records of his children's births and letters of attorney he took to England.

28. [Anon.], *New Englands First Fruits* (London, 1643), p. 26; many (like Bell) came to England 'on some special business' and intended to go back to New England. George Thomason, the London bookseller and collector (*ODNB*), recorded the publication of this tract on 31 January 1642/3. Thomas Weld of Roxbury and Hugh Peter of Salem, in London as agents for Massachusetts, produced it: Raymond P. Stearns, *The Strenuous Puritan: Hugh Peter, 1598–1660* (Urbana, Illinois: University of Illinois Press, 1954), pp. 167–8.

29. Winthrop, *Journal*, p. 423; Bell, *Legacy*, pp. 55–6; *GM 1634–1635*, 1, p. 241. On Christ as bridegroom: Susan Hardman Moore, 'Sexing the Soul: Gender and the Rhetoric of Puritan Piety', in R.N. Swanson, ed., *Gender and the Christian Religion* (Oxford: Blackwell, 1998), pp. 175–86.

30. Bell, *Legacy*, p. 56. For the ebb and flow of migration during the civil wars, see chapter 3. Bell's movements can be traced from letters of attorney recorded by the Boston notary. For example, in November 1646, Barbara Weld (the widow of Joseph Weld of Roxbury) appointed Thomas Bell to collect all debts and goods due to her or her deceased husband, 'from any person or persons whatsoever in England'. *Aspinwall NR*, p. 66; see also pp. 31, 32, 69–70 (November–December 1646, before Bell left for London); pp. 81, 82, 84–5 (August–September 1647, after his return to Boston); pp. 92–3, 105–6 (October–November 1647, before he took his family home).

31. *Aspinwall NR*, p. 396; Bell's links with other Atlantic traders, including the Boston bookseller Hezekiah Usher, are illuminated by *Aspinwall NR*, pp. 13, 69, 143, 183, 381, 388, 389, 409.

32. Bell, *Legacy*, p. 56; *GM 1634–1635*, 1, p. 241.

33. *Aspinwall NR*, pp. 92, 183; W.B. Trask, ed., *Suffolk Deeds*, 12 vols (Boston: Rockwell and Churchill, 1880–1902), 2: 341–3; *GM 1634–1635*, 1, p. 242.

34. Bell, *Legacy*, p. 57.

35. John Davenport to John Winthrop Jr, 24 July 1654, in Isabel M. Calder, ed., *Letters of John Davenport, Puritan Divine* (New Haven: Yale University Press, 1937), p. 90; Bell, *Legacy*, pp. 55–6. For more on this and the themes that follow, see chapter 5.

36. David Weir, *Early New England: A Covenanted Society* (Grand Rapids, MI and Cambridge, UK: William B. Eerdmans Publishing Company, 2005), pp. 243–303, gives an inventory of all known church and civil covenants into the eighteenth century.

37. See chapter 5.

38. Winthrop, *Journal*, p. 416; see chapter 4.

39. Bell, *Legacy*, pp. 56–7; *Aspinwall NR*, p. 388. Charles E. Hambrick-Stowe, *The Practice of Piety: Puritan Devotional Disciplines in Seventeenth-Century New England* (Chapel Hill: University of North Carolina Press, 1982), pp. 96–9, 205–6; Winton U. Solberg, *Redeem the Time: The Puritan Sabbath in Early America* (Cambridge, Mass.: Harvard University Press, 1977), pp. 112, 130.

40. See chapter 7.

41. *Roxbury . . . Church Records*, p. 80. In 1652 or 1653 Bell still owned a house, barn, and many acres of land: *GM 1634–1635*, 1, p. 237. Wheelwright's certificate: Lambeth Palace Library, Ms. COMM. III/4, fol. 406. *ODNB*, I. B. Watson, 'Yale, Elihu (1649–1721)'.

42. Eliot acknowledged Bell's help to Edward Winslow of Plymouth Colony (by then also in London), 20 October 1651: Bodleian, MS. Rawl. D. 934, fol. 11v. On Eliot's Indian Bible see Hall and Walsham, ' "Justification by Print Alone?" ', in Bremer and Botelho, eds, *World of John Winthrop*, p. 343. Hezekiah Usher collected the materials for printing it: Henry F. Waters, *Genealogical Gleanings in England* (Boston, Mass.: New England Historic Genealogical Society, 1901), p. 626n.

43. Thomas Bell's will, proved 3 May 1672: PRO, PROB 11/339. John Eliot founded the Roxbury Latin School in 1645 (now the oldest school in existence in the United States).

44. See chapter 6.

45. Claire Tomalin, *Samuel Pepys: The Unequalled Self* (London: Penguin Books, 2002), pp. 111–12, 175; Bell, *Legacy*, pp. 59–60.

46. Robert Latham and William Matthews, eds, *The Diary of Samuel Pepys* (London: HarperCollins, 2000), 7, pp. 275–6 [5 September 1666]; Bell, *Legacy*, p. 60. Plate 12 shows Seething Lane, with the tower of All Hallows Barking at its foot, just west of Tower Hill.

47. *Roxbury . . . Church Records*, p. 80. See chapter 3.

48. David L. Wykes, "'To revive the memory of some excellent men": Edmund Calamy and the early historians of nonconformity' (London: Dr Williams's Library, Friends of Dr Williams's Library, 1997). Calamy's work underlies A.G. Matthews, *Calamy Revised* (Oxford: Clarendon Press, 1934, reissued 1988).

49. Preachers still held 'sovereignty of exposition': Patrick Collinson, *The Religion of Protestants: The Church in English Society 1559–1625* (Oxford: Clarendon Press, 1982), p. 267; see also Collinson, 'Lectures by Combination: Structures and Characteristics of Church Life in 17th Century England', in his *Godly People: Essays on English Protestantism and Puritanism* (London: The Hambledon Press, 1983), pp. 467–98. Although tensions between lay and clerical settlers have often preoccupied historians, ministers and their flocks were perhaps more at ease together than at odds: James F. Cooper Jr, *Tenacious of their Liberties: The Congregationalists in Colonial Massachusetts* (Oxford and New York: Oxford University Press, 1999), pp. 23–45; Lisa M. Gordis, *Opening Scripture: Bible Reading and Interpretative Authority in Puritan New England* (Chicago: University of Chicago Press, 2003), pp. 97–111. For examples of settlers 'confessions' (spiritual testimonies), see McGiffert, *God's Plot*, pp. 149–225.

50. The will of 'Susann Bell', proved 21 March 1673 [written 10 May 1672], PRO, PROB 11/341.

51. Bell, *Legacy*, pp. 61–2 (references to Psalm 18:46 and Revelation 7:9, 14, as well as Hebrews 11:13); Winthrop, *Journal*, pp. 257–8. Hebrews 11:13, translated 'strangers and pilgrims' in the Geneva Bible and King James Version, gave the *Mayflower* Pilgrims their name.

Chapter 1

1. 'The humble remonstrance and protestation of me, Thomas Allen' [1636], Bodleian, MS. Tanner 68, fols 118r–118v.

2. Kenneth Fincham, ed., *Visitation Articles and Injunctions of the Early Stuart Church*, 2 vols, Church of England Record Society, 1, 5 (Woodbridge, Suffolk: Boydell Press, 1994, 1998), II, pp. xxv–vi, 157–60; Kenneth Fincham, 'The Restoration of Altars in the 1630s', *Historical Journal*, 44 (2001), pp. 919–40. Allen's case is discussed by Matthew Reynolds in *Godly Reformers and their Opponents in Early Modern England: Religion in Norwich c.1560–1643* (Woodbridge, Suffolk: Boydell Press, 2005), pp. 218–25. *ODNB*, Mark Robert Bell, 'Allen, Thomas (1608–1673)'; Nicholas W.S. Cranfield, 'Wren, Bishop Matthew (1585–1667)'. *CR*, 'Allen, Thomas'.

3. Thomas Allen, 'Remonstrance', Bodleian, MS. Tanner 68, fols 116r–118v; his arguments suggest he had read William Prynne's *Newes from Ipswich* (Ipswich [i.e. London?], 1636). *ODNB*, Thompson Cooper, 'Corbet, Clement (c.1576–1652)', rev. Anita McConnell; William Lamont, 'Prynne, William (1600–1699)'. In 1641 a London printer dared to put an illustration that lampooned episcopal edicts onto the title page of a fresh edition of *Newes from Ipswich*: see Plate 1.

4. Clement Corbet to Matthew Wren, 17 February 1636/7, Bodleian, MS. Tanner 68, fol. 189r (a comment directed against another emigrant minister, John Allin of Saxlingham, Norfolk).

5. Corbet to Wren, 21 November 1636, Bodleian, MS. Tanner 68, fol. 3v; Reynolds, *Godly Reformers*, p. 163; Keith L. Sprunger, *Dutch Puritanism: A History of English and Scottish Churches of the Netherlands in the Sixteenth and Seventeenth Centuries* (Leiden: E.J. Brill, 1982), pp. 7–9.

6. Bodleian, MS. Tanner 68, fols 115r, 234r; Robert Allen to Thomas Lechford, 17 November 1636, PRO, SP16/335/68. Allen's ministry had split the parish: Reynolds, *Godly Reformers*, pp. 218–19, 221. Lechford, a lawyer at Clement's Inn, London, also acted for Prynne: *ODNB*, Barbara Ritter Dailey, 'Lechford, Thomas (*d.* in or after 1642)'.

7. Corbet to Wren, 24 March 1636/7 and 14 April 1637, Bodleian, MS. Tanner 68, fols 205v, 230r.

8. Deposition by James Barwick of Norwich jail, June 1637, Bodleian, MS. Tanner 68, fol.120; Robert Allen's petition to Parliament on his brother's behalf, [1641], Bodleian, MS. Tanner 220, fols 1r–3r.

9. *Boston CR*, pp. 22, 25; James F. Hunnewell, ed., 'The First Record-Book of the First Church in Charlestown, Massachusetts', *NEHGR*, 23 (1869), p. 280; Thomas Lechford, *Plain Dealing: or, Newes from New-England* (London, 1642), p. 37. New England churches followed Reformed practice by having both a pastor and a teacher (if they could afford it). Allen became teacher, alongside Charlestown's pastor Zechariah Symmes. Not long after he settled there, he married Anna, the widow of John Harvard.

10. Robert Peck, Rector of Hingham, Norfolk; the lawyer Thomas Lechford, who fled in 1638 after the controversial trial of his client Prynne; Thomas Oliver, a 'calenderer' or presser of cloth and his wife Mary; Jonathan Porter and John Pierce, weavers. Reynolds, *Godly Reformers*, pp. 135–6, 219–20, 224–7. Lechford, Peck and the Olivers, like Allen, later returned to England.

11. Roger Thompson, *Mobility and Migration: East Anglian Founders of New England* (Amherst, Mass.: University of Massachusetts Press, 1994), pp. 72, 75–6, 98–9, 117, 153; Reynolds, *Godly Reformers*, pp. 220, 224–7. The Metcalfes joined the church at Dedham, Massachusetts: D.G. Hill, ed., *The Record of Baptisms, Marriages, and Deaths, and Admissions to the Church and Dismissals Therefrom, Transcribed from the Church Records in the Town of Dedham, Massachusetts* (Dedham, Mass., 1888), pp. 21, 22.

12. Michael Metcalfe, 'To all the true professors of Christ's gospel within the city of Norwich', 13 January 1636/7, *NEHGR*, 16 (1862), p. 281; Metcalfe's will, *NEHGR*, 6 (1852), pp. 172–3. On perceptions of Foxe in the 1630s: Damian Nussbaum, 'Appropriating Martyrdom: Fears of Renewed Persecution and the 1632 Edition of *Acts and Monuments*', in David Loades, ed., *John Foxe and the English Reformation* (Aldershot: Scolar Press, 1997), pp. 178–91; Damian Nussbaum, 'Laudian Foxe-Hunting? William Laud and the Status of John Foxe in the 1630s', in R.N. Swanson, ed., *The Church Retrospective*, Studies in Church History, 33 (Woodbridge, Suffolk: Boydell and Brewer, 1997), pp. 329–42.

13. A view of puritanism pioneered by Patrick Collinson: *The Religion of Protestants: The Church in English Society, 1559–1625* (Oxford: Clarendon Press, 1982), pp. 267, 275–83; 'The English Conventicle', in W.J. Sheils and D. Wood, eds, *Voluntary Religion*, Studies in Church History, 23 (Oxford: Blackwell, 1986), pp. 223–59; 'Towards a Broader Understanding of the Early Dissenting Tradition', in Patrick Collinson, *Godly People: Essays on English Protestantism and Puritanism* (London: The Hambledon Press, 1983), pp. 527–62; 'The Cohabitation of the Faithful with the Unfaithful', in Ole Peter Grell, Jonathan I. Israel, and Nicholas Tyacke, eds, *From Persecution to Toleration: The Glorious Revolution in England* (Oxford: Clarendon Press, 1991), pp. 51–76.

14. Paul S. Seaver, *Wallington's World: A Puritan Artisan in Seventeenth-Century London* (Stanford, California: Stanford University Press, 1985), p. 37.

15. Eamon Duffy, 'The Long Reformation: Catholicism, Protestantism and the Multitude', in Nicholas Tyacke, ed., *England's Long Reformation, 1500–1800* (London: UCL Press, 1998), pp. 41–2, 45–52; Peter Lake, '"A Charitable Christian Hatred": the Godly and their Enemies in the 1630s', in Christopher Durston and Jacqueline Eales, eds, *The Culture of English Puritanism 1560–1700* (London: Macmillan, 1996), pp. 182–3.

16. Peter Lake, *Moderate Puritans and the Elizabethan Church* (Cambridge: Cambridge University Press, 1982); Lake, 'Anti-Popery: the Structure of a Prejudice', in R. Cust and A. Hughes, eds, *Conflict in Early Stuart England: Studies in Religion and Politics 1603–1642* (London and New York: Longman, 1989), pp. 72–106; Robin Clifton, 'Fear of Popery', in C. Russell, ed., *The Origins of the English Civil War* (London: Macmillan, 1973), pp. 144–67; Anthony Milton, *Catholic and Reformed: The Roman and Protestant Churches in English Protestant Thought, 1600–1640* (Cambridge: Cambridge University Press, 1995).

17. *ODNB*, Ronald G. Asch, 'Elizabeth, Princess [Elizabeth Stuart] (1596–1662)'; Caroline M. Hibbard, 'Henrietta Maria [Princess Henrietta Maria of France] (1609–1669)'.

18. B.R. White, *The English Separatist Tradition* (Oxford: Oxford University Press, 1971); Lake, *Moderate Puritans*.

19. Kenneth Fincham, 'Clerical Conformity from Whitgift to Laud', in Peter Lake and Michael Questier, eds, *Conformity and Orthodoxy in the English Church, c.1560–1660* (Woodbridge, Suffolk: Boydell Press, 2000), pp. 125–58; Tom Webster, *Godly Clergy in Early Stuart England: The Caroline Puritan Movement c.1620–1643* (Cambridge: Cambridge University Press, 1997), pp. 180–4.

20. Robert Stansby, Rector of Westhorpe, Suffolk, distinguished between the old conformity and – referring to Wren's Injunctions – 'the new conformity as they call it': Stansby to John Winthrop, 17 March 1636/7, *Winthrop Papers*, III, pp. 380–1. For the redefinition of the agenda for conformity: Kenneth Fincham, 'Clerical Conformity from Whitgift to Laud', and Peter Lake, 'Moving the Goal Posts?', in Lake and Questier, eds, *Conformity and Orthodoxy*. Others see Laudian policy as less novel and more moderate: Kevin Sharpe, *The Personal Rule of Charles I* (New Haven and London: Yale University Press, 1992), pp. 275–402; Julian Davies, *The Caroline Captivity of the Church* (Oxford: Clarendon Press, 1992).

21. Bodleian, MS. Tanner 68, fol. 160v; Reynolds, *Godly Reformers*, p. 227; Sargent Bush Jr, ed., *The Correspondence of John Cotton* (Chapel Hill and London: University of North Carolina Press, 2001), pp. 164–5; Metcalfe, 'To all the true professors of Christ's gospel', *NEHGR*, 16 (1862), pp. 281–3; 'Answers of Samuel Ward to articles objected against him', 19 December 1634, PRO, SP16/278/65. On preaching, fear of idolatry and thoughts of emigration, see J. Sears McGee, *The Godly Man in Stuart England: Anglicans, Puritans, and the Two Tables, 1620–1670* (New Haven: Yale University Press, 1976), pp. 9–10, 77, 89–91.

22. Lake, 'A Charitable Christian Hatred', in Durston and Eales, eds, *The Culture of English Puritanism*; Sprunger, *Dutch Puritanism*, pp. 288–9 and passim; Theodore Dwight Bozeman, *To Live Ancient Lives: The Primitivist Dimension in Puritanism* (Chapel Hill and London: University of North Carolina Press, 1988), pp. 104–11; see Alexandra Walsham, *Charitable Hatred: Tolerance and Intolerance in England, 1500–1700* (Manchester and New York: Manchester University Press, 2006), pp. 160–277, on responses to living amidst hostility.

23. David Hackett Fischer, *Albion's Seed: Four British Folkways in America* (Oxford: Oxford University Press, 1989), pp. 25–36, 226–32; Thompson, *Mobility and Migration*, pp. 224–35; Carla Gardina Pestana, *The English Atlantic in an Age of Revolution, 1640–1661* (Cambridge, Mass., and London: Harvard University Press, 2004), pp. 19–20; Virginia DeJohn Anderson, *New England's Generation: The Great Migration*

and the Formation of Society and Culture in the Seventeenth Century (Cambridge: Cambridge University Press, 1991), pp. 18–26; Alison Games, Migration and the Origins of the English Atlantic World (Cambridge, Mass., and London: Harvard University Press, 2001), pp. 49–60, 72–101. On Winthrop: ANB, Charles L. Cohen, 'Winthrop, John (1588–1649)'; Francis J. Bremer, John Winthrop: America's Forgotten Founding Father (Oxford: Oxford University Press, 2003), pp. 67–170.

24. Thompson, Mobility and Migration, pp. 184–204; Webster, Godly Clergy, pp. 276–77, 283–5; GMB, 'Thomas Meakins'; Patrick Collinson, 'The Godly: Aspects of Popular Protestantism in Elizabethan England', in his Godly People, pp. 14, 17, 18.

25. About one-sixth of the migrants arrived between 1620 and 1633. The rest arrived between 1634 to 1640, according to the Great Migration Study Project which Robert C. Anderson directs at the New England Historic Genealogical Society, http://www.great migration.org. See also Robert C. Anderson, 'A Note on the Changing Pace of the Great Migration', New England Quarterly, 59 (1986), pp. 406–7.

26. See appendix 3; Richard C. Waterhouse, 'Reluctant Emigrants: The English Background of the First Generation of the New England Clergy', Historical Magazine of the Protestant Episcopal Church, 44 (1975), pp. 473–88; Thompson, Mobility and Migration, pp. 44–55 (on 37 clergy from East Anglia and Lincolnshire); Webster, Godly Clergy, pp. 149–251, 268–85 (on clerical networks in the dioceses of London, Norwich and Peterborough).

27. This contrasts with Foster's emphasis on puritan clergy 'liberated from parochial obligations'; from a 'tenebrous domain of uncertain boundaries in which lecturers on the run or tucked away in quiet corners ministered intermittently to a floating collection of self-certified saints'. Stephen Foster, The Long Argument: English Puritanism and the Shaping of New England Culture, 1570–1700 (Chapel Hill and London: University of North Carolina Press, 1991), pp. 99–106. Ian Green, 'Career Prospects and Clerical Conformity in the Early Stuart Church', Past and Present, 90 (1981), pp. 111–15, documents the incentives for conformity but minimises the effect of innovations in the 1630s.

28. Cotton to Bishop John Williams, 7 May 1633, in Bush, ed., Cotton Correspondence, p. 179; ODNB, Brian Quintrell, 'Williams, John (1582–1650)'. Dalton, Peck, Phillip, Saxton and Whitfield left for New England from parishes they had held for 20–30 years: see appendix 3.

29. Lecturers: Burdett, Higginson, Hooker, Knowles, Hugh Peter, Shepard, Stone and Wilson. On lecturers in the Jacobean religious establishment and the close scrutiny they received after 1629: Collinson, 'Lectures by Combination', Godly People, pp. 467–98; 'Royal Instructions to the Episcopate, 1629', Fincham, ed., Visitation Articles and Injunctions, II, pp. 37–8. Chaplains: Williams, Norton, Skelton, Shepard, Moxon. See appendix 3.

30. Knollys and Lothropp had renounced their ordination in the Church of England. Bachiler, Higginson, Newman and Wheelwright had been active as unlicensed preachers. See appendix 3.

31. Increase Mather, The Life and Death of . . . Mr. Richard Mather (Cambridge, Mass., 1670), p. 8. ANB, Robert Middlekauff, 'Mather, Richard'; ODNB, Michael G. Hall, 'Mather, Richard (1596–1669). John Winthrop recorded that hands were laid on John Wilson to elect and confirm him as pastor at Boston, but 'not of any intent that Mr Wilson should renounce his ministry he received in England': John Winthrop, The Journal of John Winthrop, ed. Richard S. Dunn, James Savage and Laetitia Yeandle (Cambridge, Mass., and London: Harvard University Press, 1996), p. 39. Most of New England's ministers trod a fine line: they insisted that their office depended on election by the local church (to conform to New England's aspirations to recreate primitive purity), but they also accepted that the godly ministry in England was validated in a similar way, implicitly, by the support of the local godly community – in spite of the 'superstition' of episcopal ordination. See David D. Hall, The Faithful Shepherd: A

History of the New England Ministry in the Seventeenth Century, 2nd edn (Cambridge, Mass.: Harvard University Press, 2006), pp. 102–5.

32. Waterhouse, 'Reluctant Emigrants', found evidence that at least 47 of the 76 had been suspended, but did not assume this was the full story. Cressy played down religious tensions by claiming that 'only 47' had clashed with their superiors: David Cressy, *Coming Over: Migration and Communication between England and New England in the Seventeenth Century* (Cambridge: Cambridge University Press, 1987), p. 87.

33. Thomas Allen, Blinman, Bulkeley, Burdett, Burr, Chauncy, Dalton, Samuel Eaton, Glover, Huitt, Hooker, Jones, Mather, Peck, Hugh Peter, John Phillip, Ezekiel Rogers, Saxton, Shepard, Stone, Nathaniel Ward, Thomas Weld. See appendix 3.

34. John Allin, Cotton, Davenport, Higginson, Knollys, Knowles, Larkham, Matthews, Moxon, Newman, Pierson, Symmes, Warham, Wheelwright, Whitfield, Whiting, Wilson. See appendix 3.

35. Blackwood, Bright, Denton, Dunster, Hooke, Hobart, Leveritch, Nathaniel Rogers, Thompson, Wheelwright. See appendix 3. Ann Hughes, *Politics, Society and Civil War in Warwickshire, 1620–1660* (Cambridge: Cambridge University Press, 1987), p. 79: 'the practical failure of the Laudians is less important than the threatening impact of their attempt'.

36. Webster, *Godly Clergy,* pp. 151–203; appendix 3.

37. Fincham, ed., *Visitation Articles and Injunctions,* II, pp. 37–8.

38. Thomas Shepard's 'Autobiography', Michael McGiffert, ed., *God's Plot: Puritan Spirituality in Thomas Shepard's Cambridge* (Amherst, Mass.: University of Massachusetts Press, revised and expanded edn, 1994), pp. 51–3; Webster, *Godly Clergy,* pp. 189–90, 195–6.

39. Andrew Foster, 'Archbishop Neile Revisited', in Lake and Questier, eds, *Conformity and Orthodoxy,* p. 172, citing PRO, SP16/345/85 (Neile's annual report, January 1637). For details of emigrant ministers from the dioceses of York and Chester, see appendix 3.

40. R.A. Marchant, *The Puritans and the Church Courts in the Diocese of York* (London: Longmans, 1960), pp. 54, 56; *ODNB,* Peter David Yorke, 'Bridgeman, John (*bap.* 1577, *d.* 1652)'; R.C. Richardson, 'Puritanism and the Ecclesiastical Authorities: the case of the diocese of Chester', in Brian Manning, ed., *Politics, Religion and the English Civil War* (London: Edward Arnold, 1973), pp. 3–33.

41. *ODNB,* S.J. Guscott, 'Eaton, Samuel (*d.* 1665)'. Ministers' annual income was often between £40 and £80, with a few paid more, and many less: Cressy, *Coming Over,* pp. 119–20; Green, 'Career Prospects and Clerical Conformity', p. 87. Large fines could be imposed to set an example, rather than with real hope of bringing the money in: Sharpe, *Personal Rule of Charles I,* pp. 381–2. *ANB,* R.W. Roetger, 'Eaton, Theophilus (1590–1658)'; *ODNB,* Gordon Goodwin, 'Eaton, Nathaniel (*bap. c.*1610, *d.* 1674)', rev. Francis Bremer.

42. Andrew Foster, 'Church Policies of the 1630s', in Cust and Hughes, eds, *Conflict in Early Stuart England,* p. 207, citing Joseph Lister of Bradford, and Archbishop Neile (PRO, SP16/412/45.1).

43. Reynolds, *Godly Reformers,* pp. 186–235; Fincham, ed., *Visitation Articles and Injunctions,* II, pp. xxv–vi, 157–64. Appendix 3 lists ministers who emigrated from the diocese of Norwich.

44. PRO, SP16/289/46.

45. Bodleian, MS. Tanner 68, fols 99r, 178r; J. Browne, *A History of Congregationalism in Norfolk and Suffolk* (London, 1877), pp. 422–3; *CR,* 'Phillip, John'. Phillip was brother-in-law to the puritan theologian William Ames: *ODNB,* Keith L. Sprunger, 'Ames, William (1576–1633)'.

46. PRO, SP16/289/46, SP16/302/140, SP16/308/23, 49, SP16/326/46, SP16/342/86, SP16/346/26; *Winthrop Papers,* III, pp. 439–40; [William Prynne], *Newes from Ipswich* [sig. A4]; *ODNB,* J.M. Blatchly, 'Ward, Samuel (1577–1640)'. On Dade, see Cressy,

Coming Over, pp. 140–1. Adams joined John Phillip and other East Anglian settlers at Dedham, Massachusetts.

47. Bodleian, MS. Tanner 314, fol. 153v. *ODNB*, Brian Quintrell, 'Williams, John (1582–1650)'. Cressy, *Coming Over*, p. 90, endorses Wren's claim.

48. Sir John Lambe, a legal adviser to Laud, advocated his right to intervene in the diocese: *ODNB*, J. Fielding, 'Lambe, Sir John (*c.*1566–1646)'. Laud drew the King's attention to nonconformity there: William Laud, *A History of the Troubles and Tryal of . . . William Laud* (London, 1695), pp. 527–8, 531, 548, 554.

49. Larzer Ziff, *The Career of John Cotton: Puritanism and the American Experience* (Princeton, N.J.: Princeton University Press, 1962), pp. 65–70. Bishop Williams seems to have delayed acceptance of Cotton's resignation for two months, possibly to give him time to escape: Bush, ed., *Cotton Correspondence*, p. 178. For more information on migrant ministers from the diocese of Lincoln, see appendix 3.

50. *ODNB*, John Morrill, 'Cromwell, Oliver (1599–1658)'.

51. This contrasts with the argument made by Cressy and Sharpe that the small numbers and the timelag show that pressure on puritanism was irrelevant to emigration: see Cressy, *Coming Over*, p. 87; Sharpe, *Personal Rule of Charles I*, p. 752.

52. For example: Robert Peck, Thomas Allen, Henry Whitfield, Ezekiel Rogers.

53. Thomas Allen, John Davenport, Samuel Eaton, Nathaniel Eaton, Thomas Hooker, Hugh Peter, possibly John Phillip, Thomas Weld. John Cotton considered a move to the Netherlands: Ziff, *Career of John Cotton*, pp. 66–9. Sprunger notes that most clerical migrants to the Netherlands went from the dioceses of London, Norwich and Chester, with lay immigrants from Yorkshire and East Anglia (the same areas that saw emigration to New England): *Dutch Puritanism*, pp. 285–6.

54. McGiffert, ed., *God's Plot*, p. 57.

55. Papers relating to Chauncy's clash with the authorities include: PRO, SP 16/164/40; 16/165/10, 16; 16/167/33; 16/302/16; 16/261/298b; 16/311/33; 16/312/59; 16/324/5 (his submission before Laud, 11 February 1635/6); 16/361/67 (Samuel Clarke's report to [Sir John Lambe], 12 June 1637). For the context, see John Fielding, 'Arminianism in the Localities: Peterborough Diocese, 1603–1642', in Kenneth Fincham ed., *The Early Stuart Church* (London: Macmillan, 1993), pp. 93–113; John Fielding, 'Opposition to the Personal Rule of Charles I: the Diary of Robert Woodford, 1637–1641', *Historical Journal*, 31 (1998), pp. 769–88; John Fielding, 'Conformists, Puritans and the Church Courts: the diocese of Peterborough, 1603–1642' (PhD diss., University of Birmingham, 1989). See also Webster, *Godly Clergy*, pp. 221–4; Fincham, 'Restoration of Altars in the 1630s'.

56. *ODNB*, Jim Benedict, 'Chauncy, Ichabod (1635–1691)'; Charles Chauncy, *The Retraction of Mr. Charles Chancy* (London, 1641); *Magnalia*, I, p. 468.

57. 'Answers of Samuel Ward to articles objected against him', 19 December 1634, PRO, SP16/278/65; his brother Nathaniel Ward and stepbrother Ezekiel Rogers went to Massachusetts; his brother John Ward to the Netherlands.

58. Webster, *Godly Clergy*, pp. 278–9, quoting Daniel Rogers, *Naaman the Syrian, his Disease and Cure* (London, 1642), p. 885.

59. McGiffert, ed., *God's Plot*, p. 52; T. Webster and K. Shipps, eds, *The Diary of Samuel Rogers, 1634–1638*, Church of England Record Society, 11 (Woodbridge, Suffolk: Boydell Press, 2004), pp. xvii–xx. Daniel Rogers of Wethersfield, Stephen Marshall of Finchingfield and Samuel Wharton of Felsted stayed; Thomas Shepard, Nathaniel Ward and Thomas Weld emigrated. Webster, *Godly Clergy*, pp. 268–85, discusses the choice of suffering or flight.

60. The tradition of consultation is explored in Patrick Collinson, John Craig and Brett Usher, eds, *Conferences and Combination Lectures in the Elizabethan Church: Dedham and Bury St Edmunds, 1582–1590*, Church of England Record Society, 19 (Woodbridge, Suffolk: Boydell Press, 2003).

61. Timothy Breen and Stephen Foster, 'Moving to the New World: the Character of Early Massachusetts Immigration', *William and Mary Quarterly*, 3rd series, 30 (1973), p. 203.

62. Edward Winslow, *Good News from New-England* (London, 1624), p. 64; [John White], *The Planters Plea* (London, 1630), p. 32; John F. Martin, *Profits in the Wilderness: Entrepreneurship and the Founding of New England Towns in the Seventeenth Century* (Chapel Hill and London: University of North Carolina Press, 1991); Daniel Vickers, 'Competency and Competition: Economic Culture in Early America', *William and Mary Quarterly*, 3rd series, 47 (1990), pp. 3–29; Anderson, *New England's Generation*, pp. 123–4; Stephen Innes, *Creating the Commonwealth: The Economic Culture of Puritan New England* (New York: Norton, 1995).

63. Cressy and Sharpe, in contrast, use the variety of reasons for emigration to play down the particular significance of religious context of the 1630s: Cressy, *Coming Over*, pp. 74–106; Sharpe, *Personal Rule of Charles I*, pp. 751–7.

64. John Allin and Thomas Shepard, *A Defence of the Answer made unto the Nine Questions* (London, 1648), p. 6. Webster, *Godly Clergy*, p. 281, points out that the memory of these pre-emigration consultations lasted for at least three generations.

65. Bremer, *John Winthrop*, pp. 147–65; Christopher Thompson, 'John Winthrop of Groton's Decision to Emigrate to Massachusetts: A Reconsideration of his "General Conclusions and Particular Considerations"', *Suffolk Review*, New Series 28 (Autumn 1996), pp. 19–22. The Massachusetts Bay Company was a modest enterprise, with fewer high-profile backers than the Virginia Company and Providence Island Company – which helps to account for the election of a relatively obscure Suffolk gentleman, John Winthrop, as Governor. The Company received a Royal Charter in 1629, as a trading company to underwrite and promote settlement.

66. Increase Mather, *Life of . . . Richard Mather*, pp. 12–20. Mather was influenced by letters from John Cotton and Thomas Hooker, who were already in New England. A letter from Cotton – the first to survive that postdates his arrival in Massachusetts – must be similar to the letters Mather found persuasive: Bush, ed., *Cotton Correspondence*, pp. 181–8.

67. Webster and Shipps, eds, *Samuel Rogers*, p. 84; see also pp. xx, 13, and passim; Kenneth W. Shipps, 'The Puritan Migration to New England: a New Source on Motivation', *NEHGR*, 135 (1991), pp. 83–97.

68. Lake, 'Moving the Goal Posts?' in Lake and Questier, eds, *Conformity and Orthodoxy*, pp. 204–5.

69. *Magnalia*, 1, p. 263; *ODNB*, J. Fielding, 'John Dod (1550–1645)'; Kenneth Fincham, ed., *The Early Stuart Church, 1603–1642* (Basingstoke: Macmillan, 1993), pp. 25–8. *Oxford English Dictionary*, 'baggage': 'trashy, worthless', as in John Boys, *Works* (London, 1630) p. 183, 'We may not . . . break God's net because there are some baggage fish'. Dod's advice drew on Jesus' words to Peter, John 21:18. When Cotton wrote back to someone from Dod's circle in 1634, about the reasons for emigration, he echoed these same words: Bush, ed., *Cotton Correspondence*, p. 183.

70. The debate at Ockley has been reconstructed by Webster, *Godly Clergy*, pp. 157–64.

71. John Cotton, *Gods Promise to his Plantation* (London, 1630), pp. 9–10; Increase Mather, *Life of . . . Richard Mather*, p. 14 (citing chapter and verse of Foxe's *Book of Martyrs*); see also Allin and Shepard, *Defence of the Answer*, p. 5.

72. John Davenport, *An Apologeticall Reply to a Booke Called an Answer to the Unjust Complaint of W.B.* (Rotterdam, 1636), pp. 104–6. Davenport, later of New Haven, at this point wanted to justify leaving London for the Netherlands.

73. Increase Mather, *Life of . . . Richard Mather*, p. 17. John Cotton saw the 1630s prefigured in 2 Chronicles 11: 14–16, when Jereboam threw the Levites out of their work as priests, and they left, followed by their people: *Gods Promise*, pp. 9–10; Bush, ed., *Cotton Correspondence*, pp. 210–11. The puritan theologian William Ames, who intended to join the exodus to Massachusetts but died in exile in the Netherlands,

offered advice on when it was legitimate to withdraw from a church: *Conscience with the Power and Cases Thereof* (Leiden and London, 1639), Book V, pp. 62–4. For earlier debates on the same theme: Jonathan Wright, 'Marian exiles and the legitimacy of flight from persecution', *Journal of Ecclesiastical History*, 52 (2001), pp. 220–43.

74. On the threat of popery which the godly perceived, and on the importance of raising a 'new' church from 'infancy', see 'General Observations for the Plantation of New England', and Robert Ryece to John Winthrop [1629]: *Winthrop Papers*, II, pp. 111–12, 127–30. Bozeman, *To Live Ancient Lives*, pp. 95–8, 111–14.

75. For critiques of Perry Miller's 'Errand into the Wilderness' theme, see Bozeman, *To Live Ancient Lives*, especially pp. 81–119, 198–310; Nicholas Guyatt, '"An Instrument of National Policy": Perry Miller and the Cold War', *Journal of American Studies* 36 (2002), pp. 107–49; Andrew Delbanco, 'The Puritan Errand Re-Viewed', *Journal of American Studies*, 18 (1984), pp. 343–60; Joseph A. Conforti, *Imagining New England: Explorations of Regional Identity from the Pilgrims to the Mid-Twentieth Century* (Chapel Hill: University of North Carolina Press, 2001), pp. 11–34; Donald Weber, 'Historicizing the Errand', *American Literary History*, 2 (1990), pp. 101–18. See also Patrick Collinson, 'Biblical Rhetoric: The English Nation and National Sentiment in the Prophetic Mode', in Claire McEachern and Deborah Shuger, eds, *Religion and Culture in Renaissance England* (Cambridge: Cambridge University Press, 1997), pp. 15–45. Avihu Zakai, *Exile and Kingdom*, pp. 120–206, restates in stark terms Miller's argument for an 'Errand'.

76. Bozeman, *To Live Ancient Lives*.

77. Winthrop, 'A Modell of Christian Charity', *Winthrop Papers*, II, p. 295. For the context of Winthrop's address, see Bremer, *John Winthrop*, pp. 173–84.

78. Quotations from Loren Baritz, *City on a Hill* (New York: John Wiley & Sons, 1964), p. 17; Sacvan Bercovitch, *The Puritan Origins of the American Self* (New Haven: Yale University Press, 1975), p. 97. New England as a 'city on a hill' becomes a foundation for the American sense of national destiny.

79. John Winthrop to Margaret Winthrop, 14 February 1629/30, *Winthrop Papers*, II, p. 209. Bozeman, *To Live Ancient Lives*, comments on the defensive theme: pp. 92–3, 117, 299.

80. Bell, *Legacy*, p. 46; William Wood, *New Englands Prospect* (London, 1634), p. 50. Cressy, *Coming Over*, pp. 107–77, provides a definitive account of the character of transatlantic journeys, and is the principal source for what follows.

81. *A Proportion of Provisions needfull for such as intend to plant themselves in New England, for one whole yeare. Collected by the Adventurers, with the advice of the Planters* (London, 1630); printed in Cressy, *Coming Over*, pp. 112–14. Wood, *New Englands Prospect*, pp. 49–50.

82. *A Proportion of Provisions.*

83. A witness statement from a court case over Elizabeth Glover's silver collection. A silver saltcellar and porringer survive. See Jonathan L. Fairbanks and Robert F. Trent, eds, *New England Begins: The Seventeenth Century*, 3 vols (Boston: Museum of Fine Arts, 1982), 3, pp. 480–1, 489–91. On the press, Hugh Amory, 'Printing and Bookselling in New England, 1638–1713', in Hugh Amory and David D. Hall, eds, *The Colonial Book in the Atlantic World* (Cambridge: Cambridge University Press, 2000), pp. 86–9.

84. Richard Mather's manuscript 'Journal to New England', New England Historic Genealogical Society, Boston, entry for 25 May 1635; accessed at http://www.NewEnglandAncestors.org.

85. Cressy, *Coming Over*, p. 158. John Winthrop later noted a singular act of God's Providence against the Book of Common Prayer. His son had a roomful of books, which included a volume with the Greek New Testament, Psalms and Prayer Book bound together. 'He found the common prayer eaten with mice, every leaf of it, and not any of the two other touched, nor any other of his books, though there were above a thousand'. Winthrop overstated the divinely inspired damage: the prayer book

survives in the collections of the Massachusetts Historical Society; 'less than half the pages are nibbled', and 'only at the tips of the lower right-hand corners'. Winthrop, *Journal*, pp. 340–1.

86. Richard Mather, 'Journal', entry for 24 July 1635.

87. Winthrop, *Journal*, pp. 15, 25.

88. Weld to his former parishioners in Terling, Essex, 1632, in David D. Hall, ed., *Puritans in the New World: A Critical Anthology* (Princeton and Oxford: Princeton University Press, 2004), p. 33. Weld quoted from Exodus 14:13, Moses' words to the fearful Israelites before God parted the Red Sea so that they could cross safely.

89. [Hanserd Knollys], *The Life and Death of . . . Mr. Hanserd Knollys* (London, 1692), p. 17; *ODNB*, Kenneth G.C. Newport, 'Knollys, Hanserd (1598–1691)'.

90. Winthrop, *Journal*, p. 403.

91. Increase Mather, *Life . . . of Richard Mather*, p. 22 (from Richard Mather's 'Journal', 15 August 1635).

92. Winthrop, *Journal*, pp. 32, 34–5.

Chapter 2

1. Harrison T. Meserole, ed., *Seventeenth-Century American Poetry* (New York: Doubleday & Co., 1968), pp. 397–8.

2. John Winthrop, *The Journal of John Winthrop*, eds Richard S. Dunn, James Savage and Laetitia Yeandle (Cambridge, Mass., and London: Harvard University Press, 1996), p. 261.

3. *ODNB*, David S. Katz, 'Tillam, Thomas (*fl.* 1638–1668)'; J.F. Maclear, 'New England and the Fifth Monarchy: the Quest for the Millennium in Early American Puritanism', *William and Mary Quarterly*, 3rd series, 32 (1975), pp. 230, 249. By the 1640s, Tillam was a Baptist in London, in a congregation led by another antinominan ex-colonist, Hanserd Knollys. Tillam's history shows how fluid religious allegiance could be in the seventeenth century: by his own testimony, he was born a Catholic; he became a zealous Protestant migrant to New England in the 1630s, and a religious radical in revolutionary England. In the 1660s, he was a refugee in Germany, and leader of a tiny community that believed that Christians, like Jews, should celebrate the Sabbath on Saturday, not Sunday.

4. Winthrop, *Journal*, pp. 2n., 39n.; Thomas Dudley to the Countess of Lincoln, 28 March 1630/1, Everett Emerson, ed., *Letters from New England* (Amherst, Mass.: University of Massachusetts Press, 1972), p. 73; Alison Games, *Migration and the Origins of the English Atlantic World* (Cambridge, Mass., and London: Harvard University Press, 2001), p. 86.

5. *ODNB*, Roger Thompson, 'Saltonstall, Sir Richard (*bap.* 1586, *d.*1661)'; R.E. Moody, ed., *The Saltonstall Papers, 1607–1815*, 2 vols (Boston: Massachusetts Historical Society, 1972–1974), I, pp. 1–24. See Plate 3, 'The Saltonstall Family'. Later, Saltonstall took refuge in Holland and joined the new English church at Arnhem, founded *c.*1638 by covenant as in New England, an innovative and experimental 'church-in-exile', whose ministers and members quickly returned to England when times changed: Keith L. Sprunger, *Dutch Puritanism: A History of English and Scottish Churches of the Netherlands in the Sixteenth and Seventeenth Centuries* (Leiden: E.J. Brill, 1982), pp. 226–32; *ODNB*, Barbara Donagan, 'Nye, Philip (*bap.* 1595, *d.* 1672)'.

6. *Winthrop Papers*, III, p. 21; Winthop, *Journal*, pp. 47–8; Emerson, ed., *Letters from New England*, p. 76. The Sharpes returned to Bradwell, Essex: N.C.P. Tyack, 'Migration from East Anglia to New England before 1660' (PhD diss., University of London, 1951), p. 88. Both appeared before the Archdeaconry Court of Essex in 1636, with Thomas said to be a 'common depraver of the government ecclesiastical, and of the rites and ceremonies of this church, since his coming from New England': Essex Record Office,

Chelmsford, D/AEA 41, Archdeaconry of Essex Act Book, 1636–38, fol. 102v. Another ex-colonist in trouble in the 1630s was Edward Penton, arrested in Norwich for helping to distribute William Prynne's attack on Bishop Wren, *Newes from Ipswich*. Penton was said to be a 'sanctified brother [who] hath been already at New England': Matthew Reynolds, *Godly Reformers and their Opponents in Early Modern England: Religion in Norwich c.1560–1643* (Woodbridge, Suffolk: The Boydell Press, 2005), p. 200. Most of those who went back in the 1630s left little trace in either New England or old.

7. [Francis Higginson], *New-Englands Plantation. Or, a Short and True Description of the Commodities and Discommodities of that Countrey* (London, 1630), sig. B3, Cv.

8. John White of Dorchester advised John Winthrop to train up the young and not to expect too much from older settlers: White to Winthrop, [c.1637], *Winthrop Papers*, III, p. 336.

9. Reports from 1630–1634 in Winthrop, *Journal*, pp. 42–4, 57, 94; Emerson, *Letters from New England*, p. 111; William Wood, *New Englands Prospect* (London, 1634), p. 5. See Roger Thompson, *Divided We Stand: Watertown, Massachusetts, 1630–1680* (Amherst, Mass.: University of Massachusetts Press, 2001), pp. 83–7; Karen Ordahl Kupperman, 'The Puzzle of the American Climate in the Early Colonial Period', *American Historical Review*, 87 (1982), p. 1273; David Hackett Fischer, *Albion's Seed: Four British Folkways in America* (Oxford: Oxford University Press, 1989), pp. 52–3. See also D.G. Allen, '"Vacuum Domicilium": the Social and Cultural Landscape of Seventeenth Century New England', in Jonathan L. Fairbanks and Robert F. Trent, eds, *New England Begins: The Seventeenth Century*, 3 vols (Boston: Museum of Fine Arts, 1982), 1, pp. 1–52; D.G. Allen, *In English Ways: The Movement of Societies and the Transferal of English Local Law and Custom to Massachusetts Bay in the Seventeenth Century* (Chapel Hill, N.C.: University of North Carolina Press, 1981), pp. 14–18; Karen Ordahl Kupperman, 'Climate and Mastery of the Wilderness in Seventeenth-Century New England', in David D. Hall, D.G. Allen and P.C.F. Smith, eds, *Seventeenth-Century New England*, Colonial Society of Massachusetts, *Publications*, 63 (1984), pp. 3–38.

10. Edward Johnson, *A History of New-England* (London, 1653), p. 49. Thomas Allen recalled this at a fast day sermon in Charlestown, c.1650, to collect money for settlers in the Bahamas: American Antiquarian Society, Worcester, Massachusetts, Richard Russell's Sermon Notebook, fol. 296v. Johnson wrote his history in 1650–1. For the collection for the Bahamas, see Sargent Bush Jr, ed., *The Correspondence of John Cotton* (Chapel Hill and London: University of North Carolina Press, 2001), pp. 432–6.

11. E.N. Hartley, *Ironworks on the Saugus* (Norman: University of Oklahoma Press, 1957); Bernard Bailyn, *The New England Merchants in the Seventeenth Century* (Cambridge, Mass.: Harvard University Press, 1955), pp. 71–4; N.C.P. Tyack, 'English Exports to New England, 1632–1640: Some Records in the Port Books', *NEHGR*, 135 (1981), pp. 213–38. William Aspinwall, the Boston notary, drew up many certificates for goods that passed through Boston between 1644–51: *Aspinwall NR*, pp. 394–430.

12. Winthrop, *Journal*, pp. 45–6. A few lines later, Winthrop noted that many of the settlers who returned to England the previous summer had died on the way or been ill since they got back.

13. 'Pratt's Apology', Massachusetts Historical Society, *Collections*, 2nd series, 7, pp. 126–8 (referring to Luke 4:3–4); Winthrop, *Journal*, p. 160. *GMB*, 'John Pratt', dates the letter c.1634. On scarcities and the poor quality of the soil: Games, *Migration*, p. 86; Fischer, *Albion's Seed*, p. 53.

14. 'Great Reshuffling' is Virginia DeJohn Anderson's phrase for this internal migration: *New England's Generation: The Great Migration and the Formation of Society and Culture in the Seventeenth Century* (Cambridge: Cambridge University Press, 1991), p. 92. Her findings support those of Timothy Breen and Stephen Foster, 'Moving to the New World: the Character of Early Massachusetts Immigration', *William and Mary Quarterly*, 3rd series, 30 (1973), pp. 208–13.

15. Winthrop, *Journal*, pp. 126–8; Thomas Hooker to John Winthrop, *c.* December 1638, *Winthrop Papers*, IV, pp. 75–84, and Winthrop to Hooker, March 1639, pp. 99–100; Karen Ordahl Kupperman, *Providence Island, 1630–1641: The Other Puritan Colony* (Cambridge: Cambridge University Press, 1993), pp. 333–4. The editors of Winthrop's *Journal*, p. 36n. 32, assess the argument that Winthrop wanted the thousand settlers who arrived with him in 1630 to settle in a single community.

16. Michael P. Winship highlights both the strong impulse towards unity, and the little it took to make the currents of mainstream English Protestantism turbulent: ' "The Most Glorious Church in the World": the Unity of the Godly in Boston, Massachusetts, in the 1630s', *Journal of British Studies*, 39 (2000), pp. 71–3, 96. On Roger Williams: Philip F. Gura, *A Glimpse of Sion's Glory: Puritan Radicalism in New England, 1620–1660* (Middletown, Conn.: Wesleyan University Press, 1984), pp. 31–48; *ANB*, Glenn W. LaFantasie, 'Williams, Roger (1603?–1683)'. On the Antinomian Controversy: Janice Knight, *Orthodoxies in Massachusetts: Rereading American Puritanism* (Cambridge, Mass., and London: Harvard University Press, 1994); Michael P. Winship, *Making Heretics: Militant Protestantism and Free Grace in Massachusetts, 1636–1641* (Princeton and Oxford: Princeton University Press, 2002); Theodore Dwight Bozeman, *The Precisianist Strain: Disciplinary Religion and Antinomian Backlash in Puritanism to 1638* (Chapel Hill and London: University of North Carolina Press, 2004).

17. Winthrop, 'Model of Christian Charity', *Winthrop Papers*, II, p. 293.

18. Ames to Winthrop, 29 December [1629], *Winthrop Papers*, II, p. 180; Fairbanks and Trent, eds, *New England Begins*, 2, pp. 114, 157–8. See Keith L. Sprunger, 'William Ames and the Settlement of Massachusetts Bay', *New England Quarterly*, 39 (1966), pp. 66–79. Joan Ames came over with her brother-in-law John Phillip, of Wrentham, Suffolk.

19. Philip Benedict, *Christ's Churches Purely Reformed: A Social History of Calvinism* (New Haven and London: Yale University Press, 2002), pp. 390–1; on the influence of Ames, Tom Webster, *Godly Clergy in Early Stuart England: The Caroline Puritan Movement c.1620–1643* (Cambridge: Cambridge University Press, 1997), pp. 293–309.

20. David Weir, *Early New England: A Covenanted Society* (Grand Rapids and Cambridge: William B. Eerdmans Publishing Company, 2005).

21. Weir, *Early New England: A Covenanted Society*, p. 224–5; John F. Martin, *Profits in the Wilderness: Entrepreneurship and the Founding of New England Towns in the Seventeenth Century* (Chapel Hill and London: University of North Carolina Press, 1991), p. 236; Stephen Foster, *Their Solitary Way: The Puritan Social Ethic in the First Century of Settlement in New England* (New Haven: Yale University Press, 1971), pp. 11–64. On vows in puritan piety, see for example William Gouge, *The Saints Sacrifice* (London, 1632), pp. 181–200.

22. Richard Rogers, *Seven Treatises, containing such Directions as is gathered out of the Holie Scriptures* (London, 1603), pp. 477–8; Patrick Collinson, *Godly People: Essays on English Protestantism and Puritanism* (London: The Hambledon Press, 1983), pp. 545, 559 n.109; Patrick Collinson, *The Religion of Protestants: The Church in English Society, 1559–1625* (Oxford: Clarendon Press, 1982), pp. 269–73. Collinson has explored how 'conventicles' operated without intending to be schismatic or sectarian (although some, against their intentions and principles, turned into separated gathered churches): 'The English Conventicle', in W.J. Sheils and D. Wood, eds, *Voluntary Religion*, Studies in Church History, 23 (Oxford: Blackwell, 1986), pp. 223–59. In America, there was a separatist model of covenant close to Massachusetts at Plymouth Plantation: the influence of Plymouth's separatists has long been debated, and Cotton (while still in England) rejected Salem's church covenant as a separatist act. However, as Rogers insisted, covenants need not be equated with separatism.

23. Weir, *Early New England: A Covenanted Society*, pp. 131–4, 224–5; Martin, *Profits in the Wilderness*, pp. 131–61, 217–37, 311–15. All the towns Martin studied (except for Milford, Connecticut) allowed settlers to own land without being church members.

Henry Whitfield and other settlers who founded Guilford, on Long Island Sound, made a plantation covenant on board ship before they went ashore: Massachusetts Historical Society, Boston, Ms. N–2196, Miscellaneous Bound Manuscripts Collection, 1 June 1639.

24. See below, notes 83–6.

25. Thomas Lechford, *Plain Dealing: or, Newes from New-England* (London, 1642), p. 2.

26. *Boston CR*, p. 12.

27. Lechford, *Plain Dealing*, p. 22.

28. See chapter 5.

29. John Dod and twelve other English ministers in England to New England 'Brethren', c. June 1637, in Bush, ed., *Cotton Correspondence*, p. 264; William Hooke to John Winthrop, 15 [August?] 1640, *Winthrop Papers*, IV, p. 274.

30. [John Davenport?], *An Answer of the Elders of the Severall Churches in New England unto Nine Positions* (London, 1643), p. 75, published with Richard Mather, *Church-Government and Church-Covenant Discussed* (London, 1643).

31. Lechford, *Plain Dealing*, p. 16; Darrett Rutman, *Winthrop's Boston. A Portrait of a Puritan Town, 1630–1649* (New York: Norton, 1972), p. 93; *Winthrop Papers*, III, pp. 181–2; Fischer, *Albion's Seed*, pp. 117–25. For the Old Ship Church at Hingham, Massachusetts, the oldest meetinghouse in the United States in continuous ecclesiastical use, see http://www.oldship church.org. On meetinghouses, see Marian Card Donnelly, *The New England Meeting Houses of the Seventeenth Century* (Middletown, Conn.: Wesleyan University Press, 1968).

32. The Henry Whitfield House (now the oldest house in Connecticut and the oldest stone house in New England) became a National Historic Landmark in 1997: see Plate 5, and http://www.whitfieldmuseum.com. I am indebted to Michael A. McCabe, Curator of the Henry Whitfield State Museum, for information about the likely use of the Great Hall.

33. Early colonial churches have often been seen as places where assertive lay people pushed their ministers in new directions. James F. Cooper emphasises, instead, the unanimity and mutual confidence between church members and their officers, and re-evaluates the *Cambridge Platform* of 1648, which has often been interpreted as a strategy by ministers to introduce more central control over local churches: James F. Cooper Jr, *Tenacious of their Liberties: The Congregationalists in Colonial Massachusetts* (Oxford and New York: Oxford University Press, 1999), pp. 11–67, 75–87.

34. Nicholas Tyacke, *Aspects of English Protestantism* (Manchester and New York: Manchester University Press, 2001), p. 128; Patrick Collinson, John Craig and Brett Usher, eds, *Conferences and Combination Lectures in the Elizabethan Church: Dedham and Bury St Edmunds 1582–1590*, Church of England Record Society, 19 (Woodbridge, Suffolk: Boydell Press, 2003), pp. ic–c; Patrick Collinson, 'The Godly: Aspects of Popular Protestantism', in his *Godly People*, pp. 1–17; Webster, *Godly Clergy*, pp. 287–332; S. Brachlow, *The Communion of Saints: Radical Puritan and Separatist Ecclesiology, 1570–1625* (Oxford: Oxford University Press, 1988).

35. Susanna Bell, *The Legacy of a Dying Mother to her Mourning Children, Being the Experiences of Mrs. Susanna Bell* (London, 1673), pp. 47–55. Most churches introduced the requirement of a conversion narrative. Two exceptions were Hartford, Connecticut, under the leadership of Thomas Hooker and Samuel Stone; and the church at Newbury, Massachusetts, which admitted any to church fellowship as long as they were not 'extremely ignorant or scandalous'. Baird Tipson, 'Samuel Stone's "Discourse" against Requiring Church Relations', *William and Mary Quarterly*, 3rd series, 46 (1989), pp. 786–99; Baird Tipson, 'Invisible Saints: the "Judgment of Charity" in the Early New England Churches', *Church History*, 44 (1975), pp. 460–71; Webster, *Godly Clergy*, pp. 299–301. Michael G. Ditmore, 'Preparation and Confession: Reconsidering Edmund S. Morgan's Visible Saints', *New England Quarterly*, 67 (1994), pp. 298–319,

suggests that narratives became common in 1637–38 in reaction to the Antinomian Controversy, under the influence of Thomas Shepard; rather than (as Morgan argued) in 1636, to contain a drift towards separatism, as an initiative of John Cotton.

36. Bozeman, *Precisianist Strain*, pp. 40–60, 84–120; Margo Todd, 'Puritan Self-Fashioning', in Francis J. Bremer, ed., *Puritanism: Transatlantic Perspectives on a Seventeenth-Century Anglo-American Faith* (Boston: Massachusetts Historical Society, 1993), pp. 57–87; Tom Webster, 'Writing to Redundancy: Approaches to Spiritual Journals and Early Modern Spirituality', *Historical Journal*, 39 (1996), pp. 33–56; R.P. Stearns and D.H. Brawner, 'New England Church "Relations" and Continuity in Early Congregational History', American Antiquarian Society, *Proceedings*, 75 (1965), pp. 13–45.

37. Lechford, *Plain Dealing*, pp. 4–8. Cooper, *Tenacious of their Liberties*, p. 76–7, points to a drift away from oral testimony to written submissions (for both men and women) as time went on.

38. R.C. Simmons, 'Richard Sadler's Account of the Massachusetts Churches', *New England Quarterly*, 42 (1969), p. 417. Sadler left for England in 1646.

39. George Selement and Bruce C. Woolley, eds, *Thomas Shepard's Confessions*, Colonial Society of Massachusetts, *Publications*, 58 (1981), pp. 123, 185. Andrew Delbanco, *The Puritan Ordeal* (Cambridge, Mass.: Harvard University Press, 1989), p. 216, emphasises immigrants' disappointment and bewilderment: 'the distinctively American note is not the theme of chosenness, but of collective loneliness'; see also Patricia Caldwell, *The Puritan Conversion Narrative: The Beginnings of American Expression* (Cambridge: Cambridge University Press, 1983), pp. 119–34.

40. McGiffert, ed., *God's Plot*, pp. 142–8. As McGiffert points out, recent scholarship has emphasised less the 'hardness of the procedure, the test in the testimony' and more 'the unspoken but primary intent of the exercise to create a support system for the practice of piety'.

41. Lechford, *Plain Dealing*, p. 23. Timothy H. Breen, 'Who Governs? The Town Franchise in Seventeenth-Century Massachusetts', *William and Mary Quarterly*, 3rd series, 27 (1970), pp. 460–74; Robert Emmet Wall, *Massachusetts Bay: The Crucial Decade, 1640–1650* (New Haven: Yale University Press, 1972), pp. 157–210, 228–9. See note 35 on churches that, exceptionally, did not require a conversion narrative.

42. David Underdown, *Fire from Heaven: Life in an English Town in the Seventeenth Century* (London: Fontana, 1993), pp. 91–2; Thomas Allen to John Cotton, 21 November 1642, in Bush, ed., *Cotton Correspondence*, p. 372. The tight restrictions on who could be baptised had repercussions for decades: Robert G. Pope, *The Half-Way Covenant: Church Membership in Puritan New England* (Princeton: Princeton University Press, 1969). However, New England did not ask church members who had been baptised in England to be re-baptised. This would have been a schismatic act, a judgment that their earlier baptism had been invalid.

43. Winthrop, *Journal*, pp. 275–6; 24 September 1639, G.F. Dow, ed., *The Records and Files of the Quarterly Courts of Essex County, Massachusetts*, 8 vols (Salem, Mass.: Essex Institute, 1911–21), I, p. 12. Mary Oliver's alienation escalated. In June 1646, convicted of calling New England's ministers bloodthirsty men, she was sentenced to have a slit stick put on her tongue, and to stand at the whipping post for an hour: Phillips Library, Peabody Essex Museum, Salem, Massachusetts, Essex County Court Files, 1–46–1.

44. Harry S. Stout, *The New England Soul: Preaching and Religious Culture in Colonial New England* (Oxford and New York: Oxford University Press, 1986), p. 31.

45. This is as Thomas Lechford reported it, *Plain Dealing*, pp. 18–19. Ministers' salaries became contentious: Winthrop, *Journal*, p. 423; David D. Hall, *The Faithful Shepherd: A History of the New England Ministry in the Seventeenth Century*, 2nd edn (Cambridge, Mass.: Harvard University Press, 2006), pp. 146–9.

46. Selement and Woolley, eds, *Thomas Shepard's Confessions*, p. 98; Lechford, *Plain Dealing*, p. 13. Susanna Bell could still remember, forty years later, the text of 'the first sermon that I heard after I came ashore': Bell, *Legacy*, p. 47.

47. Lechford, *Plain Dealing*, pp. 12, 16–17, 19; Fairbanks and Trent, eds, *New England Begins*, 3, p. 382; Cooper, *Tenacious of their Liberties*, pp. 28, 31.

48. Lechford, *Plain Dealing*, p.19; Winthrop, *Journal*, pp. 309–10.

49. Stout, *New England Soul*, pp. 29–30.

50. Winthrop, *Journal*, pp. 316–18; Lechford, *Plain Dealing*, p. 15; Martin, *Profits in the Wilderness*, pp. 148, 310–15.

51. John Dane, 'A Declaration of Remarkabell Prouedenses in the Corse of my Life', *NEHGR*, 8 (1854), p. 154. 'What cheer' (in modern slang corrupted to 'wotcher'): an early modern equivalent of 'how are you?'

52. Thomas Weld to his parishioners at Terling, 1632, in David D. Hall, ed., *Puritans in the New World: A Critical Anthology* (Princeton and Oxford: Princeton University Press, 2004), p. 35.

53. Winthrop, *Journal*, pp. 270–1. Rogers insisted that he did not condemn all in England: he could no longer affirm the national Church and its hierarchy, liturgy and corrupt discipline, but he praised England for 'soundness of doctrine', 'ministerial gifts' and 'power of religion'. Stephen Foster, *The Long Argument: English Puritanism and the Shaping of New England Culture, 1570–1700* (Chapel Hill and London: University of North Carolina Press, 1991), p. 158, quotes only Roger's criticism (and not the balancing affirmation), to support his case for the colonists' sectarianism.

54. David Cressy, *Coming Over: Migration and Communication between England and New England in the Seventeenth Century* (Cambridge: Cambridge University Press, 1987), pp. 213–34, explores the practicalities of sending letters across the Atlantic. The letters that survive are mostly from the papers of leading settlers and their families, and many have been printed: Bush, ed., *Cotton Correspondence*; Isabel M. Calder, ed., *Letters of John Davenport, Puritan Divine* (New Haven: Yale University Press, 1937); 'Dunster Papers', Massachusetts Historical Society, *Collections*, 4th series, 2 (1854), pp. 190–8; 'Mather Papers', Massachusetts Historical Society, *Collections*, 4th series, 8 (1868); *Saltonstall Papers; Winthrop Papers; The Wyllys Papers . . . 1590–1796*, Collections of the Connecticut Historical Society, 21 (1924). Everett Emerson printed an anthology (many from outside the main collections) in *Letters from New England*. Early correspondence in the Winthrop Papers peaked in 1637 and 1640: Carla Gardina Pestana, *The English Atlantic in an Age of Revolution, 1640–1661* (Cambridge, Mass., and London: Harvard University Press, 2004), p. 245n. 6.

55. Henry Jacie [Jessey] to John Winthrop Jr, January 1632 and *c.* June 1632, *Winthrop Papers*, III, pp. 61, 78; see also pp. 126–8, 142–3, 484–8. *ODNB*, Stephen Wright, 'Jessey [Jacie], Henry (1601–1633)'. Jessey sent Winthrop 'corantoes' – letters with public news – to circulate among colonists. From the early 1640s, newspapers started to appear regularly: Joad Raymond, *The Invention of the Newspaper: English Newsbooks, 1641–1649* (Oxford: Oxford University Press, 1996). Nathaniel Rogers of Ipswich, Massachusetts, received an edition of the newsbook *Mercurius Britannicus*: Rogers, *A Letter Discovering the Cause of God's Continuing Wrath against the Nation* (London, 1644), p. 9.

56. BL, Sloane Ms. 922, 'Letterbook of Nehemiah Wallington', contains copies of letters from Thomas Weld and Anthony Thacher in the 1630s, and of Wallington's own correspondence with the colonists James Cole and Edward Browne, 1642–50: fols 90r–93v, 104r–106v, 107, 109r–115v, 144v–145r, 145v–147v, 173r–176v. Seaver, *Wallington's World*, pp. 206–8.

57. Cressy, *Coming Over*, pp. 215–16. Among the godly shipmasters who plied the Atlantic and carried letters was Nicholas Trerise: Johan Winsser, 'Nicholas Trerise, Mariner of

Wapping and Charlestown', *NEHGR*, 143 (1989), pp. 25–39. Edward Howes to John Winthrop Jr, 18 March 1632/3, *Winthrop Papers*, III, p. 110.

58. Winthrop, *Journal*, p. 385.

59. Cressy, *Coming Over*, pp. 223, 225–6; *Winthrop Papers*, III, pp. 306n. [Robert Ryece], 190–3 [Sir John Clotworthy].

60. John White to John Winthrop, [*c*.1637], *Winthrop Papers*, III, pp. 335–6. *ODNB*, Rory T. Cornish, 'White, John (1575–1648)'.

61. Richard Bernard to [John Cotton], 1 April 1637, in Bush, ed., *Cotton Correspondence*, p. 261. Bernard's letter to Cotton has come to light recently, a small part of a more extensive exchange. Bernard sent at least two manuscripts across the Atlantic to Cotton, querying New England's innovations: Winthrop, *Journal*, p. 268. Cotton's responses no longer survive, though a riposte from Richard Mather was later printed as *An Apologie of the Churches in New-England for Church-Covenant* (London, 1643). Bernard's interest in New England is also revealed by a copy he made of Cotton's critical letter to Samuel Skelton in 1630, in which Cotton (still in England) accused Skelton of separation: Bush, ed., *Cotton Correspondence*, pp. 142–3. *ANB*, Glenn W. LaFantasie, 'Williams, Roger (1603?–1683)'; *ODNB*, Richard L. Greaves, 'Bernard, Richard (*bap.* 1598, *d.* 1641)'; Collinson, *Godly People*, p. 545. Bernard's son Masakiell, a clothier, followed his sister over in 1635, in a party of twenty-one families (some from Bernard's parish of Batcombe) led by Joseph Hull, Rector of Northleigh, Devon: Winthrop, *Journal*, p. 150; *CR*, 'Hull, Joseph'.

62. Dod et al. to New England 'Brethren', in Bush, ed., *Cotton Correspondence*, pp. 262–8. A member of Dod's circle sent a letter earlier to Cotton, to challenge his reasons for leaving England. Cotton's reply is the first letter that postdates his arrival in America to survive: John Cotton to a Minister in England, 3 December 1634, in Bush, ed., *Cotton Correspondence*, pp. 181–8.

63. Dod et al., and Cotton's reply to Dod in December 1637: Bush, ed., *Cotton Correspondence*, pp. 265, 271; for Dod's earlier endorsement of Cotton's wish to emigrate, see *Magnalia*, I, p. 263.

64. This was Dod's advice to the minister George Hughes: Dr Williams's Library, London, Quick Ms. 38.35, 'Icones Sacrae Anglicanae', fols 494–5. *ODNB*, Mary Wolffe, 'Hughes, George (1603/4–1667)'. After two months, Dod found Hughes a place as chaplain to Lord Brooke at Warwick Castle.

65. John Cotton, *A Coppy of a Letter of Mr. Cotton of Boston, in New England, sent in answer of certaine Objections made against their Discipline and Orders there, directed to a Friend* (London, 1641), reprinted in Bush, ed., Cotton Correspondence, pp. 237–42; quotation from p. 238. Cotton wrote soon after Roger Williams' banishment from Massachusetts in January 1635/6. To de-mystify what went on in New England's churches, Cotton explained what churches asked of people who wanted to become members, and wrote out a copy of the Boston church covenant. Cotton's letter was probably sent to someone from the Stour Valley on the Essex-Suffolk border, who knew that John Wilson, pastor of the Boston church, had returned to that area to recruit settlers. Wilson's activities – in two visits, in 1631–2 and 1634–5 – became controversial. Daniel Rogers of Wetherfield in Essex prevented his son Samuel from falling prey to the temptation to follow Wilson to the New World: Webster, *Godly Clergy*, pp. 278–9, 281–5.

66. _____ to John Winthrop, [*c.* May 1637], *Winthrop Papers*, III, p. 398. This report came from a critic near Colyton in Devon who dared not sign his or her name, but who was aware of the critique Richard Bernard had sent to John Cotton. With the instincts of a spin-doctor, the writer proposed that New England should hold a solemn fast day for England, and send back a sermon preached on the occasion to reassure the godly that settlers still cared for their native country. This suggestion bore fruit in *New Englands Teares, for Old Englands Feares* (London, 1641), a sermon preached by William Hooke

on Massachusetts' first official fast day for England in 1640. It is unlikely to be a coincidence that Hooke had been Vicar of Axmouth, two miles from Colyton, until he left for New England.

67. Richard Mather, 'Arguments', [Mather], *Life . . . of . . . Richard Mather*, pp. 12–20.

68. B. Richard Burg, 'A Letter of Richard Mather to a Cleric in Old England', *William and Mary Quarterly*, 3rd series, 29 (1972), pp. 81–98 (the recipient has not been identified); Emerson, ed., *Letters from New England*, pp. 201–8, to 'Mr Rathband' (William Rathband, Curate of High Lever, soon a ferocious opponent of New England), and 'Mr T.' (probably William Thompson, who followed Mather across the Atlantic in 1637 and became his collaborator in later replies to fellow Lancastrians).

69. Mather, *Church-Government and Church-Covenant Discussed*, pp. 6, 83–4. White to Winthrop, *Winthrop Papers*, III, pp. 335–6. Thomas Edwards, *Reasons against the Independant Government of Particular Congregations* (London, 1641), p. 32, identified the questioners as being from Lancashire.

70. Richard Mather and William Thompson, *An Heart-Melting Exhortation* (London, 1650), pp. 5, 10. The presses were so busy in 1645 that 'it was cast by so long, that at last the authors sent home for it again to N.E.'; in 1650 their friends still thought it worth publishing, to show Mather and Thompson's love to their countrymen. In an earlier work, Mather and Thompson acknowledged affection and respect for another Lancastrian critic of New England, the relatively conciliatory Charles Herle, minister at Winwick: Mather had been born in Herle's parish and Thompson had worked there. Mather and Thompson, *A Modest and Brotherly Answer to Mr. Charles Herle his book against the Independency of Churches* (London, 1644), sig. A2v; *ODNB*, Vivienne Larminie, 'Herle, Charles (1597/8–1659)'. Herle's *The Independency on Scriptures of the Independency of Churches* appeared in May 1643; it may have prompted Hugh Peter's publication six weeks later of Mather's *Church-Government and Church-Covenant Discussed*.

71. Presbyterians and Congregationalists shared the same Reformed theology, but in the mid-1640s fell out seriously over church government. In political terms, this fuelled the animosity between Parliament and the army. English Congregationalists also advocated religious toleration, an issue on which they diverged not only from Presbyterians, but also from religious policy in Massachusetts and Connecticut (though not in Rhode Island).

72. Peter contributed a preface to Richard Mather, *Church-Government and Church-Covenant Discussed* (London, 1643), which put into print three manuscripts that had circulated hand-to-hand in England since 1639: Mather's reply to 32 questions from Lancashire, printed as *Church-Government and Church-Covenant Discussed*; Mather's reply to Richard Bernard, printed as *An Apologie of the Churches of New England for Church Covenant*; and a reply to John Dod, printed as *An Answer of the Elders of the Severall Churches of New England unto Nine Positions*. All three appeared in one volume, although the title tract was from a different press than the other two. Mather's son Nathaniel later stated that his father had not written the reply to Bernard for public scrutiny. He had 'neither acquaintance nor any intercourse by letters with Mr Bernard', but had written 'for his private use in his own study, never intending, nor indeed consenting to its publication, nor so much as knowing unto this day how the copy of it came abroad . . . save that he conjectures some procured a copy of it from Mr Cotton': 'To the Reader', [Richard Mather], *A Disputation Concerning Church Members and their Children* (London, 1659). Nathaniel wrote this while a minister in the West Country, where perhaps he had to contend with Bernard's reputation as an opponent of New England. *An Answer of the Elders* has often been attributed to John Davenport of New Haven, but, as Theodore Dwight Bozeman points out, this attribution is flimsy: *To Live Ancient Lives: The Primitivist Dimension in Puritanism* (Chapel Hill and London: University of North Carolina Press, 1988), p. 226n. W[illiam] R[athband], *A*

Briefe Narration of some Church Courses . . . in New England (London, 1644), p. 31, said that the author was 'Mr M.', although perhaps only because it appeared in a volume with other works by Mather. On the authorship and publication of these tracts, see B.R. Burg, *Richard Mather of Dorchester* (Lexington: University Press of Kentucky, 1976), pp. 176–7; R.P. Stearns, *The Strenuous Puritan: Hugh Peter, 1598–1660* (Urbana, Illinois: University of Illinois Press, 1954), pp. 211–12. For the background to these debates, see Carol G. Schneider, 'Roots and Branches: From Principled Nonconformity to the Emergence of Religious Parties', in Bremer, ed., *Puritanism: Transatlantic Perspectives*, pp. 167–200.

73. Rathband, *A Briefe Narration*; Thomas Weld, *An Answer to W.R. His Narration* (London, 1644), p. 5. Rathband (who does not appear in the *ODNB*) identified letter writers only by initials. He and the arch-Presbyterian propagandist Thomas Edwards used similar methods: Ann Hughes, *Gangraena and the Struggle for the English Revolution* (Oxford: Oxford University Press, 2004), pp. 301–8. Weld published his riposte within four months. Richard Mather wrote a six hundred page reply to Rathband, 'A Plea for the Churches of Christ in New England' (never published and now in the Massachusetts Historical Society, Boston). Mather's earlier letters to Lancastrian clergy survive because he copied them into this manuscript.

74. John Allin and Thomas Shepard, *A Defence of the Answer made unto the Nine Questions* (London, 1648), pp. 10, 12–15, 33. Allin and Shepard complained about those who (like Rathband) 'seek all the private letters they can gather up, and search every corner to discover and publish to the world the seeming failings of brethren'.

75. John Dod et al. to New England 'Brethren', in Bush, ed., *Cotton Correspondence*, p. 265; echoed in modern times by Perry Miller, *Orthodoxy in Massachusetts, 1630–1650* (Gloucester, Mass.: Peter Smith, 1933, reprinted 1965), pp. 84, 136–44; Foster, *Long Argument*, pp. 165, 169; Delbanco, *Puritan Ordeal*, p. 99; Avihu Zakai, *Exile and Kingdom: History and Apocalypse in the Puritan Migration to America* (Cambridge: Cambridge University Press, 1992), p. 226.

76. The best example is the anthology of replies to critics from different parts of England represented in Mather's *Church-Government and Church-Covenant*. On England, Patrick Collinson, 'The Cohabitation of the Faithful with the Unfaithful', in Ole Peter Grell, Jonathan I. Israel, and Nicholas Tyacke, eds, *From Persecution to Toleration: The Glorious Revolution in England* (Oxford: Clarendon Press, 1991), pp. 62–3; see also his 'The English Conventicle', in Sheils and Wood, eds, *Voluntary Religion*, pp. 223–59.

77. Foster, *Long Argument*, pp. 138–44, 151–66, makes a case for the 'broadly based puritanism of the early migration and its more militant, sectarian successor'. For a different perspective, see Susan Hardman Moore, 'Popery, purity and Providence: deciphering the New England experiment', in Anthony Fletcher and Peter Roberts, eds, *Religion, Culture and Society in Early Modern Britain* (Cambridge: Cambridge University Press, 1994), pp. 274–6. If English puritanism is interpreted as heading inexorably in a separatist direction, it is natural to read the influence of separatism into the formation of New England, for example to account for colonial innovations as the result of radical separatist laity pushing clergy in new directions. When more weight is given to the strength of resistance to separatism in the godly circles settlers came from, and to the role of preachers in shaping religious experience, this puts New England's innovations into a different perspective.

78. Robert Stansby, a Suffolk minister, called New England a 'kingdom divided' against itself (that is, one which would not survive, Matthew 12:25): *Winthrop Papers*, III, p. 390.

79. Kupperman, *Providence Island*, pp. 146–7, 320–5, 336, 341; see also Karen Ordahl Kupperman, 'Errand to the Indies: Puritan Colonisation from Providence Island through the Western Design', *William and Mary Quarterly*, 3rd series, 45 (1988), pp. 70–99.

80. Winthrop recorded details of his letter, written 20 March 1640, in his *Journal*: pp. 324–5. Viscount Saye and Sele's reply, 9 July 1640: *Winthrop Papers*, IV, pp. 263–7; see also John Endecott to Winthrop, *Winthrop Papers*, IV, pp. 314–16. *ODNB*, 'Fiennes, William, first Viscount Saye and Sele (1582–1662)'. Although Winthrop did not crow about the fall of Providence Island, he made acerbic comments about Humfrey: *Journal*, pp. 414–16.

81. *ANB*, 'Williams, Roger'; Kupperman, *Providence Island*, pp. 320–56. The dominant colonies of Massachusetts, Connecticut and New Haven had no settlement called Providence, but competitors (for orthodoxy, or economic success) claimed the name.

82. Giles Firmin to John Winthrop, 12 February 1639/40, *Winthrop Papers*, IV, p. 191. John Cotton told Roger Williams 'the way of separation is not a way that God hath prospered': Bush, ed., *Cotton Correspondence*, p. 220.

83. John Cotton, *The Churches Resurrection* (London, 1642), p. 17: 'In the apostles' times, that was a plantation of churches . . . So when England was planted, and the churches there, it was a plantation not a reformation.'

84. Burg, 'A Letter of Richard Mather', p. 88.

85. ____ to Winthrop [May 1637], *Winthrop Papers*, III, p. 399; Rathband, *A Briefe Narration*, p. 53.

86. 'Of the Way of Reformation in the Congregations of England', John Cotton, *The Way of the Churches of Christ in New-England* (London, 1645), pp. 111–16. This tract was published without Cotton's consent, but he did not repudiate it: see his comments in John Owen, *A Defence of Mr. John Cotton from the Imputation of Selfe Contradiction* (Oxford, 1658), second pagination, pp. 36–40. The proposals covered a wide range of topics: for example, the similarity of communion discipline in the Book of Common Prayer to admission to New England's churches; reforms of patronage and ordination; the replacement of parish officers with a four-fold ministry; 'brotherly consultation' between neighbouring churches; the removal of scandalous ministers; the provision of preachers for 'profane' congregations. A hostile witness, Thomas Lechford, noted Cotton's willingness to see matters of church order as to some extent negotiable (in contrast to twelve articles of doctrine that were the 'foundation of religion'), in a sermon preached in October 1640: Lechford, *Plain Dealing*, pp. 9–10.

87. See, for example, Peter Lake's discussion of William Bradshaw: *Moderate Puritans and the Elizabethan Church* (Cambridge: Cambridge University Press, 1982), pp. 262–78; *ODNB*, Victoria Gregory, 'Bradshaw, William (*bap.* 1570, *d.* 1618)'.

88. Shepard, 'The Parable of the Ten Virgins Opened and Applied', in J.A. Albro, ed., *The Works of Thomas Shepard*, 3 vols (Boston, Mass., 1853), II, pp. 626, 170. Shepard was himself in debt: Thomas Hooker to Shepard, 2 Nov. 1640, Massachusetts Archives, Boston, Massachusetts Archives Collection, vol. 240: 37. On the rhetoric of suffering, see J. Sears McGee, *The Godly Man in Stuart England: Anglicans, Puritans, and the Two Tables, 1620–1670* (New Haven: Yale University Press, 1976), pp. 15–67.

89. Cotton, *Churches Resurrection*, p. 21. Cotton also expressed concern about migration westwards within New England.

90. John Cotton, *An Exposition upon the Thirteenth Chapter of the Revelation* (London, 1655), pp. 20, 262. Thomas Allen, who heard Cotton preach these sermons, wrote a preface 'To the Reader', which dated them between January and April 1640. The image of the 'outstretched hand' delivering Israel from Egypt came from Deuteronomy 26:8. Foster, *Long Argument*, pp. 158–9, takes Cotton's comment 'would you go back to Egypt?' as a sign of *de facto* separatism, but does not quote the counterbalancing affirmation.

91. John Tinker to John Winthrop, 26 Feb. 1639/40, *Winthrop Papers*, IV, p. 205; Winthrop, *Journal*, p. 341.

Chapter 3

1. Cotton Mather, *Memoirs of the Life of the Rev. Increase Mather D.D.* (London, 1724), pp. 2–3; C.H. Pope, ed., *Records of the First Church at Dorchester . . . 1636–1734* (Boston, 1891), p. 151.

2. *Records of the First Church at Dorchester*, p. 153. 'Unsettled humours': John Cotton to Richard Saltonstall Jr, [1649], Boston Public Library, Ms. Am. 1506, pt. 3, app. No. 5 (printed in Sargent Bush Jr, ed., *The Correspondence of John Cotton* (Chapel Hill and London: University of North Carolina Press, 2001), p. 420, but with 'Humyrs' transcribed as 'Hurryes'. Although Return stayed, most of his family left: Alison Games, *Migration and the Origins of the English Atlantic World* (Cambridge, Mass., and London: Harvard University Press, 2001), pp. 142–3, 203–4.

3. Increase Mather, *A Brief Relation of the State of New England, from the Beginning of that Plantation to this Present Year, 1689* (London, 1689), p. 5. Michael G. Hall, ed., 'The Autobiography of Increase Mather', American Antiquarian Society, *Proceedings*, 71 (1961), part 2, pp. 280–7; *ODNB*, Francis J. Bremer, 'Mather, Increase (1639–1723)'. David Cressy, *Coming Over: Migration and Communication between England and New England in the Seventeenth Century* (Cambridge: Cambridge University Press, 1987), pp. 210–12, documents Mather's 'persistent attachment' to England.

4. Nathaniel Ward, *The Simple Cobler of Aggawam in America* (London, 1647), p. 23 and titlepage. Archbishop Laud went to the block in January 1644/5. Ward started to write the pamphlet in 1645, and shipped the manuscript back in 1646. It was published in London: the bookseller George Thomason received a copy on 29 January 1646/7 (BL, Thomason Tracts, E.372[21]). Ward was still in Massachusetts in December 1646, but reached London by the following March: J.W. Dean, *A Memoir of the Rev. Nathaniel Ward* (Albany, N.Y.: J. Munsell, 1868), pp. 77, 81, 88. Ward had been a leading settler of Ipswich, a coastal town founded on land called 'Agawam' by its Native American inhabitants.

5. *ODNB*, K. Grudzien Baston, 'Ward, Nathaniel (1578–1652)'; *ANB*, Mary Rhinelander McCarl, 'Ward, Nathaniel (c.1578–1652)'; Simon P. Newman, 'Nathaniel Ward, 1580–1652: An Elizabethan Puritan in a Jacobean World', Essex Institute, *Historical Collections*, 127 (1991), pp. 313–26; Jean Béranger, *Nathaniel Ward* (Bordeaux: Études et Recherches Anglaises et Anglo-Américaines, Université de Bordeaux, 1969); Dean, *A Memoir of . . . Nathaniel Ward*. For John Ward, minister of Haverhill, Massachusetts (a community he pioneered with his father, named after Nathaniel's birthplace in Suffolk), see F.L. Weis, *Colonial Clergy and the Colonial Churches of New England* (Lancaster, Mass.: Society of the Descendants of Colonial Clergy, 1936), pp. 214–15. Nathaniel Ward's son-in-law Giles Firmin had already found a new role as a godly preacher in Essex; Ward followed him there with his daughter and a son. *ODNB*, N.H. Keeble, 'Firmin, Giles (1613/14–1697)'.

6. Between 1640 and 1643: Blackwood, Burdett, Eaton, Gibson, Knollys, Larkham, Lenthall, Hugh Peter (as a colonial agent, with Weld), John Phillip, Peck, Saxton, Weld. Francis Bright returned to England in 1630. Nathaniel Eaton, the first head of Harvard College, left in disgrace in 1639 for Virginia, but later returned to England. Appendix 3 notes which of the first generation clergy returned home, and when.

7. See appendix 2, and William Sachse, 'Harvard Men in England 1642–1714', Colonial Society of Massachusetts, *Publications*, 35 (1942–46), pp. 120–31. A list of early graduates can be found in *Harvard College Records I*, Colonial Society of Massachusetts, *Publications*, 15 (1925), pp. 82–3.

8. Many of the 600 who are known to have returned home are listed in appendix 2. In terms of migration out to New England, 'the year 1637 stands out for its relatively complete data . . . there had not been such careful recording before and there would not be again' – 273 migrants in total, 81 adult males: Timothy Breen and Stephen Foster, 'Moving to the New World: the Character of Early Massachusetts Immigration',

William and Mary Quarterly, 3rd series, 30 (1973), pp. 192–3. Virginia DeJohn Anderson, *New England's Generation: The Great Migration and the Formation of Society and Culture in the Seventeenth Century* (Cambridge: Cambridge University Press, 1991), is based on the same cohort. Alison Games based her study on almost 5,000 passengers who left the port of London for America in 1635 (to thirteen different destinations), the largest contingent to depart from a single port in a single year: *Migration*, p. 1. Cressy, *Coming Over*, pp. 130–43, discusses the patchy control of emigration from England to New England. No similar bureaucracy existed for the journey back to England.

9. Carla Gardina Pestana, *The English Atlantic in an Age of Revolution, 1640–1661* (Cambridge, Mass., and London: Harvard University Press, 2004), pp. 229–32.

10. This tallies with Thompson's finding that 60 of the 718 adult male migrants in his cohort of immigrants from 'Greater East Anglia' returned to England (one in twelve): Roger Thompson, *Mobility and Migration: East Anglian Founders of New England* (Amherst, Mass.: University of Massachusetts Press, 1994), p. 207.

11. John Winthrop, *The Journal of John Winthrop*, ed. Richard S. Dunn, James Savage and Laetitia Yeandle (Cambridge, Mass., and London: Harvard University Press, 1996), p. 354. The seven passengers were Ferdinando Adams, Hugh Peter, Thomas Weld, Thomas Lechford and probably Peter Saxton, who all stayed on for good, as well as William Hibbins and John Winthrop Jr, who later returned to New England.

12. See, for example, various ships bound for England with dozens of passengers aboard, of whom only a tiny handful can be identified: Winthrop, *Journal*, pp. 414–15, 598–9, 643–4; *Winthrop Papers*, V, p. 119; Edward Winslow, *New-Englands Salamander* (London, 1647), p. 20. The difficulties of assessing the number and identity of migrants from what survives are illustrated by another fragment from Winthrop's *Journal*. In the summer of 1638, Winthrop reckoned, 'twenty ships, and at least three thousand persons' came to New England; yet of these only seven ships can be identified, and the surviving passenger lists name only 260 migrants – or one in twelve: Winthrop, *Journal*, p. 261. The New England Historic Genealogical Society's 'Great Migration Project', as it evolves, may shed more light on this: http://www.greatmigration.org.

13. This matches the estimate David Cressy arrived at from statistics of colonial population: 'as many as one in six migrants to New England may have either permanently or temporarily returned home': Cressy, *Coming Over*, p. 192. Cressy suggests that the disparity between the number of emigrants to New England (21,000) and New England's population in 1640 (between 13,500 and 17,600) is accounted for by migration to other colonies or back to England – although he acknowledges that the best figures available are not robust, and that from the raw statistics of colonial population there is no way to discriminate between migrants who moved on within the New World and those who went home.

14. Thompson, *Mobility and Migration*, pp. 41–2, 52, notes the attraction of return for the 'better sort' and the clergy. See also Harry S. Stout, 'The Morphology of Remigration: New England University Men and their Return to England, 1640–1660', *Journal of American Studies*, 10 (1976), pp. 151–72.

15. Winthrop, *Journal*, p. 342. James E. McWilliams, 'New England's First Depression: Beyond an Export-Led Interpretation', *Journal of Interdisciplinary History*, 33 (2002), p. 16, challenges the notion that exports quickly lifted settlers out of the crisis: 'cows and wood, not fish and ships' – in other words, meeting immediate needs – were the settlers' priorities.

16. Winthrop, *Journal*, pp. 223n., 251; *NEHGR*, 3 (1849), p. 153; C.J. Hoadley, ed., *Records of the Colony and Plantation of New Haven*, 2 vols (Hartford, Conn., 1857–58), 1, pp. 40, 45; Samuel Eaton and Timothy Taylor, *The Defence of Sundry Positions and Scriptures for the Congregational-Way Justified* (London, 1646), pp. 41–2; *CSPD*, 1641–1643, p. 77; Thomas Edwards, *Gangraena* (London, 1646), iii, p. 68; *ODNB*, S.J. Guscott, 'Eaton,

Samuel (*d*.1665)'; *CR*. Eaton gathered a church which met in the chapel of Dukinfield Hall: see Plate 8.

17. PRO, SP 16/346/26; [William Prynne], *Newes from Ipswich* (Ipswich [i.e. London?], 1636), [sig. A4]; *Winthrop Papers*, III, pp. 439–40; D.G. Hill, ed., *The Record of Baptisms, Marriages, and Deaths, and Admissions to the Church and Dismissals Therefrom, Transcribed from the Church Records in the Town of Dedham, Massachusetts* (Dedham, Mass., 1888), pp. 22, 36–7; Thompson, *Mobility and Migration*, p. 265.

18. Bodleian, MS. Tanner 220, fols 1r–3r (Allen); fols 145r–145v (Peck); see also fols 54r–56r. Peck returned to Hingham in 1641. Allen left New England for Norwich in 1651.

19. Charles Chauncy, *The Retraction of Mr. Charles Chancy* (London, 1641), titlepage.

20. Winthrop, *Journal*, p. 354; R.P. Stearns, 'The Weld–Peter Mission to England', Colonial Society of Massachusetts, *Publications*, 32 (1937), pp. 188–246; *ODNB*, Michael P. Winship, 'Weld, Thomas (*bap*. 1595, *d*. 1661)'; Carla Gardina Pestana, 'Peter, Hugh (*bap*. 1598, *d*. 1660)'. William Hibbins, the owner of a leatherworks, accompanied Peter and Weld as an agent, 1641–42. On the role of colonial agents, see Graeme J. Milne, 'New England Agents and the English Atlantic, 1641–1666', (Ph.D. diss., University of Edinburgh, 1993).

21. Sir Nathaniel Barnardiston to John Winthrop, 15 March 1639/40, *Winthrop Papers*, IV, p. 218. *ODNB*, Richard L. Greaves, 'Barnardiston, Sir Nathaniel (1588–1653)'.

22. John Endecott to John Winthrop, *c*. February 1641, *Winthrop Papers*, IV, p. 315.

23. For example, Edwards, *Gangraena*, i, pp. 98–9, iii, pp. 120–46; Ann Hughes, *Gangraena and the Struggle for the English Revolution* (Oxford: Oxford University Press, 2004), pp. 63, 125, 247–9, 302–4.

24. Thomas Lechford: *ODNB*, Barbara Ritter Dailey, 'Lechford, Thomas (*d*. in or after 1642)'.

25. Michael P. Winship, '"The Most Glorious Church in the World": the Unity of the Godly in Boston, Massachusetts, in the 1630s', *Journal of British Studies*, 39 (2000), p. 96.

26. *Boston CR*, pp. 18, 23; Winthrop, *Journal*, pp. 219, 283. In 1640, what is now the New Hampshire coastline had four independent settlements: Exeter, Dover, Strawberry Bank (Portsmouth), and Hampton. (Massachusetts acquired Dover in 1641 and annexed what is now the New Hampshire coastline and southern Maine in 1652. New Hampshire became a distinct political entity in 1680.) For Marshall's connections with Woodkirk and nearby towns, see Lambeth Palace Ms. COMM. XIIa/18 fols 286–8, 320–1; R.A. Marchant, *The Puritans and the Church Courts in the Diocese of York* (London: Longmans, 1960), pp. 42, 108–11, 264, 267; G.F. Nuttall, *The Holy Spirit in Puritan Faith and Experience* (Oxford: Blackwell, 1946; reprint Chicago and London: University of Chicago Press, 1992), p. 179; G.F. Nuttall, *Visible Saints: The Congregational Way, 1640–1660* (Oxford: Blackwell, 1957), p. 123; *BDBR*; *CR*. David R. Como, *Blown by the Spirit. Puritanism and the Emergence of an Antinomian Underground in Pre-Civil-War England* (Stanford: Stanford University Press, 2004), pp. 266–324, 441–4, discusses the Grindletonians and the links with the Antinomian Controversy. *ODNB*, Leo Damrosch, 'Nayler, James (1618–1660)'; H. Larry Ingle, 'Fox, George (1624–1691)'.

27. Winthrop, *Journal*, pp. 285, 300, 318; Thomas Lechford, *Plain Dealing: or, Newes from New-England* (London, 1642), p. 43; [Hanserd Knollys], *The Life and Death of . . . Mr. Hanserd Knollys* (London, 1692), pp. 17–18; *ODNB*, Kenneth G.C. Newport, 'Knollys, Hanserd (1598–1661)'. Like Knollys, Christopher Blackwood emerged in England as a Baptist. Curate of Rye in Sussex before emigration, Blackwood left Scituate in Plymouth Colony in 1642: *ODNB*, Richard L. Greaves, 'Blackwood, Christopher (1607/8–1670)'. For the activities of Knollys and Blackwood after their return home, see Stephen Wright, *The Early English Baptists, 1603–1649* (Woodbridge, Suffolk: Boydell Press, 2006).

28. Thomas Patient, *The Doctrine of Baptism* (London, 1654), 'Epistle to the Christian Reader'. Marked 'gone', 12 July 1642: G.F. Dow, ed., *The Records and Files of the Quarterly Courts of Essex County, Massachusetts*, 8 vols (Salem, Mass.: Essex Institute, 1911–21), 1, p. 52. Carla Gardina Pestana, *Quakers and Baptists in Colonial Massachusetts* (Cambridge: Cambridge University Press, 1991), p. 66; *ODNB*, Richard L. Greaves, 'Patient, Thomas (*d.* 1666)'; Wright, *Early English Baptists*.

29. *A Note-Book kept by Thomas Lechford . . . in Boston*, American Antiquarian Society, *Transactions and Collections*, VII (Cambridge, Mass.: J. Wilson & Co., 1885), p. 274; Lechford, *Plain Dealing*, pp. 68–80 (letters to his friends in England).

30. *ODNB*, 'Lechford, Thomas'; Lechford, *Plain Dealing*, 'To the Reader'.

31. *A Note-Book kept by Thomas Lechford*, pp. 47–50 (a copy of a letter to Hugh Peter); Thomas Lechford to the Elders of the Boston Church [September 9, 1640], in Bush, ed., *Cotton Correspondence*, pp. 328–9.

32. *A Note-Book kept by Thomas Lechford*. Lechford started the notebook as soon as he arrived in Boston on 27 June 1638; the last entry was on 29 July 1641. Thomas G. Barnes, 'Thomas Lechford and the Earliest Lawyering in Massachusetts, 1638–1641', in Daniel R. Coquillette, Robert J. Brink and Catherine S. Menard, eds, *Law in Colonial Massachusetts*, Colonial Society of Massachusetts, *Publications*, 62 (1984), pp. 3–38; Angela Fernandez, 'Record-Keeping and other Trouble-Making: Thomas Lechford and Law Reform in Colonial Massachusetts', *Law and History Review*, Summer 2005, http://www.historycooperative.org/journals/lhr/23.2/fernandez.html (accessed 12 August 2006).

33. Lechford, *Plain Dealing*; [Anon.], *New Englands First Fruits* (London, 1643); William Prynne, *Independency Examined, Unmasked, Refuted* (London, 1644). For Weld's role in composing *New Englands First Fruits*, see Raymond P. Stearns, *The Strenuous Puritan: Hugh Peter, 1598–1660* (Urbana, Illinois: University of Illinois Press, 1954), p. 67.

34. Karen Ordahl Kupperman, *Providence Island, 1630–1641: The Other Puritan Colony* (Cambridge: Cambridge University Press, 1993), pp. 213, 244–5. Burdett to Laud, in Everett Emerson, ed., *Letters from New England* (Amherst, Mass.: University of Massachusetts Press, 1972), pp. 180–1.

35. Winthrop, *Journal*, pp. 348–50, 421; Lechford, *Plain Dealing*, pp. 44, 53. Larkham gave his own account of his dispute with Knollys to Winthrop, *c.* February 1640/41: *Winthrop Papers*, IV, pp. 317–19. *ODNB*, Susan Hardman Moore, 'Larkham, Thomas (1602–1669)'.

36. Edwards, *Gangraena*, iii, p. 97; F[rancis]. G[lanville]. D[igory]. P[olwhele]. W[alter]. G[odbear]. N[icholas]. W[atts]. W[illiam]. H[ore]., *The Tavistocke Naboth Turned Nabal* (London, 1658), p. 15. BL, Ms. Loan 9, Diary of Thomas Larkham, 1650–1669, fol. 16 (12 November 1654); see also fols 21, 24, 27, 32, 35v, 43v.

37. Winthrop, *Journal*, p. 150; *CR*, 'Hull, Joseph'.

38. Winthrop, *Journal*, pp. 281–2; Thomas Dudley to John Winthrop, 11 December 1638, *Winthrop Papers*, IV, p. 86 (referring to Numbers 25: 1–9); Lechford, *Plain Dealing*, p. 22; David D. Hall, *The Faithful Shepherd: A History of the New England Ministry in the Seventeenth Century*, 2nd edn (Cambridge, Mass.: Harvard University Press, 2006), pp. 102–3. In 1647, Job Lane of Dorchester made 'Mr Lenthall minister of Little Hamden in Bucking[hamshire]' his attorney, to take possession of land for him: *Aspinwall NR*, p. 106. Lenthall left New England in 1642. The reply to Bernard, written by Richard Mather, was published as part of Mather's *Church-Government and Church-Covenant Discussed* (London, 1643).

39. Winthrop, *Journal*, p. 414. Marion Gottfried, 'The First Depression in Massachusetts', *New England Quarterly*, 9 (1936), pp. 655–78; Roger Thompson, *Divided We Stand: Watertown, Massachusetts, 1630–1680* (Amherst, Mass.: University of Massachusetts Press, 2001), pp. 94–5.

40. Winthrop, *Journal*, p. 333. This man, 'one Austin', has not been identified. Winthrop commented that he arrived in 1638 'and not finding the country as he expected . . . grew discontented'. On Muslim corsairs off North Africa and the Christian shipping they targeted, see Linda Colley, *Captives: Britain, Empire and the World 1600–1850* (London: Pimlico, 2003), pp. 43–72.

41. Hugh Peter to the Massachusetts General Court, 10 September 1638, *Winthrop Papers*, IV, p. 56. On John Humfrey [Humphrey]: Kupperman, *Providence Island*, pp. 146–7, 315, 322–5, 336, 341–3; Louise A. Breen, *Transgressing the Bounds: Subversive Enterprises among the Puritan Elite in Massachusetts, 1630–1692* (Oxford and New York: Oxford University Press, 2001), pp. 104–10; Frances Rose Troup, 'John Humfrey', Essex Institute, *Historical Collections*, 65 (1929), pp. 293–308.

42. Fenwick to John Winthrop, 6 July 1640, *Winthrop Papers*, IV, p. 261; Thomas Hooker to Thomas Shepard, [early 1640s], Massachusetts Archives, Boston, Massachusetts Archives Collection, vol. 240: 102. Not long before he sailed home, Fenwick commended the virtues of staying put: moving not only weakened the plantation, 'but also . . . consumes the estate of those that remove. Rolling stones gather no moss . . . We are not to expect great things. Small things . . . should content us: a warm fireside and peaceable habitation.' But he soon became Member of the Long Parliament for Morpeth in his native county, Northumberland. George Fenwick to William Leete, 22 Oct. 1645: Guilford, Connecticut, Town Clerk's Office, Guilford Records, Volume B, fols 4–5. (The date is puzzling because Fenwick was elected an MP on 20 October 1645.) *ODNB*, Walter W. Woodward, 'Fenwick, George (*c*.1603–1657)'. Saybrook had become part of the Connecticut colony in 1644, after Connecticut bought its land and fort. On the investors' changed agenda, see Kupperman, *Providence Island*, pp. 213, 244–5, 326–35.

43. Johan Winsser, 'Walter Blackborne, a London milliner briefly in New England', *NEHGR*, 151 (1997), pp. 408–16; W.B. Trask, ed., *Suffolk Deeds*, 12 vols (Boston: Rockwell and Churchill, 1880–1902), 1: 20.

44. Richard Saltonstall took a vow to stay in New England, on principle; some borrowed money or tried to call in debts to finance the homeward journey: see chapter 5. Thompson, *Mobility and Migration*, p. 113.

45. Trask, ed., *Suffolk Deeds*, I: 37–8; *CR*. In New England, ministers' salaries averaged around £55 a year: Thompson, *Divided We Stand*, p. 223n. A London lecturer might earn £50 a year: Ian Green, 'Career Prospects and Clerical Conformity in the Early Stuart Church', *Past and Present*, 90 (1981), p. 87. Thomas Trowbridge of New Haven had his whole estate seized to pay debts, and fled. His abandoned children were taken into care: Hoadley, ed., *Records of the Colony and Plantation of New Haven*, 1, pp. 59, 92, 133.

46. Thomas Hooker to his son-in-law, the minister Thomas Shepard of Cambridge (who was mired in debt and hoped to ease it by leading a party to settle Mattabeseck, just north of New Haven), 2 November 1640: Massachusetts Archives, Boston, Massachusetts Archives Collection, vol. 240: 37. The Connecticut authorities legislated in 1641 to protect debtors by insisting on arbitration to stop the sale of debtors' goods at very cheap rates: J.H. Trumbull, ed., *The Public Records of the Colony of Connecticut prior to the Union with New Haven Colony, 1665* (Hartford, 1850), 1, p. 69.

47. On 5 July 1641, the House of Commons voted Wren unfit for office. Peck and Phillip sailed for England at the end of October 1641: Winthrop, *Journal*, pp. 414–15; 'The Hobart Journal', *NEHGR*, 121 (1967), p. 14; 'Daniel Cushing's Record', *NEHGR*, 15 (1861), p. 27. On Phillip [Phillips]: Hill, ed., *Record of . . . the Church . . . in . . . Dedham, Massachusetts*, pp. 7, 8, 23, 37; Lechford, *Plain Dealing*, p. 38; *Winthrop Papers*, IV, p. 109; J.H. Tuttle, 'The Rev. John Phillips of Dedham', Colonial Society of Massachusetts, *Publications*, 17 (1913–14), pp. 208–15. Phillip had connections at Salem and Cambridge: his sister-in-law, Joan Ames, settled at Salem (where, much to Phillip's

annoyance, the minister Hugh Peter failed to honour his promise to marry his niece, Ruth); John and William Ames (*CR*), his nephews, attended Harvard. On Peck: Lechford, *Plain Dealing*, p. 37; John J. Waters, 'Hingham, Massachusetts, 1631–1661: An East Anglian Oligarchy in the New World', *Journal of Social History*, 1 (1968), pp. 362–7; D.G. Allen, *In English Ways: The Movement of Societies and the Transferal of English Local Law and Custom to Massachusetts Bay in the Seventeenth Century* (Chapel Hill, N.C.: University of North Carolina Press, 1981), pp. 173–4.

48. Thomas Peter to John Winthrop [early 1646?], *NEHGR*, 2 (1848), p. 63. Thomas, minister at Saybrook and brother of Hugh Peter, arrived in New England in 1644, and later returned to his parish of Mylor, Cornwall: *ODNB*, Carla Gardina Pestana, 'Peter [Peters], Thomas (1597–1654/5)'. In addition to the disruption of shipping, information about quayside transactions is missing between the summer of 1641 (when Thomas Lechford stopped keeping his notebook) and late 1644 (when a new Boston notary, William Aspinwall, put pen to paper): *A Note-Book kept by Thomas Lechford*; *Aspinwall NR*.

49. John Haynes to John Winthrop, 1 December 1643, *Winthrop Papers*, IV, p. 418. James O'Toole, 'New England Reactions to the English Civil Wars', *NEHGR*, 129 (1975), pp. 3–17, 238–49.

50. William Hooke, *New-Englands Sence of Old-England and Irelands Sorrowes* (London, 1645), p. 19; a sermon preached on a fast day. Fasts in New England for England were relatively frequent: Richard P. Gildrie, 'The Ceremonial Puritan: Days of Humiliation and Thanksgiving', *NEHGR*, 136 (1982), pp. 15–16; see also William DeLoss Love, *The Fast and Thanksgiving Days of New England* (Boston: Houghton Mifflin, 1895); *Proclamations of Massachusetts Issued by Governors and other Authorities, 1620–1936*, Vol. I, 1620–1776 (Boston: Historical Records Survey, Division of Women's and Professional Projects, Works Project Administration, 1937).

51. Members of Parliament wrote in 1642 to invite John Cotton, Thomas Hooker and John Davenport to join the Westminster Assembly. Hooker doubted that it was worth travelling '3,000 miles to agree with three men' (his view of likely support for the New England Way at the Assembly); the New Haven church decided it could not spare Davenport, although he was willing to go; Cotton was also willing, but news from England of a divide between King and Parliament meant a decision was deferred, and the plan came to nothing. See Bush, ed., *Cotton Correspondence*, pp. 362–5; Winthrop, *Journal*, pp. 403–4; Sargent Bush Jr, 'Thomas Hooker and the Westminster Assembly', *William and Mary Quarterly*, 3rd series, 39 (1972), pp. 291–300. On the Artillery Company, see Breen, *Transgressing the Bounds*, pp. 3–4; Oliver A. Roberts, *History of the . . . Ancient and Honourable Artillery Company of Massachusetts, 1637–1688*, 4 vols (Boston: A. Mudge and Son, 1895–1901); T.H. Breen, 'The Covenanted Militia of Massachusetts Bay: English Background and New World Development', in his *Puritans and Adventurers: Change and Persistence in Early America* (Oxford and New York: Oxford University Press, 1980), pp. 25–45; Robert F. Trent, 'Arms and Armour', in Jonathan L. Fairbanks and Robert F. Trent, eds, *New England Begins: The Seventeenth Century*, 3 vols (Boston: Museum of Fine Arts, 1982), 1, pp. 53–65.

52. This launched the military careers of John Humfrey and William Rainborowe, and of Hugh Peter as an army chaplain: Stearns, *Strenuous Puritan: Hugh Peter*, pp. 187–201. See also Robert Thomson, *ODNB* (s.v. 'Thomson, George'). On the Irish rebellion of 1641: Nicholas Canny, 'What really happened in Ireland in 1641?', in Jane Ohlmeyer, ed., *Ireland: from Independence to Occupation, 1641–1660* (Cambridge: Cambridge University Press, 1995), pp. 24–42; Brian Mac Cuarta, ed., *Ulster 1641: Aspects of the Rising* (Belfast: Institute of Irish Studies, Queen's University of Belfast, 1993; revised edn, 1997).

53. *ODNB*, Ian J. Gentles, 'Rainborowe [Rainborow], Thomas (*d.* 1648)'; Carla Gardina Pestana, 'Rainborowe [Rainsborough], William (*fl.* 1639–1673)'. In 1642 Thomas had

been a vice-admiral in the expedition to Ireland. He was an efficient recruiter: Ian Gentles, *The New Model Army in England, Ireland and Scotland, 1645–1653* (Oxford: Blackwell, 1992), p. 35.

54. Fairbanks and Trent, eds, *New England Begins*, 1, pp. 60–1. The buff leather coat is in the collections of the Massachusetts Historical Society, Boston, and Leverett's portrait is at the Peabody Essex Museum in Salem, Massachusetts (see Plates 6, 7). The attribution to Lely is traditional and cannot be confirmed, but in the mid-1640s Lely had just started what would be an immensely successful career as a portrait painter: *ODNB*, Diana Dethloff, 'Lely, Sir Peter (1618–1680)'.

55. Winthrop, *Journal*, pp. 609–10; *GMB*, 'William Hudson' (William's father).

56. Winthrop, *Journal*, pp. 604–5. *ODNB*, Roger Thompson, 'Stoughton, Israel (*bap.* 1603, *d.* 1644); Bernard Capp, 'Bourne, Nehemiah (1611–1691)'; Richard P. Gildrie, 'Leverett, John (1616–1679)'. These three, and Hudson, served in Thomas Rainborowe's regiment.

57. *ODNB*, Carla Gardina Pestana, 'Winthrop, Stephen (1619–1658)'; *BDBR*, 'Cooke, George (*c.*1610–1652)'; Roberts, *Artillery Company*, 1, pp. 57–8; C.H. Firth and G. Davies, *The Regimental History of Cromwell's Army*, 2 vols paginated as one (Oxford: Clarendon Press, 1940), pp. 179, 184, 185, 191–2, 235, 418 (Winthrop); pp. 579–82 (Cooke). Samuel Shepard (*c.*1613–*c.*1673), half-brother to Thomas Shepard, minister of Cambridge, Massachusetts, left New England with George Cooke late in 1645: Roberts, *Artillery Company*, 1, p. 110–11.

58. Winthrop, *Journal*, pp. 687–8 (Hugh Prichard, the older and successful candidate, went to England in about 1650). Other colonists who joined the Parliamentary army in the 1640s included Benjamin Keayne (a major in Stephen Winthrop's regiment according to Roberts, *Artillery Company*, 1, pp. 67–9, possibly the 'Kaine' referred to by Firth and Davies, *Regimental History*, p. 452), Thomas Marshall (Roberts, *Artillery Company*, 1, p. 108), William Ridge and Garret Trout (*Aspinwall NR*, p. 8), William Horsford (David Underdown, *Fire from Heaven: Life in an English Town in the Seventeenth Century* (London: Fontana, 1993), p. 136, and Thomas Huckens (Roberts, *Artillery Company*, 1, p. 28).

59. Winthrop, *Journal*, pp. 599, 605. Abraham Pratt: *GMB*. Firmin: *ODNB*, N.H. Keeble, 'Firmin, Giles (1613/14–1697)'.

60. Initially, Christopher Blackwood, George Burdett, Samuel Eaton, Hanserd Knollys, Thomas Larkham, Thomas Patient, Hugh Peter and Thomas Weld. Later, John Collins, George Downing, Thomas Harrison, John Hoadley, Samuel Mather, Edmund Weld and Thomas Willis Jr (*ODNB*). See Anne Laurence, *Parliamentary Army Chaplains, 1642–1651* (Woodbridge, Suffolk: Royal Historical Society, 1990). On religious fervour in the army, see Gentles, *New Model Army*, pp. 87–119; Ian J. Gentles, 'The Iconography of Revolution: England 1642–1649', in Ian Gentles, John Morrill and Blair Worden, eds, *Soldiers, Writers and Statesmen of the English Revolution* (Cambridge: Cambridge University Press, 1998), pp. 91–113.

61. For Cromwell's close connections with emigrants and his intention of going to New England, see *ODNB*, John Morrill, 'Cromwell, Oliver (1599–1658)'.

62. Winslow, *New-Englands Salamander*, pp. 16–17, 20 (Winslow sailed back with Bourne); John Winthrop to John Winthrop Jr, 16 Nov. 1646, Thomas Peter to John Winthrop, 17 Feb. 1646/7, *Winthrop Papers*, V, pp. 119, 129; Winthrop, *Journal*, p. 681.

63. Pestana, *English Atlantic*, p. 77. James F. Cooper Jr, *Tenacious of their Liberties: The Congregationalists in Colonial Massachusetts* (Oxford and New York: Oxford University Press, 1999), pp. 68–87, assesses the 'Presbyterian challenge' within New England.

64. Thomas Goodwin and others to the Massachusetts General Court, *c.* June 1645, *Winthrop Papers*, V, pp. 23–5; for the protest of the merchants (including Thomas Fowle, Nehemiah Bourne, Robert Sedgwick and Emmanuel Downing, who all went to England later), Winthrop, *Journal*, p. 611.

65. Winthrop, *Journal*, pp. 456–8, 510–11, 554–62, 575–95. Robert Emmet Wall, *Massachusetts Bay: The Crucial Decade, 1640–1650* (New Haven: Yale University Press, 1972), pp. 93–120.

66. Edward Johnson, *A History of New-England* (London, 1653), p. 202. 'Linsey-woolsey', a cheap cloth woven from wool and flax; figuratively, 'giving the appearance of a strange medley', 'being neither one thing nor the other': *Oxford English Dictionary*.

67. Winthrop, *Journal*, pp. 624–5, 647–70. Wall, *Massachusetts Bay: The Crucial Decade*, pp. 157–224.

68. Hartley, *Ironworks on the Saugus*, pp. 77–8. Other investors included Emmanuel Downing and Thomas Weld, and the English Congregationalist William Greenhill of Stepney. *ODNB*, Stephen Clucas, 'Child, Robert (1613–1654)'; G.L. Kittredge, 'Dr Robert Child the Remonstrant', Colonial Society of Massachusetts, *Publications*, 21 (1919), pp. 1–146.

69. Winthrop, *Journal*, pp. 655–6. The magistrates and deputies were united against the Remonstrants, not divided as they had been over the Hingham militia case.

70. Winslow, *New-Englands Salamander*, pp. 14–20; 'Major John Child' [possibly William Vassall], *New-Englands Jonas cast up at London* (London, 1647), pp. 12–13 [irregular pagination]. Winslow, an agent for Massachusetts in England from 1646 to 1655, was sent over initially to represent the Bay Colony to the Parliamentary committee on foreign plantations in its dispute with Samuel Gorton of Shawomet, who had also gone to England to lobby for support: Milne, 'New England Agents', p. 307; Philip F. Gura, *A Glimpse of Sion's Glory: Puritan Radicalism in New England, 1620–1660* (Middletown, Conn.: Wesleyan University Press, 1984), pp. 276–303; *ODNB*, Carla Gardina Pestana, 'Gorton, Samuel (bap. 1593, d. 1677)'.

71. *Aspinwall NR*, pp. 30–7, 48–69: October–December 1646.

72. *Aspinwall NR*, pp. 66–7. Barbara was the widow of Joseph Weld, brother of Roxbury's minister Thomas Weld (who had gone to England as a colonial agent in 1641).

73. Later, Mary Longe was granted permission to remarry if she wished to; Joseph had not reached his relatives in England, and was presumed dead. Massachusetts Historical Society, Boston, Ms. N–2195, Miscellaneous Manuscripts Collection, 22 May 1651.

74. Ezekiel Rogers to William Sykes, 2 December 1646, BL, Add. Ms. 4276, fol. 105. Boyes was a prominent citizen of Rowley and son-in-law to the minister Elkanah Wales of Pudsey near Leeds (*CR*). Boyes carried a letter from Rogers to Wales, dated 4 December 1646: BL, Add. Ms. 4276, fol. 107.

75. Thomas and Susanna Bell, who at this point travelled back with their young children, are a good example.

76. Joshua Kent of Dedham, for example, went to England with his wife in December 1647, 'his reasons not well satisfying his friends or church here'. 'Upon the troubles rising . . . in England and the wars there', the Kents returned to New England: Hill, ed., *Record of . . . the Church . . . in . . . Dedham, Massachusetts*, p. 37. Francis J. Bremer, 'In Defence of Regicide: John Cotton on the Execution of Charles I', *William and Mary Quarterly*, 3rd series, 37 (1980), pp. 103–4.

77. Nathaniel Ward to John Winthrop Jr, 24 December 1635, *Winthrop Papers*, III, p. 216; Winthrop, *Journal*, pp. 140, 314–15, 359–60; Stearns, *Strenuous Puritan: Hugh Peter*, pp. 303–14; Newman, 'Nathaniel Ward'; *ODNB*, 'Ward, Nathaniel'.

78. Cooper, *Tenacious of their Liberties*, pp. 68–87; Williston Walker, *The Creeds and Platforms of Congregationalism* (New York: Pilgrim Press, 1991), pp. 157–237. Webster, *Godly Clergy*, pp. 304–5, makes the point that, until the 1640s, clerical meetings were not seen as 'Presbyterianising'; see also R.F. Scholz, 'Clerical Consociation in Massachusetts Bay: Reassessing the New England Way and its Origins', *William and Mary Quarterly*, 3rd series, 19 (1972), pp. 391–414.

79. *ODNB*, Paul C.H. Lim, 'Woodbridge, Benjamin (1622–1684)'; *CR*, Thomas Rashley, Benjamin and John Woodbridge. On Henry Sewall and Stephen Dummer, see the

diarist Samuel Sewall's later account of his family, *NEHGR*, 1 (1847), pp. 111–13. On Newbury: Cooper, *Tenacious of their Liberties*, pp. 70–1.

80. Winslow, *New-Englands Salamander*, pp. 17, 18.

81. R.C. Simmons, 'Richard Sadler's Account of the Massachusetts Churches', *New England Quarterly*, 42 (1969), pp. 411–25.

82. Winthrop, *Journal*, pp. 600–1.

83. Samuel Eliot Morison, *Harvard College in the Seventeenth Century*, 2 vols (Cambridge, Mass.: Harvard University Press, 1936), 1, pp. 76–8.

84. Nathaniel Rowe to John Winthrop [*c*.1642], *Winthrop Papers*, IV, pp. 343–4; *Aspinwall NR*, p. 5; Michael McGiffert, ed., *God's Plot: Puritan Spirituality in Thomas Shepard's Cambridge* (Amherst, Mass.: University of Massachusetts Press, revised and expanded edn, 1994), pp. 166–8; *ODNB*, Michael J. Jarvis, 'Rowe, Owen (1592/3–1661)'. The schoolmaster at Lynn was Thomas Willis, who returned to England in 1641 or 1642: *ODNB*, C.S. Knighton, 'Willis, Thomas (1582/3–1666)'; for his son Thomas, see *ODNB*, C.S. Knighton, 'Willis, Thomas [*c*.1618–73]'. The disgraced head of Harvard was Nathaniel Eaton (*ODNB*), replaced in 1640 by the College's first President, Henry Dunster (*ODNB*).

85. Benjamin Woodbridge, George Downing, John Bulkeley, William Hubbard, Henry Saltonstall, Nathaniel Brewster and Tobias Barnard. Other Harvard graduates in the 1640s who eventually left for England include John Allin, Samuel Mather (BA 1643), Abraham James (who took no degree but studied with the class of 1642 or 1643), Jeremiah Holland, William Ames, James Ward (BA 1645), Nathaniel Mather, Comfort Starr, John Barden, Abraham Walver (BA 1647), Urian Oakes and John Collins (BA 1649). Joshua Swinnock also returned to England without a degree: *Harvard College Records III*, Colonial Society of Massachusetts, *Publications*, 31 (1935), p. 55n. The graduates from 1642 to 1660 are listed in *Harvard College Records I*, Colonial Society of Massachusetts, *Publications*, 15 (1925), pp. 82–4.

86. Lucy Downing to John Winthrop, 24 February 1644, *Winthrop Papers*, IV, p. 445; *ODNB*, Jonathan Scott, 'Downing, Sir George (1623–1684)'.

87. Winthrop, *Journal*, p. 504; Nathaniel Norcrosse to John Cotton, July 1647, with Cotton's draft reply, in Bush, ed., *Cotton Correspondence*, pp. 396–9; Lucy Downing to John Winthrop Jr, 17 December 1648, *Winthrop Papers*, V, p. 291; Thompson, *Divided We Stand*, p. 236n. 10.

88. *ODNB*, 'Bourne, Nehemiah'; Winthrop, *Journal*, p. 402n; his will of 1691, as a merchant of London, PRO, PROB 11/407; Breen, *Transgressing the Bounds*, pp. 114–18; W.R. Chaplin, 'Nehemiah Bourne', Colonial Society of Massachusetts, *Publications*, 42 (1952–6), pp. 28–155; Bernard Capp, *Cromwell's Navy: The Fleet and the English Revolution, 1648–1660* (Oxford: Clarendon Press, 1989), p. 177.

89. Nehemiah Bourne to John Winthrop, 4 March 1639/40: *Winthrop Papers*, IV, p. 214.

90. Breen, *Transgressing the Bounds*, p. 115, suggests Bourne wrote an account of Turnham Green, *An Exact . . . Relation of the Battell Fought . . . at Acton* (London, 1642), but this is not clear: the titlepage gives the author only as 'one Master Bourne an Officer under Colonel Hollis'.

91. Winthrop, *Journal*, p. 611. Bourne's fellow-petitioners included Thomas Fowle, Emmanuel Downing and Robert Sedgwick.

92. Nehemiah Bourne to John Winthrop, 12 August 1648, *Winthrop Papers*, V, p. 244; Capp, *Cromwell's Navy*, p. 56. Other colonial entrepreneurs with a similar history include Emmanuel Downing, Thomas Bell, Edward Bendall and David Yale.

93. Hannah Dugard to Mary Wyllys, 17 May 1646, *The Wyllys Papers . . . 1590–1796*, Collections of the Connecticut Historical Society, 21 (1924), p. 91.

94. William Bisbey to Mary Wyllys, 11 May 1646, *Wyllys Papers*, p. 89.

95. Lawrence Wright to John Winthrop, 10 March 1646/7, *Winthrop Papers*, V, pp. 137–8.

96. William Cutter to Henry Dunster, 19 May 1654, 'Dunster Papers', Massachusetts Historical Society *Collections*, 4th series, 2 (1854), p. 196.
97. William Perkins, *A Cloud of Faithfull Witnesses, Leading to the Heavenly Canaan, or a Commentary on the 11. Chapter to the Hebrewes* (London, 1607), p. 199; on Hebrews 11:9.
98. Theodore Dwight Bozeman, *To Live Ancient Lives: The Primitivist Dimension in Puritanism* (Chapel Hill and London: University of North Carolina Press, 1988), pp. 98–109, 111, 116.

Chapter 4

1. Marmaduke Matthews to John Winthrop Jr, 7 December 1649, *Winthrop Papers*, V, p. 379. *ODNB*, Richard C. Allen, 'Matthews, Marmaduke (*c*.1606–*c*.1683)'.
2. Pequot (now New London, Connecticut) had been founded in 1646. Matthews to John Winthrop Jr, and to Jonathan Brewster and others of New London, 7 December 1649, *Winthrop Papers*, V, pp. 379–82. On the ordinance for toleration: W.A. Shaw, *A History of the English Church during the Civil Wars and under the Commonwealth, 1640–1660*, 2 vols (London: Longman, Green, 1900), II, pp. 58–70; for reports of toleration and the advent of the Second Civil War, *Winthrop Papers*, V, p. 198. Armed conflict broke out again in May 1648: Ian Gentles, *The New Model Army in England, Ireland and Scotland, 1645–1653* (Oxford: Blackwell, 1992), pp. 235–65.
3. Matthews was at St John's, Swansea, by 25 Dec. 1655: Lambeth Palace, Ms. COMM. VIa/7, fol. 379.
4. *ODNB*, Stephen K. Roberts, 'Jones, Philip (1617/18–1674)'.
5. Marmaduke Matthews, *The Messiah Magnified by the Mouthes of Babes in America* (London, 1659), 'Epistle Dedicatory'.
6. James Axtell, *The School upon a Hill: Education and Society in Colonial New England* (New Haven and London: Yale University Press, 1974), pp. 21–9, 156, 169–71. In 1642 Massachusetts had passed a law which required towns to see that families taught children to read and write.
7. Austin Woolrych, *Britain in Revolution 1625–1660* (Oxford: Oxford University Press, 2002), pp. 461–501. The defeat of Charles II at Worcester in September 1651 brought the War of Three Kingdoms to an end.
8. Francis J. Bremer, 'In Defence of Regicide: John Cotton on the Execution of Charles I', *William and Mary Quarterly*, 3rd series, 37 (1980), pp. 103–5, 122; Sargent Bush Jr, ed., *The Correspondence of John Cotton* (Chapel Hill and London: University of North Carolina Press, 2001), pp. 461, 463–4. Carla Gardina Pestana, *The English Atlantic in an Age of Revolution, 1640–1661* (Cambridge, Mass., and London: Harvard University Press, 2004), p. 188, discusses the transportation of prisoners of war.
9. Bremer, 'In Defense of Regicide', pp. 110–11, 123; for Cotton's earlier views, in a sermon preached in 1639/40, see John Cotton, *An Exposition upon the Thirteenth Chapter of the Revelation* (London, 1655), p. 20. Cotton referred to a request he had received for ministers to go to the four northern counties of Northumberland, Cumberland, Westmorland and Durham, which had for a long time been 'under darkness and the shadow of death for want of the gospel'. A few months after he preached the sermon, Cotton wrote to Cromwell: see his letter of 28 July, 1651, and Cromwell's reply in October (which enclosed a printed narrative of his victory over the Scots and Charles II at Worcester), in Bush, ed., *Cotton Correspondence*, pp. 458–64, 468–70.
10. John Winthrop, *The Journal of John Winthrop*, ed. Richard S. Dunn, James Savage and Laetitia Yeandle (Cambridge, Mass., and London: Harvard University Press, 1996), p. 518n.

11. Massachusetts Historical Society, Boston, Ms. N–2195, Miscellaneous Manuscripts Collection, 15, 16, and 26 May 1651; 28, 31 Oct. 1651. Henry Dunster recorded the report of the churches of Charlestown, Cambridge, Lynn and Reading after they met (at the request of the General Court) with Matthews and Malden church members [1651]: Massachusetts Historical Society, Boston, Ms. N–1143, 'Henry Dunster Notebook, 1628–1654', fol. 143. Michael P. Winship, 'Contesting Control of Orthodoxy among the Godly: William Pynchon Reexamined', *William and Mary Quarterly*, 3rd series, 54 (1997), p. 814n., describes Matthews as an 'otherwise conventional minister', with 'a fondness for idiosyncratic theological speculation, some of which had a tincture of Antinomianism'.

12. *Harvard College Records I*, Colonial Society of Massachusetts, *Publications*, 15 (1925), p. 83; *Harvard College Records III*, Colonial Society of Massachusetts, *Publications*, 31 (1935), pp. 137–9; Sibley; *ODNB*, 'Matthews, Marmaduke'.

13. David D. Hall, *The Faithful Shepherd: A History of the New England Ministry in the Seventeenth Century*, 2nd edn (Cambridge, Mass.: Harvard University Press, 2006), pp. 190–4, comments on the growing popularity of written contracts from the 1650s, in reaction to the greater mobility of second generation ministers. In the early days, ministers had been granted a house and land in their own right (which their children could inherit) but it became common to specify in contracts that these should revert to the town when the minister ended his work, unless he had stayed for a good number of years.

14. Virginia DeJohn Anderson, *New England's Generation: The Great Migration and the Formation of Society and Culture in the Seventeenth Century* (Cambridge: Cambridge University Press, 1991), pp. 120–1, singles out Hull; the quotation is a comment by the Rector of Truro, cited in *CR*. Another rolling stone was the idiosyncratic minister Stephen Bachiler, who moved repeatedly before arriving at Strawberry Bank (now Portsmouth, New Hampshire): *GMB*. Bachiler sailed back across the Atlantic in the early 1650s, when he was in his nineties – surely the most elderly migrant of his day.

15. *ODNB*, Michael P. Winship, 'Wheelwright, John (1592?–1679)'. On the process that led to the revocation of Wheelwright's banishment, see Sargent Bush Jr, '"Revising what we have done amisse": John Cotton and John Wheelwright, 1640', *William and Mary Quarterly*, 3rd series, 45 (1988), pp. 733–50. Lambeth Palace Library, Ms. COMM III/4, fol. 406, records Wheelwright's admission to the parishes of Belleau, Aby and Swaby, Lincolnshire, on 7 December 1655.

16. Winthrop, *Journal*, p. 423; Roger Thompson, *Divided We Stand: Watertown, Massachusetts, 1630–1680* (Amherst, Mass.: University of Massachusetts Press, 2001), pp. 60, 68–71. The right of non-freemen to speak at town meetings had been enshrined in the Massachusetts *Body of Liberties*, 1641: Timothy H. Breen, 'Who Governs? The Town Franchise in Seventeenth-Century Massachusetts', *William and Mary Quarterly*, 3rd series, 27 (1970), pp. 462–63.

17. In 1646 the New Haven Court – in a dispute about whether a court official took down testimony accurately or not – recorded that a witness had said that 'Mrs Eaton would not lie with her husband since she was admonished but caused her bed to be removed to another room': C.J. Hoadley, ed., *Records of the Colony and Plantation of New Haven*, 2 vols (Hartford, Conn., 1857–8), 1, p. 270. For more on the controversial Mrs Eaton, see Lilian Handlin, 'Dissent in a Small Community', *New England Quarterly*, 58 (1985), pp. 193–220. She died within months of making the move to greater religious liberty in England.

18. *Aspinwall NR*, pp. i–x; Philip F. Gura, *A Glimpse of Sion's Glory: Puritan Radicalism in New England, 1620–1660* (Middletown, Connecticut: Wesleyan University Press, 1984), pp. 138–42; *ANB*, Stephen L. Robbins, 'Aspinwall, William'; *GMB*; *ODNB*, Francis J. Bremer, 'Aspinwall, William (d. in or after 1662)'. Aspinwall later worked as a minister in Ireland.

19. C.E. Banks, 'Thomas Venner: the Boston Wine-Cooper and Fifth Monarchy Man', *NEHGR*, 47 (1893), pp. 437–44; J.F. Maclear, 'New England and the Fifth Monarchy: the Quest for the Millennium in Early American Puritanism', *William and Mary Quarterly*, 3rd series, 32 (1975), pp. 223–60; *ODNB*, Richard L. Greaves, 'Venner, Thomas (1608/9–1661)'; *BDBR*, B.S. Capp, 'Venner, Thomas'. Venner had been Warden of Boston's Company of Coopers (barrel-makers) – a skilled trade much in demand: see Stephen Innes, *Labor in a New Land: Economy and Society in Seventeenth-Century Springfield* (Princeton, N.J.: Princeton University Press, 1983), p. 100.

20. *Boston CR*, pp. 43, 51, 52; Judith L. Olsen, *Five Generations of the Descendants of Richard and Abigail Lippincott* (Woodbury, N.J.: Gloucester County Historical Society, 1982), pp. 7–17. Strictly speaking, Lippincott was a church member at Dorchester, but had been 'recommended' to Boston in 1644, and so came under its discipline: on settlers' habit of moving to another settlement without changing their church membership, see chapter 5.

21. *Boston CR*, pp. 21, 53–4; Rufus M. Jones, *The Quakers in the American Colonies* (London: Macmillan, 1911), p. 45; Carla Gardina Pestana, *Quakers and Baptists in Colonial Massachusetts* (Cambridge: Cambridge University Press, 1991), pp. 28–9. George Burden made a will, 15 October 1652, with provision for his family 'if my wife and children stay in England', but also 'if we return to New England': *NEHGR*, 8 (1854), pp. 277–8.

22. For an outline of Pynchon's career, see *ANB*, William Penack, 'Pynchon, William'; *ODNB*, Robert Charles Anderson, 'Pynchon, William (1590–1662)'. The Gratz Sermon Collection, Historical Society of Pennsylvania, Philadelphia, Manuscript Collection 250B, Box 1, contains John Pynchon's notes of Sabbath morning and afternoon sermons by Moxon in 1649: John noted when his father William or brother-in-law Henry Smith preached instead. Moxon: *CR*; *ODNB*, Alexander Gordon, revised by Susan Hardman Moore, 'Moxon, George (*bap.* 1602, *d.* 1687)'.

23. William Pynchon, *The Meritorious Price of Our Redemption* (London, 1650). Winship, 'Contesting Control of Orthodoxy', pp. 795–822; Gura, *Glimpse of Sion's Glory*, pp. 311–22. Michael P. Winship, 'William Pynchon's *The Jewes Synagogue*', *New England Quarterly*, 71 (1998), pp. 290–7, draws attention to Pynchon's views on church government: he did not hide his distaste for the Massachusetts authorities' crackdown on the Remonstrants in 1646.

24. See the letter sent by John Cotton, Richard Mather, Zechariah Symmes, John Wilson and William Thompson in the summer of 1651 to 'some Brethren' in England who had written to Massachusetts in support of Pynchon: Bush, ed., *Cotton Correspondence*, pp. 454–8.

25. Joseph Pynchon, Henry and Ann (Pynchon) Smith: *GMB*. Pynchon's business interests are explored in Innes, *Labor in a New Land*; C. Bridenbaugh, ed., *The Pynchon Papers*, I, *Letters of John Pynchon, 1654–1700*; II, *Selections from the Account Books of John Pynchon*, Colonial Society of Massachusetts, *Publications*, 60, 61 (1982).

26. Thomas Goodwin and others to the Massachusetts General Court, *c.* June 1645, *Winthrop Papers*, V, pp. 23–5; Gura, *A Glimpse of Sion's Glory*, p. 310. Winship, 'Contesting Control of Orthodoxy', pp. 815, 818–20, discusses the letters and Pynchon's lack of impact in England.

27. Of the 250 households, 67% stayed in one community throughout their time in America. 23% moved once within New England before going home, usually within a short time of their first arrival. 10% moved more than twice before returning to England. Some settlers migrated between settlements close to Boston; others left for outlying communities like Ipswich, Newbury or Rowley, or western settlements like Hartford, Connecticut, and Springfield, Massachusetts. A few traders moved into Boston. This fits the patterns of settlement observed by Anderson (who coined the term 'Great Reshuffling'), in *New England's Generation*, pp. 89–130, and Roger Thompson, *Mobility and Migration: East Anglian Founders of New England* (Amherst,

Mass.: University of Massachusetts Press, 1994), pp. 209–23. In other words, those who left were not more restless than their neighbours – except that in the end they went home.

28. For more on this, see chapters 6 and 7.

29. John Cotton to the corporation and church of Boston, Lincolnshire [1650?], printed as a preface to his *Of the Holiness of Church-Members* (London, 1650); reprinted in Bush, ed., *Cotton Correspondence*, pp. 421–25. Cotton's will, 30 November 1652: *NEHGR*, 5 (1851), p. 241.

30. John Davenport to John Winthrop Jr, 24 May 1654, in Isabel M. Calder, ed., *Letters of John Davenport, Puritan Divine* (New Haven: Yale University Press, 1937), p. 90.

31. Increase Mather, *The Life and Death of . . . Mr. Richard Mather* (Cambridge, Mass., 1670), p. 25; *Magnalia*, 1, p. 468. Richard Mather's sons Samuel, Nathaniel and Increase went to England in the 1650s, as did Chauncy's sons Ichabod, Isaac and (later) Elnathan. Other first generation ministers whose Harvard-trained sons went home included John Allin of Dedham, Peter Bulkeley of Concord and Samuel Whiting of Lynn: see Sibley. On Chauncy's reasons for naming his son 'Ichabod', see p. 26.

32. Ten first generation ministers left in the 1650s, compared with fifteen in the 1640s, out of a total of 76 who emigrated to New England in the 1630s. See appendices 3, 4.

33. Bernard C. Steiner, *A History of the Plantation of Menunkatuck and of the Original Town of Guilford* (Baltimore, 1897), pp. 62–3, citing William Hubbard's *A General History of New England* [1682], 2nd printed edn (Boston, Mass.: Massachusetts Historical Society, 1848), p. 328; Acts 20: 36–8. Whitfield became a preacher at Winchester Cathedral, and was buried there in 1657. His granite house at Guilford is illustrated in Plate 5.

34. Norfolk Record Office, Norwich, NCR Case 16d/6, Norwich City Assembly Book of Proceedings, 1642–68, fols 102, 106v, 120, 123.

35. John Knowles left Watertown in 1651 after more than a decade: *ODNB*, Roger Thompson, 'Knowles, John (c.1606–1685)'; *CR*. George Moxon left Springfield in 1652 after sixteen years, in the wake of the controversy that embroiled William Pynchon and the acquittal of Hugh Parsons, who had been charged with bewitching Moxon's daughters: *ODNB*, 'Moxon'; *CR*. William Hooke, teaching elder at New Haven for twelve years alongside John Davenport, left in 1656; his son John started to study at Oxford in 1652; his wife Jane, a first cousin of Oliver Cromwell, had gone back in 1654 with the rest of their children; *ODNB*, Susan Hardman Moore, 'Hooke [Hook], William (1600/1–1678)'; *CR*. Richard Blinman, who worked at Gloucester, Massachusetts, between 1642–50 and at New London in Connecticut between 1650–8, took over briefly from Hooke at New Haven before leaving for England himself in 1659: *CR*.

36. Samuel Mather to Jonathan Mitchell, Massachusetts Historical Society, Boston, Ms. N-2196, Miscellaneous Bound Manuscripts Collection, 26 March, 1651. With one or two minor changes, Samuel's report on the graduates followed the order, class by class, in which the graduates were listed by the College: *Harvard College Records I*, pp. 82–3. Nathaniel Mather to [John Rogers?] 23 December 1650, and to John Rogers, 23 March 1650/1: Boston Public Library Ms. Am. 1502 vol. 1, nos 6, 7; printed (with the first letter misdated to '1651?'), in 'Mather Papers', Massachusetts Historical Society, *Collections*, 4th series, 8 (1868), pp. 1–5.

37. Michael G. Hall, ed., 'The Autobiography of Increase Mather', American Antiquarian Society, *Proceedings*, 71 (1961), part 2, p. 281.

38. Samuel Eliot Morison, *Harvard College in the Seventeenth Century*, 2 vols (Cambridge, Mass.: Harvard University Press, 1936), I, pp. 300–2.

39. *Harvard College Records I*, p. 83; *Harvard College Records III*, pp. 137–9 (from 'Chesholme's Steward's Book, 1651–1660', where the bills of students like Manasseh Matthews provide evidence of their presence even if they left before graduation).

40. Fast days on 17 March 1651/2, 10 November 1652, 23 March 1652/3: *Proclamations of Massachusetts*, pp. 22–3. Massachusetts General Court, 'A Declaration concerning the

Advancement of Learning in New England', October 1652, Massachusetts Archives, Boston, Massachusetts Archives Collection, vol. 58: 21; Nathaniel Mather to [John Rogers ?], 'Mather Papers', Massachusetts Historical Society, *Collections*, 4th series, 8 (1868), p. 4.

41. Hall, *Faithful Shepherd*, p. 184.

42. Fletcher: *Boston CR*, p. 30; W.B. Trask, ed., *Suffolk Deeds*, 12 vols (Boston: Rockwell and Churchill, 1880–1902), 3: 120; Henry Jessey, *The Lords Loud Call to England* (London, 1660), pp. 18–24; his will, *NEHGR*, 16 (1862), pp. 231–3; *CR*. Bendall: still in New England, December 1651, Trask, ed., *Suffolk Deeds*, 1: 163–4; in London by 12 February 1653/4, when he was dismissed to a church there, *Boston CR*, p. 55; probably admitted Rector of Cotgrave, Nottinghamshire, 17 April 1654, Lambeth Palace Ms. COMM. III/3, fol. 11; his widow sold their house and land in Boston in 1661, Trask, ed., *Suffolk Deeds*, 4: 88; *GMB*. For 'Bendall's Dock', see Annie Haven Thwing, *The Crooked and Narrow Streets of the Town of Boston, 1630–1822* (originally published Boston: Marshall Jones Company, 1920; CD Rom, Boston: Massachusetts Historical Society and New England Historic Genealogical Society, 2001), pp. 126–8. John Winthrop described Bendall's ingenious diving contraption: Winthrop, *Journal*, pp. 399–400.

43. *ODNB*, 'Aspinwall, William'. Milam [Mylam, Mileham, Millard] was in Waterford, Ireland, by 1655: Edward Roberts to Henry Dunster, May 1655, 'Dunster Papers', Massachusetts Historical Society, *Collections*, 4th series, 2 (1854), pp. 196–7; St J. D. Seymour, *The Puritans in Ireland, 1647–1661* (Oxford: Clarendon Press, 1921; reprint edn, Oxford: Clarendon Press, 1969), pp. 103, 217. Probably John Milam, a well-to-do cooper in Boston, who sold a shop and land in 1655. He and his wife Christian were church members. *Boston CR*, p. 20; Massachusetts Historical Society, Boston, Ms. N–2195, Miscellaneous Manuscripts Collection, 18 October 1648; Trask, ed., *Suffolk Deeds*, I: 285; Rutman, *Winthrop's Boston*, pp. 199–200.

44. Clement: Seymour, *Puritans in Ireland*, p. 209; *The Probate Records of Essex County, Massachusetts*, 1, *1635–1664* (Salem, Mass., Essex Institute, 1916), pp. 290–2; G.F. Dow, ed., *The Records and Files . . . of the Quarterly Courts of Essex County, Massachusetts*, 8 vols (Salem. Mass.: Essex Institute, 1911–21), 2, p. 202.

45. Hoadley: Steiner, *History . . . of Guilford*, p. 70; BL, Egerton Ms. 2519, fol. 11. Thornton: in Ireland from 1654 as a minister, Seymour, *Puritans in Ireland*, p. 222; *NEHGR*, 149 (1995), pp. 413–14; *GMB*.

46. Chaplin described himself in his will, 16 August 1656, as 'of Thetford in the County of Norfolk, clerk': Henry F. Waters, *Genealogical Gleanings in England* (Boston, Mass.: New England Historic Genealogical Society, 1901), p. 32; *NEHGR*, 56 (1902), pp. 183–4.

47. Horsford: *GMB* [Hosford]; David Underdown, *Fire from Heaven: Life in an English Town in the Seventeenth Century* (London: Fontana, 1993), pp. 136, 138, 201; *CR*. As an elder, he often gave the weekly lecture (midweek sermon) at Windsor. The church had close relations with Springfield, Massachusetts, and Horsford may have stepped in to preach there after George Moxon's departure in 1652. He was Rector of Calverleigh, Devon, between 1657–60. An annex to his will, dated 6 September 1654, contained provision in case 'my wife stays in New England, but I hope she will come unto me in England'; Jane Horsford made her will on 23 July 1655, 'going after my husband unto old England'. *A Digest of the Early Connecticut Probate Records* (online database: http://www. NewEnglandAncestors.org, New England Historic Genealogical Society, 2006).

48. Zephaniah Smith was probably the colonist who became minister at Roscrea, Ireland, before 1656. *Aspinwall NR*, pp. 183–4; Seymour, *Puritans in Ireland*, p. 221.

49. Bernard Capp, *Cromwell's Navy: The Fleet and the English Revolution, 1648–1660* (Oxford: Clarendon Press, 1989), pp. 73–86; Woolrych, *Britain in Revolution*, pp. 507–14.

50. The lookout window can be seen in Plate 5. For the discussion about the college at New Haven, at the Guilford General Court meeting on 28 June 1652, see: Guilford,

Connecticut, Town Clerk's Office, Guilford Records, Volume A, fol. 128. New Haven settlers discussed a move south to Delaware: F.B. Dexter, ed., *New Haven Town Records*, vol. 1, 1649–62 (New Haven, 1917), pp. 54, 223, 226–7.

51. William Leete to Samuel Desborough, 10 October 1654, BL, Egerton Ms. 2519, fol. 10; Samuel Maverick, 'A Brief Description of New England' [*c.*1660], cited by Bernard Bailyn, *The New England Merchants in the Seventeenth Century* (Cambridge, Mass.: Harvard University Press, 1955), p. 95.

52. Robert Newman (an elder of the New Haven church), Thomas Yale, Benjamin Ling, John Caffinch, Robert Seely, and perhaps Richard Malbon. Stephen Goodyear, London merchant turned colonial adventurer, went to England in 1657 to promote the development of the East Haven ironworks, but died there. Edward Hopkins, brother-in-law of Thomas Yale, left Hartford in 1652.

53. *ODNB*, Natalie Zacek, 'Ludlow, Roger (*bap.* 1590, *d.* after 1664?)'.

54. Steiner, *History of . . . Guilford*, pp. 64–5. John Winthrop Jr considered buying Whitfield's property, but it was eventually sold to Robert Thomson, a London merchant who had lived briefly in Boston (*ODNB*, s.v. 'Thomson, George'): Massachusetts Historical Society, *Collections*, 4th series 7 (1865), p. 399; Calder, ed., *Letters of John Davenport*, p. 217n. Others who left included Samuel Desborough, Nathaniel Whitfield, Thomas Jones, John Hoadley and Thomas Jordan. Whitfield's place as Guilford's minister was filled by his son-in-law John Higginson (who also set sail for England in 1659, but was delayed by a storm, which forced him to shelter at Salem, Massachusetts, where he was persuaded to stay on as minister).

55. William Leete to Samuel Desborough, BL, Egerton Ms. 2519, fol. 10v.

56. Bailyn, *New England Merchants*, p. 53, notes plans in 1645 for establishing trade in furs.

57. R.E. Moody, ed., *The Saltonstall Papers, 1607–1815*, 2 vols (Boston: Massachusetts Historical Society, 1972–1974), I, pp. 25–41; Woolrych, *Britain in Revolution*, pp. 429–33; D. Alan Orr, 'The Juristic Foundation of Regicide', in Jason Peacey, ed., *The Regicides and the Execution of Charles I* (Basingstoke: Palgrave, 2001), pp. 117–38.

58. John Tuttle and others to Cromwell, 31 December 1650, J. Nickolls, ed., *Original Letters and Papers of State addressed to Oliver Cromwell* (London, 1743), p. 44. Tuttle was in London with Nathaniel Mather, March 1650/1: 'Mather Papers', Massachusetts Historical Society, *Collections*, 4th series, 8 (1868), p. 2. *Records . . . of the Quarterly Courts of Essex County*, 2, pp. 142–3, 172–4; *Probate Records of Essex County*, 1, pp. 277–8.

59. Boyes: D.G. Allen, *In English Ways: the Movement of Societies and The Transferal of English Local Law and Custom to Massachusetts Bay in the Seventeenth Century* (Chapel Hill, N.C.: University of North Carolina Press, 1981), p. 245; Waters, *Genealogical Gleanings*, p. 230; G.B. Blodgette and M. Mighill, eds, *The Early Records of the Town of Rowley, Massachusetts, I, 1639–1672* (Rowley, 1894), passim [to 1653]; letters from Ezekiel Rogers, BL, Add Ms. 4276, fols 105, 107. Other leading lights who left the town were Edward Carleton, Sebastian Brigham and Francis Parrat. On Rowley's cloth industry, see Bailyn, *New England Merchants*, pp. 72–4.

60. M. Middlebrooke to Michael Wigglesworth of Malden, 6 April 1657, *NEHGR*, 11 (1857), p. 111n.

61. Harwood: *Boston CR*, pp. 50, 59, 69; *NEHGR*, 23 (1869), p. 410, 42 (1888), pp. 64–5; Trask, ed., *Suffolk Deeds*, 1: 45, 2: 192–3. Yale: Bailyn, *New England Merchants*, p. 29. Fogg: *GMB*. Downing: *Winthrop Papers*, III, passim; Bailyn, *New England Merchants*, pp. 74, 76, 129.

62. Deed of sale, January 1656/7, Trask, ed., *Suffolk Deeds*, 2: 329–30. PRO, RG 4/4414, London, Stepney, Bull Lane (Independent), Births and Baptisms, 1644–1837 [William Greenhill's church]: 20 Feb. 1656/7 (Rebecca Lord), 6 October 1657 (Nathaniel Thurston). Two or more families sharing the same house was common: Darrett Rutman, *Winthrop's Boston. A Portrait of a Puritan Town, 1630–1649* (New York: Norton, 1972), p. 192.

63. Massachusetts Archives, Boston, Massachusetts Archives Collection, vol. 15B: 155–9 (papers relating to a dispute over her husband Thomas Nelson's estate, between the Dummers and Thomas's children by an earlier marriage).

64. I.M. Calder, *The New Haven Colony* (New Haven: Yale University Press, 1934), pp. 198, 212; Calder, ed., *Letters of John Davenport*, p. 101n. Sarah's husband, James Astwood, asked to be buried 'at the feet of Mr [John] Cotton, as near to him as I may, though not to hinder my betters'. The estate he left covered less than a third of his debts: *NEHGR*, 7 (1853), p. 337; 9 (1855), p. 40.

65. Middlesex South District Registry of Deeds, Cambridge, Massachusetts, Middlesex Deeds, Lib. II, 32–4. One of Palgrave's attorneys was the mariner John Pierce [Pearse] of Wapping ('late of New England'), a member of William Greenhill's church at Stepney.

66. *Probate Records of Essex County*, 1, p. 72.

67. Peter Bulkeley's will, 14 April 1658: *NEHGR*, 10 (1856), p. 167. John Bulk[e]ley, *CR*.

68. Vermace [Fermayes]: Richard D. Pierce, ed., *Records of the First Church in Salem, Massachusetts, 1629–1736* (Salem, Mass.: Essex Institute, 1974), p. 8; Norfolk Record Office, Norwich, Ms. FC 31/1, Great Yarmouth, Middlegate Congregational Church Book, 1643–1855, 20 January, 1651/2.

69. Allen, *In English Ways*, p. 285; Middlesex South District Registry of Deeds, Middlesex Deeds, Lib. II, fol. 300. The Parishes emigrated in 1635 and returned by 1654. Their son Thomas stayed on as a student at Harvard and ended up in court for his attitude to the town and church, and later for a night fight between 'scholars and some of the town': Middlesex County Courthouse, Cambridge, Massachusetts, Middlesex County Court Records, I, fols 82–3 (9 June 1656); Middlesex County Court Files, File 7 # 3, affidavit from Charles Chauncy, 14 March 1658 [Abstracts of Court Files of Middlesex County, Massachusetts, 1649–75, online database, http://www.NewEnglandAncestors.org, New England Historic Genealogical Society, 2003]. Thomas Parish Jr left for England after he graduated with a BA in 1659: Sibley.

70. Will of Nicholas Busby, 25 July 1657, *NEHGR*, 8 (1854), pp. 278–9. Thompson, *Mobility and Migration*, pp. 83, 233.

71. See Louise A. Breen on 'cosmopolitan puritans in a provincial colony': *Transgressing the Bounds: Subversive Enterprises among the Puritan Elite in Massachusetts, 1630–1692* (Oxford and New York: Oxford University Press, 2001), pp. 97–143.

72. Thompson, *Mobility and Migration*, pp. 102, 108, 112, 234; T.H. Breen and Stephen Foster, 'Moving to the New World: the Character of Early Massachusetts Immigration', *William and Mary Quarterly*, 3rd series, 30 (1973), p. 216. D.G. Hill, ed., *The Record of Baptisms, Marriages, and Deaths, and Admissions to the Church and Dismissals Therefrom, Transcribed from the Church Records in the Town of Dedham, Massachusetts* (Dedham, Mass., 1888), p. 35. John Phillip sent a letter to Henry Dunster by means of Chickering: see Dunster to Phillip, 8 Feb. 1649/50, Massachusetts Historical Society, Boston, Ms. N–1143, 'Henry Dunster Notebook, 1628–1654', fol. 117. The yeoman Joseph Peck lived out his days in Hingham, Massachusetts, after his brother, the minister Robert Peck, returned to his parish at Hingham in Norfolk.

73. These impressions tally broadly with Allen, *In English Ways*, pp. 13–14.

74. John Maverick, William Walton and John Warham stayed on; William Hooke, Joseph Hull and Thomas Larkham went to England.

Chapter 5

1. John Cotton to Richard Saltonstall Jr [1649], Boston Public Library, Ms. Am. 1506, pt 3, app. no. 5, printed in Sargent Bush Jr, ed., *The Correspondence of John Cotton* (Chapel Hill and London: University of North Carolina Press, 2001), p. 420; Cotton wrote

unsettled 'Humrys' (rather than 'Hurryes', as Bush transcribed it): humours as a state of mind, derived from the ancient and medieval physiology of bodily humours.

2. A contemporary copy of a paper signed by George Wyllys Jr before he sailed for England, Connecticut Historical Society, Hartford, Wyllys Papers, Ms. VII, 24A; printed in *The Wyllys Papers . . . 1590–1796*, Collections of the Connecticut Historical Society, 21 (1924), p. 6. Wyllys had been in England in 1638 and was in England again by March 1639/40: he signed the oath in New England between these dates. His father later sent the original to England, which may explain why the document survives in the archives as a copy with no signature or date. See Plate 4.

3. R.E. Moody, ed., *The Saltonstall Papers, 1607–1815*, 2 vols (Boston: Massachusetts Historical Society, 1972–4), I, pp. 27, 34–6. John Gurdon, Saltonstall's brother-in-law, was one of the Members of Parliament who invited Hooker, Cotton and Davenport to attend the Westminster Assembly: Bush, ed., *Cotton Correspondence*, p. 363. See also Plate 3, 'The Saltonstall Family'.

4. Saltonstall kept property in New England and returned in the 1660s; he was in England again between 1672–80, in New England between 1680–87 and died in England in 1694. Moody, ed., *Saltonstall Papers*, 1, pp. 39–41.

5. The Massachusetts General Court noted in mid-October his 'intended voyage' to England: Moody, ed., *Saltonstall Papers*, I, p. 36.

6. *Wyllys Papers*, p. 6. See Plate 4.

7. Governor George Wyllys to George Wyllys Jr, 28 October 1644: *Wyllys Papers*, pp. 66–78. For the godly circles near Fenny Compton known to the Wyllys family, see Ann Hughes, *Politics, Society and Civil War in Warwickshire, 1620–1660* (Cambridge: Cambridge University Press, 1987).

8. *Wyllys Papers*, p. 69.

9. Will of Governor George Wyllys, 14 December 1644, Connecticut Historical Society, Wyllys Papers, Ms. VII, 44–5. George Wyllys Jr to Mrs Mary Wyllys (his mother), 4 May 1646, 9 May 1646: *Wyllys Papers*, pp. 82–7. Governor Wyllys had waxed lyrical about the Wethersfield estate to his son: *Wyllys Papers*, pp. 66–7.

10. Will of Thomas Hooker, 7 July 1647, cited by M.J.A. Jones, *Congregational Commonwealth: Connecticut, 1636–1662* (Middletown, Conn.: Wesleyan University Press, 1968), p. 156. John Hooker was still in Oxford in 1655: Sargent Bush Jr, 'Thomas Hooker and the Westminster Assembly', *William and Mary Quarterly*, 3rd series, 29 (1972), p. 295. Governor Wyllys' daughter Esther married Robert Harding, a Boston merchant who was often in London in the 1640s. She died by 1647 and Robert Harding had moved to live in London by 1651: W.B. Trask, ed., *Suffolk Deeds*, 12 vols (Boston: Rockwell and Churchill, 1880–1902), 1: 319–20; *GMB*.

11. Samuel Mather and William Greenhill, 'To the Reader', Thomas Shepard, *Subjection to Christ, in all his Ordinances* (London, 1654).

12. On providentialism: Alexandra Walsham, *Providence in Early Modern England* (Oxford: Oxford University Press, 1999), pp. 8–32; David D. Hall, *Worlds of Wonder, Days of Judgment: Popular Religious Belief in Early New England* (Cambridge, Mass.: Harvard University Press, 1990), pp. 71–116; Michael P. Winship, *Seers of God: Puritan Providentialism in the Restoration and Early Enlightenment* (Baltimore, Maryland: Johns Hopkins University Press, 1996).

13. A committee of six, appointed 10 October 1639: J.H. Trumbull, ed., *The Public Records of the Colony of Connecticut prior to the Union with New Haven Colony, 1665* (Hartford, 1850), pp. 39–40. On Winthrop's providentialism: *The Journal of John Winthrop*, ed. Richard S. Dunn, James Savage and Laetitia Yeandle (Cambridge, Mass., and London: Harvard University Press, 1996), pp. xxxiii–xxxvii.

14. Samuel Symonds to John Winthrop, 6 Feb. 1646/7, *Winthrop Papers*, V, pp. 125–7.

15. *Magnalia*, 1, p. 146.

16. Roger Clap, *Memoirs of Roger Clap* (Boston, 1844), pp. 20–1.

17. Clement Chaplin, an elder in the Hartford church, was in Thetford, Norfolk, by 1656: Henry F. Waters, *Genealogical Gleanings in England* (Boston, Mass.: New England Historic Genealogical Society, 1901), p. 32. Roger Ludlow, who at the time the committee met was Deputy-Governor of Connecticut, ended up in Cromwellian Ireland: *ODNB* Natalie Zacek, 'Ludlow, Roger (*bap.* 1590, *d.* after 1664?)'. Eaton's widow, children and stepchildren all went back: Ann, Theophilus and Hannah Eaton, David and Thomas Yale and Edward and Ann Hopkins.

18. Winthrop to John Winthrop Jr, *c.*1643, *Winthrop Papers*, IV, p. 366.

19. Winthrop, *Journal*, pp. 414–17.

20. John Endecott to John Winthrop, *c.* Feb. 1640/1, *Winthrop Papers*, IV, pp. 314–16; on the debate about whether to send Thomas Weld, Hugh Peter and William Hibbins as agents, see also Winthrop, *Journal*, pp. 345–7.

21. William Morton to John Winthrop Jr, *c.* August 1646, *Winthrop Papers*, V, p. 94. George Fenwick, secular leader of the community, had already left; Thomas Peter, the minister, proved hard to replace.

22. William Pynchon to John Winthrop, 27 October 1646, *Winthrop Papers*, V, p. 115. Pynchon probably referred to John Haynes, Governor of Connecticut, who never left, but whose son Hezekiah (later a deputy major-general under Cromwell) went back to England in 1637 and in the 1640s joined the Parliamentary army: *ODNB*, Christopher Durston, 'Haynes, Hezekiah (*d.* 1693)'. Herbert Pelham of Cambridge, Massachusetts, went to England late in 1646. Pelham was expected to come back to New England, because he was elected an assistant of the Bay Colony in his absence in 1647, 1648 and 1649: *ODNB*, Robert Charles Anderson, 'Pelham, Herbert (*c.*1600–1674)'.

23. Winthrop, *Journal*, p. 655.

24. A fast day called for 15 March 1653/4, Trumbull, ed., *Public Records of . . . Connecticut*, p. 251; *Magnalia*, 1, p. 146. Massachusetts included 'lack of . . . persons for public service' in calls for fast days on 17 March 1651/2, 10 November 1652 and 23 March 1652/3: *Proclamations of Massachusetts Issued by Governors and other Authorities, 1620–1936*, Vol. I, 1620–1776 (Boston: Historical Records Survey, Division of Women's and Professional Projects, Works Project Administration, 1937), pp. 22–3.

25. David Cressy, *Coming Over: Migration and Communication between England and New England in the Seventeenth Century* (Cambridge: Cambridge University Press, 1987), pp. 178–90.

26. Leete to Samuel Desborough, 10 October 1654, BL, Ms. Egerton 2519, fol. 10v.

27. Thomas Edwards, *Gangraena* (London, 1646), i, pp. 99–100; Raymond P. Stearns, *The Strenuous Puritan: Hugh Peter, 1598–1660* (Urbana, Illinois: University of Illinois Press, 1954), pp. 173, 366. A colonial visitor, William Coddington, reported in 1651: 'I was merry with him and called him the Archbishop of Canterbury.'

28. William Eyre, *Vindiciae Justificationis Gratuitae* (London, 1654) p. 84; Benjamin Woodbridge, *The Method of Grace in the Justification of Sinners* (London, 1656), 'Epistle to Reader'.

29. William Perkins, 'A Treatise of the Vocations or Callings of Men', *Works*, I (London, 1608), in I. Breward, ed., *The Works of William Perkins* (Abingdon: Sutton Courtenay Press, 1970), p. 473. For similar arguments current in England and New England, see Stephen Foster, *Their Solitary Way: The Puritan Social Ethic in the First Century of Settlement in New England* (New Haven: Yale University Press, 1971), pp. 99–106.

30. Williston Walker, *The Creeds and Platforms of Congregationalism* (New York: Pilgrim Press, 1991), p. 225. This reiterated a point made in the late 1630s, for example [John Davenport?], *An Answer of the Elders of the Severall Churches in New England unto Nine Positions* (London, 1643), pp. 75–6 (written in 1639). A similar platform of polity, drawn up in England at the Savoy Conference in 1658, took a softer line: it made no reference to 'pretended want of competent subsistence' and allowed people to leave a

church for reasons of 'conveniency of habitation'. Walker, *Creeds and Platforms of Congregationalism*, pp. 407–8.

31. [Davenport?], *An Answer of the Elders*, p. 74.

32. Walsham, *Providence in Early Modern England*, pp. 12, 229–30, 294–5.

33. Guilford General Court, 20 February 1649/50: Guilford, Connecticut, Town Clerk's Office, Guilford Records, Volume A, fol. 40. Whitfield left in August 1650.

34. Charles E. Hambrick-Stowe, *The Practice of Piety: Puritan Devotional Disciplines in Seventeenth-Century New England* (Chapel Hill: University of North Carolina Press, 1982), pp. 137–43, 150–5, comments on the prevalence of private meetings and private conference; see also Barbara Donagan, 'Godly Choice: Puritan Decision-Making in Seventeenth-Century England', *Harvard Theological Review*, 76 (1983), pp. 307–34.

35. Edward Hopkins to John Winthrop, 21 June 1648, *Winthrop Papers*, V, p. 231. See also the case of Robert Seeley: Cressy, *Coming Over*, p. 202.

36. Thomas Allen's sermon on Psalm 143:8, 9 November 1650: American Antiquarian Society, Worcester, Massachusetts, Richard Russell's Sermon Notebook, fol. 139v. Norfolk Record Office, Norwich, NCR Case 16d/6, Norwich City Assembly Book of Proceedings, 1642–1668, fols 102r, 106v.

37. John Davenport to John Winthrop Jr, 24 July, 11, 19 Sept. 1654, in Isabel M. Calder, ed., *Letters of John Davenport, Puritan Divine* (New Haven: Yale University Press, 1937), pp. 90–1, 94, 95.

38. Cotton to the corporation and church at Boston, Lincolnshire [1650], Bush, ed., *Cotton Correspondence*, p. 423; Winthrop, *Journal*, p. 655.

39. As the *Cambridge Platform* put it, 'order requires, that a member . . . removing, have letters testimonial; and of dismission from the church whereof he yet is, unto the church whereunto he desireth to be joined . . . If a member be called to remove only for a time, where a church is, letters of recommendation are requisite and sufficient': Walker, ed., *Creeds and Platforms of Congregationalism*, p. 226. *Savoy Declaration*: Walker, ed., *Creeds and Platforms of Congregationalism*, pp. 407–8.

40. D.G. Hill, ed., *The Record of Baptisms, Marriages, and Deaths, and Admissions to the Church and Dismissals Therefrom, Transcribed from the Church Records in the Town of Dedham, Massachusetts* (Dedham, Mass., 1888), pp. 36–7.

41. R.G. Pope, ed., *The Notebook of the Reverend John Fiske, 1644–1675* (Salem, Mass.: Essex Institute, 1974), pp. xxiv–xv, 168. Fiske's church at Wenham moved to Chelmsford in 1655.

42. Thomas Weld, *An Answer to W[illiam] R[athband] His Narration* (London, 1644), p. 49; see also [Davenport?], *An Answer of the Elders*, p. 74.

43. Walker, ed., *Creeds and Platforms of Congregationalism*, p. 225.

44. Thomas Weld, *A Brief Narration of the Practices of the Churches in New-England* (London, 1645), p. 10.

45. Winthrop, *Journal*, pp. 414–15; see also his harsh verdict on Abraham Pratt, p. 599.

46. Nathaniel Mather to John Rogers, 23 March 1650/1, 'Mather Papers', Massachusetts Historical Society, *Collections*, 4th series, 8 (1868), pp. 2–3.

47. George Selement and Bruce C. Woolley, eds, *Thomas Shepard's Confessions*, Colonial Society of Massachusetts, *Publications*, 58 (1981), pp. 87–8 (Stansby, undated, but before 1641); p. 195 (Wyeth, January 1644/5). Arrows are a sign of God's judgment in Job 6:4, Psalm 38:2. Stansby was a nephew of Robert Stansby, a Suffolk minister who registered his disquiet at the strict conditions for church membership in New England: *Winthrop Papers*, III, p. 390.

48. Walker, ed., *Creed and Platforms of Congregationalism*, p. 226; Weld, *Answer to W[illiam] R[athband] His Narration*, p. 19. The hinterland to Weld's comment was Richard Mather's more general response (*Church-Government and Church-Covenant Discussed* (London, 1643), pp. 28–30) to critical questions from Lancashire – which

Rathband may have had a hand in drafting – about what testimonials were required for admission to churches.

49. Giles Firmin, *A Sober Reply to the Sober Answer of Reverend Mr. Cawdrey* (London, 1653), p. 28; the *Cambridge Platform* of 1648, in Walker, ed. *Creeds and Platforms of Congregationalism*, p. 226. See also Giles Firmin, *Separation Examined* (London, 1652), pp. 62–3. Firmin spoke from experience: he lived in Ipswich, Massachusetts, from 1638 but was only dismissed to the church there, 'where he hath long inhabited', by the Boston church in 1643/4: *Boston CR*, p. 41. John Fiske, minister at Wenham, Massachusetts, allowed members from Newbury, Dorchester and Salem (all living in Wenham) to receive communion: Pope, ed., *Notebook of . . . John Fiske*, p. 13; Pope discusses the problems that the settlers' mobility created for the Wenham church, pp. xx–xxv.

50. Stephen Foster notes the prevalence of the habit and sees it as a sign of lay resistance to clerical control: *The Long Argument: English Puritanism and the Shaping of New England Culture, 1570–1700* (Chapel Hill and London: University of North Carolina Press, 1991), pp. 178–9.

51. This is the danger the *Cambridge Platform* recognised, rather than a desire for lay autonomy. Another indicator of tacit conservatism is the reluctance of settlers who moved to give spiritual testimony for a second time to gain admission to a church: Pope, ed., *Notebook of . . . John Fiske*, p. xxiii–xxiv.

52. Giles Firmin referred to 'the letters . . . of recommendation, which the churches make for the members, when they come over hither [to England], requiring of the churches here what communion, counsel, or comfort they shall need': Firmin, *Separation Examined*, p. 63. Fifteen out of forty-four churches established before 1660 have records that survive: see Harold Field Worthley, *An Inventory of the Records of the Particular (Congregational) Churches of Massachusetts Gathered 1620–1805*, Harvard Theological Studies, 25 (Cambridge, Mass., and London: Harvard University Press, 1970). Usually, the records contain little more than a note that a member was 'recommended' or 'dismissed'; Pope, ed., *Notebook of . . . John Fiske*, p. 31, contains a copy of a 'letter dismissive'.

53. Elizabeth Edwards: Pierce, ed., *Records of . . . Salem*, pp. 8, 19; Norfolk Record Office, Norwich, Ms. FC 31/1, Great Yarmouth, Middlegate Congregational Church Book, 1643–1855, 19 March 1649/50. Elizabeth sold off land in Salem in July 1649, with power of attorney from her husband Thomas, a shoemaker, who left New England before her: Southern Essex County Registry of Deeds, Salem, Essex Deeds, Book I, fol. 12 (recorded 14 Nov. 1649); online at http://www.salemdeeds.com. Mark Vermace ('Fermayes' or Fermage) of Salem also joined the church at Yarmouth, 20 January, 1651/2.

54. Norfolk Record Office, Norwich, Ms. FC 31/1, Great Yarmouth, Middlegate Congregational Church Book, 1643–1855, 26 February 1645/6; *Boston CR*, p. 49 (26 September 1647). Thomas Benton, a Congregationalist, was Curate and later Rector of Pulham St Mary, Norfolk: *CR*.

55. *Roxbury Land and Church Records*, Sixth Report of the Boston Record Commissioners (Boston: Rockwell and Churchill, 1884), p. 80; *Boston CR*, p. 84. Ralph Josselin, minister of Earls Colne in Essex, admitted deputy major-general Hezekiah Haynes to communion in 1652 by virtue of his church membership in New England: Alan Macfarlane, ed., *The Diary of Ralph Josselin 1616–1683* (Oxford: Oxford University Press, 1976), p. 268. This is intriguing, because Haynes only spent a short time in New England, from 1633 to 1637: *ODNB*, Christopher Durston, 'Haynes, Hezekiah (d. 1693)'.

56. Allen sold some property before he left, but it was not until 1657 that he sent instructions to his attorney to sell 'what houses, grounds, cattle or any other estate whatsoever' he still had in New England. Notwithstanding this, his son inherited (and sold off) two houses and shares in mills in 1677 and 1680. Middlesex South District Registry of Deeds, Cambridge, Massachusetts, Middlesex County Deeds, Lib. II, fols

104–5, 111–13; T.B. Weyman, *The Genealogy and Estates of Charlestown* (Boston: D. Clapp & Sons, 1879), 'Allen, Thomas'.

57. Waters, *Genealogical Gleanings*, p. 137n.

58. Henry Dunster, President of Harvard, sent a string of letters back to John Phillip in Suffolk to sort out what to do with his tumbledown property in Cambridge, Massachusetts: Dunster to Phillip, 8 February 1649/50, Massachusetts Historical Society, Boston, Ms. N–1143, 'Henry Dunster Notebook, 1628–1654', fol. 117. The Cambridge town meeting voted in May 1650 to sell 'the house which Mr Phillips built' for £50, and send him the money: Cambridge Town Records (transcript), City Hall, Cambridge, Massachusetts, fol. 137. Before he left in 1641, Phillip sold land and part of a house in Dedham to the church there: Massachusetts Historical Society, Ms. N–2196, Miscellaneous Bound Manuscripts Collection, 1641. Peck's son-in-law John Mason sold Peck's house and land at Hingham, Massachusetts, on 5 July 1647: Trask, ed., *Suffolk Deeds*, 1: 82.

59. Phillips Library, Peabody Essex Museum, Salem, Massachusetts, Essex County Quarterly Court Records, 2: 397: Bellingham, Sebastian Brigham, Edward Carleton.

60. John Davenport to John Winthrop Jr, 24 July 1654, in Calder, ed., *Letters of John Davenport*, p. 92.

61. Petition to the General Court on Pelham's behalf by Henry Dunster, 19 Oct. 1648, Massachusetts Archives, Boston, Massachusetts Archives Collection, vol. 45: 12; will of Herbert Pelham of 'Ferrers Bewers Hamlet', Essex, 30 March 1676 (made 1 Jan. 1672/3), PRO, PROB 11/352; Sumner Chilton Powell, *Puritan Village: The Formation of a New England Town* (Middletown, Conn.: Wesleyan University Press, 1963), pp. 90, 125.

62. John Endecott to John Winthrop, 22 April 1644, *Winthrop Papers*, IV, p. 456. Ottley, son-in-law to John Humfrey, was deeply in debt.

63. Trask, ed., *Suffolk Deeds*, I: 60.

64. A letter from Richard Blinman, printed by Thomas Edwards: *Gangraena*, iii, p. 94.

65. G.F. Dow, ed., *The Records and Files of the Quarterly Courts of Essex County, Massachusetts*, 8 vols (Salem, Mass.: Essex Institute, 1911–21), 1, pp. 199, 266. Cressy, *Coming Over*, pp. 266–7, notes that some settlers used migration as a substitute for divorce.

66. Rosamund Saltonstall to Samuel Saltonstall, 22 April 1644, in Moody, ed., *Saltonstall Papers*, I, p. 137. See Plate 3, 'The Saltonstall Family'. Thomas Larkham, who sailed home with one son ahead of the rest of the family, later wrote that his family had been scattered like dry bones (a reference to Ezekiel 37), 'yet did the Lord bring them altogether again here in England': BL, Ms. Loan 9, Diary of Thomas Larkham, 1650–1669, fol. 27.

67. *The Complete Works of Ann Bradstreet*, eds Joseph R. McElrath Jr and Allan P. Robb (Boston, Mass.: Twayne, 1981), pp. 228, 230–1. Samuel Bradstreet, a Harvard graduate, went to England in 1657 and returned in 1661. She wrote more poems to mark her husband's absence in England from 1661–2: pp. 232–7.

68. Plate 9. Winslow, who commissioned the portrait to mark his son Josiah's marriage to Penelope Pelham in London, was one of the trustees who oversaw the dispersal of Charles I's lavish art collection: Jerry Brotton, *The Sale of the Late King's Goods: Charles I and his Art Collection* (London: Macmillan, 2006), p. 216.

69. Moody, ed., *Saltonstall Papers*, I, p. 36. In September 1649, 'being by God's providence upon a voyage for England', Saltonstall appointed the pastor and deacons of the Ipswich church as his attorneys: Massachusetts Historical Society, Boston, Ms. N–2232, Saltonstall Papers, copy from Ipswich Deeds, Lib. 2, fol. 6. Hugh Peter and Samuel Shepard, likewise, each left a young child behind and made officers of the church their attorneys: Stearns, *Strenuous Puritan: Hugh Peter*, pp. 181–2; Oliver A. Roberts, *History of the . . . Ancient and Honourable Artillery Company of Massachusetts, 1637–1688*, 4 vols (Boston: A. Mudge and Son, 1895–1901), 1, p. 110.

70. Stephen Winthrop to John Winthrop, 29 July 1647, *Winthrop Papers*, V, pp. 174–5.
71. Will of Christopher Youngs [Yongs] of Wenham, 9 June 1647: *Probate Records of Essex County*, 1, pp. 76–8.
72. Edward Carl[e]ton to John Winthrop, *c.* 29 August 1640, and two further letters early in September, *Winthrop Papers*, IV, pp. 279–81, 282–4. Carleton returned to New England but went back to England permanently in the 1650s.
73. *A Note-Book kept by Thomas Lechford . . . in Boston*, American Antiquarian Society, *Transactions and Collections*, VII (Cambridge, Mass.: J. Wilson & Co., 1885), p. 431. William Prynne (*ODNB*) was his former client.
74. *Town Records of Salem, Massachusetts: 1634–1691*, 3 vols (Salem, Mass.: Essex Institute, 1868–1934), 1, pp. 124, 140, 142, 147. Elizabeth Avis, a lame maid costing her master four shillings a week, 'much desireth to go for England to her friends', so the Commonwealth of Massachusetts paid for her transport: Cressy, *Coming Over*, p. 197.
75. Francis J. Bremer, 'In Defence of Regicide: John Cotton on the Execution of Charles I', *William and Mary Quarterly*, 3rd series, 37 (1980), p. 123. The Council of Ireland offered £50 to Henry Dunster in 1655 to come over with his family: 'Dunster Papers', Massachusetts Historical Society, *Collections*, 4th series, 2 (1854), pp. 196–7.
76. Trask, ed., *Suffolk Deeds*, 2: 294; Waters, *Genealogical Gleanings*, p. 178. Rodolphus Elmes emigrated from Southwark in 1635, aged fifteen, as a servant: C.E. Banks, *The Planters of the Commonwealth . . . 1620–1640* (Boston: Houghton Mifflin, 1930), p. 144. Benjamin Jupe and his sister Mary Morse had been left two houses in London by a cousin: they borrowed £15 from their uncle, the wealthy Boston merchant Robert Keayne, to pay the cost of their passage home. The loan was to be repaid by rents due to them from their cousin's estate. See Waters, *Genealogical Gleanings*, p. 152; *NEHGR*, 35 (1881), p. 277; Trask, ed., *Suffolk Deeds*, 2: 86, 182, 183, 184.
77. Robert Clements' costs were £105 10 shillings. *The Probate Records of Essex County, Massachusetts, 1635–1664* (Salem, Mass.: Essex Institute, 1916), 1, p. 292.
78. Massachusetts Historical Society, Boston, Ms. SBd–151, 'Abraham Browne: volume of reminiscences, 1653–1668'; extracts published by Stephen T. Riley, 'Abraham Browne's Captivity by the Barbary Pirates, 1655', in P.C.F. Smith, ed., *Seafaring in Colonial Massachusetts*, Colonial Society of Massachusetts, *Publications*, 52 (1980), pp. 31–42. On attacks by Muslim privateers on Christian ships and the fate of their prisoners: Linda Colley, *Captives: Britain, Empire and the World, 1600–1850* (London: Pimlico, 2003), pp. 43–134.
79. Guilford General Court, 31 December 1646: Guilford, Connecticut, Town Clerk's Office, Guilford Records, Volume A, fol. 19; Winthrop, *Journal*, pp. 630–1, 643–4. Thomas Dunck claimed Austin had promised to repay him £2 10 shillings in goods to be shipped over from England. For Austin, see I.M. Calder, *The New Haven Colony* (New Haven: Yale University Press, 1934), pp. 160–1. According to the editors of Winthrop's *Journal*, 'cranksided' means easily tipped.
80. Thomas Goodwin, 'Preface' to Thomas Hooker, *A Survey of the Summe of Church-Discipline* (London, 1648). This was printed from a copy sent over after Hooker's death: Winthrop, *Journal*, p. 609.

Chapter 6

1. *Magnalia*, 2, p. 41.
2. BL, Ms. Loan 9, Diary of Thomas Larkham, 1650–1669, fols 16, 21, 24, 27, 32, 35v, 43v.
3. As John Eliot reported to Josiah's father, Edward Winslow, 20 October 1651: Bodleian, MS. Rawl. D. 934, fol. 11r. Josiah's bride was Penelope Pelham, who had returned to England with her parents several years earlier. See Plates 10–11.
4. Ian K. Steele, *The English Atlantic 1675–1740* (Oxford: Oxford University Press, 1986), p. 7.
5. Henry Jacie [Jessey] to John Winthrop Jr, 12 June 1633, *Winthrop Papers*, III, p. 126.

6. John Winthrop Jr to Elizabeth Winthrop, 8 October 1641, *Winthrop Papers*, IV, p. 342.

7. David Cressy, *Coming Over: Migration and Communication between England and New England in the Seventeenth Century* (Cambridge: Cambridge University Press, 1987), p. 156.

8. Steele, *The English Atlantic*, pp. 9–10; Gillian T. Cell, *English Enterprise in Newfoundland 1577–1660* (Toronto: University of Toronto Press, 1969), pp. 4–6; Mark Kurlansky, *Cod: A Biography of the Fish that Changed the World* (London: Vintage, 1999), pp. 70–2.

9. John Davenport to John Winthrop Jr, 24 July and 11 September 1650, in Isabel M. Calder, ed., *Letters of John Davenport, Puritan Divine* (New Haven: Yale University Press, 1937), p. 93.

10. John Winthrop, *The Journal of John Winthrop*, ed. Richard S. Dunn, James Savage and Laetitia Yeandle (Cambridge, Mass., and London: Harvard University Press, 1996), pp. 598–9. Abraham and Joanna Pratt died; Giles Firmin survived.

11. Austin Woolrych, *Britain in Revolution 1625–1660* (Oxford: Oxford University Press, 2002), is a good guide to the turbulent events of the 1640s and 1650s. Derek Hirst, 'The English Republic and the Meaning of Britain', in Brendan Bradshaw and John Morrill, eds, *The British Problem, c.1534–1707: State Formation in the Atlantic Archipelago* (Basingstoke: Macmillan, 1996), pp. 192–219, explores the cost to the Republic of creating regimes to support the union of three states, England, Ireland and Scotland.

12. Susanna Bell, *The Legacy of a Dying Mother to her Mourning Children, Being the Experiences of Mrs. Susanna Bell* (London, 1673), pp. 56, 1. Harwood and Usher: Henry F. Waters, *Genealogical Gleanings in England* (Boston, Mass.: New England Historic Genealogical Society, 1901), p. 626n. Bernard Bailyn, *The New England Merchants in the Seventeenth Century* (Cambridge, Mass.: Harvard University Press, 1955), p. 37.

13. On the Atlantic mercantile community: Bailyn, *New England Merchants*; Robert Brenner, *Merchants and Revolution: Commercial Change, Political Conflict and London's Overseas Traders, 1550–1653* (Princeton, N.J.: Princeton University Press, 1991); Carla Gardina Pestana, *The English Atlantic in an Age of Revolution, 1640–1661* (Cambridge, Mass., and London: Harvard University Press, 2004), pp. 157–82; Nuala Zahediah, 'Making Mercantilism Work: London Merchants and Atlantic Trade in the Seventeenth Century', *Transactions of the Royal Historical Society*, 6th series, 9 (1999), pp. 143–60.

14. Of 204 certificates of imports and exports noted by William Aspinwall of Boston between 1645 and 1651, only eight were on the account of New England traders: Bailyn, *New England Merchants*, p. 91; see *Aspinwall NR*, pp. 394–430.

15. *Aspinwall NR*, p. 362. Henry Shrimpton amassed a fortune of £11,979 from sending back timber, fish and furs, but his success was built on his ability to get credit from his brother: Bailyn, *New England Merchants*, pp. 35, 192.

16. See, for example, *Aspinwall NR*: Foote, pp. 113, 150, 402, 403, 404, 406, 407, 421; Ashurst and Pocock, p. 399; Peake, pp. 398, 400, 404. Ashurst: *ODNB*.

17. _____ to John Winthrop, [*c.* May 1637], *Winthrop Papers*, III, pp. 402–3.

18. John and Thomas Rucke: *Aspinwall NR*, pp. 173, 268, 273, 277.

19. William Gray and Benjamin Keayne: *Aspinwall NR*, pp. 92, 160; Bailyn, *New England Merchants*, p. 87; Bernard Bailyn, ed., *The Apologia of Robert Keayne: The Self-Portrait of a Puritan Merchant* (New York: Harper & Row, 1965), p. 32. Robert shrewdly pointed out that if Benjamin intended to live in England, 'he will be forced to sell his land [in New England] it may be for half the value of it'. But he allowed that if the overseers of his will or godly elders thought his son had a 'call of God, to carry him away' to England, he would not oppose it: 'I would not . . . be found a fighter against God . . . for any ends of my own'.

20. Benjamin Keayne to John Cotton, 12 March 1646/7, in Sargent Bush Jr, ed., *The Correspondence of John Cotton* (Chapel Hill and London: University of North Carolina Press, 2001), pp. 394–5; Stephen Winthrop to John Winthrop Jr, 27 March 1646,

Winthrop Papers, V, p. 70; Benjamin Keayne to Thomas Dudley, 18 March 1646/7, *Winthrop Papers*, V, pp. 144, 189n.; Brampton Gurdon to John Winthrop, 6 June 1649, *Winthrop Papers*, V, p. 351; *Boston CR*, pp. 46, 49.

21. *Magnalia*, 1, p. 146; John Davenport to John Winthrop Jr, 24 July 1654, in Calder, ed., *Letters of John Davenport*, p. 90. In 1667, after the Restoration of Charles II made a return to England unattractive for someone of Davenport's religious convictions, he made a controversial move from New Haven to Boston.

22. Robert Newman: *NEHGR* 24 (1870), p. 34; 41 (1887), p. 56; 49 (1895), p. 501; Massachusetts Historical Society, *Collections*, 5th series, 8 (1882), p. 67. John Evance: Calder, ed., *Letters of John Davenport*, p. 102n. Richard Malbon, a merchant and leading magistrate, left *c*.1649, according to James Savage, *A Genealogical Dictionary of the First Settlers of New England* (4 vols, Boston: 1860–62). Malbon's son Samuel left Harvard for Oxford in 1650: *CR*, Sibley.

23. Calder, ed., *Letters of John Davenport*, p. 84; Winthrop, *Journal*, p. 644. Gregson sailed for England in January 1646, to secure a Parliamentary patent for the New Haven colony: Graeme J. Milne, 'New England Agents and the English Atlantic, 1641–1666' (PhD diss., University of Edinburgh, 1993), p. 135.

24. *Magnalia*, 1, p. 146. *ODNB*, James P. Walsh, 'Hopkins, Edward (*c*.1602–1657)'; *ODNB*, David Yale, s.v. 'Yale, Elihu'; Winthrop, *Journal*, p. 570n.; Bailyn, *New England Merchants*, pp. 29, 107.

25. *Boston CR*, p. 55; Winthrop, *Journal*, p. 399n.; *GMB*. Bendall may well have been the person admitted as Rector of Cotgrave, Nottinghamshire, on 17 April 1654: Lambeth Palace Ms. COMM. III/3, fol. 11. Freegrace, born in Boston in 1635 (his name underlining his father's sympathies with the Antinomians), went back to New England in the 1660s, and eventually became Clerk of the Supreme Court in Massachusetts. Hoptfor, born in Boston in 1641, moved to trade from Antigua.

26. Nathaniel Mather to [John Rogers?], 23 December 1650, in 'Mather Papers', Massachusetts Historical Society, *Collections*, 4th series, 8 (1868), p. 5 (misdated '1651?' by the editor; see p. 241, n. 36).

27. W.B. Trask, ed., *Suffolk Deeds*, 12 vols (Boston: Rockwell and Churchill, 1880–1902), 2: 315a–16. The merchants were Jonathan Wade, Henry Powning and John Woodmancey. The London merchant William Peake and former colonist Samuel Sedgwick witnessed a will Wade made in England: Savage, *Genealogical Dictionary*.

28. William Aspinwall's notarial records (*Aspinwall NR*) are crammed with copies of promissory notes.

29. William Bury of Boston promised to pay off £25 he owed to another colonist after he reached England, 'at the sign of the cock at Mr Joshua Foote's shop'; Zephaniah Smith of Windsor, Connecticut, agreed to send money to Foote's shop in 1648 for Thomas Bell; Francis Lisle of Boston promised to pay off a debt of £40 over four years – 'in commodities merchantable in England if money fail' – at Richard Hutchinson's premises in Cheapside. *Aspinwall NR*, pp. 90, 102 (Bury), pp. 183–4 (Smith); Trask, ed., *Suffolk Deeds*, 1: 20 (Lisle).

30. Mark Peterson, 'Big Money Comes to Boston', *Common-Place*, vol. 6, no. 3, April 2006: accessed at http://www.common-place.org/vol-06/no-03/peterson/, 4 December 2006.

31. John Winthrop Jr to ____?, 19 Oct. 1660, Massachusetts Historical Society, *Collections*, 5th series, 8 (1882), pp. 66–7. For the Exchange, see Plate 13.

32. F[rancis]. G[lanville]. D[igory]. P[olwhele]. W[alter]. G[odbear]. N[icholas]. W[atts]. W[illiam]. H[ore]., *The Tavistocke Naboth Turned Nabal* (London, 1658), pp. 15, 17.

33. Winthrop, *Journal*, pp. 706–7.

34. Bodleian, MS. Rawl. D. 934, fol. 19r–21r, 26r–31v. Pestana, *English Atlantic*, p. 187, comments on this scheme in the context of other schemes for forced labour. R.P. Stearns, 'The Weld–Peter Mission to England', Colonial Society of Massachusetts, *Publications*, 32 (1937), pp. 213–16, 237–8. *ODNB*, A.W. McIntosh, 'Andrewes, Sir Thomas (*d*. 1659)': a regicide, and the first Lord Mayor of London under the Commonwealth.

35. E.N. Hartley, *Ironworks on the Saugus* (Norman: University of Oklahoma Press, 1957), pp. 64, 67–8, 70, 71.
36. 'Papers relating to proceedings of the Corporation for the Propagation of the Gospel in New England, 1649–1656', Bodleian, MS. Rawl. D. 934, fol. 1v: a list of members, including the London merchants Robert Thomson (who had lived briefly in Boston), Robert Houghton and Richard Hutchinson (brother-in-law of Anne Hutchinson), and Henry Ashurst as treasurer; with ex-colonists Herbert Pelham, Edward Winslow and Richard Floyd. John Eliot wrote to tell Winslow that the merchant Thomas Bell (once of Roxbury, now of London) had sent him news of the Company's work: 20 October 1651, Bodleian, MS. Rawl. D. 934, fol. 11v.
37. *Roxbury Land and Church Records*, Sixth Report of the Boston Record Commissioners (Boston: Rockwell and Churchill, 1884), p. 80.
38. Tai Liu, *Puritan London: A Study of Religion and Society in the City Parishes* (London and Toronto: Associated University Presses, 1986), pp. 103–25. Richard Hutchinson, the son of Anne Hutchinson, was dismissed in 1645 from Boston to 'the church of Christ whereof Mr Thomas Goodwin is pastor': *Boston CR*, p. 44. Goodwin was at St Dunstan-in-the-East, followed by Thomas Harrison (*CR*), a minister who had been in New England. In 1649, Philip Hatley and Henry Stonehill of Milford church were also dismissed to Thomas Goodwin's church (in Stonehill's case this was said to be 'Coleman Street', which confused Thomas with John Goodwin): Connecticut State Library, Hartford, Milford First Congregational Church Records, 1639–1837, fol. 2. Thomas Weld of Roxbury (*ODNB, CR*), briefly held office at St Giles, Cripplegate. New England records rarely mentioned a particular church in England. A search of various parish records held at the Guildhall Library, City of London, has yielded no references to transfer of membership: Guildhall Library Ms. 1175/1, Vestry Minutes, St Margaret New Fish Street; GL Ms. 4449, Births, marriages and deaths, St Stephen's, Coleman Street, 1636–89; GL Ms. 4458/1, Vestry Minutes, St Stephen's, Coleman Street, 1622–1726; GL Ms. 4887, Vestry Minutes, St Dunstan in the East, 1537–1651.
39. The church book has been divided. The record of baptisms (from 1644) and marriages (from 1646) is in the PRO: RG 4/4414, London, Stepney, Bull Lane (Independent). The record of admissions, dismissions and discussion among the members is in the London Borough of Tower Hamlets Local History Library and Archive: W/SMH/A/1, Records of Stepney Meeting: Church Book, 1644–1894.
40. *ODNB*, Richard L. Greaves, 'Greenhill, William (1597/8–1671)'; *CR*.
41. Tower Hamlets Archive, W/SMH/A/1 (Stepney Church Book), fols 3, 4. Bernard Capp, *Cromwell's Navy: The Fleet and the English Revolution, 1648–1660* (Oxford: Clarendon Press, 1989), p. 303n.
42. PRO, RG 4/4414 (Stepney Births and Marriages), fol. 118, Hannah Pelham, 11 July 1647; fol. 120, Willmot Witheredge, 28 August 1651. Two months before Hannah's baptism, Herbert Pelham wrote from London that he hoped to return to New England: 'I know no place where I more desire to be than among yourselves': *Winthrop Papers*, V, p. 157. By 1656 the church book described Edward Witheredge as a local resident, of Limehouse; for his career as an American trader and naval captain, see Capp, *Cromwell's Navy*, p. 165 [Witheridge]. Stepney's record of baptisms also includes children of Samuel Higginson, Robert and Rebecca Lord and Richard and Martha Thurston.
43. PRO, RG 4/4414 (Stepney Births and Marriages), fol. 118, Theophilus Hutchinson, 1 Sept. 1648, fol. 121, Ann, 5 July 1654; *Boston CR*, p. 44. (Less likely, but possible, is that these were children of her brother-in-law Richard Hutchinson, a prominent London merchant.)
44. Tower Hamlets Archive, W/SMH/A/1 (Stepney Church Book), fol. 192: Capp, *Cromwell's Navy*, p. 303, suggests this is Nehemiah; his relatives were John Bourne and Anthony Earning. 'Mrs Willowbie', also a member, was probably the mother of the colonist Francis Willoughby, originally from Wapping, who, like Samuel Higginson and Bourne, joined Cromwell's navy: Tower Hamlets Archive, W/SMH/A/1 (Stepney Church Book), fols 1v, 4.

45. *CR* 'Knowles, John'. PRO, RG 4/4414 (Stepney Births and Marriages), 19 April 1664; 5 January 1674/5. Dr Williams's Library, London, Ms. 38. 59: A.G. Matthews' detailed abstracts of the wills of ejected ministers, collected as part of the research for *CR* [Greenhill].

46. *Boston CR*, p. 69 (16 March 1672/3). In 1663 Harwood had been involved in efforts to persuade the English Congregationalist John Owen to become Boston's minister.

47. Will of 'Susann Bell', proved 21 March 1673, PRO, PROB 11/341; *CR*, 'John Knowles'.

48. Claire Tomalin, *Samuel Pepys: The Unequalled Self* (London: Penguin Books, 2002), p. 178.

49. Bell, *Legacy*, pp. 44–62.

50. Desborough to Cromwell, 18 Jan. 1650/1, in J. Nickolls, ed., *Original Letters and Papers of State Addressed to Oliver Cromwell* (London, 1743), p. 54.

51. J.S. Morrill, 'The Making of Oliver Cromwell', in J.S. Morrill, ed., *Oliver Cromwell and the English Revolution* (Harlow: Longman, 1990), pp. 19–48. Samuel Desborough's brother married Cromwell's sister when Oliver was still a country squire. Willoughby's certificate, 25 July 1650: *Aspinwall NR*, p. 306.

52. Michael P. Winship, *Making Heretics: Militant Protestantism and Free Grace in Massachusetts, 1636–1641* (Princeton and Oxford: Princeton University Press, 2002), pp. 243–6; Violet A. Rowe, *Sir Henry Vane the Younger. A Study in Political and Administrative History* (London: The Athlone Press, 1970); *ODNB*, Ruth E. Mayers, 'Vane, Sir Henry, the younger (1613–1662)'; *ANB*, Ronald P. Dufour, 'Vane, Sir Henry'.

53. Raymond P. Stearns, *The Strenuous Puritan: Hugh Peter, 1598–1660* (Urbana, Illinois: University of Illinois Press, 1955); *ODNB*, Carla Gardina Pestana, 'Peter [Peters], Hugh (*bap.* 1598, *d.* 1660)'; *ANB*, Richard P. Gildrie, 'Peter, Hugh'.

54. John B. Beresford, *The Godfather of Downing Street: Sir George Downing, 1623–1684* (London: R. Cobden-Sanderson, 1925); *ODNB*, Jonathan Scott, 'Downing, Sir George'.

55. Jane Ohlmeyer, ed., *Ireland from Independence to Occupation, 1641–1660* (Cambridge: Cambridge University Press, 1995); T.C. Barnard, *Cromwellian Ireland* (Oxford: Oxford University Press, 1975); David Stevenson, 'Cromwell, Scotland and Ireland', in Morrill, ed., *Oliver Cromwell and the English Revolution*.

56. John Humfrey to John Winthrop Jr, 21 July 1642, *Winthrop Papers*, IV, p. 352. Winthrop was in England from 1641 to 1643, to find expertise and investors for the ironworks at Saugus.

57. Stearns, *Strenuous Puritan: Hugh Peter*, pp. 187–201. *ODNB*, Carla Gardina Pestana, 'Rainborowe [Rainsborough], William (*fl.* 1639–1673)'.

58. George Cooke, brother to Hugh Peter's first wife, left for England in the autumn of 1645 (with a commission to act as an agent for Massachusetts). He went with his fellow-townsman of Cambridge, Massachusetts, Samuel Shepard (stepbrother to the minister Thomas Shepard). Cheng Yuan, 'The Politics of the English Army in Ireland during the Interregnum' (PhD diss., Brown University, 1981), pp. 69–70; C.H. Firth and G. Davies, *The Regimental History of Cromwell's Army*, 2 vols paginated as one (Oxford: Clarendon Press, 1940), pp. 579–82; *Winthrop Papers*, V, pp. 115, 266; *BDBR*. An inventory of Cooke's estate in New England is in the Middlesex County Probate and Family Court, Cambridge, Massachusetts, Middlesex County Probate Records, 1st series, 4 October 1652, docket 4988. For assessment of the attacks on Wexford and Drogheda, see *ODNB*, John Morrill, 'Cromwell, Oliver (1599–1658)'; David Stevenson, 'Cromwell, Ireland and Scotland', pp. 156–8.

59. Barnard, *Cromwellian Ireland*, pp. 288–9; *ODNB*, Natalie Zacek, 'Ludlow, Roger (*bap.* 1590, *d.* after 1664?)'. Ludlow was well connected, as a cousin of Edmund Ludlow, the Lieutenant-General of Ireland. He went to Ireland in 1654, followed by his son-in-law, the preacher Nathaniel Brewster, in 1655.

60. St J.D. Seymour, *The Puritans in Ireland, 1647–1661* (Oxford: Clarendon Press, 1921; reprint edn, Oxford: Clarendon Press, 1969), p. 224; Barnard, *Cromwellian Ireland*, p. 138. Henry Dunster received an invitation after his resignation as President of

Harvard: Edward Roberts to Dunster, March 1655/6, 'Dunster Papers', Massachusetts Historical Society, *Collections*, 4th series, 2 (1854), pp. 196–7.

61. Zephaniah Smith and Thomas Thornton, tanners from Windsor, Connecticut; John 'Millard' or 'Milam', perhaps once a cooper in Boston (who carried the letter to Dunster); see also John Clements of Haverhill, Massachusetts. Seymour, *Puritans in Ireland*, pp. 104, 206, 209, 217, 221, 222; 'Dunster Papers', Massachusetts Historical Society, *Collections*, 4th series, 2 (1854), p. 197; Barnard, *Cromwellian Ireland*, p. 210. Other settlers who went to Ireland as ministers included Harvard graduates Edmund Weld, Joshua Hobart and (although Seymour did not identify him as from New England) Abraham Walver: Seymour, *Puritans in Ireland*, pp. 56, 104, 162, 214, 222, 223; Sibley.

62. Barnard, *Cromwellian Ireland*, pp. 139–40; Anne Laurence, *Parliamentary Army Chaplains, 1642–1651* (Woodbridge, Suffolk: Royal Historical Society, 1990), pp. 123–4.

63. Barnard, *Cromwellian Ireland*, p. 138. In New England, Jenner protested that voluntary contributions at Weymouth did not provide a decent income, and left for Maine: Winthrop, *Journal*, p. 244; David D. Hall, *The Faithful Shepherd: A History of the New England Ministry in the Seventeenth Century*, 2nd edn (Cambridge, Mass.: Harvard University Press, 2006), p. 149. His salary at Saco, Maine, was £47: *Winthrop Papers*, IV, p. 308. He returned to England on the same ship as Thomas Harrison, who later recommended him for work in Ireland: BL, Lansdowne Ms. 821, fol. 200. For his stipend of £65 as Rector of Horstead with Stanninghall and Coltishall, Norfolk, see Lambeth Palace Ms. COMM. XIIb/9, fol. 1. The list of books he sold to the Corporation, and letters from John Eliot and Edward Winslow about the sale, are in Bodleian, MS. Rawl. D. 934, fols 11v, 32r–33v; Ebenezer Hazard, *Historical Collections* (2 vols, Philadephia, 1792–4), 2, p. 178.

64. Seymour, *Puritans in Ireland*, p. 215.

65. Only ten ministers in Ireland received more than £200 a year: Barnard, *Cromwellian Ireland*, p. 136. Harrison was paid £300.

66. B.R. White, 'Thomas Patient in England and Ireland', *Irish Baptist Historical Society Journal*, 2 (1969–70), pp. 36–48; Barnard, *Cromwellian Ireland*, pp. 101–2, 146–7. Christopher Blackwood, who had been in New England, also became a prominent Baptist preacher: Seymour, *Puritans in Ireland*, pp. 60, 207; Barnard, *Cromwellian Ireland*, pp. 101–2, 103n., 108.

67. Peter Bulkeley and others to Cromwell, 31 December 1650, in Nickolls, ed., *Original Letters*, pp. 44–5; *Records . . . of the Quarterly Courts of Essex County*, II, pp. 142–3, 174. Beside John Tuttle and Bulkeley, minister of Concord, the letter was signed by Samuel Whiting and Thomas Cobbet, ministers of Lynn, John Knowles, minister at Watertown; and the layman Daniel Dennison of Ipswich.

68. R. Scott Spurlock, *Cromwell and Scotland: Conquest and Religion, 1650–1660* (Edinburgh: John Donald Publishers, 2007), pp. 7–38; R. Scott Spurlock, 'Sectarian Religion in Scotland: the Impact of Cromwell's Occupation (1650–1660)', (PhD diss., University of Edinburgh, 2005), appendix 1; Ian Gentles, *The New Model Army in England, Ireland and Scotland, 1645–1653* (Oxford: Blackwell, 1992), pp. 387–412; John D. Grainger, *Cromwell against the Scots: The Last Anglo-Scottish War, 1650–1652* (East Linton: Tuckwell Press, 1997). The Kirk's efforts to impose a Presbyterian state church arguably alienated Cromwell more than the presence in Scotland of Charles II, who was proclaimed King of Great Britain and Ireland by the Scots on 5 February 1649.

69. *ODNB*, Walter W. Woodward, 'Fenwick, George (c.1603–1657)'. Reade: Firth and Davies, *Regimental History*, pp. 384–5, 387–8, 389, 563–8; Frances D. Dow, *Cromwellian Scotland, 1651–1660* (Edinburgh: Donald, 1979), pp. 64, 150, 226, 257, 258. The garrison at Edinburgh Castle fell three months after Dunbar, in December 1650. The English entered Stirling Castle on 15 September 1651.

70. Spurlock, *Cromwell and Scotland*.

71. Laurence, *Parliamentary Army Chaplains*, pp. 105, 123–4.
72. Capp, *Cromwell's Navy*, pp. 67, 307; David Stevenson, 'The English and the Public Records of Scotland, 1650–1660', in his *Union, Revolution and Religion in 17th Century Scotland* (Aldershot: Variorum Collected Studies Series, 1997), X, p. 160.
73. Francis J. Bremer, 'In Defence of Regicide: John Cotton on the Execution of Charles I', *William and Mary Quarterly*, 3rd series, 37 (1980), p. 122. A hundred and fifty Scots prisoners were shipped to New England as labourers: Bush, ed., *Cotton Correspondence*, pp. 461, 463–4.
74. Spurlock, 'Sectarian Religion in Scotland', pp. 337–8.
75. Dunster to 'some Christian friends in and about Bury in Lancashire', [late 1650]: Massachusetts Historical Society, Boston, Ms. N–1143, 'Henry Dunster Notebook, 1628–1654', fol. 135. His letter continued the debate about church order he had kept up with old contacts in his native county since the 1630s.
76. Papers relating to the settlement of Roger Glover's estate, 20 October 1652, 4 November 1654: Robert W. Lovett, ed., *Documents from the Harvard University Archives, 1638–1750 (Harvard College Records IV)*, Colonial Society of Massachusetts, *Publications*, 49 (1975), pp. 26–8, 52–3.
77. Dow, *Cromwellian Scotland*, is an invaluable guide to the workings and personnel of the regime.
78. For a map of English garrisons, see Spurlock, *Cromwell and Scotland*, p. xiii.
79. Woolrych, *Britain in Revolution*, p. 501.
80. Letters from Emmanuel Downing to John Winthrop Jr, 15 March 1652/3 and 27 March 1658, Massachusetts Historical Society, *Collections*, 4th series, 6 (1863), pp. 79, 85; Dow, *Cromwellian Scotland*, p. 185. George Downing's mother Lucy and sister Martha also came to Scotland.
81. Emmanuel Downing to Fitz John Winthrop, 2 February and 6 September 1658, Massachusetts Historical Society, *Collections*, 4th series, 6 (1863), pp. 84, 86; *ODNB*, James P. Walsh, 'Winthrop, Fitz John (1639?–1707)'.
82. Dow, *Cromwellian Scotland*, passim. T. M'Crie, ed., *The Life of Mr. Robert Blair*, (Edinburgh: Wodrow Society, 11, 1848), pp. 300–1. Blair set out for New England in 1636, but was driven back by storms: *ODNB*, David Stevenson, 'Blair, Robert (1593–1666)'.
83. Nathaniel Mather to [John Rogers?], 23 December 1650 [not 1651], in 'Mather Papers', Massachusetts Historical Society, *Collections*, 4th series, 8 (1868), p. 4. Another Harvard graduate, John Glover (whose brother Roger died at the siege of Edinburgh Castle) went to Scotland to take charge of a hospital. On his way north, he visited William Cutter, an old colonial neighbour from Cambridge, Massachusetts, in Newcastle-on-Tyne – a fact duly reported back to his stepfather Henry Dunster at Harvard: 'Dunster Papers', Massachusetts Historical Society, *Collections*, 4th series, 2 (1854), pp. 195–6; Sibley.
84. Laurence, *Parliamentary Army Chaplains*, p. 152; Spurlock, 'Sectarian Religion in Scotland', p. 354. John Collins, another Harvard graduate, became minister to a new congregational church at Leith in 1654, around the time Mather left for Ireland. John Hoadley, formerly with Samuel Desborough at Guilford, served as chaplain to the garrison at Edinburgh Castle, c.1654–9: Laurence, *Parliamentary Army Chaplains*, p. 136; Spurlock, 'Sectarian Religion in Scotland', pp. 192–3, pp. 354–5; Bernard C. Steiner, *A History of the Plantation of Menunkatuck and of the Original Town of Guilford* (Baltimore, 1897), p. 70.
85. Desborough: MP for Edinburgh 1654, Midlothian 1656, Edinburgh 1659. Downing: Edinburgh 1654, Carlisle 1656, 1659. Reade: Linlithgow, Clackmannan and Stirling 1654. Winthrop: Banff and Aberdeen 1656. On the advent of one Parliament for three nations, see Woolrych, *Britain in Revolution*, p. 601.
86. William Leete to Desborough, 10 October 1654, BL, Egerton Ms. 2519, fol. 10v. Leete sent greetings to John Hoadley and Thomas Jones, formerly of Guilford.
87. Capp, *Cromwell's Navy*, p. 56, citing PRO, SP25/123/226, Vane to the 'Generals at Sea'.

88. Capp, *Cromwell's Navy*, pp. 46–52, 122–3, 128; A.C. Dewar, 'Naval Administration in the Interregnum', *Mariner's Mirror*, XII (1926), p. 419. See also Richard Bonney, 'The European Reaction to the Trial and Execution of Charles I', in Jason Peacey, ed., *The Regicides and the Execution of Charles I* (Basingstoke: Palgrave, 2001), pp. 247–9.

89. Capp, *Cromwell's Navy*, pp. 49, 165–6, 295.

90. Capp, *Cromwell's Navy*, details the naval careers of Willoughby, Bourne and Hopkins.

91. *Magnalia*, 1, p. 145; Winthrop, *Journal*, p. 570.

92. *Magnalia*, 1, p. 147. Hopkins was Member of Parliament for Dartmouth; Willoughby, for Portsmouth.

93. Tomalin, *Samuel Pepys*, pp. 111, 284.

94. Winthrop, *Journal*, p. 570. Hopkins left money to found schools in Connecticut and £500 to Harvard College.

95. Capp, *Cromwell's Navy*, pp. 157, 313, 315. Besides Norcrosse, Capp mentions George Moxon, the former minister of Springfield, Massachusetts (or his son) and Nathaniel Mather, who was recommended for appointment as a naval chaplain after he lost his parish living at Barnstaple in Devon early in 1660, for speaking against the reinstated Rump Parliament.

96. Bush, ed., *Cotton Correspondence*, p. 462.

97. William Leete to Samuel Desborough, 10 October 1654, BL, Egerton Ms. 2519, fol. 10.

98. *ODNB*, Len Travers, 'Winslow, Edward (1595–1655)', Richard P. Gildrie, 'Leverett, John (1616–1679)'; H.D. Sedgwick, 'Robert Sedgwick', Colonial Society of Massachusetts, *Publications*, 3 (1895–7), pp. 156–74. John Humfrey Jr and William Pelham were also on the expedition: Firth and Davies, *Regimental History*, pp. 722–5. On the Western Design: Capp, *Cromwell's Navy*, pp. 87–91; Timothy Venning, *Cromwellian Foreign Policy* (Basingstoke: Macmillan, 1995), pp. 71–90; Pestana, *English Atlantic*, pp. 174, 177–81; Karen Ordahl Kupperman, 'Errand to the Indies: Puritan Colonisation from Providence Island through the Western Design', *William and Mary Quarterly*, 3rd series, 45 (1988), pp. 70–99.

99. Bonney, 'European Reaction', in Peacey, ed., *Regicides*, p. 265.

100. Venning, *Cromwellian Foreign Policy*, pp. 87–8 (but mistakes Daniel for his cousin Vincent). Daniel Gookin, *To all Persons whom these may Concern in the Several Townes and Plantations of the United Colonies, in New England* (Cambridge, Mass., 1656); letters from Gookin to Thurloe, 1656–7, in T. Birch, ed., *A Collection of the State Papers of John Thurloe*, 7 vols (London, 1742), 4, pp. 440, 449; 5, pp. 6–7, 147–8; 6, p. 362. ODNB, Roger Thompson, 'Gookin, Daniel (*bap.* 1612, *d.* 1687)'.

101. A point noted by G.E. Aylmer, *The State's Servants: The Civil Servants of the English Republic, 1649–1660* (London: Routledge and Kegan Paul, 1973), p. 184.

102. Herbert Pelham, who sat as an MP for Essex, had strong local ties. *ODNB*, Robert Charles Anderson, 'Pelham, Herbert (*c.*1600–1674)'.

103. *ODNB*, Ruth E. Mayers, 'Vane, Sir Henry the younger (1613–1662)'; Woolrych, *Britain in Revolution*, pp. 437–8. Vane retired from politics in 1653 over the Dutch war, but returned in 1656 as a critic of the Protectorate, and re-entered the restored Rump Parliament in 1659.

104. Haynes was deputy major-general for East Anglia, nominally deputising for Charles Fleetwood: Christopher Durston, *Cromwell's Major-Generals: Godly Government during the English Revolution* (Manchester and New York: Manchester University Press, 2001), pp. 31, 49–50.

105. Robert Jeffreys was Registrar-Accountant from 1649 to 1652: Aylmer, *State's Servants*, p. 63. Richard Saltonstall became Customs Commissioner for England in 1656, a promotion from the role he held in Scotland: Moody, ed., *Saltonstall Papers*, I, p. 37; Aylmer, *State's Servants*, pp. 72–3. Nathaniel Whitfield of Guilford initially worked as a clerk to the naval commissioners, but major-general William Goffe (whose head-quarters were in Winchester, where Henry Whitfield, Nathaniel's father, was a leading preacher) put him forward for work in customs administration at a salary of £100 a year: Aylmer, *State's Servants*, p. 126. Edward Winslow and John Humfrey were

trustees for the sale of Charles I's goods and for St James' Palace: Jerry Brotton, *The Sale of the Late King's Goods: Charles I and his Art Collection* (London: Macmillan, 2006), p. 216; Stearns, *Strenuous Puritan: Hugh Peter*, p. 338.

106. Pelham (*ODNB*) served as a JP throughout the 1650s: the earliest references in the Assize and Quarter Session Records are Essex Record Office ASS 35/92/1/34 (5 March 1650/1); Q/SR 351/111 (13 Jan. 1651/2).

107. Williston Walker, *The Creeds and Platforms of Congregationalism* (New York: Pilgrim Press, 1991), pp. 345n., 347n.; *ODNB*, Susan Hardman Moore, 'Hooke [Hook], William (1600/1–78)'.

108. *ODNB*, Stephen K. Roberts, 'Disbrowe [Desborough], John (*bap*. 1608, *d*. 1680)'; Stephen Wright, 'Desborough [Disbrowe], Samuel (1619–1690)'. Roger Williams told John Winthrop Jr that Cromwell looked on New England 'only with an eye of pity, as poor, cold and useless': 15 Feb. 1654/5, Massachusetts Historical Society, *Collections*, 4th series, 6 (1863), p. 291.

109. *ODNB*, Bernard Capp, 'Bourne, Nehemiah (1611–1691)'.

110. The manor of Elsworth was bought in 1655 by trustees acting on Desborough's behalf; he grew up at Eltisely. *ODNB*, 'Desborough [Disbrowe], Samuel'.

111. Waters, *Genealogical Gleanings*, pp. 545–6. John Hoadley and Thomas Jordan, who like Caffinch had emigrated to Guilford, also returned to Kent: Hoadley (after his time in Edinburgh) went to Rolvenden, near Tenterden; Jordan to Lenham. *CR*, ['Hoadly']; Steiner, *History of . . . Guilford*, p. 45.

112. [Giles Bitleston] to Thomas Cheasman or Edward Winshop in 'New Town' [Cambridge], New England, 1 Sept. 1638, *CSPD*, 1638–1639, p. 418; William Cutter to Henry Dunster, 19 May 1654, in 'Dunster Papers', Massachusetts Historical Society, *Collections*, 4th series, 2 (1854), pp. 195–6. Others who stayed close to their roots were George Wyllys Jr, Stephen Dummer and Matthew and Elizabeth Boyes.

113. Alison Games, *Migration and the Origins of the English Atlantic World* (Cambridge, Mass., and London: Harvard University Press, 2001), pp. 142–3, 203–4, 278n. 44. Return married Sarah Hobart, daughter of Peter Hobart, the minister at Hingham, Massachusetts.

114. See appendix 4.

115. Later in the 1650s, Allen became Rector of St George Tombland (Plate 15) and pastor to a gathered church that met there. The exceptions who moved further away from their roots were George Burdett, Thomas James, Hanserd Knollys, Hugh Peter and Thomas Weld.

116. Susan Hardman Moore, 'Arguing for Peace: Giles Firmin on New England and Godly Unity', in R.N. Swanson, ed., *Unity and Diversity in the Church*, Studies in Church History, 32 (Oxford: Blackwell, 1996), pp. 251–61. Only Thomas Harrison and Nathaniel Norcrosse strayed further from their place of birth than the adjacent county. Harrison, born in Hull, worked in London and Ireland after his return; Norcrosse, born in London, worked as a naval chaplain and then in parishes in Kent and Norfolk.

117. Samuel Mather to Jonathan Mitchell, Massachusetts Historical Society, Boston, Ms. N–2196, Miscellaneous Bound Manuscripts Collection, 26 March 1651.

118. John Bulkeley, Comfort Starr: *CR*. Michael G. Hall, ed., 'The Autobiography of Increase Mather', American Antiquarian Society, *Proceedings*, 71 (1961), part 2, p. 281 (this in spite of the fact that Richard Mather's relations with fellow Lancashire clergy had become strained after his emigration). Joshua and Nehemiah Ambrose went back to Lancashire. Benjamin Woodbridge became Rector of Newbury, Berkshire, where his uncle, Thomas Parker, had assisted before emigration. William Ames joined his uncle, John Phillip, in Suffolk. John Angier Jr served Ringley chapel, Lancashire, close to his father John Angier of Denton. *CR*, Sibley.

119. Christopher Marshall (*CR*) went to Woodkirk, Yorkshire. Samuel Newman emigrated from this parish in 1638, and Abraham Pearson in 1639 (see appendix 3). John Allin (*CR*), whose family came from John Phillip's parish of Wrentham in Suffolk, became Vicar of Rye, Sussex, where the colonist Christopher Blackwood had been a curate

before emigration. John Sams (*CR*) followed John Owen as minister of Coggeshall in Essex, which had strong links with the puritan colonies through local families like the Cranes and Sparhawkes: Waters, *Genealogical Gleanings*, pp. 224–9, 1197.

120. Henry Butler: *CR*, Sibley. Butler was admitted as Vicar of Yeovil with a certificate from William Benn of All Hallows, Dorchester (*CR*): Lambeth Palace Library, Ms. COMM. III/6, fol. 5.

121. W.A. Shaw, *A History of the English Church during the Civil Wars and under the Commonwealth, 1640–1660*, 2 vols (London: Longman, Green, 1900), II, pp. 284–6. The names of certificate-givers (though not the content of their testimonials) were recorded in the Registers of Presentations and Approvals of Ministers, now in Lambeth Palace Library: Mss COMM. III/1–7 (cited in *Calamy Revised* as Lambeth Mss 968, 983, 997, 996, 996a, 998, 999). J. Houston, ed., *Catalogue of Ecclesiastical Records of the Commonwealth, 1643–1660, in the Lambeth Palace Library* (Farnborough, Hants.: Gregg, 1968) pp. 65, 200.

122. Rowe, *Sir Henry Vane the Younger*, pp. 172, 200, 202. Vane's country home was at Belleau: Roger Williams stayed with Lady Vane in 1652; from 1653, after his retreat from politics, Vane lived there.

123. Lambeth Palace Library, Ms. COMM. III/4, fol. 406.

124. Lambeth Palace Library, Ms. COMM. III/3, fol. 11. Nothing survives to identify the Boston entrepreneur Edward Bendall conclusively with the Rector of Cotgrave, but the circumstantial evidence of the certificates is intriguing. Also, a new Rector (John Clark, *CR*) was admitted in 1659, after the death of the incumbent; Jane Bendall was a widow before 1661 (Trask, ed., *Suffolk Deeds*, 4: 88).

125. Lambeth Palace Library, Ms. COMM. III/3, lib.2, fol. fol. 20. *ODNB*, John S. Morrill, 'Brereton, Sir William, first baronet (1604–1661)'. Moxon's certificate-givers included the Welsh congregationalist Walter Cradock. Insight into his context at Astbury is given by Samuel Clarke's life of Machin: Clarke, *The Lives of Sundry Eminent Persons* (London, 1683), pp. 83–92.

126. Lambeth Palace Library, Ms. COMM. III/5, fol. 8; *ODNB*, Mary Wolffe, 'Hughes, George (1603/4–1667)'; 'Peter [Peters], Hugh'.

127. *Boston CR*, pp. 30, 46; Thomas Edwards, *Gangraena* (London, 1646), ii, pp. 67, 163–4; iii, Preface; 'The Canterbury Church Book', *Congregational Historical Society Transactions*, VII (1916–18), pp. 190, 192–3; Lambeth Palace Library, Ms. COMM. III/5 fols 37, 177; *Congregational Historical Society Transactions*, VIII (1920–3), p. 263.

128. John Rogers, *Ohel or Beth-shemesh: A Tabernacle for the Sun* (London, 1653), pp. 397–8.

Chapter 7

1. Suffolk Record Office, Lowestoft Branch, Ms. 1337/1/1, Wrentham Congregational Church, Church Book 1649–1971, fols 7–11, 25–7.

2. Samuel Baker, 23 August 1667, in John Browne, *The Congregational Church at Wrentham in Suffolk: Its History and Biographies* (London: Jarrold & Sons, 1854), pp. 7, 11.

3. The parochial survey of October 1650 referred to 'Mr John Phillips an ancient and reverend preaching minister', who 'supplies the cure every Lord's Day with the assistance of Mr William Ames son to the late Reverend Doctor Ames': Lambeth Palace Library, Ms. COMM. XII a /15, fol. 571. Ames: *CR*.

4. D.G. Hill, ed., *The Record of Baptisms, Marriages, and Deaths, and Admissions to the Church and Dismissals Therefrom, Transcribed from the Church Records in the Town of Dedham, Massachusetts* (Dedham, Mass., 1888), p. 23; George Selement and Bruce C.

Woolley, eds, *Thomas Shepard's Confessions*, Colonial Society of Massachusetts, *Publications*, 58 (1981), pp. 210–12.

5. Sargent Bush Jr, ed., *The Correspondence of John Cotton* (Chapel Hill and London: University of North Carolina Press, 2001), pp. 362–5; John Winthrop, *The Journal of John Winthrop*, ed. Richard S. Dunn, James Savage and Laetitia Yeandle (Cambridge, Mass., and London: Harvard University Press, 1996), pp. 403–4; Sargent Bush Jr, 'Thomas Hooker and the Westminster Assembly', *William and Mary Quarterly*, 3rd series, 29 (1972), pp. 291–300. On the Assembly: Robert S. Paul, *The Assembly of the Lord: Politics and Religion in the Westminster Assembly and the 'Great Debate'* (Edinburgh: T. & T. Clark, 1985); Chad B. Van Dixhoorn, 'Reforming the Reformation: Theological Debate at the Westminster Assembly, 1643–1652', 7 vols (PhD diss., University of Cambridge, 2005). Dr Van Dixhoorn's thesis contains a new transcript of the Minutes of the Assembly, from the original three-volume manuscript in Dr Williams's Library, London. The Westminster Assembly Project, of which Dr Van Dixhoorn is Director, is preparing a new edition of the Assembly's minutes and papers for publication: http://www.westminsterassembly.org. John Phillip attended the Assembly as one of two representatives from Suffolk.

6. See appendix 4.

7. See Ann Hughes, '"The public profession of these nations": the national Church in Interregnum England', in Christopher Durston and Judith Maltby, eds, *Religion in Revolutionary England* (Manchester and New York: Manchester University Press, 2007), pp. 93–114; John Morrill, 'The Church in England, 1642–9', in Morrill, ed., *Reactions to the English Civil War, 1642–1649* (Basingstoke: Macmillan, 1986), pp. 89–114.

8. Suffolk Record Office, Lowestoft, Ms. 1337/1/1, Wrentham Church Book, fols 7–11. The congregational church at Cockermouth, Cumberland, wrote down an account of its early years in 1662, 'as they have been kept in some loose papers by some of us from time to time', admitting that 'for nine or ten years space, things were little minded (as they might and should have been) in a way of penning down': Cumbria Record Office and Local Studies Library (Whitehaven), YDFCCL 3/1, 'The Register of Cockermouth Congregational Church, 1651–1771', fols 2–3.

9. Thomas Edwards, *Gangraena* (London, 1646), i, pp. 98, 147–8; iii, p. 82. See also, for example, his comments in *Gangraena*, i, pp. 69 [Giles Firmin], 97–8 [Hanserd Knollys], iii, pp. 67–8 [Samuel Eaton], 93–4 [an ex-colonist who deserted his wife], 97 [Thomas Larkham]. Pamphlets like Thomas Lechford's *Plain Dealing: or, Newes from New-England* (London, 1642) and William Rathband's *A Briefe Narration of some Church Courses . . . in New England* (London, 1644) had focused on practices in New England. Ann Hughes, *Gangraena and the Struggle for the English Revolution* (Oxford: Oxford University Press, 2004), pp. 12, 249–50, points out how Edwards' book shaped contemporary perceptions. For the roots of radical movements in pre-1640 England see David R. Como, *Blown by the Spirit. Puritanism and the Emergence of an Antinomian Underground in Pre-Civil-War England* (Stanford: Stanford University Press, 2004); Stephen Wright, *The Early English Baptists, 1603–1649* (Woodbridge, Suffolk: Boydell Press, 2006).

10. John Owen, *A Review of the True Nature of Schisme* (Oxford, 1657), pp. 35, 36. Owen was responding to Daniel Cawdrey's critique of his *The Duty of Pastors and People Distinguished* (London, 1643) in which Owen had called himself presbyterian by 'a misapplication of names and things'.

11. John Cotton, *The Keyes of the Kingdom of Heaven* (London, 1644). Carla Gardina Pestana, *The English Atlantic in an Age of Revolution, 1640–1661* (Cambridge, Mass., and London: Harvard University Press, 2004), pp. 72–3, comments that Goodwin and Nye published Cotton's tract with some reservations, a sign of the growing distance between Independents and New England by the mid-1640s. On pp. 56–60 she paints a heady picture of the early 1640s, which downplays any defensiveness or ambiguity in the message of colonial leaders: 'New England symbolised aggressive puritanism'; 'the religious sensibility of New Englanders was ready for export into the wider Atlantic

world'; 'for a euphoric period in the first years of the Long Parliament, New England stood near the center of the movement to reform the English church'.

12. Consultations before emigration, and the stock of ideas inherited from earlier godly ideas about the Church were important, but once the settlers were in America, letters and tracts mediated the New England Way to England. See Carol G. Schneider, 'Roots and Branches: From Principled Nonconformity to the Emergence of Religious Parties', in Francis J. Bremer, ed., *Puritanism: Transatlantic Perspectives on a Seventeenth-Century Anglo-American Faith* (Boston: Massachusetts Historical Society, 1993), pp. 185–8; Tom Webster, *Godly Clergy in Early Stuart England: The Caroline Puritan Movement c.1620–1643* (Cambridge: Cambridge University Press, 1997), p. 305–9.

13. Thomas Goodwin et al., *An Apologeticall Narration* (London, 1643) [January 1643/4], pp. 3, 5. On their experience in Holland: Keith L. Sprunger, *Dutch Puritanism: A History of English and Scottish Churches of the Netherlands in the Sixteenth and Seventeenth Centuries* (Leiden: E.J. Brill, 1982), pp. 168–73, 227–30, 378.

14. Goodwin, *Apologeticall Narration*, pp. 3–5.

15. Goodwin, *Apologeticall Narration*, pp. 23, 25–6. John Allin and Thomas Shepard, *A Defence of the Answer* (London, 1648), pp. 14–15, made the same point from New England about the misunderstandings created by being at a distance.

16. On the aspirations of this coalition, which (in the ambiguity of arguments about church reform before parties took firm shape) included campaigners for reformed episcopacy as well as presbyterians and adherents of the New England Way, see: Carol Geary Schneider, 'Godly Order in a Church Half-Reformed: the Disciplinarian Legacy, 1570–1641' (PhD diss., Harvard University, 1986), pp. 442–50; Rosemary Bradley, '"Jacob and Esau Struggling in the Wombe": a study of Presbyterian and Independent Religious Conflicts, 1640–48' (PhD diss., University of Kent at Canterbury, 1975), pp. 26–33.

17. Pestana, *English Atlantic*, pp. 58–9. Manuscripts that settlers sent back in the late 1630s to answer English critics led the foray into print: notably, Richard Mather, *Church-Government and Church-Covenant Discussed* (London, 1643). In other words, papers written to defend emigration and innovations in New England were commandeered to steer old England's reform. The Dissenting Brethren were invited to bring their own template for change to the Assembly, but (to the delight of their critics) declined: [Westminster Assembly], *A Copy of a Remonstrance lately Delivered in to the Assembly . . . Declaring the Grounds and Reasons of their declining to bring into the Assembly, their Model of Church-Government* (London, 1645), 'To the Reader'.

18. Goodwin, *Apologeticall Narration*, p. 5.

19. Pestana, *English Atlantic*, pp. 235–40, 'London pamphlets about New England, 1641–1649', lists 125 tracts: only thirteen are by former colonists. Thomas Weld, a Massachusetts agent, was the first colonist to publish from England in defence of the New England Way.

20. Edwards, *Gangraena*, i, pp. 68–9.

21. Giles Firmin, *A Serious Question Stated* (London, 1651), 'To the Courteous Reader'; also Giles Firmin, *Separation Examined* (London, 1652), 'To the Reader', and Giles Firmin, *The Answer of Giles Firmin* (London, 1689), p. 6. Firmin did not fit neatly into a party: Susan Hardman Moore, 'Arguing for Peace: Giles Firmin on New England and Godly Unity', in R.N. Swanson, ed., *Unity and Diversity in the Church*, Studies in Church History, 32 (Oxford: Blackwell, 1996), pp. 251–61. Hughes, *Gangraena and the Struggle for the English Revolution*, pp. 325–6; Geoffrey F. Nuttall, 'The Essex Classes (1648)', *United Reformed Church History Society Journal*, 3 (1983), p. 199.

22. See appendix 4.

23. John Morrill, 'The Impact of Puritanism', in J.S. Morrill, ed., *The Impact of the English Civil War* (London: Collins & Brown, 1991), p. 56; I.M. Green, 'The Persecution of

"Scandalous" and "Malignant" Parish Clergy during the English Civil War', *English Historical Review*, 94 (1979), pp. 507–31.

24. Nathaniel Mather to John Rogers, 23 March 1650/1, 'Mather Papers', Massachusetts Historical Society, *Collections*, 4th series, 8 (1868), p. 3.

25. See appendix 4.

26. Nathaniel Ward, *The Simple Cobler of Aggawam in America* (London, 1647, BL E.372[21]), p. 35. (The *Oxford English Dictionary Online* cites Ward for his use here of 'plebsbyterian', 'interpendent' and 'commoderate'.) He signed the 'Essex Testimony' in support of the Solemn League and Covenant with the Scots, printed as John Biddle, *A Testimony of the Ministers in the Province of Essex* (London, 1648). He coordinated a petition from the Eastern Association which attacked religious toleration: [N. Ward], *To the High and Honorable Parliament . . . the Humble Petitions . . . of the Eastern Association* (London, 1648). On his conservatism, see *ODNB*, 'Ward, Nathaniel'.

27. R.C. Simmons, 'Richard Sadler's Account of the Massachusetts Churches', *New England Quarterly*, 42 (1969), pp. 411–25; *CR*.

28. William Hooke to John Davenport, 2 March 1662/3, A.G. Matthews, ed., 'A Censored Letter', *Congregational Historical Society Transactions*, 9 (1924–6), p. 266; *ODNB*, 'Hooke, William'. John Hooke worked for many years after 1662 at the Savoy Chapel, a bitter blow for his father, who had been ejected as Master of the Savoy. For others who conformed, see appendix 4.

29. Edmund Calamy named nineteen. Ten or more can be added if others are included whom Calamy omitted, but who nevertheless showed strong leanings towards Congregationalism, or were left out of his count because they had died or were not in livings at the Restoration. See appendix 4. Those who took this line included a majority of the ministers who had been in parish ministry in the 1630s (before emigration), most of the older laymen who entered the ministry, and at least half the younger graduates and Harvard students.

30. Geoffrey Nuttall first drew attention to this phenomenon in 'Congregational Commonwealth Incumbents', *Congregational Historical Society Transactions*, 14 (1940–4), pp. 155–67.

31. To put this into perspective, only 130 of 1,909 ministers ejected from parish livings at the Restoration were said by Calamy to be 'Congregationalist' – that is, roughly one in fifteen: Nuttall, 'Congregational Commonwealth Incumbents', p.155. But one in two of the New Englanders in parish ministry followed this path, and former colonists make up almost a quarter of the total.

32. Norfolk Record Office, Norwich: Ms. FC 19/1, Norwich Old Meeting Congregational Church Book, 1642–1839, 23 April, 29 May, 10 June 1644; Ms. FC 31/1, Great Yarmouth, Middlegate Congregational Church Book, 1643–1855, 19 March 1645/6. Entries in Wrentham's parish register suggest that Phillip limited baptism to the children of godly families after he came back from New England: from 1641 the register listed most children by date of birth, not baptism (although 'baptised' seems sometimes to have been added later). Wrentham's Congregational church had a separate record of baptisms, at one time bound with its church book, but now in the National Archives. Suffolk Record Office, Lowestoft Branch, 168/D1/1, Wrentham Parish Records; PRO RG 4/3098, Suffolk, Wrentham (Independent): Births and Baptisms, 1650–1785.

33. Phillip's name crops up most often in the autumn of 1643. He was probably there to put up his hand on 25 September 1643, to affirm the Solemn League and Covenant with the Scots to bring 'a Reformation of three Kingdoms': Alexander Henderson and Philip Nye, *The Covenant: with a narrative of the proceedings and Solemn Manner of Taking it by the Honourable House of Commons, and Reverent Assembly of Divines* (London, 1643), pp. 10, 14; Van Dixhoorn, 'Reforming the Reformation', 2, p. 96.

34. Van Dixhoorn, 'Reforming the Reformation', 2, pp. 79, 101 (14 September, 2 October 1643); 'Propositions concerning evidence of God's love', 7 September 1640, *Winthrop*

Papers, IV, pp. 286–7. Michael P. Winship, *Making Heretics: Militant Protestantism and Free Grace in Massachusetts, 1636–1641* (Princeton and Oxford: Princeton University Press, 2002), pp. 223–4, suggests the propositions are close to the theology of Richard Sibbes (*ODNB*). Phillip's fellow signatories in Massachusetts were Thomas Weld and John Eliot of Roxbury, John Allin of Dedham, Thomas Shepard of Cambridge, Richard Mather and Jonathan Burr of Dorchester and John Wilson of Boston.

35. Van Dixhoorn, 'Reforming the Reformation', 3, p. 320 (14 November 1643). Phillip made short contributions to other debates in November and December 1643, but then seems to have been absent. In August 1645 he was added to a committee to consider on what grounds people could be suspended from communion: Van Dixhoorn, 'Reforming the Reformation', 6, p. 161.

36. John Browne, *A History of Congregationalism . . . in Norfolk and Suffolk* (London: Jarrold & Sons, 1877) pp. 163, 607–8; W.A. Shaw, *A History of the English Church during the Civil Wars and under the Commonwealth, 1640–1660*, 2 vols (London: Longman, Green, 1900), II, p. 425.

37. Suffolk Record Office, Lowestoft, Ms. 1337/1/1, Wrentham Church Book, fol. 7.

38. Suffolk Record Office, Lowestoft, Ms. 1337/1/1, Wrentham Church Book, fol. 7.

39. John Cotton, *The Way of the Churches of Christ in New-England* (London, 1645), pp. 111–12.

40. Allin and Shepard, *Defence of the Answer*, p. 10; on primordial churches in New England, Theodore Dwight Bozeman, *To Live Ancient Lives: The Primitivist Dimension in Puritanism* (Chapel Hill and London: University of North Carolina Press, 1988), pp. 120–50.

41. For all except Whitfield, see *CR*; *ODNB*, Francis J. Bremer, 'Whitfield [Whitfeld], Henry (1590/1–1657)'.

42. *ODNB*, Michael P. Winship, 'Weld, Thomas (*bap.* 1595, *d.* 1661); Roger Howell, 'Thomas Weld of Gateshead: the return of a New England puritan', *Archaeologia Aeliana*, 4th series, 48 (1970), pp. 303–32; R.P. Stearns, 'The Weld–Peter Mission to England', Colonial Society of Massachusetts, *Publications*, 32 (1937), pp. 188–246.

43. *ODNB*, Susan Hardman Moore, 'Larkham, Thomas (1602–1669)'; Susan Hardman Moore, '"Pure folkes" and the parish: Thomas Larkham in Cockermouth and Tavistock', in Diana Wood, ed., *Life and Thought in the Northern Church c.1100–c.1700* (Woodbridge, Suffolk: Boydell Press, 1999), pp. 489–509.

44. Thomas Larkham, *The Wedding-Supper* (London, 1652), 'Dedication to Parliament'. This tract carried a portrait of its author: see Plate 14.

45. Anne Laurence, *Parliamentary Army Chaplains, 1642–1651* (Woodbridge, Suffolk: Royal Historical Society, 1990), pp. 145–6. George Hughes (1603/4–1667): *ODNB*, *CR*. H.J. Hopkins, 'Thomas Larkham's Tavistock: Change and Continuity in an English Town, 1600–1670' (PhD diss., University of Texas, 1981), pp. 1–43, assesses the town's history in the first half of the seventeenth century.

46. Thomas Larkham, *The Parable of the Wedding-Supper Explained* (London, 1656), 'To the Saints and People of England'.

47. Larkham's diary recorded a sharp drop in his income from 1650 to 1651. Tithe income from Lamerton parish had been allocated to augment the income of the Vicar of Tavistock (as part of a fine levied on the patron, a royalist). But the trustees refused to pay Larkham, judging him 'unworthy to be continued in the employment of gospel preaching'. BL, Ms. Loan 9, Diary of Thomas Larkham, 1650–1669, fol. 9v; Larkham, *Wedding-Supper*, 'Dedication to Parliament'; PRO, SP19/95/89, 91, 93, 106–9, 115–18, 120, 122–33 (papers relating to the dispute, presented to the Committee for Advance of Money). Hardman Moore, '"Pure folkes" and the parish', pp. 494–5.

48. Cumbria Record Office and Local Studies Library (Whitehaven), YDFCCL 3/1, 'The Register of Cockermouth Congregational Church, 1651–1771', fols 1–4; B. Nightingale, *The Ejected of 1662 in Cumberland and Westmorland*, 2 vols (Manchester: Manchester

University Press, 1911), 1, pp. 687–9, 710–11. The overlap between old and new ecclesiastical structures meant that the gathered church did not ordain Benson as a teaching elder, 'because he had been before ordained by the bishops, and the church was fearful of iterating his ordination lest they should have offended'. George Larkham, fresh to the ministry, was ordained pastor by his father and neighbouring parish clergy.

49. Seven out of twenty, almost a third: George Larkham, Richard Gilpin, John Wilkinson, William Hopkins, Simon Atkinson, perhaps also Theophilus Polwhele and Comfort Starr. For Wilkinson, see Nightingale, *Ejected of 1662*, 1, pp. 749–53; for the others, *CR*. A gathered church at Kirkoswald, led by Hopkins and Atkinson, included a good number of other parish clergy as members: John Davis, Daniel Broadly, John Rogers and George Nicholson. Nightingale, *Ejected of 1662*, 1, pp. 319–24, 334–8, 384; 2, pp. 1258–9.

50. Gilpin and others to Richard Baxter, 1 September 1653, in Nightingale, *Ejected of 1662*, 1, p. 88.

51. Cumbria Record Office and Local Studies Library (Whitehaven), YDFCCL 3/1, 'The Register of Cockermouth Congregational Church, 1651–1771', fol. 7.

52. *The Agreement of the Associated Ministers ... of ... Cumberland and Westmorland* (London, 1656), cited by Nightingale, *Ejected of 1662*, 1, pp. 91–2. Geoffrey F. Nuttall, *Richard Baxter* (London: Nelson, 1965), pp. 67–70, discusses the Worcestershire Voluntary Association and other county voluntary associations of the 1650s.

53. *Agreement*, Nightingale, *Ejected of 1662*, 1, p. 103. In October 1653 the northern Congregational churches argued that the Commissioners for the Propagation of the Gospel had 'proved the greatest blessing that ever the North had': Christopher Hill, 'Puritans and "The Dark Corners of the Land"', in his *Change and Continuity in Seventeenth Century England* (London: Weidenfeld and Nicolson, 1974), p. 39.

54. Larkham, *Parable of the Wedding-Supper*, 'To the Saints and People of England'. He left Cumberland on 5 April 1652. George Larkham stayed on in Cumberland, pastor to a Congregational church for almost fifty years, known in nonconformist circles as 'the star of the North': Nightingale, *Ejected of 1662*, 1, p. 684.

55. F[rancis]. G[lanvile]. D[igory]. P[olwhele]. W[alter]. G[odbear]. N[icholas]. W[atts]. W[illiam]. H[ore]., *The Tavistocke Naboth Proved Nabal* (London, 1658), p. 11. Larkham successfully defended himself against a charge of riot brought to the Committee for Plundered Ministers, but incurred costs of £50, which the church helped him to meet: BL, Ms. Loan 9, Diary of Thomas Larkham, fols 11v–13r. (He enjoyed a similar vindication after a brawl at Dover, Maine, when the arbitrators from Massachusetts ruled in his favour.)

56. F.G. et al., *Tavistocke Naboth*, p. 67. Larkham started the fracas in print with *Naboth, in a Narrative and Complaint of the Church of God at Tavistock* (London, 1657), and replied to his opponents' riposte (*Tavistocke Naboth*) with *Judas Hanging Himself* ([London?], 1658): these two rare tracts survive in the Wallace Notestein Collection at the College of Wooster, Ohio. Larkham's opponents continued the dispute with [Anon.], *A Strange Metamorphosis in Tavistock, or the Nabal-Naboth improved a Judas* (London, 1658): British Library, Thomason Tracts, E. 940[2]. I am grateful to Dr Adam Smyth of the University of Reading for alerting me to the whereabouts of these tracts.

57. F.G. et al., *Tavistocke Naboth*, pp. 59–60. The Tavistock church book does not appear to have survived.

58. F.G. et al., *Tavistocke Naboth*, p. 67.

59. BL, Ms. Loan 9, Diary of Thomas Larkham, fol. 35v; Edward Windeatt, 'Early Nonconformity in Tavistock', *Report and Transactions of the Devonshire Association*, 21 (1889), p. 153; PRO, SP25/99/226–225 (17 March 1659/60). Preachers at the lecture included Tavistock-born ministers who were protégés of Hughes, and local ministers who were members of Hughes' Devon Association: John Tickel of Exeter (*CR*), John Rowe of Crediton (*CR* s.v. his son of the same name), Digory Polewhele of Whitchurch and Andrew Gove of Petertavy (Shaw, *History of the English Church*, II, p. 449).

60. Thomas Larkham, *A Discourse of Paying of Tithes* (London, 1656), p. 25.
61. See, for example, BL, Ms. Loan 9, Diary of Thomas Larkham, fols 12v, 14v, 15v, 16r, 17r, 20v, 26r, 36r.
62. From entries in Larkham's diary, the gathered church seems to have celebrated communion about once a quarter, sometimes more often: BL, Ms. Loan 9, Diary of Thomas Larkham, fols 15v, 16v, 17v (3 September, 31 December 1654, April/May 1655); fols 31, 31v (18 July and August 1658). Larkham recorded these occasions to account for the money he gave as a 'communion gift': sixpence, a shilling and, on one occasion, ten shillings.
63. Larkham, *Wedding-Supper*, p. 250. Parliament ordered that, from 29 September 1653, births, not baptisms, were to be entered in the record. The Tavistock parish register followed the Parliamentary order, but in some cases added a date of baptism. It is not clear whether those baptised were all the children of members of the gathered church, but this seems unlikely. Before the 1653 order, the register recorded where a child was baptised, if not in Tavistock parish church. Some baptisms had taken place in nearby parishes: neighbour ministers, with whom Larkham had fallen out, may have been baptising when he would not. The entries from 1653 to 1660 contain no information of this kind. The register reverted to recording the date of baptism after Larkham surrendered the living in 1660. Devon Record Office, Exeter, 482A add 2 /PR1, Tavistock Parish Register, 1614–1793.
64. BL, Ms. Loan 9, Diary of Thomas Larkham, fols 30v, 31v, 32v, 33r, 34r. The church had contact with gathered churches at Bideford and Exeter (William Bartlet, Lewis Stucley: *CR*).
65. Roger Howell, *Newcastle upon Tyne and the Puritan Revolution* (Oxford: Clarendon Press, 1967), p. 228; Howell, 'Thomas Weld', p. 322; Stearns, 'Weld–Peter Mission'.
66. Thomas Weld and others, *The Perfect Pharisee under Monkish Holinesse* (Gateshead, 1653). Thomas Weld and others, *A False Jew* (London, 1653); Howell, 'Thomas Weld', pp. 324–8. The 'false Jew' turned out to be Thomas Ramsay, a Scottish Catholic. For Tillam and his poem, 'Upon the first sight of New England, 29 June 1638', see chapter 2.
67. Howell, 'Thomas Weld', pp. 329–30.
68. 'By a friend to truth and an enemy to lyes' [Thomas Weld], *A Vindication of Mr. Weld. Wherein the case between him and his opposers, is truly stated, and the Church-Way of Christ soberly Asserted* (London, 1658), pp. 4–5. This answered James Cole, Thomas Potts, Thomas Arrowsmith, George Johnson and Ralph Clavering, whose pamphlet does not appear to survive.
69. [Weld], *Vindication*, pp. 15, 22. The 'supporter' was probably Weld himself, who (despite his efforts to disguise it) is the most likely author of the tract.
70. Thomas Weld to his parishioners at Terling, 1632: David D. Hall, ed., *Puritans in the New World: A Critical Anthology* (Princeton and Oxford: Princeton University Press, 2004), p. 35.
71. [Weld], *Vindication*, p. 15.
72. [Weld], *Vindication*, p. 24.
73. [Weld], *Vindication*, p. 16.
74. [Weld], *Vindication*, p. 7.
75. [Weld], *Vindication*, p. 11.
76. Weld's catalogue of the books (patristic, puritan and continental Reformed texts) survives: Bodleian, MS. Rawl. D. 934, fols 34r–38v. He received £34.
77. [Weld], *Vindication*, p. 12. Gateshead's 'pit-men' worked the coal mines.
78. Howell, 'Thomas Weld', pp. 329–30; *CSPD*, 1657–8, p. 251; *CSPD*, 1658–9, pp. 69–70. The 'four and twenty', parish officers, had civic duties as well as religious.
79. [Weld], *Vindication*, p. 27.
80. Giles Firmin (as editor), Stephen Marshall, *The Power of the Civil Magistrate in Matters of Religion Vindicated* (London, 1657), pp. 22–3. Firmin is more often cited for his anecdotes than for views, because he scattered his tracts with stories about people he

had known in colony and homeland – with the intent of reminding readers of the ties that bound the godly in both Englands. After his return to England he corresponded with Thomas Shepard, John Norton, Governor John Winthrop and others: Giles Firmin, *The Real Christian* (London, 1670), p. 214; Firmin, *Separation Examined*, 'To the Reader'; Giles Firmin, *Of Schism*, 'To the . . . Associated Ministers in the County of Essex' (London, 1658); *Winthrop Papers*, V, pp. 88–9. Hardman Moore, 'Arguing for Peace: Giles Firmin on New England and Godly Unity'; *ODNB*, N.H. Keeble, 'Firmin, Giles (1613/14–1697)'.

81. Edwards, *Gangraena*, iii, p. 68, 165; Eaton replied to Edwards in a tract written with his colleague Timothy Taylor, *A Just Apologie for the Church of Duckenfeild in Cheshire* (London, 1647), pp. 2–3. Hughes, *Gangraena and the Struggle for the English Revolution*, pp. 208, 213, 267.

82. Firmin, *Real Christian*, p. 270.

83. See, for example, references to the Barrington family and to the Elizabethan preacher Richard Rogers of Wethersfield and his family, in Firmin, *Real Christian*, 'Epistle Dedicatory' and pp. 67–8, 75–6.

84. *The Agreement of the Associated Ministers of the County of Essex* (London, 1658).

85. Edwards, *Gangraena*, i, p. 69. Firmin claimed Edwards attacked him because he challenged Edwards' reports of Anne Hutchinson's excommunication from the Boston church. Firmin had been an eyewitness at this event: *Separation Examined*, pp. 101–2.

86. Firmin, *Separation Examined*, 'To the . . . Ministers of London'.

87. Firmin, *Separation Examined*, pp. 68, 98; Firmin, *Serious Question Stated*, 'To the Courteous Reader'. To show how New England ministers kept faith with their English origins, Firmin looked back in Essex tradition to Alexander Richardson of Barking, 'whom Dr Ames and Mr Hooker, honoured much, and follow much': *Separation Examined*, p. 80; see Webster, *Godly Clergy*, pp. 29–30.

88. Giles Firmin, *A Sober Reply to the Sober Answer of Reverend Mr Cawdrey* (London, 1653), p. 24; Firmin, *Separation Examined*, p. 45.

89. Firmin, *Separation Examined*, pp. 20 (mispaginated as 13), 82. He cited Cotton, *Way of the Churches of Christ*, p. 111.

90. Firmin, *Separation Examined*, pp. 81–2; on the Wethersfield covenant, Patrick Collinson, *The Religion of Protestants: the Church in English Society 1559–1625* (Oxford: Clarendon Press, 1982), pp. 269–70.

91. As the titlepage of Firmin, *Serious Question Stated* put it: 'whether the ministers of England are bound . . . to baptise the children of all such parents which say, they believe in Jesus Christ; but are . . . scandalous in their conversations'. Firmin commented that Stephen Marshall left his parish because he was 'unsatisfied . . . to baptise all, yet refuse above half the Lord's Supper. But now he is out of the snare being only a lecturer': Firmin to Baxter, 24 July 1654, N.H. Keeble and Geoffrey F. Nuttall, eds, *Calendar of the Correspondence of Richard Baxter*, 2 vols (Oxford: Oxford University Press, 1991), 1, letter 192.

92. Firmin, *Separation Examined*, pp. 107–8; Firmin, *Serious Question Stated*, 'To the Courteous Reader'.

93. Firmin, *Sober Reply*, p. 7.

94. Firmin, *Sober Reply*, p. 8. Rogers and Stephen Marshall of Finchingfield ordained Firmin at Shalford (the Essex Congregationalists refused to ordain him by laying on hands, although this was the practice in New England): Firmin, *Separation Examined*, p. 27.

95. Giles Firmin, *Separation Examined*, p. 109; Firmin, *The Answer of Giles Firmin* (London, 1689), p. 6.

96. Cotton, *Way of the Churches of Christ*, pp. 111–16; see chapter 2, n. 86.

97. Cotton's Thanksgiving Sermon, 1651: Francis J. Bremer, 'In Defence of Regicide: John Cotton on the Execution of Charles I', *William and Mary Quarterly*, 3rd series, 37

(1980), p. 122; John Cotton, *Certain Queries Tending to Accommodation and Communion of Presbyterian and Congregationall Churches* (London, 1654), pp. 3–4.

98. *CR*. Eaton accepted state augmentation of his salary as a preacher: Shaw, *History of the English Church*, II, p. 585.

99. Bodleian, MS. Tanner 65, fols 214r–214v; printed, in an abbreviated form, by Sir Thomas Aston in *A Remonstrance Against Presbitery* (np, 1641), pp. 5–6.

100. Laurence, *Parliamentary Army Chaplains*, pp. 123–4.

101. *CSPD*, 1641–3, p. 77; *ODNB*, J.J. Mason, 'Duckenfield [Duckenfeild], Robert (1619–1689)'. See Plate 8.

102. Samuel Eaton and Timothy Taylor, *The Defence of Sundry Positions and Scriptures for the Congregational-way Justified* (London, 1646), pp. 19–21; Samuel Eaton and Timothy Taylor, *A Defence of Sundry Positions and Scriptures alleged to justify the Congregationall-way* (London, 1645), p. 2. Adam Martindale, of Gorton in Lancashire, observed that the parishioners who deserted his flock to join the covenanted church at Dukinfield still hired and paid for seats in Gorton church: R. Parkinson, ed., *The Life of Adam Martindale*, Chetham Society, Old Series, IV, (Manchester, 1845), p. 74. *ODNB*, Michael Mullett, 'Angier, John (1605–1677)'. Eaton's exchanges with Hollingworth were linked to the debate between New England ministers and Lancashire clergy: Hughes, *Gangraena and the Struggle for the English Revolution*, p. 208n.

103. *Life of Adam Martindale*, pp. 61, 64. As a young minister, Angier worked with John Cotton in Lincolnshire, and almost went to New England.

104. John Angier Jr transferred to Harvard in 1647, and graduated BA in 1653 and MA in 1655. He returned to join his father as a minister in the Lancashire classis. Before his ordination in 1657 he had to repent publicly of whatever it was that got him thrown out of Emmanuel. *Harvard College Records III*, Colonial Society of Massachusetts, *Publications*, 31 (1935), pp. 64–5n; E. Axon, ed., *Oliver Heywood's Life of John Angier of Denton*, Chetham Society, New Series, 97 (1937), pp. 93–4, 129.

105. *ODNB*, S.J. Guscott, 'Eaton, Samuel (d. 1665)'. Michael Mullett comments that although Angier's ministry came under threat after 1662, he was protected by his episcopal ordination, the sympathy of local gentry, the need to keep a preaching minister in his poor living (a perpetual curacy), and his willingness to use the Prayer Book: *ODNB*, 'Angier, John'. Denton was a chapelry within the parish of Manchester.

106. Patrick Collinson, 'The English Conventicle', in W.J. Sheils and D. Wood, eds, *Voluntary Religion*, Studies in Church History, 23 (Oxford: Blackwell, 1986), p. 257.

107. Michael P. Winship, 'Were there any Puritans in New England?' *New England Quarterly*, 74 (2001), pp. 127–9.

108. Thomas Allen to John Cotton, 21 November 1642, in Bush, ed., *Cotton Correspondence*, p. 374.

109. Robert G. Pope, *The Half-Way Covenant: Church Membership in Puritan New England* (Princeton: Princeton University Press, 1969). Richard Blinman (who fell out with his church at New London over this issue) put down on paper his strong objections to the Synod's proposals. His manuscript survives at the American Antiquarian Society, Worcester, Massachusetts: 'An answeare to divers Rd Elders of New England' [c.1657].

110. [Nathaniel Mather], 'To the Reader', in Richard Mather, *A Disputation concerning Church-Members and their Children in Answer to XXI Questions* (London, 1659). Nathaniel Mather accused Firmin of misrepresenting New England's churches: 'he above others is not without advantages to know New-England, and the ways of the churches there, better than it seems he doth'. But it may not be a coincidence that the first church in New England to affirm the Half-Way Covenant (after Richard Mather's church at Dorchester) was the church at Ipswich, Massachusetts, where Firmin and his father-in-law Ward had been members, and where John Norton – who wrote to Firmin to support the pragmatic pastoral plans of the Essex Association – had been Firmin's minister.

111. Winship, 'Were there any Puritans in New England?'; Anne S. Brown and David D. Hall, 'Family Strategies and Religious Practice: Baptism and the Lord's Supper in Early New England', in David D. Hall, ed., *Lived Religion in America: Towards a History of Practice* (Princeton: Princeton University Press, 1997), pp. 41–68.

112. Firmin, *Serious Question Stated*, 'To the Courteous Reader'.

113. Cumberland Association, *Agreement*, cited by Nightingale, *Ejected of 1662*, 1, p. 94; Eaton and Taylor, *A Defence of Sundry Positions . . . Justified*, p. 2.

114. When Ames was admitted as Rector of Frostenden in 1656, some of his certificates came from members of Wrentham's gathered church: Lambeth Palace Library, Ms. COMM. III/5, fol. 107; Suffolk Record Office, Lowestoft, Ms. 1337/1/1, Wrentham Church Book, fol. 25. He was also Rector of South Cove: *CR*.

115. [Weld], *Vindication*, p. 15.

116. Allen added his comments on this point to John Cotton's discussion of 'accommodation and communion' between Presbyterians and Congregationalists: Cotton [ed. T. Allen], *Certain Queries*, pp. 15–20. The Norwich church book has few entries covering Allen's time as pastor up to 1663, because until then he kept his own record of church business. His record of baptisms was later copied into it. Norfolk Record Office, Norwich, Ms. FC 19/1, Norwich Old Meeting Congregational Church Book.

117. Hugh Peter, mocked by Thomas Edwards for always being on the verge of returning to New England, may have deliberately avoided a commitment to a gathered church or parish because of his obligation to the church at Salem, Massachusetts. Shortly before he was executed for treason, he wrote: 'It hath much lain to my heart above anything almost, that I left that people I was engaged to in New England, it cuts deeply, I look upon it as a root-evil: and though I was never parson nor vicar, never took ecclesiastical promotion, never preached upon any agreement for money in my life, though not without offers and great ones; yet I had a flock, I say, I had a flock, to whom I was ordained who were worthy of my life and labours': *A Dying Fathers Last Legacy to an Onely Child* (London, 1660), pp. 108–9.

118. Cotton's willingness to concede this in documents of the late 1630s (*Way of the Churches of Christ*, pp. 111–16) and early 1650s (*Certain Queries*) puts a different perspective on the flurry of tracts about the New England Way in the mid-1640s, particularly as some of these had originated in the late 1630s as defences of what settlers had done on American soil, rather than as models for implementing the New England Way back home.

Chapter 8

1. Claire Tomalin, *Samuel Pepys: The Unequalled Self* (London: Penguin Books, 2002), pp. 111–12.

2. Bernard Capp, *Cromwell's Navy: The Fleet and the English Revolution, 1648–1660* (Oxford: Clarendon Press, 1989), p. 371; Bernard Bailyn, *The New England Merchants in the Seventeenth Century* (Cambridge, Mass.: Harvard University Press, 1955), p. 160. Willoughby went back to Charlestown, Massachusetts.

3. *Proclamations of Massachusetts Issued by Governors and other Authorities, 1620–1936*, Vol. I, 1620–1776 (Boston: Historical Records Survey, Division of Women's and Professional Projects, Works Project Administration, 1937), pp. 25–6.

4. John Maidston to John Winthrop Jr, 24 March 1659/60, T. Birch, ed., *A Collection of the State Papers of John Thurloe*, 7 vols (London, 1742), 1, p. 768. Winthrop wrote on 19 September to suggest to an enquirer (possibly Maidston) that former colonists in London could give the best advice: Massachusetts Historical Society, *Collections*, 5th series, 8 (1882), p. 68.

5. Isabel M. Calder, ed., *Letters of John Davenport, Puritan Divine* (New Haven: Yale University Press, 1937), pp. 198, 199.

6. Christopher Durston, *Cromwell's Major-Generals: Godly Government during the English Revolution* (Manchester and New York: Manchester University Press, 2001), pp. 235–6; *ODNB*. Daniel Gookin, formerly in government service at Dunkirk, travelled with them. *Magnalia*, 1, p. 237, lists fourteen ministers who came over for the first time after the Restoration.

7. Capp, *Cromwell's Navy*; *BDBR*, 'Hatsell, Henry'; Calder, ed., *Letters of John Davenport*, p. 216n. Others who returned to New Haven included Benjamin Ling, Hannah Eaton (daughter of Governor Theophilus Eaton, who brought over her husband William Jones), Robert Seely and Thomas Yale (who returned to see to the estate of his mother, Ann Eaton, and stayed on).

8. See appendix 2. Most made the transatlantic journey between 1660 and 1663, with a trickle of migrants into the 1670s. Mabel Reed, widowed in England, rejoined the three children she left behind in Woburn, Massachusetts (see the will of William Reed, recorded in New England 1661, Middlesex Probate and Family Court, Cambridge, Massachusetts, Middlesex Probate Records, First Series, docket 18636). The Quakers Richard and Abigail Lippincot, who had once lived in Boston, went to Rhode Island and later to New Jersey.

9. *ODNB*, Richard P. Gildrie, 'Leverett, John (1616–79)'; he stayed in England as an agent for Massachusetts until 1662. *ODNB*, James P. Walsh, 'Winthop, Fitz John' (1639?–1707); he returned in 1663.

10. David D. Hall, *The Faithful Shepherd: A History of the New England Ministry in the Seventeenth Century*, 2nd edn (Cambridge, Mass.: Harvard University Press, 2006), pp. 185–6, notes the prestige of those who had been ministers in England.

11. Michael G. Hall, ed., 'The Autobiography of Increase Mather', American Antiquarian Society, *Proceedings*, 71 (1961), part 2, p. 286. Though Increase soon had twelve invitations to church work, he delayed making a commitment until 1664, 'finding a great averseness in my spirit to comply therewith. I had . . . a great desire to return to England if liberty for nonconformity should be granted.'

12. Middlesex South District Registry of Deeds, Cambridge, Massachusetts, Middlesex County Deeds, Lib. II, fols 104–5, 111–13. T.B. Weyman, *The Genealogy and Estates of Charlestown* (Boston: D. Clapp & Sons, 1879), 'Allen, Thomas'.

13. Like many of the ministers who lost church livings at the Restoration, most left before St Bartholomew Day in August 1662, usually because they occupied sequestered posts which the former incumbent successfully claimed. Those who lost their livings in 1660 to 1661 were: Thomas Larkham, Joseph Hull, Thomas Willis Jr, Thomas Waterhouse, John Sams, Thomas Rashley, John Woodbridge, John Knowles, George Moxon, Edward Fletcher, William Horsford, John Bulkeley, Samuel Malbon, Nathaniel Mather, John Hooke, Leonard Hoar, Urian Oakes, Comfort Starr, Joseph Farnworth, John Weld, Henry Butler and Isaac Chauncy. Those ejected in 1662 were: Thomas James, Stephen Marshall, Giles Firmin, Richard Sadler, Thomas Harrison, Thomas Allen, Marmaduke Matthews, Benjamin Woodbridge, John Allin and Samuel Mather. John Phillip died in 1660; Thomas Weld died before 1662.

14. Larkham recorded his experiences in his diary (though not while he was away from Tavistock in 1665–6, to evade the Five Mile Act). He was excommunicated by the authorities but, by intervention of the patron, the Earl of Bedford, was buried in Tavistock parish church in 1669. Almost two hundred letters from Allin to Frith, 1663–70, and some from Allin to Samuel Jeake of Rye, are preserved in the Frewen archive at the East Sussex Record Office: FRE/5421–FRE/5634. Allin (*CR*) was a Harvard graduate and the son of John Allin of Dedham, Massachusetts.

15. Larkham, Henry Butler, Thomas Harrison and John Sams were among those prosecuted: *CR*.

16. Nathaniel Mather went to Rotterdam, Samuel Malbon to Amsterdam: *CR*.

17. *CR*. Like Larkham, Firmin practised as an apothecary. On occasional conformity, see Alexandra Walsham, *Charitable Hatred: Tolerance and Intolerance in England, 1500–1700* (Manchester and New York: Manchester University Press, 2006), pp. 192–3.

18. *ODNB*, Richard L. Greaves, 'Venner Thomas (1608/9–61)'; Kenneth C.G. Newport, 'Knollys, Hanserd (1598–1661)'. The ex-colonist John Baker was also a 'Vennerite', and put to death.

19. Francis J. Bremer, *Congregational Communion: Clerical Friendship in the Anglo-American Puritan Community, 1610–1692* (Boston, Mass.: Northeastern University Press, 1994), pp. 202–52; David Cressy, *Coming Over: Migration and Communication between England and New England in the Seventeenth Century* (Cambridge: Cambridge University Press, 1987).

20. Louise A. Breen, *Transgressing the Bounds: Subversive Enterprises among the Puritan Elite in Massachusetts, 1630–1692* (Oxford and New York: Oxford University Press, 2001), pp. 115–16, citing Nehemiah Bourne to John Winthrop Jr, 19 April 1662, Massachusetts Historical Society, *Collections*, 4th series, 7 (1865), pp. 305–6.

21. The will of 'Susann Bell, widow of All Hallows Barking, City of London', proved 21 March 1673 [written 10 May 1672], PRO, PROB 11/341.

22. Carla Gardina Pestana, *The English Atlantic in an Age of Revolution, 1640–1661* (Cambridge, Mass., and London: Harvard University Press, 2004), p. 225; Michael P. Winship, *Making Heretics: Militant Protestantism and Free Grace in Massachusetts, 1636–1641* (Princeton and Oxford: Princeton University Press, 2002), pp. 244, 255. Hugh Peter, *A Dying Fathers Last Legacy to an Onely Child* (London, 1660), p. 117, suggested his daughter might return to New England, but she did not: Raymond P. Stearns, *The Strenuous Puritan: Hugh Peter, 1598–1660* (Urbana, Illinois: University of Illinois Press, 1954) p. 422n.

23. *ODNB*, Jonathan Scott, 'Downing, Sir George'.

Appendix 1

1. William Bradford, *History of Plymouth Plantation*, ed. S. Morison (New York: Knopf, 1952), p. 36. Alexander Young claimed that 'the term Pilgrims belongs exclusively to the Plymouth colonists': *Chronicles of the Pilgrim Fathers of the Colony of Plymouth, from 1602 to 1625* (Boston: C.C. Little & James Brown, 1841), p. 88. Charles L. Cohen, 'Pilgrims', in Paul Boyer, ed., *The Oxford Companion to United States History* (Oxford and New York: Oxford University Press, 2001), accessed online at http://www.anb.org/articles, 22 October 2005; Jeremy Dupertuis Bangs, 'Pilgrim Fathers' (*act.* 1620), *ODNB*, online edition, Oxford University Press, January 2007 [http://www.oxforddnb. com/view/theme/93695, accessed 17 Jan. 2007]. 'Plimoth Plantation', the living museum at Plymouth, Massachusetts, prefers to refer to its inhabitants as 'English colonists', not 'Pilgrims'.

2. *Oxford English Dictionary Online*, 'pilgrim, *n*.'. Charles E. Hambrick-Stowe, *The Practice of Piety: Puritan Devotional Disciplines in Seventeenth-Century New England* (Chapel Hill: University of North Carolina Press, 1982), pp. 54–90, discusses the metaphor of puritan as pilgrim.

Appendix 3

1. *Magnalia*, I, p. 404.

2. Peter Clark, *English Provincial Society from the Reformation to the Revolution: Religion, Politics and Society in Kent, 1500–1640* (Hassocks: Harvester Press, 1977), pp. 199, 372.

3. Ralph J. Coffman and Mary F. Rhinelander, 'The Testament of Richard Mather and William Thompson', *NEHGR*, 140 (1986), pp. 3–16 (quotation from p. 16).

4. Kenneth Fincham, ed., *Visitation Articles and Injunctions of the Early Stuart Church*, 2 vols, Church of England Record Society, 1, 5 (Woodbridge, Suffolk: Boydell Press, 1994, 1998), II, pp. 108–9; *ODNB*, A.J. Hegarty, 'Brent, Sir Nathanael (1573/4–1652)'.

5. *Magnalia*, I, p. 396; on altar policy under Bishop Robert Wright in Coventry and Lichfield, see Kenneth Fincham, 'The Restoration of Altars in the 1630s', *Historical Journal*, 44 (2001), p. 931.

6. Fincham, ed., *Visitation Articles and Injunctions*, II, p. xvii.

7. William Laud, *A History of the Troubles and Tryal of . . . William Laud* (London, 1695), p. 531, called Lincoln 'the greatest Diocese in the Kingdom': it sprawled across many counties, from Lincolnshire in the north to Bedfordshire near London. Entries are divided into archdeaconries.

8. Isabel M. Calder, ed., *Letters of John Davenport, Puritan Divine* (New Haven: Yale University Press, 1937), pp. 82–3.

9. Laud, *Troubles and Tryal*, p. 531. *ODNB*, 'Brent, Sir Nathanael'; Fincham, ed., *Visitation Articles and Injunctions*, II, pp. 106–7.

10. Archdeacon Robert Newell's articles of 1637 advocated kneeling to receive communion and a communion table set altar-wise at the east end. Newell's authority was backed by Laud's Dean of the Arches, Sir John Lambe. *ODNB*, Andrew Foster, 'Newell, Robert (1576–1642)', J. Fielding, 'Lambe, Sir John (*c*.1566–1646)'; Fincham, ed., *Visitation Articles and Injunctions*, II, p. xx; Fincham, 'The Restoration of Altars in the 1630s', p. 935.

11. *Magnalia*, I, p. 519.

12. Laud, *Troubles and Tryal*, p. 544.

13. Fincham, ed., *Visitation Articles and Injunctions*, I, pp. 175–7; on settlement at Newbury, Massachusetts, and the English origins of its settlers, see D.G. Allen, *In English Ways: The Movement of Societies and the Transferal of English Local Law and Custom to Massachusetts Bay in the Seventeenth Century* (Chapel Hill, N.C.: University of North Carolina Press, 1981) pp. 89–116, 261–8. On Twisse, Tom Webster, *Godly Clergy in Early Stuart England: The Caroline Puritan Movement c.1620–1643* (Cambridge: Cambridge University Press, 1997) pp. 174–7.

14. Printed in Everett Emerson, ed., *Letters from New England* (Amherst, Mass.: University of Massachusetts Press, 1972), pp. 167–74.

15. *GMB*; Kenneth Fincham, *Prelate as Pastor: The Episcopate of James I* (Oxford: Clarendon Press, 1990), p. 326. Bachiler was known to the Winthrop family in 1621: *Winthrop Papers*, I, p. 235. He allied himself with London merchants who formed a company to send settlers to Saco, Maine: V.C. Sanborn, 'Stephen Bachiler and the Plough Company of 1630', *The Genealogist*, New Series, 19 (1903), pp. 270–84.

16. The Bishop of Winchester, Walter Curll, enforced the reading of the Book of Sports: Fincham, ed., *Visitation Articles and Injunctions*, II, pp. xviii–xix; *ODNB*, M. Dorman, 'Curll, Walter (1575–1647)'.

17. Laud, *Troubles and Tryal*, p. 554.

18. R.A. Marchant, *The Puritans and the Church Courts in the Diocese of York* (London: Longmans, 1960), p. 34n.

BIBLIOGRAPHY

Manuscript sources

American archives

AMERICAN ANTIQUARIAN SOCIETY, WORCESTER, MASSACHUSETTS

Misc. Mss Boxes, 'B'. Richard Blinman, 'An Answeare to divers Reverend Elders of New England', *c*.1657.
Russell Family, Sermons and Sermon Notes. Richard Russell's Sermon Notebook, 1649–51.

BOSTON PUBLIC LIBRARY, BOSTON

Ms. Am. 1502 / 1. Miscellaneous letters.
Ms. Am. 1506. Cotton Papers.

CAMBRIDGE, MASSACHUSETTS, CITY CLERK'S OFFICE, CITY HALL

Cambridge Town Records, 1632–1703 (transcript).

CONNECTICUT HISTORICAL SOCIETY, HARTFORD

The Wyllys Papers.

CONNECTICUT STATE LIBRARY, HARTFORD

Milford, First Congregational Church Records, 1639–1837.

GUILFORD, CONNECTICUT, TOWN CLERK'S OFFICE

Guilford Records, Volume A.
Guilford Records, Volume B.

HISTORICAL SOCIETY OF PENNSYLVANIA, PHILADELPHIA

Gratz Sermon Collection, Historical Society of Pennsylvania Manuscript Collection 250B, Box 1. John Pynchon's notes of sermons by George Moxon at Springfield, Massachusetts, 1649.

MASSACHUSETTS ARCHIVES, BOSTON

Massachusetts Archives Collection
  Volume 10. Ecclesiastical, 1637–1679.
  Volume 15B. Estates, 1636–1671.
  Volume 45. Lands, 1622–1726.
  Volume 58. Literacy, 1645–1774.
  Volume 240. Hutchinson Papers (Vol. 1, 1625–1650).
  Volume 241. Hutchinson Papers (Vol. 2, 1651–1680).

MASSACHUSETTS HISTORICAL SOCIETY, BOSTON

Ms. SBd–151. Abraham Browne: volume of reminiscences, 1653–1668.
Ms. N–1143. Henry Dunster Notebook, 1628–1654.
Ms. N–2232. Saltonstall Family Papers.
Ms. N–2195. Miscellaneous Manuscripts Collection, 1600–1972.
Ms. N–2196. Miscellaneous Bound Manuscripts Collection, 1629–1908.

MASSACHUSETTS, MIDDLESEX COUNTY COURTHOUSE, CAMBRIDGE

Middlesex County Court Records, I, 1649–1663 (transcript).
Middlesex County Court Files, 1649–1663.
[Abstracts of Court Files of Middlesex County, Massachusetts, 1649–1675, online database,
  http://www.NewEnglandAncestors.org, New England Historic Genealogical Society, 2003.]

MASSACHUSETTS, MIDDLESEX PROBATE AND FAMILY COURT, CAMBRIDGE

Middlesex County Probate Records, First Series, 1648–1876.

MASSACHUSETTS, MIDDLESEX SOUTH DISTRICT REGISTRY OF DEEDS,
  CAMBRIDGE

Middlesex Deeds, Lib. I, II, III.

MASSACHUSETTS, SOUTHERN ESSEX COUNTY REGISTRY OF DEEDS, SALEM

Essex Deeds. [Document images and indices online at http://www.salemdeeds.com.]

NEW ENGLAND HISTORIC GENEALOGICAL SOCIETY, BOSTON,
  MASSACHUSETTS

Richard Mather's Ms. Journal to New England, 1635. [Document images online at http://
  www. NewEnglandAncestors.org.]

PHILLIPS LIBRARY [formerly ESSEX INSTITUTE], PEABODY ESSEX MUSEUM,
  SALEM, MASSACHUSETTS

Essex County Quarterly Court Records.
Essex County Quarterly Court File Papers.
Essex County Probate Records (microfilm).

British archives

BODLEIAN LIBRARY, UNIVERSITY OF OXFORD

Rawlinson Ms. D. 934. Papers relating to proceedings of the Corporation for the Propagation of the Gospel in New England, 1649–1656.
Tanner Mss 65, 68, 220, 314.

BRITISH LIBRARY, LONDON

Additional Ms. 4276.
Egerton Ms. 2519. Papers of General Samuel Desborough, 1651–1660.
Lansdowne Ms. 821. Letters to Henry Cromwell.
Sloane Ms. 922. Letterbook of Nehemiah Wallington.
Loan 9. Diary of Thomas Larkham, 1650–1669.

CUMBRIA RECORD OFFICE AND LOCAL STUDIES LIBRARY, WHITEHAVEN

Ms. YDFCCL 3/1. The Register of Cockermouth Congregational Church, 1651–1771.

DEVON RECORD OFFICE, EXETER

482A add 2 / PR1. Tavistock Parish Register, 1614–1793.

DR WILLIAMS'S LIBRARY, LONDON

Ms. 38.59. Abstracts of wills collected by A.G. Matthews.
Quick Ms. 38.35. Nineteenth-century transcript of 'Icones Sacrae Anglicanae' (Ms. 38.31).

EAST SUSSEX RECORD OFFICE, LEWES

FRE/5421–FRE/5634. Letters from John Allin to Dr Philip Frith and Samuel Jeake of Rye, Sussex, 1663–74.

ESSEX RECORD OFFICE, CHELMSFORD

D/AEA 41. Archdeaconry of Essex Act Book, 1636–1638.
Essex Assize Files, 1650s; Quarter Sessions Rolls and Order Books, 1650s.

GUILDHALL LIBRARY, CITY OF LONDON

Ms. 1175/1. Vestry Minutes, St Margaret, New Fish Street.
Ms. 4449. Births, marriages and deaths, St Stephen's, Coleman Street, 1636–1689.
Ms. 4458/1. Vestry Minutes, St Stephen's, Coleman Street, 1622–1726.
Ms. 4887. Vestry Minutes, St Dunstan in the East, 1537–1651.

LAMBETH PALACE LIBRARY, LONDON

Mss COMM. III/1–7. Registers of Presentations and Approvals of Ministers, 1654–1660.
Mss COMM. V/5, VII/2. Day Books of the Trustees for the Maintenance of Ministers; Augmentation Order Books.
Mss COMM. XIIa, XIIb. Copies of parochial surveys, 1647–1657.

LONDON BOROUGH OF TOWER HAMLETS, LOCAL HISTORY LIBRARY AND ARCHIVE

W/SMH/A/1. Records of Stepney Meeting: Church Book, 1644–1894.

THE NATIONAL ARCHIVES [PUBLIC RECORD OFFICE], KEW, LONDON

PROB 11/339, 11/341, 11/352, 11/407. Wills of Thomas and Susanna Bell, Herbert Pelham, Nehemiah Bourne. [Accessed at http://www.nationalarchives.gov.uk/documentsonline]

RG 4/3098. Suffolk, Wrentham (Independent), Births and Baptisms, 1650–1785.

RG 4/4414. London, Stepney, Bull Lane (Independent), Births and Baptisms, 1644–1837; Marriages, 1646–1677.

SP16/261, 278, 302, 312, 324, 334, 346, 349, 361. State Papers Domestic: Charles I, 1625–1649.

SP19/95. State Papers Domestic: The Commonwealth [1642–1660]. Order Book of the Committee for the Advance of Money.

SP25/99. State Papers Domestic: The Commonwealth [1642–1660]. Committee for the Advance of Money.

NORFOLK RECORD OFFICE, NORWICH

NCR Case 16d/6. Norwich City Assembly Book of Proceedings, 1642–1668.

FC 19/1. Norwich Old Meeting Congregational Church. Church Book, 1642–1839.

FC 31/1. Great Yarmouth, Middlegate Congregational Church. Church Book, 1643–1855.

SUFFOLK RECORD OFFICE, LOWESTOFT BRANCH

1337/1/1, Wrentham Congregational Church. Church Book, 1649–1971.

168/D1/1, Wrentham Parish Register: births, 1602–1731; marriages, 1603–1714; deaths, 1603–1676.

Primary printed sources

Adventurers. A Proportion of Provisions needfull for such as intend to plant themselves in New England, for one whole yeare. Collected by the Adventurers, with the advice of the Planters. London, 1630.

Allin, John and Thomas Shepard. A Defence of the Answer Made unto the Nine Questions. London, 1648.

Ames, William. Conscience with the Power and Cases Thereof. [Leiden and London], 1639.

[Anon.]. New Englands First Fruits. London, 1643.

[Anon.]. A Strange Metamorphosis in Tavistock, or the Nabal-Naboth improved a Judas. London, 1658. [Thomason E.940(2)]

Aspinwall, William. A Volume Relating to the Early History of Boston, Containing the Aspinwall Notarial Records from 1644 to 1651. Boston, Mass.: Report of the Record Commissioners, 32, Municipal Printing Office, 1903.

Aston, Sir Thomas. A Remonstrance Against Presbitery. [London], 1641.

Bell, Susanna. The Legacy of a Dying Mother to her Mourning Children, Being the Experiences of Mrs. Susanna Bell. London, 1673.

Biddle, John. A Testimony of the Ministers in the Province of Essex. London, 1648.

Birch, T., ed. A Collection of the State Papers of John Thurloe (7 vols). London, 1742.

[Boston]. Pierce, Richard D., ed. The Records of the First Church in Boston 1630–1868, I. Boston: Colonial Society of Massachusetts, Publications, 39, 1961.

Bradford, William. History of Plymouth Plantation, ed. S. Morison. New York: Knopf, 1952.

Bradstreet, Ann. The Complete Works of Ann Bradstreet. Edited by Joseph R. McElrath Jr and Allan P. Robb. Boston, Mass.: Twayne, 1981.

Bush, Sargent, Jr, ed. The Correspondence of John Cotton. Chapel Hill and London: University of North Carolina Press, 2001.

Calder, Isabel M., ed. *Letters of John Davenport, Puritan Divine.* New Haven: Yale University Press, 1937.

Calendar of State Papers: Colonial Series, 1574–1660. London: Longman, Green, Longman & Roberts, 1860.

Calendar of State Papers: Domestic Series, of the Reign of Charles I (23 vols). London: Longman & Co., 1858–97.

Calendar of State Papers: Domestic Series, of the Commonwealth (13 vols). London: Longman & Co., 1875–86.

[Cambridge]. George Selement and Bruce C. Woolley, eds. *Thomas Shepard's Confessions.* Boston: Colonial Society of Massachusetts, *Publications*, 58, 1981.

[Canterbury, Kent]. 'The Canterbury Church Book', *Congregational Historical Society Transactions*, VII (1916–18), pp. 183–93.

[Charlestown]. James F. Hunnewell, ed. 'The First Record-Book of the First Church in Charlestown, Massachusetts', *NEHGR*, 23 (1869), pp. 187–91, 279–83.

Chauncy, Charles. *The Retraction of Mr. Charles Chancy.* London, 1641.

Child, Major John [William Vassall?]. *New-Englands Jonas cast up at London.* London, 1647.

Clap, Roger. *Memoirs of Capt. Roger Clap.* Boston, 1844.

Clarke, Samuel. *The Lives of Sundry Eminent Persons.* London, 1683.

Collinson, Patrick, John Craig and Brett Usher, eds. *Conferences and Combination Lectures in the Elizabethan Church: Dedham and Bury St Edmunds, 1582–1590*, Church of England Record Society, 19. Woodbridge, Suffolk: Boydell Press, 2003.

[Connecticut]. *A Digest of Early Connecticut Probate Records.* Online database: http://www.NewEnglandAncestors.org. Boston: New England Historic Genealogical Society, 2006.

[Connecticut]. J.H. Trumbull, ed. *The Public Records of the Colony of Connecticut prior to the Union with New Haven Colony, 1665* (15 vols to 1776). Hartford, 1850–1890.

Cotton, John. *Gods Promise to his Plantation.* London, 1630.

——. *A Coppy of a Letter of Mr. Cotton of Boston in New England, sent in answer of certaine Objections made against their Discipline and Orders there, directed to a Friend.* London, 1641.

——. *The Churches Resurrection.* London, 1642.

——. *The Keyes of the Kingdom of Heaven.* London, 1644.

——. *The Way of the Churches of Christ in New-England.* London, 1645.

——. *Of the Holiness of Church-Members.* London, 1650.

——. *Certain Queries Tending to Accommodation and Communion of Presbyterian and Congregationall Churches.* [Edited by Thomas Allen.] London, 1654.

——. *An Exposition upon the Thirteenth Chapter of the Revelation.* London, 1655.

Dane, John. 'A Declaration of Remarkabell Prouedenses in the Corse of my Life', *NEHGR*, 8 (1854), pp. 149–56.

Davenport, John. *An Apologeticall Reply to a Booke Called an Answer to the Unjust Complaint of W.B.* Rotterdam, 1636.

——. *An Answer of the Elders of the Severall Churches in New England unto Nine Positions.* London, 1643.

[Dedham]. D.G. Hill, ed. *The Record of Baptisms, Marriages, and Deaths, And Admissions to the Church and Dismissals Therefrom, Transcribed from the Church Records in the Town of Dedham, Massachusetts.* Dedham, Mass., 1888.

[Dorchester]. C.H. Pope, ed. *Records of the First Church at Dorchester . . . 1636–1734.* Boston, 1891.

'Dunster Papers'. Massachusetts Historical Society, *Collections*, 4th series, 2 (1854), pp. 190–8.

Eaton, Samuel and Timothy Taylor. *A Defence of Sundry Positions and Scriptures alleged to justify the Congregationall-Way.* London, 1645.

——. *The Defence of Sundry Positions and Scriptures for the Congregational-Way Justified.* London, 1646.

——. *A Just Apologie for the Church of Duckenfeild in Cheshire.* London, 1647.

Edwards, Thomas. *Reasons against the Independant Government of Particular Congregations.* London, 1641.

——. *Gangraena.* London, 1646.

Emerson, Everett, ed. *Letters from New England.* Amherst, Mass.: University of Massachusetts Press, 1972.

[Essex County]. *The Probate Records of Essex County, Massachusetts,* 1, 1635–1664. Salem, Mass.: Essex Institute, 1916.

[Essex County]. G.F. Dow, ed. *The Records and Files of the Quarterly Courts of Essex County, Massachusetts* (8 vols). Salem: Essex Institute, 1911–21.

[Essex, England]. *The Agreement of the Associated Ministers of the County of Essex.* London, 1658.

Eyre, William. *Vindiciae Justificationis Gratuitae.* London, 1654.

Fincham, Kenneth, ed. *Visitation Articles and Injunctions of the Early Stuart Church* (2 vols). Church of England Record Society 1, 5. Woodbridge, Suffolk: Boydell Press, 1994, 1998.

Firmin, Giles. *A Serious Question Stated.* London, 1651.

——. *Separation Examined.* London, 1652.

——. *A Sober Reply to the Sober Answer of Reverend Mr. Cawdrey.* London, 1653.

——. *Of Schism.* London, 1658.

——. *The Real Christian.* London, 1670.

——. *The Answer of Giles Firmin.* London, 1689.

——. *The Questions Between the Conformist and Nonconformist.* London, 1681.

Fiske, John. *The Notebook of the Reverend John Fiske, 1644–1675,* ed. R.G. Pope. Salem, Massachusetts: Essex Institute, 1974.

G[lanville], F[rancis], D[igory] P[olwhele], W[alter] G[odbear], N[icholas] W[atts], W[illiam] H[ore]. *The Tavistocke Naboth Turned Nabal.* London, 1658.

Goodwin, Thomas, Philip Nye, Sidrach Simpson, Jeremiah Burroughes, William Bridge. *An Apologeticall Narration, Humbly Submitted to the Honourable Houses of Parliament.* London, 1643.

Gookin, Daniel. *To all Persons whom these may concern in the Several Townes and Plantations of the United Colonies, in New England.* Cambridge, Mass., 1656.

Gouge, William. *The Saints Sacrifice.* London, 1632.

Harvard College Records, I. Boston: Colonial Society of Massachusetts, *Publications,* 15, 1925.

Harvard College Records, III. Boston: Colonial Society of Massachusetts, *Publications,* 31, 1935.

Harvard College Records IV. Robert W. Lovett, ed. *Documents from the Harvard University Archives, 1638–1750.* Boston: Colonial Society of Massachusetts, *Publications,* 49, 1975.

Hazard, Ebenezer. *Historical Collections* (2 vols). Philadephia, 1792–4.

Henderson, Alexander, and Philip Nye. *The Covenant with a narrative of the proceedings and solemn manner of taking it by the Honourable House of Commons, and reverent Assembly of Divines.* London, 1643.

Herle, Charles. *The Independency on Scriptures of the Independency of Churches.* London, 1643.

[Heywood, Oliver]. *Oliver Heywood's Life of John Angier of Denton,* ed. E. Axon. Chetham Society, New Series, 97. Manchester: Chetham Society, 1937.

[Higginson, Francis]. *New-Englands Plantation. Or, a Short and True Description of the Commodities and Discommodities of that Countrey.* London, 1630.

Hooke, William. *New Englands Teares, for Old Englands Feares.* London, 1641.

——. *New-Englands Sence of Old-England and Irelands Sorrows.* London, 1645.

Hooker, Thomas. *A Survey of the Summe of Church-Discipline.* London, 1648.

Hutchinson, Thomas. *The Hutchinson Papers. A Collection of Original Papers Relative to the History of the Colony of Massachusetts-Bay* (2 vols). Albany, New York: Publications of the Prince Society, 1865.

Jessey, Henry. *The Lords Loud Call to England.* London, 1660.

Johnson, Edward. *A History of New-England.* London, 1653.

Josselin, Ralph. *The Diary of Ralph Josselin 1616–1683,* ed. Alan Macfarlane. Oxford: Oxford University Press, 1976.

Keayne, Robert. *The Apologia of Robert Keayne,* ed. Bernard Bailyn. New York: Harper and Row, 1965.

Keeble, N.H. and Geoffrey F. Nuttall, eds. *Calendar of the Correspondence of Richard Baxter* (2 vols). Oxford: Oxford University Press, 1991.

[Knollys, Hanserd]. *The Life and Death of . . . Mr. Hanserd Knollys.* London, 1692.

Larkham, Thomas. *The Wedding-Supper.* London, 1652.

——. *The Parable of the Wedding-Supper Explained.* London, 1656.

——. *A Discourse of Paying of Tithes.* London, 1656.

——. *Naboth, in a Narrative and Complaint of the Church of God at Tavistock.* London, 1657.

——. *Judas Hanging Himself.* [London?], 1658.

Laud, William. *A History of the Troubles and Tryal of . . . William Laud.* London, 1695.

Lechford, Thomas. *Plain Dealing: or, Newes from New-England.* London, 1642.

——. *A Note-Book Kept by Thomas Lechford . . . in Boston . . . 1638 to 1641. Transactions and Collections* of the American Antiquarian Society, VII. Cambridge, Mass.: J. Wilson & Co., 1885.

Marshall, Stephen. *The Power of the Civil Magistrate in Matters of Religion Vindicated.* [Edited by Giles Firmin]. London, 1657.

[Martindale, Adam]. *The Life of Adam Martindale,* ed. R. Parkinson. Chetham Society, Old Series, IV. Manchester: Chetham Society, 1845, reprint Manchester: Chetham Society, 2001.

[Massachusetts]. N.B. Shurtleff, ed. *Records of the Governor and Company of the Massachusetts Bay in New England (1626–1686)* (5 vols in 6). Boston, 1853–4. Reprint, New York: AMS Press, 1968.

Massachusetts Historical Society. *Collections of the Massachusetts Historical Society.* Boston: The Society, 1792–.

Mather, Cotton. *Memoirs of the Life of the Rev. Increase Mather D.D.* London, 1725.

——. *Magnalia Christi Americana; or, the Ecclesiastical History of New England,* ed. T. Robbins (2 vols). Hartford: Silas Andrus & Son, 1853.

Mather, Increase. *The Life and Death of . . . Mr. Richard Mather.* Cambridge, Mass., 1670.

——. *A Brief Relation of the State of New England, from the Beginning of that Plantation to this Present Year, 1689.* London, 1689.

——. 'The Autobiography of Increase Mather', ed. Michael G. Hall, American Antiquarian Society, *Proceedings,* 71 (1961), part 2, pp. 280–7.

Mather, Richard. *Church-Government and Church-Covenant Discussed.* London, 1643.

——. *An Apologie of the Churches in New-England for Church-Covenant.* London, 1643.

—— and William Thompson. *A Modest and Brotherly Answer to Mr. Charles Herle his book against the Independency of Churches.* London, 1644.

—— and William Thompson. *An Heart-Melting Exhortation.* London, 1650.

——. *A Disputation concerning Church-Members and their Children in Answer to XXI questions.* London, 1659.

'Mather Papers'. Massachusetts Historical Society, *Collections,* 4th series, 8 (1868).

Matthews, A.G. ed. 'A Censored Letter', *Congregational Historical Society Transactions,* IX (1924–6), p. 266.

Matthews, Marmaduke. *The Messiah Magnified by the Mouthes of Babes in America*. London, 1659.

McGiffert, Michael, ed. *God's Plot: Puritan Spirituality in Thomas Shepard's Cambridge*. Amherst, Mass.: University of Massachusetts Press, revised and expanded edition, 1994.

M'Crie, T., ed. *The Life of Mr. Robert Blair*. Edinburgh: Wodrow Society, 1848.

Meserole, Harrison T., ed. *Seventeenth Century American Poetry*. New York: Doubleday & Co., 1968.

Metcalfe, Michael. 'To all the true professors of Christ's gospel within the city of Norwich', 13 January 1636/7, *NEHGR*, 16 (1862), pp. 279–84.

[New Haven]. C.J. Hoadley, ed. *Records of the Colony and Plantation of New Haven* (2 vols). Hartford, Conn., 1857–1858.

[New Haven] F.B. Dexter, ed., *New Haven Town Records*. Vol. 1, 1649–1662. New Haven, Conn., 1917.

Nickolls, J., ed. *Original Letters and Papers of State Addressed to Oliver Cromwell*. London, 1743.

Owen, John. *A Review of the True Nature of Schisme*. Oxford, 1657.

——— . *A Defence of Mr. John Cotton from the Imputation of Selfe Contradiction*. Oxford, 1658.

Patient, Thomas. *The Doctrine of Baptism*. London, 1654.

Pepys, Samuel. *The Diary of Samuel Pepys*. Vol. VI, 1665. Edited by Robert Latham and William Matthews. London: HarperCollins, 2000.

Perkins, William. *A Cloud of Faithfull Witnesses, Leading to the Heavenly Canaan, or a Commentary on the 11. Chapter to the Hebrewes*. London, 1607.

——— . 'A Treatise of the Vocations or Callings of Men', in *Works*, I. London, 1608. Reprinted, I. Breward, ed., *The Works of William Perkins*. Abingdon: Sutton Courtenay Press, 1970.

Peter, Hugh. *A Dying Fathers Last Legacy to an Onely Child*. London, 1660.

[Pratt, John]. 'Pratt's Apology', Massachusetts Historical Society, *Collections*, 2nd series, 7 (1818), pp. 126–8.

[Prynne, William]. *Newes from Ipswich*. Ipswich [i.e. London?], 1636.

——— . *Independency Examined, Unmasked, Refuted*. London, 1644.

The Pynchon Papers, ed. C. Bridenbaugh, I, *Letters of John Pynchon, 1654–1700*; II, *Selections from the Account Books of John Pynchon*. Boston: Colonial Society of Massachusetts, Publications, 60, 61, 1982.

Pynchon, William. *The Meritorious Price of Our Redemption*. London, 1650.

R[athband], W[illiam]. *A Briefe Narration of some Church Courses . . . in New England*. London, 1644.

Rogers, Daniel. *Naaman the Syrian, his Disease and Cure*. London, 1642.

Rogers, John. *Ohel or Beth-shemesh: A Tabernacle for the Sun*. London, 1653.

Rogers, Nathaniel. *A Letter Discovering the Cause of God's Continuing Wrath against the Nation*. London, 1644.

Rogers, Richard. *Seven Treatises, containing such Directions as is gathered out of the Holie Scriptures*. London, 1603.

Rogers, Samuel. *The Diary of Samuel Rogers, 1634–1638*, ed. Tom Webster and K. Shipps. Church of England Record Society, 11. Woodbridge, Suffolk: Boydell Press, 2004.

[Roxbury]. *Roxbury Land and Church Records*. Sixth Report of the Boston Record Commissioners. Boston: Rockwell and Churchill, 1884.

[Rowley]. Blodgette, G.B. and M. Mighill, eds. *The Early Records of the Town of Rowley, Massachusetts, I, 1639–1672*. Rowley, Mass., 1894.

[Salem]. Pierce, Richard D., ed. *Records of the First Church in Salem, Massachusetts, 1629–1736*. Salem, Mass.: Essex Institute, 1974.

[Salem]. *Town Records of Salem, Massachusetts: 1634–1691* (3 vols). Salem, Mass.: Essex Institute, 1868–1934.

The Saltonstall Papers, 1607–1815, ed. R. E. Moody (2 vols). Massachusetts Historical Society, *Collections*, 80, 81. Boston, Mass.: Massachusetts Historical Society, 1972–4.

Shepard, Thomas. *Subjection to Christ, in all his Ordinances*. London, 1654.

—— . *The Works of Thomas Shepard*, ed. J.A. Albro (3 vols). Boston, Mass., 1853.

Suffolk Deeds, ed. W.B. Trask (12 vols). Boston: Rockwell and Churchill, 1880–1902.

Ward, Nathaniel. *The Simple Cobler of Aggawam in America*. London, 1647.

[——]. *To the High and Honorable Parliament . . . the Humble Petitions . . . of the Eastern Association*. London, 1648.

Weld, Thomas. *An Answer to W[illiam] R[athband] His Narration*. London, 1644.

—— . *A Brief Narration of the Practices of the Churches in New-England*. London, 1647.

—— . *The Perfect Pharisee under Monkish Holinesse*. Gateshead, 1653.

—— . *A False Jew*. London, 1653.

[Weld, Thomas]. 'By a friend to truth, and an enemy to lyes'. *A Vindication of Mr. Weld. Wherein the case between him and his opposers, is truly stated, and the Church-Way of Christ soberly asserted*. London, 1658.

[Westminster Assembly]. *A Copy of a Remonstrance lately Delivered in to the Assembly . . . Declaring the Grounds and Reasons of their declining to bring into the Assembly, their Model of Church-Government*. London, 1645.

[White, John]. *The Planters Plea*. London, 1630.

Winslow, Edward. *Good Newes from New-England*. London, 1624.

—— . *New-Englands Salamander*. London, 1647.

Winthrop, John. *The Journal of John Winthrop*, ed. Richard S. Dunn, James Savage and Laetitia Yeandle. Cambridge, Mass., and London: Harvard University Press, 1996.

The Winthrop Papers, 1498–1654, ed. Allyn B. Forbes et al. (6 vols). Boston: Massachusetts Historical Society, 1929–.

Wood, William. *New Englands Prospect*. London, 1634.

Woodbridge, Benjamin. *The Method of Grace in the Justification of Sinners*. London, 1656.

The Wyllys Papers . . . 1590–1796. Collections of the Connecticut Historical Society, 21. Hartford: Connecticut Historical Society, 1924.

Young, Alexander. *Chronicles of the Pilgrim Fathers of the Colony of Plymouth, from 1602 to 1625*. Boston: C.C. Little & James Brown, 1841.

Secondary sources

Allen, D.G. *In English Ways: The Movement of Societies and the Transferal of English Local Law and Custom to Massachusetts Bay in the Seventeenth Century*. Chapel Hill: University of North Carolina Press, 1981.

—— . '"Vacuum Domicilium": the Social and Cultural Landscape of Seventeenth Century New England', in Jonathan L. Fairbanks and Robert F. Trent, eds, *New England Begins: The Seventeenth Century* (3 vols), 1, pp. 1–52. Boston: Museum of Fine Arts, 1982.

American National Biography (24 vols). Oxford and New York: Oxford University Press, 1999. [*ANB Online* at http://www.anb.org, 2005 –.]

Amory, Hugh. 'Printing and Bookselling in New England, 1638–1713', in Hugh Amory and David D. Hall, eds, *The Colonial Book in the Atlantic World*, pp. 83–116. Cambridge: Cambridge University Press, 2000.

Anderson, Robert C. 'A Note on the Changing Pace of the Great Migration', *New England Quarterly*, 59 (1986), pp. 406–7.

—— , G.F. Sanborn and M.L. Sanborn, eds. *The Great Migration: Immigrants to New England, 1634–1643*. Boston, Mass.: Great Migration Study Project, New England Historic Genealogical Society, 1999– .

—— , ed. *The Great Migration Begins: Immigrants to New England 1620–1633, Volumes I–III*. Online database: http://www.greatmigration.org, New England Historic

Genealogical Society, 2002. Originally published as Robert Charles Anderson, ed., *The Great Migration Begins: Immigrants to New England 1620–1633, Volumes I–III* (3 vols). Boston, Mass: New England Historic Genealogical Society, 1995.

Anderson, Virginia DeJohn. *New England's Generation: The Great Migration and the Formation of Society and Culture in the Seventeenth Century.* Cambridge: Cambridge University Press, 1991.

Axtell, James. *The School upon a Hill: Education and Society in Colonial New England.* New Haven and London: Yale University Press, 1974.

Aylmer, G.E. *The State's Servants: The Civil Servants of the English Republic, 1649–1660.* London: Routledge and Kegan Paul, 1973.

Bailyn, Bernard. *The New England Merchants in the Seventeenth Century.* Cambridge, Mass.: Harvard University Press, 1955.

—— . *Atlantic History: Concept and Contours.* Cambridge, Mass.: Harvard University Press, 2005.

Banks, C.E. 'Thomas Venner: the Boston Wine-Cooper and Fifth Monarchy Man', *NEHGR*, 47 (1893), pp. 437–44.

Baritz, Loren. *City on a Hill.* New York: John Wiley & Sons, 1964.

Barnard, T.C. *Cromwellian Ireland: English Government and Reform in Ireland.* Oxford: Oxford University Press, 1975.

Barnes, Thomas G. 'Thomas Lechford and the Earliest Lawyering in Massachusetts, 1638–1641', in Daniel R. Coquillette, Robert J. Brink and Catherine S. Menard, eds, *Law in Colonial Massachusetts*, pp. 3–38. Boston: Colonial Society of Massachusetts, *Publications*, 62, 1984.

Benedict, Philip. *Christ's Churches Purely Reformed: A Social History of Calvinism.* New Haven and London: Yale University Press, 2002.

Béranger, Jean. *Nathaniel Ward.* Bordeaux: Études et Recherches Anglaises et Anglo-Américaines, Université de Bordeaux, 1969.

Bercovitch, Sacvan. *The Puritan Origins of the American Self.* New Haven: Yale University Press, 1975.

—— . *The American Jeremiad.* Madison: University of Wisconsin Press, 1978.

Beresford, John B. *The Godfather of Downing Street: Sir George Downing, 1623–1684.* London: R. Cobden-Sanderson, 1925.

Bernard, G.W. 'The Church of England c.1529–c.1642', *History*, 75 (1990), pp. 183–206.

Bonney, Richard. 'The European Reaction to the Trial and Execution of Charles I', in Jason Peacey, ed., *The Regicides and the Execution of Charles I*, pp. 247–79. Basingstoke: Palgrave, 2001.

Bozeman, Theodore Dwight. *To Live Ancient Lives: The Primitivist Dimension in Puritanism.* Chapel Hill and London: University of North Carolina Press, 1988.

—— . *The Precisianist Strain: Disciplinary Religion and Antinomian Backlash in Puritanism to 1638.* Chapel Hill and London: University of North Carolina Press, 2004.

Brachlow, S. *The Communion of Saints: Radical Puritan and Separatist Ecclesiology, 1570–1625.* Oxford: Oxford University Press, 1988.

Bradley, Rosemary. ' "Jacob and Esau Struggling in the Wombe": A Study of Presbyterian and Independent Religious Conflicts, 1640–1648'. PhD diss., University of Kent at Canterbury, 1975.

Brautigam, Dwight. 'Prelates and Politics: Uses of "Puritan", 1625–1640', in Laura Lunger Knoppers, ed., *Puritanism and its Discontents*, pp. 49–66. Newark, N.J. and London: University of Delaware Press, 2003.

Breen, Louise A. *Transgressing the Bounds: Subversive Enterprises among the Puritan Elite in Massachusetts, 1630–1692.* Oxford and New York: Oxford University Press, 2001.

Breen, Timothy H. 'Who Governs? The Town Franchise in Seventeenth-Century Massachusetts', *William and Mary Quarterly*, 3rd series, 27 (1970), pp. 460–74.

—— . 'The Covenanted Militia of Massachusetts Bay: English Background and New World Development', in his *Puritans and Adventurers: Change and Persistence in Early America*, pp. 25–45. Oxford and New York: Oxford University Press, 1980.

—— and Stephen Foster, 'Moving to the New World: the Character of Early Massachusetts Immigration', *William and Mary Quarterly*, 3rd Series, 30 (1973), pp. 189–222.

Bremer, Francis J. 'The New Haven Colony and Oliver Cromwell', *Bulletin of the Connecticut Historical Society*, 38 (1973), pp. 65–72.

—— . 'In Defence of Regicide: John Cotton on the Execution of Charles I', *William and Mary Quarterly*, 3rd series, 37 (1980), pp. 103–24.

—— . *Puritan Crisis: New England and the English Civil Wars, 1630–1670*. New York & London: Garland, 1989.

—— , ed. *Puritanism: Transatlantic Perspectives on a Seventeenth-Century Anglo-American Faith*. Boston: Massachusetts Historical Society, 1993.

—— . *Congregational Communion: Clerical Friendship in the Anglo-American Puritan Community, 1610–1692*. Boston, Mass.: Northeastern University Press, 1994.

—— . *John Winthrop: America's Forgotten Founding Father*. Oxford: Oxford University Press, 2003.

—— and Lynn A. Botelho. *The World of John Winthrop: Essays on England and New England 1588–1649*. Boston, Mass.: Massachusetts Historical Society, 2005.

Brenner, Robert. *Merchants and Revolution: Commercial Change, Political Conflict and London's Overseas Traders, 1550–1653*. Princeton, N.J.: Princeton University Press, 1991.

Brotton, Jerry. *The Sale of the Late King's Goods: Charles I and his Art Collection*. London: Macmillan, 2006.

Brown, Anne S. and David D. Hall, 'Family Strategies and Religious Practice: Baptism and the Lord's Supper in Early New England', in David D. Hall, ed., *Lived Religion in America: Towards a History of Practice*, pp. 41–68. Princeton: Princeton University Press, 1997.

Browne, John. *The Congregational Church at Wrentham in Suffolk: Its History and Biographies*. London: Jarrold & Sons, 1854.

—— . *A History of Congregationalism, and Memorials of the Churches in Norfolk and Suffolk*. London: Jarrold & Sons, 1877.

Burg, B. Richard. 'A Letter of Richard Mather to a Cleric in Old England', *William and Mary Quarterly*, 3rd series, 29 (1972), pp. 81–98.

—— . *Richard Mather of Dorchester*. Lexington: University Press of Kentucky, 1976.

Bush, Sargent, Jr. 'Thomas Hooker and the Westminster Assembly', *William and Mary Quarterly*, 3rd series, 29 (1972), pp. 291–300.

—— . '"Revising what we have done amisse": John Cotton and John Wheelwright, 1640', *William and Mary Quarterly*, 3rd series, 45 (1988), pp. 733–50.

Calder, I.M. *The New Haven Colony*. New Haven: Yale University Press, 1934.

Caldwell, Patricia. *The Puritan Conversion Narrative: The Beginnings of American Expression*. Cambridge: Cambridge University Press, 1983.

Canny, Nicholas. 'What really happened in Ireland in 1641?', in Jane Ohlmeyer, ed., *Ireland: from Independence to Occupation, 1641–1660*, pp. 24–65. Cambridge: Cambridge University Press, 1995.

Capp, Bernard. *Cromwell's Navy: The Fleet and the English Revolution, 1648–1660*. Oxford: Clarendon Press, 1989.

Cell, Gillian T. *English Enterprise in Newfoundland 1577–1660*. Toronto: University of Toronto Press, 1969.

Chaplin, W.R. 'Nehemiah Bourne', Colonial Society of Massachusetts, *Publications*, 42 (1952–6), pp. 28–155.

Clifton, Robin. 'Fear of Popery', in Conrad Russell, ed., *The Origins of the English Civil War*, pp. 144–67. London: Macmillan, 1973.

Colley, Linda. *Captives: Britain, Empire and the World 1600–1850*. London: Pimlico, 1983.

Collins, Jeffrey R. 'The Church Settlement of Oliver Cromwell', *History*, 87 (2002), pp. 18–40.

Collinson, Patrick. 'A Comment: Concerning the Name Puritan', *Journal of Ecclesiastical History*, 31 (1980), pp. 483–8.

——— . *The Religion of Protestants: The Church in English Society 1559–1625*. Oxford: Clarendon Press, 1982.

——— . *Godly People: Essays on English Protestantism and Puritanism*. London: The Hambledon Press, 1983.

——— . 'The English Conventicle', in W.J. Sheils and D. Wood, eds, *Voluntary Religion*, pp. 223–59. Studies in Church History, 23. Oxford: Blackwell, 1986.

——— . 'The Cohabitation of the Faithful with the Unfaithful', in Ole Peter Grell, Jonathan I. Israel and Nicholas Tyacke, eds, *From Persecution to Toleration: the Glorious Revolution in England*, pp. 51–76. Oxford: Clarendon Press, 1991.

——— . 'Biblical Rhetoric: The English Nation and National Sentiment in the Prophetic Mode', in Claire McEachern and Deborah Shuger, eds, *Religion and Culture in Renaissance England*, pp. 15–45. Cambridge: Cambridge University Press, 1997.

Como, David R. *Blown by the Spirit. Puritanism and the Emergence of an Antinomian Underground in Pre-Civil-War England*. Stanford: Stanford University Press, 2004.

Conforti, Joseph A. *Imagining New England: Explorations of Regional Identity from the Pilgrims to the Mid-Twentieth Century*. Chapel Hill: University of North Carolina Press, 2001.

Cooper, James F., Jr. *Tenacious of their Liberties: The Congregationalists in Colonial Massachusetts*. Oxford and New York: Oxford University Press, 1999.

Crandall, Ralph J. and Randall J. Coffman. 'From Emigrants to Rulers: the Charlestown Oligarchy in the Great Migration', *NEHGR*, 131 (1977), pp. 3–27, 121–32, 207–13.

Cressy, David. *Coming Over: Migration and Communication between England and New England in the Seventeenth Century*. Cambridge: Cambridge University Press, 1987.

Davies, Julian. *The Caroline Captivity of the Church*. Oxford: Clarendon Press, 1992.

Dean, J.W. *A Memoir of the Rev. Nathaniel Ward*. Albany, N.Y.: J. Munsell, 1868.

Delbanco, Andrew. 'The Puritan Errand Re-Viewed', *Journal of American Studies*, 18 (1984), pp. 343–60.

——— . *The Puritan Ordeal*. Cambridge, Mass.: Harvard University Press, 1989.

Deming, Dorothy. *The Settlement of the Connecticut Towns*. New Haven: Yale University Press, 1933.

Dewar, A.C. 'The Naval Administration of the Interregnum 1641–1659', *Mariner's Mirror*, 12 (1926), pp. 406–30.

Ditmore, Michael G. 'Preparation and Confession: Reconsidering Edmund S. Morgan's Visible Saints', *New England Quarterly*, 62 (1994), pp. 298–319.

Donagan, Barbara. 'Godly Choice: Puritan Decision-Making in Seventeenth-Century England', *Harvard Theological Review*, 76 (1983), pp. 307–34.

Donnelly, Marian Card. *The New England Meeting Houses of the Seventeenth Century*. Middletown, Conn.: Wesleyan University Press, 1968.

Dow, Frances D. *Cromwellian Scotland, 1651–1660*. Edinburgh: Donald, 1979.

Duffy, Eamon. 'The Long Reformation: Catholicism, Protestantism and the Multitude', in Nicholas Tyacke, ed., *England's Long Reformation, 1500–1800*, pp. 33–70. London: UCL Press, 1998.

Durston, Christopher. *Cromwell's Major-Generals: Godly Government during the English Revolution*. Manchester and New York: Manchester University Press, 2001.

——— and Judith Maltby, eds. *Religion in Revolutionary England*. Manchester and New York: Manchester University Press, 2007.

Fairbanks, Jonathan L. and Robert F. Trent, eds. *New England Begins: The Seventeenth Century* (3 vols). Boston: Museum of Fine Arts, 1982.

Feintuch, Burt, and David H. Watters, eds, *The Encyclopaedia of New England: The Culture and History of an American Region.* New Haven and London: Yale University Press, 2005.

Fender, Stephen. *Sea Changes: British Emigration and American Literature.* Cambridge: Cambridge University Press, 1992.

Fernandez, Angela. 'Record-Keeping and other Trouble-Making: Thomas Lechford and Law Reform in Colonial Massachusetts', *Law and History Review*, Summer 2005, http://www.historycooperative.org/journals/lhr/23.2/fernandez.html (accessed 12 August 2006).

Fielding, John. 'Conformists, Puritans and the Church Courts: the diocese of Peterborough, 1603–1642'. PhD diss., University of Birmingham, 1989.

—— . 'Arminianism in the Localities: Peterborough diocese, 1603–1642', in Kenneth Fincham, ed., *The Early Stuart Church*, pp. 93–113. London: Macmillan, 1993.

—— . 'Opposition to the Personal Rule of Charles I: the Diary of Robert Woodford, 1637–1641', *Historical Journal* 31 (1998), pp. 769–88.

Fincham, Kenneth. *Prelate as Pastor: The Episcopate of James I.* Oxford: Clarendon Press, 1990.

—— , ed. *The Early Stuart Church, 1603–1642.* Basingstoke: Macmillan, 1993.

—— . 'Clerical Conformity from Whitgift to Laud', in Peter Lake and Michael Questier, eds, *Conformity and Orthodoxy in the English Church, c.1560–1660*, pp. 125–58. Woodbridge, Suffolk: Boydell Press, 2000.

—— . 'The Restoration of Altars in the 1630s', *Historical Journal*, 44 (2001), pp. 919–40.

—— . 'Material Evidence: the Religious Legacy of the Interregnum at St George Tombland, Norwich', in Kenneth Fincham and Peter Lake, eds, *Religious Politics in Post-Reformation England*, pp. 224–40. Woodbridge: Boydell Press, 2006.

Firth, C.H. and G. Davies, *The Regimental History of Cromwell's Army* (2 vols). Oxford: Clarendon Press, 1940.

Fischer, David Hackett. *Albion's Seed: Four British Folkways in America.* Oxford: Oxford University Press, 1989.

Foster, Andrew. 'Church Policies of the 1630s', in Richard Cust and Ann Hughes, eds, *Conflict in Early Stuart England: Studies in Religion and Politics 1603–1642*, pp. 193–223. London and New York: Longman, 1989.

—— . 'Archbishop Neile Revisited', in Peter Lake and Michael Questier, *Conformity and Orthodoxy in the English Church, c.1560–1660*, pp. 159–78. Woodbridge, Suffolk: Boydell Press, 2000.

Foster, Stephen. *Their Solitary Way: The Puritan Social Ethic in the First Century of Settlement in New England.* New Haven: Yale University Press, 1971.

—— . *The Long Argument: English Puritanism and the Shaping of New England Culture, 1570–1700.* Chapel Hill and London: University of North Carolina Press, 1991.

Games, Alison. *Migration and the Origins of the English Atlantic World.* Cambridge, Mass., and London: Harvard University Press, 2001.

Gentles, Ian. *The New Model Army in England, Ireland and Scotland, 1645–1653.* Oxford: Blackwell, 1992.

—— . 'The Iconography of Revolution: England 1642–1649', in Ian Gentles, John Morrill and Blair Worden, eds, *Soldiers, Writers and Statesmen of the English Revolution*, pp. 91–113. Cambridge: Cambridge University Press, 1998.

Gildrie, Richard P. 'The Ceremonial Puritan: Days of Humiliation and Thanksgiving', *NEHGR*, 136 (1982), pp. 3–16.

Gordis, Lisa M. *Opening Scripture: Bible Reading and Interpretative Authority in Puritan New England.* Chicago: University of Chicago Press, 2003.

Gottfried, Marion. 'The First Depression in Massachusetts', *New England Quarterly*, 9 (1936), pp. 655–78.

Grainger, John D. *Cromwell against the Scots: The Last Anglo-Scottish War, 1650–1652.* East Linton: Tuckwell Press, 1997.

Greaves, Richard L. and Robert Zaller, eds. *Biographical Dictionary of British Radicals in the Seventeenth Century* (3 vols). Brighton: Harvester Press, 1982–4.

Green, I.M. 'The Persecution of "Scandalous" and "Malignant" Parish Clergy during the English Civil War', *English Historical Review*, 94 (1979), pp. 507–31.

—— . 'Career Prospects and Clerical Conformity in the Early Stuart Church', *Past and Present*, 90 (1981), pp. 71–115.

—— . *Print and Protestantism in Early Modern England*. Oxford: Oxford University Press, 2000.

Gura, Philip F. *A Glimpse of Sion's Glory: Puritan Radicalism in New England, 1620–1660*. Middletown, Conn.: Wesleyan University Press, 1984.

Guyatt, Nicholas. ' "The Peculiar Smiles of Heaven": Providence and the Invention of the United States, 1607–1865'. PhD diss., Princeton University, 2003.

—— . ' "An Instrument of National Policy": Perry Miller and the Cold War', *Journal of American Studies*, 36 (2002), 1, pp. 107–49.

Hall, David D. *Worlds of Wonder, Days of Judgment: Popular Religious Belief in Early New England*. Cambridge, Mass.: Harvard University Press, 1990.

—— . 'Narrating Puritanism', in Harry S. Stout and D.G. Hart, eds, *New Directions in American Religious History*, pp. 51–83. New York: Oxford University Press, 1997.

—— . 'Readers and Writers in Early New England', in Hugh Amory and David D. Hall, eds, *The Colonial Book in the Atlantic World*, pp. 117–51. Cambridge: Cambridge University Press, 2000.

—— . *The Faithful Shepherd: A History of the New England Ministry in the Seventeenth Century*. 2nd edn, Cambridge, Mass.: Harvard University Press, 2006.

—— , ed. *Puritans in the New World: A Critical Anthology*. Princeton University Press: Princeton and Oxford, 2004.

—— , D.G. Allen, P.C.F. Smith, eds, *Seventeenth-Century New England*. Boston: Colonial Society of Massachusetts, *Publications*, 63, 1984.

—— and Alexandra Walsham. ' "Justification by Print Alone?": Protestantism, Literacy and Communications in the Anglo-American World of John Winthrop', in Francis J. Bremer and Lynn A. Botelho, eds, *The World of John Winthrop: Essays on England and New England 1588–1649*, pp. 334–85. Boston, Mass.: Massachusetts Historical Society, 2005.

Hambrick-Stowe, Charles E. *The Practice of Piety: Puritan Devotional Disciplines in Seventeenth-Century New England*. Chapel Hill: University of North Carolina Press, 1982.

Handlin, Lilian. 'Dissent in a Small Community', *New England Quarterly*, 58 (1985), pp. 193–220.

Hardman, Susan. 'Return Migration from New England to England, 1640–1660'. PhD diss., University of Kent at Canterbury, 1986.

Hardman Moore, Susan. 'Popery, purity and Providence: deciphering the New England experiment', in Anthony Fletcher and Peter Roberts, eds, *Religion, Culture and Society in Early Modern Britain*, pp. 257–89. Cambridge: Cambridge University Press, 1994.

—— . 'Arguing for Peace: Giles Firmin on New England and Godly Unity', in R.N. Swanson, ed., *Unity and Diversity in the Church*, pp. 251–61. Studies in Church History, 32. Oxford: Blackwell, 1996.

—— . 'Sexing the Soul: Gender and the Rhetoric of Puritan Piety', in R.N. Swanson, ed., *Gender and Christian Religion*, pp. 175–86. Studies in Church History, 34. Oxford: Blackwell, 1998.

—— . ' "Pure folkes" and the Parish: Thomas Larkham in Cockermouth and Tavistock', in Diana Wood, ed., *Life and Thought in the Northern Church c.1100–c.1700*, pp. 489–509. Woodbridge, Suffolk: Boydell Press, 1999.

—— . 'New England's Reformation: "Wee shall be as a Citty upon a Hill, the Eies of All People are upon Us" ', in Kenneth Fincham and Peter Lake, eds, *Religious Politics in Post-Reformation England*, pp. 143–58. Woodbridge: Boydell Press, 2006.

Hartley, E.N. *Ironworks on the Saugus*. Norman: University of Oklahoma Press, 1957.

Hill, Christopher. 'Puritans and "The Dark Corners of the Land"', in his *Change and Continuity in Seventeenth Century England*, pp. 3–47. London: Weidenfeld and Nicolson, 1974.

Hirst, Derek. 'The English Republic and the Meaning of Britain', in Brendan Bradshaw and John Morrill, eds, *The British Problem, c.1534–1707: State Formation in the Atlantic Archipelago*, pp. 192–219. Basingstoke: Macmillan, 1996.

Hopkins, H.J. 'Thomas Larkham's Tavistock: Change and Continuity in an English Town, 1600–1670'. PhD diss., University of Texas, 1981.

Houlbrooke, Ralph. 'The Puritan Death-Bed, c.1560–c.1660', in Christopher Durston and Jacqueline Eales, eds, *The Culture of English Puritanism, 1560–1700*, pp. 122–44. London: Macmillan, 1996.

Houston, J., ed. *Catalogue of Ecclesiastical Records of the Commonwealth, 1643–1660, in the Lambeth Palace Library*. Farnborough, Hants.: Gregg, 1968.

Howell, Roger. *Newcastle upon Tyne and the Puritan Revolution*. Oxford: Clarendon Press, 1967.

—— . 'Thomas Weld of Gateshead: the return of a New England puritan', *Archaeologia Aeliana*, 4th series, 48 (1970), pp. 303–32.

Hughes, Ann. *Politics, Society and Civil War in Warwickshire, 1620–1660*. Cambridge: Cambridge University Press, 1987.

—— . *Gangraena and the Struggle for the English Revolution*. Oxford: Oxford University Press, 2004.

—— . '"The public profession of these nations": the national Church in Interregnum England', in Christopher Durston and Judith Maltby, eds, *Religion in Revolutionary England*, pp. 93–114. Manchester and New York: Manchester University Press, 2007.

Innes, Stephen. *Labor in a New Land: Economy and Society in Seventeenth-Century Springfield*. Princeton, N.J.: Princeton University Press, 1983.

—— . *Creating the Commonwealth: The Economic Culture of Puritan New England*. New York: Norton, 1995.

Jones, M.J.A. *Congregational Commonwealth: Connecticut, 1636–1662*. Middletown, Conn.: Wesleyan University Press, 1968.

Jones, Rufus M. *The Quakers in the American Colonies*. London: Macmillan, 1911.

Kittredge, G.L. 'Dr. Robert Child the Remonstrant', Colonial Society of Massachusetts, *Publications*, 21 (1919), pp. 1–146.

Knight, Janice. *Orthodoxies in Massachusetts: Rereading American Puritanism*. Cambridge, Mass.: Harvard University Press, 1994.

Kupperman, Karen Ordahl. 'The Puzzle of the American Climate in the Early Colonial Period', *American Historical Review*, 87 (1982), pp. 1262–89.

—— . 'Climate and Mastery of the Wilderness in Seventeenth-Century New England', in David D. Hall, D.G. Allen and P.C.F. Smith, eds, *Seventeenth-Century New England*, pp. 3–38. Boston: Colonial Society of Massachusetts, *Publications*, 63, 1984.

—— . 'Errand to the Indies: Puritan Colonisation from Providence Island through the Western Design', *William and Mary Quarterly*, 3rd series, 45 (1988), pp. 70–99.

—— . *Providence Island, 1630–1641: The Other Puritan Colony*. Cambridge: Cambridge University Press, 1993.

Kurlansky, Mark. *Cod: A Biography of the Fish that Changed the World*. London: Vintage, 1999.

Lake, Peter. *Moderate Puritans and the Elizabethan Church*. Cambridge: Cambridge University Press, 1982.

—— . 'Anti-Popery: the Structure of a Prejudice', in Richard Cust and Ann Hughes, eds, *Conflict in Early Stuart England: Studies in Religion and Politics 1603–1642*, pp. 72–106. London and New York: Longman, 1989.

——— . 'Defining Puritanism – Again?', in Francis J. Bremer, ed., *Puritanism: Transatlantic Perspectives on a Seventeenth-Century Anglo-American Faith*, pp. 3–29. Boston: Massachusetts Historical Society, 1993.

——— . '"A Charitable Christian Hatred": the Godly and their Enemies in the 1630s', in Christopher Durston and Jacqueline Eales, eds, *The Culture of English Puritanism, 1560–1700*, pp. 145–83. London: Macmillan, 1996.

——— . 'Moving the Goal Posts? Modified Subscription and the Construction of Conformity in the Early Stuart Church', in Peter Lake and Michael Questier, eds, *Conformity and Orthodoxy in the English Church, c.1560–1660*, pp. 179–205. Woodbridge, Suffolk: Boydell Press, 2000.

Laurence, Anne. *Parliamentary Army Chaplains, 1642–1651*. Woodbridge, Suffolk: Royal Historical Society, 1990.

Liu, Tai. *Puritan London: A Study of Religion and Society in the City Parishes*. London and Toronto: Associated University Presses, 1986.

Love, William DeLoss. *The Fast and Thanksgiving Days of New England*. Boston: Houghton Mifflin, 1895.

Mac Cuarta, Brian, ed. *Ulster 1641: Aspects of the Rising*. Belfast: Institute of Irish Studies, Queen's University of Belfast, 1993; revised edn, 1997.

Maclear, J.F. 'New England and the Fifth Monarchy: the Quest for the Millennium in Early American Puritanism', *William and Mary Quarterly*, 3rd series, 32 (1975), pp. 223–60.

Marchant, R.A. *The Puritans and the Church Courts in the Diocese of York*. London: Longmans, 1960.

Martin, John F. *Profits in the Wilderness: Entrepreneurship and the Founding of New England Towns in the Seventeenth Century*. Chapel Hill and London: University of North Carolina Press, 1991.

Matthews, A.G. *Calamy Revised*. Oxford: Clarendon Press, 1934; reprint, Oxford: Clarendon Press, 1988.

McGee, J. Sears. *The Godly Man in Stuart England: Anglicans, Puritans, and the Two Tables, 1620–1670*. New Haven: Yale University Press, 1976.

McWilliams, James E. 'New England's First Depression: Beyond an Export-Led Interpretation', *Journal of Interdisciplinary History*, 23 (2002), pp. 1–20.

Miller, Perry. *Orthodoxy in Massachusetts, 1630–1650*. Cambridge, Mass.: Harvard University Press, 1933. Reprint, New York: Harper and Row, 1970.

——— . *Errand into the Wilderness*. Cambridge, Mass.: Harvard University Press, 1956.

Milne, Graeme J. 'New England Agents and the English Atlantic, 1641–1666'. PhD diss., University of Edinburgh, 1993.

Milton, Anthony. *Catholic and Reformed: The Roman and Protestant Churches in English Protestant Thought, 1600–1640*. Cambridge: Cambridge University Press, 1995.

Morison, Samuel Eliot. *The Founding of Harvard College*. Cambridge, Mass.: Harvard University Press, 1935.

——— . *Harvard College in the Seventeenth Century* (2 vols). Cambridge, Mass.: Harvard University Press, 1936.

Morrill, John. 'The Church in England, 1642–9', in J.S. Morrill, ed., *Reactions to the English Civil War, 1642–1649*, pp. 89–114. Basingstoke: Macmillan, 1986.

——— . 'The Making of Oliver Cromwell', in J.S. Morrill, ed., *Oliver Cromwell and the English Revolution*, pp. 19–48. London and New York: Longman, 1990.

——— . 'The Impact of Puritanism', in J.S. Morrill, ed., *The Impact of the English Civil War*, pp. 50–66. London: Collins & Brown, 1991.

——— . 'A Liberation Theology? Aspects of Puritanism in the English Revolution', in Laura Lunger Knoppers, ed., *Puritanism and its Discontents*, pp. 27–48. Newark, N.J. and London: University of Delaware Press, 2003.

New England Historical and Genealogical Register. Boston, Mass.: New England Historic Genealogical Society, 1847–. Online database: http://www.NewEnglandAncestors.org, New England Historic Genealogical Society, 2001–.

Newman, Simon P. 'Nathaniel Ward, 1580–1652: An Elizabethan Puritan in a Jacobean World', Essex Institute, *Historical Collections*, 127 (1991), pp. 313–26.

Nightingale, B. *The Ejected of 1662 in Cumberland and Westmorland* (2 vols). Manchester: Manchester University Press, 1911.

Nussbaum, Damian. 'Appropriating Martyrdom: Fears of Renewed Persecution and the 1632 Edition of *Acts and Monuments*', in David Loades, ed., *John Foxe and the English Reformation*, pp.178–91. Aldershot: Scolar Press, 1997.

——. 'Laudian Foxe-Hunting? William Laud and the Status of John Foxe in the 1630s', in R.N. Swanson, ed., *The Church Retrospective*, pp. 329–42. Studies in Church History, 33. Woodbridge, Suffolk: Boydell and Brewer, 1997.

Nuttall, G.F. *The Holy Spirit in Puritan Faith and Experience.* Oxford: Blackwell, 1946. Reprint, Chicago and London: University of Chicago Press, 1992.

——. *Visible Saints: The Congregational Way, 1640–1660.* Oxford: Blackwell, 1957.

——. 'Congregational Commonwealth Incumbents', *Congregational Historical Society Transactions*, 14 (1940–4), pp. 155–67.

——. *Richard Baxter.* London: Nelson, 1965.

——. 'The Essex Classes (1648)', *Journal of the United Reformed Church History Society*, 3 (1983–7), pp. 194–202.

Ohlmeyer, Jane, ed., *Ireland from Independence to Occupation, 1641–1660.* Cambridge: Cambridge University Press, 1995.

Olsen, Judith L. *Five Generations of the Descendants of Richard and Abigail Lippincott.* Woodbury, N.J.: Gloucester County Historical Society, 1982.

Orr, D. Alan. 'The Juristic Foundation of Regicide', in Jason Peacey, ed., *The Regicides and the Execution of Charles I*, pp. 117–38. Basingstoke: Palgrave, 2001.

O'Toole, James. 'New England Reactions to the English Civil Wars', *NEHGR*, 129 (1975), pp. 3–17, 238–49.

Oxford Dictionary of National Biography (61 vols). Oxford: Oxford University Press, 2004–. [*Oxford DNB Online* at http://www.oxforddnb.com, 2005– .]

Paul, Robert S. *The Assembly of the Lord: Politics and Religion in the Westminster Assembly and the 'Great Debate'.* Edinburgh: T. & T. Clark, 1985.

Pestana, Carla Gardina. *Quakers and Baptists in Colonial Massachusetts.* Cambridge: Cambridge University Press, 1991.

——. *The English Atlantic in an Age of Revolution, 1640–1661.* Cambridge, Mass., and London: Harvard University Press, 2004.

Peterson, Mark. 'Big Money Comes to Boston', *Common-Place*, vol. 6, no. 3, April 2006: accessed at http://www.common-place.org/vol-06/no-03/peterson/, 4 December 2006.

Pettit, Norman. 'God's Englishman in New England: His Enduring Ties to the Motherland', Massachusetts Historical Society, *Proceedings*, 101 (1989), pp. 56–70.

Pope, Robert G. *The Half-Way Covenant: Church Membership in Puritan New England.* Princeton: Princeton University Press, 1969.

Powell, Sumner Chilton. *Puritan Village: The Formation of a New England Town.* Middletown, Conn.: Wesleyan University Press, 1963.

Proclamations of Massachusetts Issued by Governors and other Authorities, 1620–1936, Vol. I, 1620–1776 (Boston: Historical Records Survey, Division of Women's and Professional Projects, Works Project Administration, 1937).

Raymond, Joad. *The Invention of the Newspaper: English Newsbooks, 1641–1649.* Oxford: Oxford University Press, 1996.

Reynolds, Matthew. *Godly Reformers and their Opponents in Early Modern England: Religion in Norwich c.1560–1643.* Woodbridge, Suffolk: Boydell Press, 2005.

Richardson, R.C. 'Puritanism and the Ecclesiastical Authorities: the case of the diocese of Chester', in Brian Manning, ed., *Politics, Religion and the English Civil War*, pp. 3–33. London: Edward Arnold, 1973.

Riley, Stephen T. 'Abraham Browne's Captivity by the Barbary Pirates, 1655', in P.C.F. Smith, ed., *Seafaring in Colonial Massachusetts*, pp. 31–42. Boston: Colonial Society of Massachusetts, *Publications*, 52, 1980.

Roberts, Oliver A. *History of the . . . Ancient and Honourable Artillery Company of Massachusetts, 1637–1688* (4 vols). Boston: A. Mudge and Son, 1895–1901.

Rose Troup, Frances. 'John Humfrey', Essex Institute, *Historical Collections*, 65 (1929), pp. 293–308.

Rowe, Violet A. *Sir Henry Vane the Younger. A Study in Political and Administrative History*. London: The Athlone Press, 1970.

Rutman, Darrett. *Winthrop's Boston. A Portrait of a Puritan Town, 1630–1649*. New York: Norton, 1972.

Sachse, William. 'Harvard Men in England 1642–1714', Colonial Society of Massachusetts, *Publications*, 35 (1942–6), pp. 120–31.

——— . 'The Migration of New Englanders to England, 1640–1660', *American Historical Review*, 53 (1947–8), pp. 251–78.

——— . *The Colonial American in Britain*. Madison, Wisconsin: University of Wisconsin Press, 1956.

Savage, James. *A Genealogical Dictionary of the First Settlers of New England* (4 vols). Boston, Mass., 1860–2.

Schneider, Carol Geary. 'Godly Order in a Church Half-Reformed: the Disciplinarian Legacy, 1570–1641'. PhD diss., Harvard University, 1986.

——— . 'Roots and Branches: From Principled Nonconformity to the Emergence of Religious Parties', in Francis J. Bremer, ed., *Puritanism: Transatlantic Perspectives on a Seventeenth-Century Anglo-American Faith*, pp. 167–200. Boston: Massachusetts Historical Society, 1993.

Scholz, R.F. 'Clerical Consociation in Massachusetts Bay: Reassessing the New England Way and its Origins', *William and Mary Quarterly*, 3rd series, 19 (1972), pp. 391–414.

Seaver, Paul S. *Wallington's World: A Puritan Artisan in Seventeenth-Century London*. Stanford, California: Stanford University Press, 1985.

Sedgwick, H.D. 'Robert Sedgwick', Colonial Society of Massachusetts, *Publications*, 3 (1900), pp. 156–74.

Seymour, St J.D. *The Puritans in Ireland, 1647–1661*. Oxford: Clarendon Press, 1921. Reprint, Oxford: Clarendon Press, 1969.

Sharpe, Kevin. *The Personal Rule of Charles I*. New Haven and London: Yale University Press, 1992.

Shaw, W.A. *A History of the English Church during the Civil Wars and under the Commonwealth, 1640–1660* (2 vols). London: Longman, Green, 1900.

Shipps, Kenneth W. 'The Puritan Migration to New England: a New Source on Motivation', *NEHGR*, 135 (1991), pp. 83–97.

Sibley, J.L. *Biographical Sketches of Graduates of Harvard University . . . 1642–1689* (3 vols). Cambridge, Mass.: C.W. Sever, 1873–85.

Simmons, R.C. 'Richard Sadler's Account of the Massachusetts Churches', *New England Quarterly*, 42 (1969), pp. 411–25.

Solberg, Winton U. *Redeem the Time: The Puritan Sabbath in Early America*. Cambridge, Mass.: Harvard University Press, 1977.

Sprunger, Keith L. 'William Ames and the Settlement of Massachusetts Bay', *New England Quarterly*, 39 (1966), pp. 66–79.

——— . *Dutch Puritanism: A History of English and Scottish Churches of the Netherlands in the Sixteenth and Seventeenth Centuries*. Leiden: E.J. Brill, 1982.

Spurlock, R. Scott. *Cromwell and Scotland: Conquest and Religion, 1650–1660*. Edinburgh: John Donald Publishers, 2007.

——. 'Sectarian Religion in Scotland: the Impact of Cromwell's Occupation (1650–1660)'. PhD diss., University of Edinburgh, 2005.

Stearns, R.P. 'The Weld–Peter Mission to England', Colonial Society of Massachusetts, *Publications*, 32 (1937), pp. 188–246.

——. *The Strenuous Puritan: Hugh Peter, 1598–1660*. Urbana, Illinois: University of Illinois Press, 1954.

—— and D.H. Brawner, 'New England Church "Relations" and Continuity in Early Congregational History', American Antiquarian Society, *Proceedings*, 75 (1965), pp. 13–45.

Steele, Ian K. *The English Atlantic 1675–1740*. Oxford: Oxford University Press, 1986.

Steiner, Bernard C. *A History of the Plantation of Menunkatuck and of the Original Town of Guilford*. Baltimore: privately printed, 1897.

Stevenson, David. 'Cromwell, Scotland and Ireland', in J.S. Morrill, ed., *Oliver Cromwell and the English Revolution*, pp. 149–80. London and New York: Longman, 1990.

——. 'The English and the Public Records of Scotland, 1650–1660', in his *Union, Revolution and Religion in 17th Century Scotland*, X. Aldershot: Variorum Collected Studies Series, 1997.

Stout, Harry S. 'The Morphology of Remigration: New England University Men and their Return to England, 1640–1660', *Journal of American Studies*, 10 (1976), pp. 151–72.

——. *The New England Soul: Preaching and Religious Culture in Colonial New England*. Oxford and New York: Oxford University Press, 1986.

Thomas, Keith. *Religion and the Decline of Magic*. London: Weidenfeld and Nicolson, 1971.

Thompson, Christopher. 'John Winthrop of Groton's Decision to Emigrate to Massachusetts: A Reconsideration of his "General Conclusions and Particular Considerations"', *Suffolk Review*, New Series 28 (Autumn 1996), pp. 19–22.

Thompson, Roger. *Mobility and Migration: East Anglian Founders of New England*. Amherst, Mass.: University of Massachusetts Press, 1994.

——. *Divided we Stand: Watertown, Massachusetts, 1630–1680*. Amherst, Mass.: University of Massachusetts Press, 2001.

Thwing, Annie Haven. 'Inhabitants and Estates of the Town of Boston, 1630–1800' [electronic resource] and *The Crooked and Narrow Streets of the Town of Boston, 1630–1822* (originally published Boston: Marshall Jones Company, 1920). CD ROM. Boston: Massachusetts Historical Society and New England Historic Genealogical Society, 2001.

Tipson, Baird. 'Samuel Stone's "Discourse" against Requiring Church Relations', *William and Mary Quarterly*, 3rd series, 46 (1989), pp. 787–99.

——. 'Invisible Saints: the "Judgment of Charity" in the Early New England Churches', *Church History*, 44 (1975), pp. 460–71.

Todd, Margo. 'Puritan Self-Fashioning', in Francis J. Bremer, ed., *Puritanism: Transatlantic Perspectives on a Seventeenth-Century Anglo-American Faith*, pp. 57–87. Boston: Massachusetts Historical Society, 1993.

Tomalin, Claire. *Samuel Pepys: The Unequalled Self*. London: Penguin Books, 2002.

Tuttle, J.H. 'The Rev. John Phillips of Dedham', Colonial Society of Massachusetts, *Publications*, 17 (1913–14), pp. 208–15.

Tyack, N.C.P. 'Migration from East Anglia to New England before 1660'. PhD diss., University of London, 1951.

——. 'The Humbler Puritans of East Anglia and the New England Movement: Evidence from the Court Records of the 1630s', *NEHGR*, 138 (1984), pp. 79–106.

——. 'English Exports to New England, 1632–1640: Some Records in the Port Books', *NEHGR*, 135 (1981), pp. 213–38.

Tyacke, Nicholas. *Anti-Calvinists: The Rise of English Arminianism c.1590–1640*. Oxford: Clarendon Press, 1987.

——— . *Aspects of English Protestantism c.1530–1700*. Manchester and New York: Manchester University Press, 2001.

Underdown, David. *Fire from Heaven: Life in an English Town in the Seventeenth Century*. London: Fontana, 1993.

Van Dixhoorn, Chad B., 'Reforming the Reformation: Theological Debate at the Westminster Assembly, 1643–1652' (7 vols). PhD diss., University of Cambridge, 2005.

Venning, Timothy. *Cromwellian Foreign Policy*. Basingstoke: Macmillan, 1995.

Vickers, Daniel. 'Competency and Competition: Economic Culture in Early America', *William and Mary Quarterly*, 3rd series, 47 (1990), pp. 3–29.

Walker, Williston. *The Creeds and Platforms of Congregationalism*. New York: Pilgrim Press, 1991.

Wall, Robert Emmet. *Massachusetts Bay: The Crucial Decade, 1640–1650*. New Haven: Yale University Press, 1972.

Walsham, Alexandra. *Providence in Early Modern England*. Oxford: Oxford University Press, 1999.

——— . *Charitable Hatred: Tolerance and Intolerance in England, 1500–1700*. Manchester and New York: Manchester University Press, 2006.

Waterhouse, Richard. 'Reluctant Emigrants: the English Background of the First Generation of the New England Puritan Clergy', *Historical Magazine of the Protestant Episcopal Church*, 44 (1975), pp. 473–88.

Waters, Henry F. *Genealogical Gleanings in England*. Boston, Mass.: New England Historic Genealogical Society, 1901.

Waters, John J. 'Hingham, Massachusetts, 1631–1661: An East Anglian Oligarchy in the New World', *Journal of Social History*, 1 (1968), pp. 362–7.

Weber, Donald. 'Historicizing the Errand', *American Literary History*, 2 (1990), pp. 101–18.

Webster, Tom. 'Writing to Redundancy: Approaches to Spiritual Journals and Early Modern Spirituality', *Historical Journal*, 39 (1996), pp. 33–56.

——— . *Godly Clergy in Early Stuart England: The Caroline Puritan Movement c.1620–1643*. Cambridge: Cambridge University Press, 1997.

——— . 'The Piety of Practice and the Practice of Piety', in Francis J. Bremer and Lynn A. Botelho, eds, *The World of John Winthrop: Essays on England and New England 1588–1649*, pp. 111–46. Boston, Mass.: Massachusetts Historical Society, 2005.

Weir, David. *Early New England: A Covenanted Society*. Grand Rapids and Cambridge: William B. Eerdmans Publishing Company, 2005.

Weis, F.L. *The Colonial Clergy and the Colonial Churches of New England*. Lancaster, Mass.: Society of the Descendants of Colonial Clergy, 1936.

White, B.R. 'Thomas Patient in England and Ireland', *Irish Baptist Historical Society Journal*, 2 (1969–1970), pp. 36–48.

——— . *The English Separatist Tradition*. Oxford: Oxford University Press, 1971.

Windeatt, Edward. 'Early Nonconformity in Tavistock', *Report and Transactions of the Devonshire Association*, 21 (1889), pp. 148–58.

Winship, Michael P. *Seers of God: Puritan Providentialism in the Restoration and Early Enlightenment*. Baltimore, Maryland: Johns Hopkins University Press, 1996.

——— . 'Contesting Control of Orthodoxy among the Godly: William Pynchon Reexamined', *William and Mary Quarterly*, 3rd series, 54 (1997), pp. 795–822.

——— . 'William Pynchon's *The Jewes Synagogue*', *New England Quarterly*, 71 (1998), pp. 290–7.

——— . '"The Most Glorious Church in the World": the Unity of the Godly in Boston, Massachusetts, in the 1630s', *Journal of British Studies*, 39 (2000), pp. 71–98.

——— . 'Were there any Puritans in New England?' *New England Quarterly*, 74 (2001), pp. 118–38.

——— . *Making Heretics: Militant Protestantism and Free Grace in Massachusetts, 1636–1641*. Princeton and Oxford: Princeton University Press, 2002.

Winsser, Johan. 'Nicholas Trerise, Mariner of Wapping and Charlestown', *NEHGR*, 143 (1989), pp. 25–39.

—— . 'Walter Blackbourne, a London milliner briefly in New England', *NEHGR*, 151 (1997), pp. 408–16.

Woolrych, Austin. *Britain in Revolution 1625–1660*. Oxford: Oxford University Press, 2002.

Worthley, Harold Field. *An Inventory of the Records of the Particular (Congregational) Churches of Massachusetts Gathered 1620–1805*. Harvard Theological Studies, 25. Cambridge, Mass., and London: Harvard University Press, 1970.

Wright, Jonathan. 'Marian exiles and the legitimacy of flight from persecution', *Journal of Ecclesiastical History*, 52 (2001), pp. 220–43.

Wright, Stephen. *The Early English Baptists, 1603–1649*. Woodbridge, Suffolk: Boydell Press, 2006.

Wykes, David L. '"To revive the memory of some excellent men": Edmund Calamy and the early historians of nonconformity'. London: Dr Williams's Library, Friends of Dr Williams's Library, 1997.

Yuan, Cheng. 'The Politics of the English Army in Ireland during the Interregnum'. PhD diss., Brown University, 1981.

Zahediah, Nuala. 'Making Mercantilism Work: London Merchants and Atlantic Trade in the Seventeenth Century', *Transactions of the Royal Historical Society*, 6th series, 9 (1999), pp. 143–60.

Zakai, Avihu. *Exile and Kingdom: History and Apocalypse in the Puritan Migration to America*. Cambridge: Cambridge University Press, 1992.

Ziff, Larzer. *The Career of John Cotton. Puritanism and the American Experience*. Princeton: Princeton University Press, 1962.

INDEX

New England settlements are entered individually, alphabetically, along with modern State names. Places in England are listed under historic counties.

Could be arrested.
p60 for not having child
baptized in timely
fashion

Some left because of religion
others because their beliefs
pissed off participation
in civic affairs

p62 doctrinal schisms —
different requirements
for admittance to church —